Virginia Hasn't Always Been for Lovers

Virginia Hasn't Always Been for Lovers

Interracial Marriage Bans and the Case of Richard and Mildred Loving

Phyl Newbeck

Southern Illinois University Press • Carbondale

Library of Congress Cataloging-in-Publication Data
Newbeck, Phyl, 1961–
Virginia hasn't always been for lovers : interracial marriage bans and the case of Richard
and Mildred Loving / Phyl Newbeck.
    p. cm.
Includes bibliographical references and index.
   1. Interracial marriage—Law and legislation—Virginia—History—20th century. I. Title.
KFV2495.5.N49 2004
346.75501'6—dc22   2003028064
ISBN 0-8093-2528-4 (cloth binding : alk. paper)

Printed on recycled paper. ♻

The paper used in this publication meets the minimum requirements of American National Standard for Information Sciences—Permanence of Paper for Printed Library
Materials, ANSI Z39.48-1992. ∞

To the late George D. Jackson,
who taught me a lot more than just backspins

Contents

List of Illustrations ix
Preface xi
Acknowledgments xiii

Introduction 1

Part One: Mildred Jeter and Richard Loving

1. I Do 9
2. The Passing Capital of America 17

Part Two: The Rise and Fall of Antimiscegenation Statutes in the United States

3. Making Sense of Senseless Laws 25
4. How It All Began 37
5. The Prosecutions Continue 55
6. Taking Away the Children and the Money 64
7. The West Leads the Way 75
8. The Organizations Challenge, and the Challenges Become Organized 89
9. The Sad Case of Ruby and Ham 103
10. Connie and Dewey Share a Room 117

Part Three: *Loving v. Virginia*

11. Richard and Mildred Want to Go Home 135
12. On to the Supreme Court 147
13. The Amicus Briefs 161
14. Virginia and North Carolina Defend the Indefensible 169
15. May It Please the Court 173
16. The Supreme Court Speaks 186

Part Four: The Aftermath

17. Not All States Listen 193
18. "A Big Interracial Display of Their Romance" 197
19. The Feds Finally Step In 206
20. Happily Ever After 214

Appendix A: Virginia's Racial Integrity Statute 223
Appendix B: Florida's Antimiscegenation Laws 225
Appendix C: Miscegenation Statutes, by State 227
Notes 233
Bibliography 275
Index 291

Illustrations

Following page 132
"The genesis of the word"
Harry Bridges and Noriko Sawada with their attorney
One-room schoolhouse in Central Point, Virginia
Caroline County jail and closeup of sign
Judge Leon Bazile
Mildred Loving's plea for help
Richard and Mildred Loving relaxing with friends
Richard and Mildred with Richard's mother and their daughter Peggy
A crime "against the peace and dignity of the Commonwealth of Virginia"
The beginnings of the court case
The lawyers who represented the Lovings: Bernie Cohen and
    Philip Hirschkop
Berta Linson and Roger Mills
The Loving children
Mildred Loving in 1992

Preface

By 1967, most of the obvious symbols of segregation had disappeared. Bus stations were integrated, bathrooms and water fountains no longer carried the odious "white" and "colored" signs, and anyone could sit down at the Woolworth counter and order a hamburger. However, one major barrier to equality still existed. Sixteen states continued to outlaw the marriage of whites and blacks (and sometimes of whites with other racial groups). Richard Perry Loving was white, and his wife, Mildred Dolores Jeter Loving, was "colored," in the parlance of the day. Together they were able to challenge the law that had driven them from their home state of Virginia under penalty of imprisonment for the crime of marrying one another.

One snowy evening in December 1997, my former husband and I rented the Showtime movie *Mr. and Mrs. Loving.* I knew enough history to recognize that the producers were probably playing fast and loose with some of the facts but not enough to recognize where the inaccuracies were. I set out to find the true story of Richard and Mildred Loving. My initial goal was certainly not to write a book, a task I had never before contemplated. It was simply to find a suitable volume that discussed the Lovings and their case. A quick review of the available literature revealed that there were no books about the people or the case, and thus I rashly decided that I would have to write one.

I would rank the Supreme Court case of *Loving v. Virginia* as one of the major landmarks of the civil rights movement, right up there with *Brown v. Board of Education, Topeka, Kansas* in 1954, the Freedom Rides of 1961, the March on Washington in 1963, Freedom Summer in Mississippi in 1964, and the march from Selma to Montgomery, Alabama, in 1965. There are a variety of books, from scholarly tomes to personal memoirs, about all of these events, but there is only a void regarding the Lovings and their battle to live together legally in Virginia. Entire tomes about the 1960s devote not a single sentence to this epic case.[1]

Perhaps the reason lies in the fact that, by 1967, the nation was growing tired of the civil rights struggle. The cry of "black power" had replaced "we shall overcome," eroding the support of the northern white liberals who traditionally opened up their checkbooks when the National Association for the Advancement of Colored People, the Southern Christian Leadership Conference, the Congress on Racial Equality, or the more militant Student Nonviolent Coordinating Committee came calling. In truth, none of these groups was a major factor in the *Loving* case, although the NAACP and its Legal Defense and Education Fund did contribute amicus briefs. Perhaps the reason is that by 1967, the country was more preoccupied with the war in Vietnam than the situation at home. Perhaps it is easier to visualize the struggle to use a restroom, eat a hamburger sitting down, or ride in any section of a bus than it is to conceptualize a desire to marry. And perhaps the reason is that the Lovings, a quiet and reclusive pair, lacked the charisma of a Fannie Lou Hamer, the oratory of a Rev. Martin Luther King Jr., or the audacity of a Stokely Carmichael. Whatever the reason, the story of Mildred and Richard Loving has yet to be told in full detail. The following pages are my humble attempt to do so.

By way of full disclosure, I should note that I am white and my former husband is black. Our ages (born in 1961 and 1959, respectively) and geography (married in New York state) ensured that we would not have the type of experience the unfortunate Lovings endured. Still, my mind dwells on the fact that were we twenty years older and a few states farther south, this story could have been ours.

Acknowledgments

I thank my mother, Anni Newbeck, for constantly pushing me toward intellectual pursuits. She started bringing home library books for me at an early age, gradually moving me from children's baseball stories to biographies of baseball players and then to biographies of more historical traditional figures. I also am in her debt for the loan of an old manual typewriter and workbook that allowed me to teach myself to type at home, without a doubt one of the most valuable skills I have ever learned. In more recent times, Anni provided editing services free of charge. She also accompanied me when I scouted out Central Point, Virginia, and Mildred Loving's old haunts, providing questionable navigation assistance but unquestionable moral support. In lieu of a tape recorder, Anni dutifully scribbled hieroglyphic notes as I spewed forth my thoughts on the road to Central Point.

I wish I could personally thank my late father, Jerry Newbeck, who played devil's advocate and challenged me on issues that in my youthful zeal, I was positive were one-dimensional. Both he and my mother, survivors of Nazi Germany, subscribed to the liberal politics common to German Jewish immigrants and passed their beliefs on to their only child. I vividly recall a business trip with my father during which I challenged one of his associates on his racism. Although I'm sure he would have preferred to have me exercise my First Amendment rights at another time and place, I knew my father was proud of me for my opinions.

When I was very young, I confused the last names of a black woman and a white man on *Mr. Rogers' Neighborhood,* thinking they were the same. I have a distinct memory of asking my mother if it was possible for a black person to be married to a white person. The truth is that at the time I asked the question, there were at least sixteen states where the answer was no. My mother, however, had no experience with the American South, having moved directly from Germany to Bedford Stuyvesant in Brooklyn, New York, and ultimately to Astoria, Queens, New York. She answered in the affirmative. Years later, when I reminded her of this question, she told me that I had asked the wrong parent. My father had been stationed in Cleo, Alabama, during his Army days and, even to an inquisitive five-year-old, would have provided a far more detailed answer about the diverse laws in different parts of the country. Perhaps, if I had asked him, I would have lost whatever curiosity compelled me to write this book.

I thank my former husband, Chuck West, for taking care of me and the house while I shirked all duties in favor of pounding the keyboard. Chuck kept me fed and in clean clothes and made sure the house was presentable while I used my epic-to-be as a way to avoid a great deal of what needed to be done.

I thank my friends who, even after learning that the simple query "How's the book going?" would lead to a lengthy diatribe on the history of race relations in America, continued to ask that question. A special note of appreciation to Christine and Reggie, Emily and Martin, Martha and Steve, and Ruth and Frank for showing the world that color is irrelevant in a strong relationship.

Special thanks go to the staff at the University of Vermont's Bailey-Howe Library, particularly Martha Day, who reawakened my research skills. Also deserving of special thanks are Angus Robertson, who tirelessly tracked down interlibrary-loan books for me, and the smiling faces at the UVM circulation desk, who dealt with me on an almost daily basis. I owe a debt to the work-study students at the Office of Affirmative Action/Equal Opportunity—Lydia Kelsey, Michelle Messer, and Lauren Waters—who willingly copied voluminous materials for me. Additional thanks go to Ron Jacobs, a fellow UVM staffer and the author of *The Way the Wind Blew,* for showing me that if a subject is meaningful to me, I could and should take the time to write about it.

I extend my thanks to the folks at Cleveland Public Library, particularly Rhonda Green, who copied microfilm files of the NAACP for me. Additionally, the Mudd Manuscript Library at Princeton provided unlimited access to ACLU records and the staff was gracious and helpful. I am profoundly grateful for the in-depth research done by Chang Moon Sohn and Byron Curti Martyn in their respective PhD theses, which formed a solid base for this book, and to Robert Sickels, whose *Race, Marriage and the Law* was the only book on the subject when I began my research. I thank young Brittany Houser for willing her way to a meeting with Mildred Loving and forming a friendship with her. And I thank her mother, Leslie Houser, for sharing some of the details of that friendship with me. In addition, Leslie introduced me to Caroline County historian Stan Beason, who provided my mother and me with a guided tour of the courthouse where Judge Bazile made his pronouncement about separate races and continents and the jail where the Lovings were incarcerated.

Special thanks are due Gregory Michael Dorr, who allowed me to use his wonderful article on *Naim v. Naim* before it was published in the *American Journal of Legal History.* Greg traveled to Portsmouth, Virginia, to copy the trial record in the case for me, saving me considerable time and expense. Special thanks also go to Boston College law professor Arthur Berney, who followed up my interview with him by sending me in-depth written recollections of his role in *Loving* and alerted me to an informative law review article that was published after we had spoken. Professor Michael Meltsner was also kind enough to alert me to a very useful law review article several months after I had the pleasure of interviewing him. Kenneth MacDonald of Seattle was so intrigued by my questions about a 1953 case in which he had been involved that he did significant research to help me understand what had transpired.

I thank all the wonderful people who allowed me to interview them (by telephone, by e-mail, or in person) or wrote back to give me their recollections. Each of them is listed in the bibliography section of this book. Of those, I was particularly charmed by the Arizona contingent of Harry Ackerman, Charles Ares, Marvin Cohen, Lawrence Ollason, and Paul Rees, who helped me consider in a new light those who had the unenviable task of arguing to uphold antimiscegenation statutes. Many others, too numerous to mention here, did not recall the events I wished to discuss with them and politely turned down my interview requests. I thank them for taking the time to respond to my inquiries. It was an honor to be able to correspond with so many people who had such a positive influence on this country. Certainly one of the high points of writing this book was receiving an e-mail from Casey Hayden, one of my heroes from the civil rights and feminist movements.

While not all of those interviewed were able to provide full and complete recollections, their input was useful. James Nabrit III, for instance, broke the news that Supreme Court documents were available in venues other than the Supreme Court. Most of my interviews were done by telephone, but I had the honor of visiting former Secretary of Transportation William Coleman at his beautiful summer house in Vermont. I thoroughly enjoyed my trip to Alexandria, Virginia, for a visit with Phil Hirschkop, which was followed by lunch with Bernie Cohen. I was stunned when Cohen called Mildred Loving to ask whether she would reconsider speaking to me and she agreed. Just as memorable was a visit to my University of Vermont office by Paul Rees of Tucson, Arizona, and his wife. They happened to be in Boston and drove more than two hundred miles to hand deliver some documents that Rees had been carrying for me throughout their European vacation. Others who graciously provided me with relevant written materials of which I was not previously aware were Harry Ackerman, David Carliner, Noriko Bridges Flynn, Brad Jordan, Roger Mills, and William Zabel.

I owe a debt of gratitude to my late ice-skating teacher, George D. Jackson, an electrician by trade, who was the most significant nonparental role model in my life. When I was a thirteen-year-old undisciplined recreational figure skater, I saw him doing fast-paced footwork at Rockefeller Center. I summoned up all my courage and asked if he could show me what he was doing. He must have been impressed at the way I practiced, because the following week, he taught me a new move. From then on, we were inseparable on the ice. For more than ten years, Mr. Jackson imparted an expanding array of knowledge, asking nothing in return. He taught me not only the flip and the back-sit-spin but also that all persons, regardless of race, are human beings first. I wish he were alive today to see my newest cross-foot backspin and to read this book.

When my former husband and I bought our house in Vermont in 1995, I thought the third-floor attic space was one of its most endearing features. Sufficiently removed from the rest of the house to minimize internal distractions, the room, now my office, has a spectacular view of Mt. Mansfield, Vermont's highest peak, with the rolling hills and fields of my rural town in the foreground. When my research became too depressing, my mountain view would always lead me to more pleasant thoughts. My final thanks are to the state of Vermont for welcoming a flatlander like me.

Virginia Hasn't Always Been for Lovers

Introduction

It is stated as well authenticated fact that if the issue of a black man and a white woman, intermarry, they cannot possibly have any progeny, and such a fact sufficiently justifies those laws which forbid the intermarriage of blacks and whites....
—Missouri Supreme Court decision, 1883

*T*his book started out as a very simple project: I wanted to tell the story of *Loving v. Virginia,* the 1967 Supreme Court case that struck down laws banning marriage between people of different racial backgrounds. I fancied myself journeying to Central Point, Virginia, to interview Mildred and Richard Loving, their attorneys, the state's attorneys, others peripheral to the case, and the family, and to review the legal documents. Alas, nothing is as easy as it seems. Richard Loving died in an automobile accident in 1974. Mildred Loving does not see what she did as particularly heroic or even newsworthy. After years of being approached in June of every year ending in a *2* or a *7* by reporters celebrating a five-year anniversary of the case, she feels as though she has spent her life being interviewed. In 1997, the thirty-year anniversary of her case, she turned down a request for an interview by *Emerge* magazine[1] and has kept her silence ever since. Her children are grown, but they still defer to their mother's request that they not talk to the media about the family and the case. My initial attempts to contact her were rebuffed.[2]

Unable to speak to the hero and heroine of the story, I sought out the villains. Sheriff Brooks, who walked into the Loving house in the dead of night to arrest the pair for the crime of being married, no longer talks to the press for fear of "riling up the black folks."[3] Judge Bazile, who used the occasion of sentencing the pair to preach about how God made separate races and wanted to keep them separate, is deceased. It is doubtful that he lies in an integrated cemetery. Neither R. D. McIlwaine, the Virginia attorney general who argued in favor of Virginia's antimiscegenation laws, nor Judge Carrico, who affirmed the initial conviction, was willing to be interviewed, though both were gracious in their refusals. I was unable to trace any of the other parties who were involved in either the brief from the state of Virginia or the amicus brief filed by the state of North Carolina.

Back on the side of the "good guys," I found a further impediment in that the two principal attorneys for the Lovings—Bernie Cohen and Phil Hirschkop—do not speak to one another. Hirschkop has the complete case file[4] but chose not to share it with me while he contemplated whether to take legal action against Cohen for his consulting role in a movie about the case that omitted any reference to Hirschkop. I was able to interview a number of the authors of amicus briefs on behalf of the Lovings, but the passage of time and their ensuing careers dimmed the memories of many of those I spoke to.

As my attempts at writing a book with real human interest began to dry up, I was forced to head to the last refuge of the academician: the library. I learned that laws barring interracial marriage (called antimiscegenation statutes) were first promulgated in the United States in the 1600s. Legislators frequently revised the statutes (often to include more nonwhite persons within the prohibited categories and to strengthen the penalties) throughout the seventeenth, eighteenth, nineteenth, and even twentieth centuries. Forty-one states had such laws at one time or another (some before achieving statehood), and every state but one (my home state of Vermont) had such statutes proposed at one time in its history. In 1967, when the Lovings brought their case to the Supreme Court, sixteen states continued to ban interracial marriage.

Many states were quite specific about which racial and ethnic groups belonged in the class of unmarriables. Some states defined these groups in terms of "percentage of blood," while others traced the offender's genealogy to determine whether she or he had any inappropriate ancestors to the third or fourth generation. Depending on the jurisdiction, "any ascertainable trace" of black blood could be sufficient to keep someone from marrying a white person (and "white" was almost never defined), whereas in other jurisdictions, at least one full-blooded African great-grandparent was required for intermarriage to be banned. The wording of the statutes also varied, with some prohibiting whites from marrying "Negroes," "Africans," persons of "Ethiopian descent," or simply "the colored race." Some states included Asians in the prohibited class, and some included Native Americans. Oregon forbade the marriage of whites and Kanakans (Hawaiians). At one point, Arizona banned marriages between whites and Hindus. Only a few states were particular about whether persons in the unmarriable classes could mate with one another.

Statutes were hardly consistent regarding the penalties inflicted on a couple who dared to marry in contravention of state laws. In seventeen states, such action was a felony; in others it was a misdemeanor. Fines and prison terms ran the gamut from a slap on the wrist to ten years behind bars. Virtually all states declared the offending marriage null and void, thus delegitimizing the children. Several states specifically ensured that undesirables could not marry in another jurisdiction (as the Lovings had done) and legally return as husband and wife. Some states were not satisfied with prosecuting the newly wedded couple but also imposed sanctions on persons who knowingly provided marriage licenses to interracial pairings and those who solemnized such unions. Mississippi considered it a crime to advocate in favor of mixed marriages. Several states believed that their statutory prohibitions were insufficient and included intermarriage bans in their constitutions.

Just as I began to despair that this book would consist of nothing more than a depressing history of prejudice in this country, I learned that not all Americans had passively suffered the existence of antimiscegenation laws for so many years. Various so-called special interest groups fought against such laws in state legislatures and in the courts. The NAACP and the ACLU are obvious examples, but the National Catholic Conference, the American Jewish Congress, and the Japanese American Citizens League are other groups that, long before 1967, tried to strike down this last remnant of legalized prejudice.

Loving was by no means the first antimiscegenation case to reach the Supreme Court, coming as it did almost eighty years after the earliest challenge. In *Pace v. Alabama,* an unenlightened nineteenth-century court upheld a statute that inflicted greater penalties on those who engaged in interracial, rather than intraracial, fornication, using the argument that both the black and white fornicators were equally punished. The Supreme Court did not have the opportunity to hear another challenge until 1954, when it unceremoniously denied certiorari in the case of *Jackson v. Alabama*. One year later, the justices were forced at least to feign interest in the case of *Naim v. Naim*, a direct challenge to Virginia's ban on intermarriage. Timing is everything, and *Naim* was simply too close chronologically to the Court's momentous decision to ban segregation in public education. Afraid of further alienating the southern half of the country, the justices turned tail and refused to make a determination. *Naim* was followed by *McLaughlin v. Florida* in 1964. The facts of *McLaughlin* dealt specifically with interracial fornication, so although the Court overruled the ancient precedent of *Pace*, it refused to make a decision on the constitutionality of Florida's intermarriage ban.

Federal courts were not the only ones to deal with the question of antimiscegenation laws. The first state to rule that its ban on interracial marriage was unconstitutional was Alabama in 1872. This fact is particularly noteworthy, since Alabama was one of two states (South Carolina being the other) that retained intermarriage bans in their state constitutions when I began work on this book in 1997. The Alabama ruling lasted less than a decade before being overturned, as the Reconstruction era was replaced by a new and improved discriminatory South. The next successful judicial challenge did not come until 1948, when California ruled that its antimiscegenation statute was unconstitutional. This seeming milestone, however, did not lead to a rush of other court decisions. The lack of response was partly due to the California statute's having been a relatively benign one. It prohibited interracial marriages but did not impose a punishment on the couples and never defined exactly what constituted a prohibited marriage. Ten years later, by sheer force of personality, union leader Harry Bridges was able to overturn Nevada's antimiscegenation law, and the following year, Arizona's statute was successfully challenged.

Judicial action was not the only means of challenging antimiscegenation statutes. In some states, the legislature acted to remove these odious laws from the books. In 1780, Pennsylvania became the first state to repeal its intermarriage ban. Several northeastern and a few midwestern states followed suit in the 1800s. After the court decisions in California, Nevada, and Arizona, the remaining midwestern and western states slowly began the process of repealing their bans. Even Maryland, the site of the oldest antimiscegenation law in the country, repealed its statute a few months before the Loving decision.

The result of all this research is that what you hold before you is not quite the book I wanted to write but a historical account of *Loving*, its precedents, and its descendants. I found the last surprising, since it had never occurred to me that there would be any litigation on this issue after *Loving*. I was wrong. As the 1970s unfolded, twelve states still had legislative bans on intermarriage, and a few were still trying to enforce them. The last judicial battle on the subject occurred in 1972, and the last political battle was fought in Alabama, where the state constitution continued to prohibit interracial marriage until 2000.

The first section of this book tells the story of Richard and Mildred Loving, their courtship, their marriage, and their arrest. The second section describes the growth of antimiscegenation laws in the United States and the beginning of the fight against these racially discriminatory laws. The third is dedicated to the Lovings' court case. The book concludes with a section that describes how the issue that would not die was finally put to rest. Although this topic lends itself to a variety of interdisciplinary studies, my only goal is to lay out the history of these laws. I will leave it to other scholars to discuss the psychological, sociological, and economic perspectives of this legislation.

This country has seen thousands of laws enforcing racial discrimination, many of which persisted late into the twentieth century. Although much of the discrimination was only quasi-legal, a variety of legal barriers existed well into the 1950s and 1960s. I think that at this point, everyone is aware of the United States' shameful history of segregated school systems and restaurants, "colored" and "white" bathrooms and drinking fountains, and segregated transportation and waiting rooms. However, a variety of other dual systems received less recognition. Some states segregated their orphanages, and some their old age homes. Many segregated their prisons, their homes for juvenile delinquents, their poor houses, and their mental hospitals. Some states segregated their tuberculosis patients, and a number of states had separate schools for the blind as well as for what were then called the "deaf and dumb." Other states did not allow integrated fraternal organizations to operate within their boundaries.[5]

Communities maintained facilities as esoteric as racetracks and billiard halls separately for each race. Texas did not allow interracial boxing matches. Oklahoma would not allow different races to fish together in public waters. In Louisiana, the circus tent entrances for blacks and whites could not be less than twenty-five feet apart. Florida ensured that black and white textbooks were stored separately, and North Carolina did not allow books used by one race to ever be used by the other. Oklahoma had separate telephone booths for black and white patrons. Some states had segregated baths and lockers at the coal mines, while others had them in their cotton mills. As late as 1950, Kentucky had a law against presenting or participating in a play that was "based upon antagonism between master and slave or that excites race prejudice." Mississippi could imprison for up to six months anyone who printed or published information "in favor of social equality." In Montgomery, Alabama, it was unlawful for white and black persons to play cards, dice, dominoes, checkers, pool, billiards, softball, basketball, football, or golf, or to accompany one another at swimming pools or at athletic events. In neighboring Selma, a black man could be arrested for "socializing" with a white woman in public *or* in private.[6]

Any one of these many legal indignities to the rights of humankind could and should be the topic of in-depth research. However, I find something particularly galling about the prohibition against interracial marriage: an act that is purely voluntary and affects nobody but the consenting couple. Although none of the above-referenced laws can be justified, one might argue that they involve a variety of people who may choose, for whatever reason, not to come into contact with one another. But marriage is different. By its very nature, marriage is a matter of choice for two human beings, and the fact that these prohibitions continued as long as they did is, in my mind, a very shameful commentary on America.

Part One

Mildred Jeter and Richard Loving

1

I Do

There is no subject which, in the present state of the times, calls more loudly for legislative interposition than the one before them. It is an infraction of the laws of the Almighty, for one moment to allow the pernicious doctrine of such amalgamation to have an abiding place in our government, or upon our State books, being marked, as they are, by the eternal and unchangeable laws of God, the one *white* and the other *black*. Your committee believe that any man or set of men, who would encourage, counsel, aid, or abet in such unholy marriages as said bill prohibits, deserve the just animadversion of every christian philanthropist and patriot, and should be punished by several penalties imposed by legislative enactment.
     —Indiana state senator proposing an intermarriage ban in 1840

*O*n June 2, 1958, Richard Perry Loving and Mildred Dolores Jeter journeyed from their hometown of Central Point, Virginia, to Washington, D.C., to get married. What should have been a simple declaration of love turned into a living nightmare for the young couple for one simple reason: by the laws of the state of Virginia, Richard was "white" and Mildred was "colored."

Mildred and Richard had known each other for most of their lives. Their families lived about seven miles from one another in rural Central

Point, and both had spent virtually their entire lives in the area. Richard Loving was born in October 1933 to a young laborer and a housewife. Almost six years later, a fifty-four-year-old tenant farmer and his twenty-eight-year-old wife, also a homemaker, became the proud parents of Mildred Jeter.[1] When Mildred was eleven, seventeen-year-old Richard began to take notice of her. Richard first started visiting Mildred's family farmhouse to hear her seven brothers play what she called "hillbilly music," but soon he was coming to see Mildred.[2] During the next few years, they became friendly, and eventually the relationship blossomed into romance. In Central Point, fraternizing between the races was not uncommon, so their budding relationship drew little attention from black or white neighbors.[3] However, as the young pair was soon to learn, dating was one thing but marriage quite another.

Mildred's heritage was a mixture of African and Cherokee. She was a slender woman who was called String Bean, or Bean for short. Richard was a gangly man of English and Irish heritage. He worked as a bricklayer, but virtually every spare moment was spent drag racing in a car that he co-owned with a black friend. Segregation meant that the two had gone to separate schools and attended different churches, but within the friendly confines of Central Point, there were plenty of opportunities for the races to mix, and Richard and Mildred found plenty of time for each other. When he was twenty-four and she was eighteen, Mildred became pregnant. They decided to marry.[4] It was Richard's idea to travel to Washington, D.C., for the ceremony.[5] On a spring day in 1958, the couple headed north with Mildred's father and one of her brothers in tow as witnesses. They picked the name of a minister from a phone book and, immediately after the ceremony, got back in the car, and returned to Central Point.[6]

Mildred did not realize that it was illegal for persons of different races to marry in Virginia. She thought that they were making the trip to Washington, D.C., because there was less red tape involved and the marriage could be performed more expeditiously. In contrast to Virginia, the District did not require blood tests.[7] Richard knew that they would be unable to obtain a license in Virginia, but he did not trouble his young bride-to-be with that information. What he did not know was that Virginia had taken its prohibition of intermarriage one step further. The state was one of several that specifically penalized couples who attempted to evade their antimiscegenation laws by leaving to marry and then returning to live as husband and wife.[8]

Richard and Mildred returned to Central Point with a framed marriage license as Mr. and Mrs. Loving. They started their married life living in the home of Mildred's parents, sleeping in the downstairs bedroom while Richard made plans to build a home for his new family. Meanwhile, word of the wedding reached local authorities, who were outraged that a white man had chosen a Negro bride. On June 11, 1958, Justice of the Peace Robert W. Farmer issued arrest warrants to law enforcement officers of Caroline County at the complaint of the county prosecutor, Bernard Mahon. Mahon, acting on an anonymous tip, alleged that the Lovings had, on June 2, 1958, "unlawfully and feloniously" left the state with the purpose of marrying and returning to cohabit "as man and wife against the peace and dignity of the Commonwealth of Virginia."[9]

Three policemen (the sum total of law enforcement officials in the county)[10] entered the unlocked house in the dead of night and shone flashlights in Richard's and Mildred's faces. Sheriff Garnett Brooks demanded of Richard what he was doing in bed with "that woman." Richard didn't immediately speak, so Mildred answered, "I'm his wife." Richard pointed to the framed marriage license that they had hung on the wall. "That's no good here," said Brooks. The newlyweds were charged with unlawful cohabitation and taken to the jail in nearby Bowling Green. Authorities entered indictments against them for violations of sections 20-57 and 20-58 of the civil code (*see* Appendix A). Section 20-57 declared interracial marriages null and void, while 20-58 explicitly forbade couples from crossing state lines to evade the antimiscegenation law.[11]

One local historian believes that although Brooks was disgusted by the thought of an interracial couple, it is likely that he would not have arrested the pair if Mahon, a man with political ambitions, had not asked him to do so.[12] Mahon's eventual successor, Jack Lilly, disagrees, maintaining that someone of Mahon's stature in the community would not have relished the publicity from the Loving case. Lilly attributes the impetus behind the arrest to Brooks, whom he characterizes as "a classic redneck" who harbored a great deal of animosity toward people of color.[13] A deputy sheriff whose term followed that of Brooks would not go quite so far but confirmed that Brooks did not like black people.[14] Slightly more cryptic was the testimony of the man who succeeded Brooks: he only expressed surprise that there were differing opinions as to whether or not Brooks was a racist.[15] Raymond Green, a laconic mechanic who was part of Richard's drag race team did not mince words. When asked whether Brooks was a racist, he replied, "Hell, yes."[16]

Brooks has said that he requested that his deputy and the county jailer accompany him for the arrest because he feared violence from the tightly knit community of Central Point. He made the visit at night because he knew that he would be able to catch the couple in the act of cohabitation. Local lore has it that Brooks often raided moonshine operations in the company of only his German shepherd,[17] so it is curious that he should expect to be met with violence on only this occasion. Brooks was known as a man who did not put up with foolishness. He had a penchant for stopping people who seemed to have no real sense of purpose in their activities. When his queries as to a person's business in a particular place and time were met with what he considered inappropriate answers, it was not unusual for him to strike the smart-talker with his blackjack and cart him off to jail. "Nobody messed with Garnett Brooks."[18] He was a physically imposing man with huge arms and hands. The only thing that jarred with this image was his high-pitched voice.[19]

Richard's warrant was executed during a visit from Brooks on July 13. Mildred's was executed four days later. Both pled not guilty to the charges. Because Richard was white, he was bailed out of jail after only one night, while Mildred, referred to as "a Negress" by the county attorney, spent four more nights incarcerated until her hearing. Although Richard protested, he was told that if he tried to bail her out, he would have to return to prison. They separated briefly to live with their respective parents until the court date[20] and were ordered to post a bond of one thousand dollars each, or the equivalent, to assure their appearance in court.[21]

Built in 1900, the Bowling Green jail has a red brick exterior, but the interior walls are lined with stainless steel. In 1958 there were two large cells, one upstairs and one downstairs, for the men. The rate of crime in the area was low, and female crime was negligible. All jailed women were housed in a single five- by seven-foot upstairs cell that Mildred remembers as rat-infested. Although a local historian disputes this recollection, Mildred is not the only one to report an abundance of rodents. Basketball star Wilt Chamberlain was once detained overnight in Bowling Green. His autobiography makes reference to the four-legged creatures with whom he shared the hours.[22]

The Bowling Green courthouse of 1958 was a relatively new edifice, built to replace one that burned during the fire of 1955. Today it remains a center of activity in the small town, just off the main business street. Stately trees and a lush green lawn soften the brick exterior. A large painting in the front of the green commemorates the "Union occupation" of the town.

The jail's evidence locker, a tiny cubbyhole underneath the stairs, was used primarily for storing moonshine. The jailer often spent the night at jail, although occasionally, as in the case of the raid on the Lovings, he accompanied the sheriff and deputy to make arrests. Such forays, which left a trustee in charge of the facilities, were sharply curtailed after one trustee emptied the evidence locker and sold moonshine from the back window of the jail. In 1967 larger penal facilities were needed and a new jail was built down the street. The old jail now houses the museum of the Caroline County Historical Society.[23] Even after the new jail was built, security remained rather lax. Jack Lilly recalls being appointed to represent a prisoner who had been charged with grand larceny. When he got to the jail, the sheriff told him that the prisoner would be returning shortly. He had been sent to the post office to retrieve the mail.[24]

On July 17, 1958, Richard appeared before Justice of the Peace Edward Stehl III at the Bowling Green courthouse adjacent to the jail. Mildred's court appearance was on October 13. The run-on statement of an indictment read,

[T]he said Richard Perry Loving, being a white person and the said Mildred Dolores Jeter being a colored person, did unlawfully and feloniously go out of the state of Virginia, for the purpose of being married, and with the intention of returning to the State of Virginia and were married out of the State of Virginia, to-wit, in the District of Columbia on June 2, 1958, and afterwards returned to and resided in the County of Caroline, State of Virginia, cohabitating as man and wife against the peace and dignity of the Commonwealth.[25]

On the advice of their lawyer, Frank Beazely, Richard and Mildred entered pleas of not guilty, but the court did not agree. Regarding Richard's case (and later Mildred's), Judge Stehl ruled, "Upon defendant's plea of not guilty to the within charge, and upon examination of witnesses I find probable cause to charge the accused with a felony and it is ordered that he be held for action of the grand jury."[26]

Edward Stehl died in 1993. His wife has stated that, in his professional practice, Stehl represented clients of all races, and the outside world considered him to be a moderate on the race issue. However, events gave the lie to this reputation when, in the 1980s, his eldest daughter from his first marriage, a successfully employed, college-educated woman, married a black man. Stehl refused to recognize the marriage. He did not attend the wedding and forbade his daughter from visiting his home with her husband. Eventually, Stehl relented and allowed her entry into his home but refused to recognize her marriage or allow her to bring her husband along. Mrs. Stehl says that the daughter's marriage "broke her father's heart" and "totally destroyed him." She was the only child left completely out of Stehl's will.[27]

The choice of Frank Beazely as the couple's attorney was a well-advised one. Beazely was considered *the* lawyer in Caroline County for many years, even though there were at least three other attorneys to choose from. Beazely was certainly the only lawyer a knowledgeable person would want if she or he was appearing before Judge Leon M. Bazile, who would be hearing the Lovings' case. Rumor has it that at one point in his career, the Virginia legislature planned not to renew Bazile's appointment. As a member of the legislature, Beazely made an impassioned plea that persuaded the body to retain Bazile. This intervention appeared to create a bond between the two men. Lilly remembers a 1995 trial in which Beazely bought Cokes for the jury without Bazile's objecting to such improper actions.[28] The sheriff and deputy sheriff who took office in 1964 confirm the local legend, which had it that Bazile ruled the way Beazely wanted him to rule.[29]

Bazile not only appeared to be in the thrall of Frank Beazely but also showed some bias in favor of Sheriff Brooks. When Brooks's first cousin applied for a divorce and custody of his child, Bazile moved quickly. He issued an injunction that allowed Brooks and his deputy to proceed to the cousin's home and take possession of the child. When the child's mother objected, "[t]he sheriff and his deputy forcibly took [the child], who was crying, from his mother's arms." Within half an hour, the men returned with a truck to remove the mother from the house. When she hid in the bedroom, Brooks kicked the door down, as suggested by her husband. She was told she could take some possessions with her, but when she refused to state what property she wanted, she was handcuffed, driven to the courthouse, and released behind the jail. Bazile's decision to grant the husband a divorce and custody of the child was reversed on appeal.[30]

At a grand jury hearing later in the year, forewoman Gladys Livermon brought formal charges against Richard and Mildred. Although they had the option of appearing before a jury, the Lovings waived that right because the facts were not in dispute and they knew it was unlikely that a jury in Virginia would be sympathetic to their plight. As it turned out, neither was the judge. The Lovings pled guilty to the charge, and on January 6, 1959, Judge Bazile pronounced the following sentence:

The court doth accept the pleas of "guilty" and fix the punishment of both accused at one year each in jail. The court does suspend said sentence for a period of twenty-five years upon the provision that both accused leave Caroline County and the State of Virginia at once and do not return together or at the same time to said county and state for a period of twenty-five years.[31]

Given Bazile's animosity toward mixed marriages, one might have expected him to sentence the unlucky couple to the maximum penalty allowable by law (five years). In all likelihood, their punishment—in effect, a suspended sentence—would have been far more severe had Beazely not represented them.[32]

Bazile asked whether the couple had anything to say before final sentencing. Displaying the same rectitude that they maintained throughout their lengthy court battle, they did not. They each paid court costs of $36.29, were released from custody, and reluctantly headed back to Washington, D.C., where they took up residence with Mildred's cousin Alex Byrd and his wife, Laura.[33] Richard crossed the Potomac every day to work as a laborer in Virginia. Although they could not live with their families, the Lovings were not completely cut off. Mildred returned to Virginia at the end of each of her pregnancies so that Richard's mother, a midwife, could deliver all three of the Lovings' babies[34]: Sidney, born in 1958, Donald, born in 1959, and Peggy, born in 1960.[35]

The ruling allowed the Lovings to visit the state separately, but Frank Beazely advised them that it was permissible for them to visit Virginia together as long as they did not stay at the same house overnight. Unfortunately, this advice was contrary to Judge Bazile's order. When the couple returned in March 1959 to spend Easter with their families, they were rearrested and charged with violating their parole. Initially they were asked to post a two-hundred-dollar bond and appear before the court on April 13. Beazely pled their case in front of Judge Bazile, assuring the judge that he was at fault for misinterpreting the order. The charges were dismissed without the Lovings having to spend any time in jail.[36] In all probability, a lawyer other than Beazely would not have been able to spare the couple from jail time for this infraction.[37]

Born and bred in the countryside, the Lovings were very unhappy in their exile. Mildred missed the grass beneath her feet and simple pleasures like walking down a country lane to pick up her mail. She felt that the concrete of Washington, D.C., was no substitute for the open spaces of Caroline County.[38] After their son Donald was hit by a car, the pair was even further convinced that they needed to go back to the country.[39] Many rural sections of the South would not have been particularly hospitable to a mixed-race couple, but Central Point, Virginia, was another story.

2

The Passing Capital of America

[No clergy or lay person] making the slightest pretensions to respectability, can be found so debased and so regardless of the opinions of their fellow citizens [as to perform intermarriage ceremonies]....It is cruel, unjust and improper to augment the excitement already existing against an unfortunate and comparatively helpless portion of the human family...to punish that as a high crime, which is at most but evidence of vicious feeling, bad taste, and personal degradation.
>   —Senator John Pearson of Pennsylvania, speaking in 1841 against
>   a bill to fine those who solemnize interracial marriages

*B*y many accounts, Richard Loving looked like the last guy in the world to risk going to jail to defend the honor of a black woman. His attorney, Philip Hirschkop, has stated that he "looked like a real redneck. You could just picture him in a Klan outfit." Richard was devoted to his wife, however, and was "a very decent human being." Hirschkop calls them "the strangest damn couple I've ever seen in my life; the most mismatched I've ever seen." But they were clearly committed to one another and made their decisions in tandem. There was no doubt about their strength as a couple. Hirschkop reports that he never heard them argue.[1] Although both of them were painfully shy, Richard was more quiet and introspective than his wife. Even when he was in the room, he let Mildred do all the talking.[2] It wasn't that he didn't understand what was taking place; he just didn't comment on it.[3] He was "very country, sort of rough."[4] Neither of the Lovings finished high school. Richard dropped out after one year, and Mildred left after eleventh grade.[5] Local attorney Jack Lilly believes that Mildred was significantly more intelligent than Richard, whose shyness rendered him mute in many situations.[6]

Hirschkop's former partner, Bernie Cohen, describes both Richard and Mildred as "uncomplicated people" who had no interest in "making a statement or becoming civil rights heroes."[7] That is almost an understatement. As their case headed toward the Supreme Court, the *Baltimore Afro-American* noted that they were not members of any civil rights organization and were not attempting to create social reforms.[8] To this day, Mildred objects to any characterization of her actions as heroic or even noteworthy.[9] She and Richard had no interest in establishing any kind of principle. They were simply two people in love who wanted to live together as husband and wife in their hometown.[10]

It was easy for Richard and Mildred to fall in love in rural Central Point, Virginia. Race lines were less distinct in Central Point than in other parts of the state or the South. The town has been called "the passing capital of America" for the ability of its black residents to quietly pass as white once they leave town. One Central Point resident claimed that the town had "done more integrating than any other part of the United States."[11] The official dividing line was still there, and the races were segregated in schools, hospitals, churches, and all forms of organized civic life. However, different institutions did not prevent social interaction, and the Loving and Jeter families were no exception. For his part, Richard said that while he was growing up, "everybody looked alike to me."[12]

Richard's father drove a truck for a wealthy black farmer for almost twenty-five years, an employment situation that was highly unusual in the South. Richard, a brick mason, was a member of a drag-racing partnership with two black friends, Percy Fortune and Raymond Green. Fortune was a local merchant, and Green was a mechanic.[13] Raymond Green continues to maintain an auto repair shop just down the street from Mildred Loving's home. *Ebony* magazine called the trio "the country's most successful integrated drag racing team" and dubbed Richard "the spark plug." Usually, Fortune drove the car, with Loving and Green as mechanics, but occasionally Richard got behind the wheel. In 1966 the team won thirty-eight trophies and collected almost three thousand dollars to split among them.[14]

Described in a 1992 *New York Times* article as "little more than a scattering of simple homes with a boarded up general store," Central Point is a speck in the middle of Caroline County.[15] It is such a small place that it is not included on state maps. Caroline County is a rural section of eastern Virginia, northeast of Richmond and southeast of Fredericksburg, roughly thirty miles long and twenty miles wide.[16] As of 2001, the population of Caroline County was just 22,100. The county seat, Bowling Green, site of the courthouse and jail, had just over 750 citizens.[17]

Historically, Caroline County's major industries have included agriculture, forestry products, and mining. Well into the 1990s, the county continued to have fifty-one thousand acres of farmland and 261,000 acres of commercial forest land among its 549 square miles.[18] However, the county is courting the future. The section of its Web page that addresses economic development consists of an invitation to manufacturers and retailers to relocate rather than a list of current industries.[19] County taxes are quite low, with the local sales tax a mere 1%. Changing times are reflected in the rise in Sheriff's Department personnel from three in 1958 to thirty-three in 1998. In addition, the state has assigned eleven state police officers to the county.[20] A review of the local civic organizations shows a social life heavily weighted toward school groups, boy and girl scout troops, 4-H clubs, and organizations like Children of the Confederacy and United Daughters of the Confederacy.[21] A better reflection of the community is the listing of the sixty-four area churches, the majority of which are Independent Baptist, with Southern Baptist and United Methodist congregations following in number. The county hosts only one Catholic church, no synagogue, and no mosque.[22]

Central Point is just one of many tiny spots that exist as towns in name only. At one time, it was among seventy-seven communities in Caroline County that had their own post offices. Today, only six towns within the county hold that distinction. Improved transportation and the growth of chain stores have taken business away from the small general stores that once housed post offices.[23] Aside from St. Stephen's Baptist Church and Raymond Green's auto repair shop, Central Point is just a collection of single-family homes. The road on which the Lovings settled after their case was finished is a narrow, winding lane without shoulders or painted lines, its surface a middle ground between pavement and gravel. Some of the land is farmed, some of it is being logged, and some lies fallow, although it appears as though many of the fallow fields were working farms not too long ago. Along the road are pines, maples, oaks, and a number of ornamental dogwood and cherry trees. Wisteria vines are cultivated next to some of the houses, but the purple blossoms also run wild along the side of the road. The raising of livestock, like farming, is fading in popularity. Although a few families still raise cows or chickens, or both, broken fences and empty pens provide evidence of the number of residents who have opted for the supermarket over homegrown meat and eggs.

A quick drive down the main road of Central Point, appropriately called Passing Road, clearly shows that it is inhabited by people of mixed ancestry. Although the homes are far apart, there is an unmistakable sense of neighborliness. Central Point is the kind of place where a request for directions to a house will consist of "wait until you see the first brick house on the right. Then go to the second driveway on your left." People have lived on the road all their lives without bothering to notice the actual house numbers of their friends and relatives.[24] Richard and Mildred's roots in the area are evident. Just outside Central Point are at least two homes that have the name "Loving" on the mailbox, and there is a road called Jeter Lane after Mildred's family.

Sparta, the village nearest to Central Point, looks as though it is ready to be discovered by real estate developers. Trailer homes and modest old shacks coexist with statelier brick homes with long driveways and manicured hedges. Sparta is enough of a town to be listed on local maps, but the churches and cemeteries outnumber by far the retail establishments. The Mattaponi River, named after an indigenous Native American tribe, cuts through Sparta. While Central Point looks as though the housing boon has passed it by, Sparta is starting to show signs of prosperity. Sparta still has its own post office and a few small general stores. It also houses one of the few multistory buildings in the county: a tiny apartment house.

Many of the black farmers in the area in and around Central Point were "white enough 'to pass'" in the 1950s and 1960s. Race was not considered a major factor in daily life. A resident of Central Point attested to the fact that although the Lovings weren't the recipients of many congratulatory calls after the Supreme Court ruled in their favor in June of 1967, neither did they receive any death threats. Admittedly, their lack of a telephone and daily mail delivery probably contributed to the dearth of responses. One of Mildred's cousins noted that Richard was not the first white person in their family and would not be the last. Inhabitants have described Central Point as a place where black and white families were friendly with one another and sexual relations across the color bar were not uncommon. Mixed-race children were prevalent, but they were generally the product of nonmarital sexual relations.[25]

Shortly after the Lovings were married, a local farmer commended Richard, noting that "[a] lot of folks down here just don't have the guts Richard had. There has been plenty of mingling among races for years and nobody griped or tried to legalize it. Negroes got kind of slick and passed and fooled outsiders. Rich just wasn't the type. What he wanted, he wanted on paper and legal. As a result, he broke up the system." The farmer praised Richard for standing up "when everyone else thought he couldn't win," noting that most blacks found it easier to pass than to engage overtly in an interracial marriage, while most whites were afraid to buck the system.[26]

Interracial unions, albeit of the nonmatrimonial sort, were very common in Central Point, and at least in the black community, the marriage of Richard and Mildred did not raise eyebrows. University of Georgia professor Robert Pratt remembers seeing Mildred and her three children visit her sister's family down the road from his grandmother's house in the nearby town of Battery. Richard visited, too, but he avoided driving with Mildred, particularly during daylight hours.[27] However, as the years progressed, Richard became less cautious, perhaps out of confidence that the black community "would keep his secret."[28]

The producer of the film *Mr. and Mrs. Loving* describes Central Point during the middle of the twentieth century as a place of surprising racial harmony for that era, a harmony perhaps due to the fact that residents of all races were equally poor. His research indicates that Central Point was the site of a massive amount of black–American Indian intermarriage in the early years of the country. The town was virtually untouched by the civil rights movement.[29] Of course, the reason for that omission is that the civil rights movement typically sought out areas of resistance. While Central Point may not have been as ideal as many remember it, it did not display the violence and overt tension of similar towns in Mississippi and Alabama.

In the 1960s, Central Point was a predominantly black community. It was also a springboard from which literally hundreds of men and women left home to quietly cross the color line simply by neglecting to inform their spouses, employers, landlords, and so forth that by law they were legally black. Even black Central Point youngsters shopped and attended

theaters in nearby towns by posing as white. Within the small town, however, there was no hiding one's heritage. As a result, when relatives who
were passing for white returned home with their white spouses, children
often stayed home from school to save the boundary-crossing relative the
embarrassment of being associated with a blacks-only school or school
bus. A school official was quite understanding about the problem. "These
people have infiltrated the white race more than any other group of
Negroes. When a student plays hookey from school for a week and says
an in-law is visiting the family, we understand. The kids just can't afford
to catch the Negro school bus without giving away the racial identity."[30]

People who "passed" were threatened with many forms of exposure.
The integration of the military also created problems for the passing
Central Point blacks when their "white" units accepted black GIs who
knew the Central Pointers. In general, the graduates of Central Point's
black high school crossed the color line upon graduation, and a teacher
reported that "[w]e hardly ever hear about them after they finish." For
its history of Caroline County, the St. Stephen's Baptist Church in Central Point received the following write-up: "The people of the church and
community are, as a whole, very nearly white and out of their community could not be recognized or distinguished as colored people. It is said
that the predominant blood in them is that of Indian and white races."[31]
While it is true that there is a strain of Native American blood in the
county, many blacks who were too dark to pass as white claimed such a
heritage to explain their complexion rather than admitting to African
American descent.[32]

Central Point may have been a small town and the Lovings a quiet and
unassuming couple, but Richard and Mildred would change the course
of history. Before history can be changed, however, it must be made. In
the 1600s, white settlers came voluntarily to the shores of America. Soon
they imported less-willing Africans to bear the burden of building a new
country. To ensure that the line between master and slave would be indelible, the colonists enacted a number of laws. Not least among them
were the regulations that prohibited interracial marriage.

Part Two

The Rise and Fall of Antimiscegenation Statutes
in the United States

3

Making Sense of Senseless Laws

The natural law which forbids their intermarriage and the social amalgamation which leads to the corruption of races, is as clearly divine as that which imparted to them different natures. The tendency of intimate social intermixture is to amalgamation, contrary to the laws of the races. From social amalgamation it is but a step to illicit intercourse, and but another to intermarriage. The right to be free from social contact is as clear as to be free from intermarriage. The former may be less repulsive as a condition, but no less entitled as a right.

—1865 Pennsylvania case on railroad segregation

*T*he United States is virtually unique in its proscription of interracial marriages. In Spanish-colonized Latin American territories, marriage between the colonists and the indigenous people was initially forbidden, but the ban was lifted in 1514, more than 450 years prior to *Loving*.[1] Anthropologist J. A. Rogers writes that despite the abundance of people of African descent in Europe, no nation had laws against intermarriage, with the exception of France, which apparently had briefly promulgated such a law during the colonization of Haiti. In the 1940s, when Rogers wrote his three-volume treatise on sex and race, only two other countries—Australia and South Africa—had any marital restrictions based on race, while roughly half of the United States continued to proscribe interracial unions.[2]

Historians debate whether racism or economics motivated the creation of antimiscegenation laws. A look at the language of the early statutes shows that economics was certainly a major issue, but the longevity of these statutes, well beyond the odious days when one human being could be owned by another, indicates that racism soon became a major one as well. During the period of slavery, laws that prohibited the coupling of owner and owned were promulgated in response to the likelihood that such unions would obscure the racial barriers necessary for the maintenance of the system.[3] Antimiscegenation laws also prevented poor white servants from seeing their interests as dovetailing with those of black slaves. Underlying the economic interests at stake, the laws prevented these two subordinate groups from combining their forces in rebellion against white slave owners.[4]

Antimiscegenation laws were also a means of controlling the sexuality of women. Most of the early statutes reserved harsher penalties for women who crossed the color line than for their male partners. Paternalism toward white women greatly motivated the enactment of these statutes. A review of the first such laws shows that their major concern was the coupling of white women with black men, not that of white men with black women. In part this double standard derived from the status of a child generally being based on the status of its mother. Thus white women who bore mulatto children were guilty of "tainting" the white race and merited far more severe punishment than black women bearing such children.[5] Although in some states both black men and white women were punished for producing mixed-race offspring, no similar penalty was ever exacted against white men who impregnated black women.

One of the most intriguing aspects of the laws that banned interracial marriage is their name: antimiscegenation. The word *miscegenation* was coined in 1864 by two Democrats who tried to discredit Abraham Lincoln. David Goodman Croly and George Wakeman penned an anonymous, allegedly Republican election pamphlet called "Miscegenation: The Theory of the Blending of the Races, Applied to the American White Man and Negro."[6] In their guise as pseudo-Republicans, the duo sang the praises of intermixing.[7]

The little pamphlet caused quite a stir and sparked debate on both sides of the Atlantic, with the *London Morning Herald* being the first paper to unravel Croly and Goodman's hoax. The New York newspapers engaged in a small war, accusing each other's editorial staffs of favoring amalgamation. The *New York Herald* accused all its rivals of having "indorsed [*sic*] and advocated" miscegenation, writing that the Republicans "and their families have taken it up, and have sent a regiment of darkeys, to be transformed first into heroes, and then into husbands, and then into miscegenators." Even the *New York Times* sounded the theme of Republican miscegenation, printing an editorial that claimed the local Republican Union Club

> has fitted up a nightbell at its door . . . and keeps a black minister on the premises, who marries all couples of different colors at any hour of the day or night. . . . [I]f things go on at their present rate, it is feared that in three months every white man who is not connected by marriage with a colored family will be "read out" of the party.[8]

States employed a variety of defenses to explain their continued criminalization of intermarriage. In general, they rationalized antimiscegenation statutes as a way to "protect" their white citizenry from a growing nonwhite population. North Dakota, however, acted to prohibit interracial marriages at a time when only 201 blacks resided in the state. Nebraska included Mongolians in its prohibition despite the fact that the combined Japanese and Chinese population of the state was less than one-twenty-fifth of one percent. Mississippi's intermarriage ban included Japanese even though in 1940, only one Japanese person resided in the entire state.[9] Wyoming did Mississippi one better, banning marriages between whites and Malays at a time when not a single Malay could be found in any corner of the territory.[10]

Many states argued that their statutes protected the public health. According to a report of the Public Health Service, however, fourteen of the seventeen states that did not require premarital blood tests in 1948 had antimiscegenation laws. In the *Mercer Law Review,* Edward Wright noted that "the worst offenders of the states failing to protect their citizens with a good health law are the very states which insist they must protect the health of their citizens by prohibiting interracial marriage."[11]

Other states defended their statutes by saying they supported public morals. Nonetheless, although forty-one states prohibited interracial marriage, only twenty-two banned interracial sex, which, from a morality standpoint, would certainly be at least as noxious as marriage.[12] In addition, only eight states prohibited interracial cohabitation.[13] Interracial marriage was clearly regarded more harshly than less permanent forms of black-white sexual liaisons.

Such contradictions make it highly unlikely that health, morals, or even race per se were the dominant impulses in the initial enactment of antimiscegenation laws. When people are divided by caste, the higher-class men generally guard the chastity of their women and girls against any encroachment by the subordinate class. Social interaction would undermine the power of the ruling class. Historians observe that when the United States was founded, miscegenation was "not only a serious breach of Puritan morality, but also a serious threat to slavery and the stability of the servile labor force."[14]

When Gunnar Myrdal conducted his research for *An American Dilemma* in the 1930s and 1940s, he asked white southerners to list the things they thought blacks wanted most. The number one item on the list was intermarriage and sexual intercourse with whites. In a complete reversal of this ranking, black southerners placed bedroom equality sixth on their list, well below economic opportunity, fair treatment in court, political enfranchisement, desegregation of public facilities, and social equality and etiquette, in that order.[15] Myrdal believed that the entire system of segregation was designed and perpetuated to prevent interracial liaisons. "Sex becomes . . . the principle around which the whole structure of segregation of the Negroes—down to disenfranchisement and denial of equal opportunities in the labor market—is organized."[16] Interviewed in 1963, Myrdal reiterated his finding that intermarriage was far more on the minds of the white man than the Negro. "This is a kind of bug in the white man's brain—that the Negro is particularly anxious to marry his daughter."[17] In a book published in 1959, NAACP attorney Jack Greenberg used more than three hundred pages to describe racial discrimination in numerous areas of American life, only to conclude that the "[u]nderlying opposition to the desegregation discussed in previous chapters is segregationist hostility to sexual relations between Negro men and white women and intermarriage. Indeed, some who could not be called strong supporters of segregation oppose such contacts."[18]

Pseudoscience carried the day in court. In *Scott v. Georgia*,[19] the judge dabbled in social science to hold that interracial children were "sickly and effeminate" and physically inferior to their full-blooded counterparts.[20] In North Carolina, a judge quoted physiologists in support of the statement that a woman who gave birth to mulatto children had her blood "tainted by mingling with that of her first child, and she is incapable of bearing children that will not show mixture of African blood in appearance or character." Therefore, a white man whose wife had given birth to a mixed-race child was justified in asking for a divorce because he had "lost the common right lawfully to continue his pure race."[21] An Alabama court held that "there can not be any tyranny or injustice in requiring both alike to join this union with those of their own race only, whom God hath joined together by indelible peculiarities, which declare that He has made the two races distinct."[22] Missouri got into the act, insisting that the offspring of interracial couples were the equivalent of mules in their inability to reproduce.[23]

Before a state can get to the business of outlawing marriages, it has to determine what type of people constitute the "undesirable" class of prospective spouses. Although a majority of the states in the union have had various laws that mandated segregation, the definition of who was to be segregated was usually placed in the section of the state statute pertaining to miscegenation.[24] Crossing the boundary from one state to another could change a person's racial classification. Some states were so worried that future generations might allow persons of darker complexion to sneak into the white race that they included racial definitions in their constitutions.[25]

Most states held that a single African American great-grandparent or even great-great-grandparent tainted the blood of a person sufficiently to classify him or her as black. Only Oregon stated that a person had to have a full-blooded African American grandparent to be considered black. Virginia and Georgia were the most extreme examples, requiring registration of race on documents such as birth, marriage, divorce, and death certificates, and holding that a single drop of blood from a black relative was sufficient to render a person unfit to marry a white.[26] Some states had more restrictive definitions regarding interracial marriage than those about school or transportation segregation.[27]

As one might expect, the most exclusive definitions of race emerged from the Deep South. The Georgia definition is written in a particularly stringent manner. "The term 'white person' shall include only persons of the white or Caucasian race who have no ascertainable trace of either Negro, African, West Indian, Asiatic Indian, Mongolian, Japanese or Chinese blood in their veins."[28] "Any Negro blood" was also sufficient in Alabama, Arizona, Montana, Oklahoma, and Virginia. While not using those terms, Louisiana's law simply applied to people "of color."[29] It is unclear whether Nevada's lawmakers realized that they were making their prohibition narrower than most when they banned marriage between whites and people of Ethiopian descent.[30]

Some states were in such a hurry to classify on the basis of race that they arrived at multiple and conflicting definitions. In Florida, the state constitution defined a "Negro" as someone who had at least one-sixteenth African American blood (i.e., at least one great-great-grandparent). The antimiscegenation law, however, was more generous, including only those who were no more than one-eighth black.[31] Louisiana became so enamored of definitions that its statute defined mulattoes, quadroons, octoroons, and griffes.[32] This legislative overkill may have been the result of a case in which a white man escaped conviction of interracial concubinage by stating that his paramour, only one-eighth black, did not qualify under the statute.[33] Although Louisiana's reductio ad absurdum was uncommon, ten states (Arkansas, California, Colorado, Delaware, Idaho, Kentucky, Mississippi, South Carolina, Tennessee, and Wyoming) specifically mentioned mulattoes in their bans.[34] Nevada also used the term *mulatto,* but only for its concubinage statute.[35] South Carolina was the only state to include mestizos in its prohibition, although legislators neglected to define the term.[36]

It wasn't just the individual states that got into the classification act. The federal census was quite uneven in its determination of who was black. In 1870 there were separate categories for blacks and mulattoes, but the following census featured a category for blacks only. In 1890 the census defined blacks as those with three-fourths or more Negro blood and included separate categories for mulattoes, quadroons, and octoroons. In 1900, only blacks were counted, and in 1910 and 1920 mulattoes were once again a separate category.[37]

For those who might not understand polysyllabic racial classifications, Nevada forbade fornication, adultery, and marriage between whites and "any person of the Ethiopian or black race, Malay or brown race, or Mongolian or yellow race."[38] The law in Arkansas made some interesting distinctions. A person with "any Negro blood whatsoever" was forbidden from engaging in concubinage with a white person but was allowed to marry a white person as long as his or her Negro blood was not "visible and distinct."[39] To further muddle matters, for school segregation purposes, Arkansas found any trace of Negro blood sufficient, but for railroad segregation purposes, there had to be a "visible and distinct admixture."[40] Although defining who was black appeared to be a national pastime, only four states (Georgia, Oklahoma, Texas, and Virginia) thought it worth their while to define who was white.[41]

A number of states were fairly vague in their racial definitions. Alabama's last statutory revision defined a "person of color" as someone descended from Negro ancestors, with no reference to the limit of time or number of generations.[42] Arizona looked to see whether the offending party had "a visible and distinct admixture of African blood." As in Arkansas, for the purpose of concubinage, the statute was broader, referring to anyone who had "any negro blood whatever."[43] A Missouri judicial decision stipulated that the race of parties could be judged by appearance.[44] Equally absurd was the case of West Virginia, which relied on a person's reputation, considering someone a member of the Negro race if she or he was "known" to be such.[45]

Some states revised their statutes ad nauseam. At one point, Arizona had a law so restrictive that a person of mixed blood could not marry, period.[46] Virginia changed the definition of *Negro* three times and the definition of *Indians* twice. One of the more bizarre aspects of the Virginia antimiscegenation law is that an exception was made for the descendants of Pocahontas and John Rolfe, despite the fact that under the law, the two would have been jailed for their union.[47] Georgia originally forbade marriages between whites and persons of African descent.[48] Later, the law provided that "[i]t shall be unlawful for a white person to marry anyone except a white person."[49]

As the years progressed, the penalties for miscegenation increased, and the definition of *Negro* became more inclusive. In addition, many states began to include other racial classifications among their list of unmarriables. The initial prohibitions targeted only black and white unions, but subsequently some states, led by South Carolina, extended the prohibition to American Indians. This feeling was not universal. Thomas Jefferson, despite having spoken strongly against the marriage of whites and blacks, suggested that Indians and whites should "meet and blend together, to intermix, and become one people." The laws of several states read differently, and in response, a number of Native American tribes, most notably those in Virginia, banned marriage between their members and blacks. The Cherokee were the first to take this step, in 1824.[50] They punished marriages between free persons and slaves with fifty strokes of the whip and would not allow parties to such a union to hold office. The Creeks banned sex and marriage between their tribe and blacks (free or slave) and barred the offspring of such a union from inheritance rights.[51] In 1886 the Pamunkeys decreed that any tribal member who married someone other than an Indian or a white person would forfeit his or her rights in town.[52] This prohibition may well have been a direct response to an 1843 petition signed by more than 140 white people to abolish the Pamunkey and Mattaponi reservations on the grounds that their members were more than one quarter black and thus were legally mulattoes.[53] The Chickahominy followed the Pamunkeys' lead, stating that any member who married a black person would forfeit his or her tribal membership.[54]

As Asians migrated to the West, Chinese were added to some antimiscegenation statutes. When Japanese began arriving as well, the catchall term *Mongolian* was included.[55] The western United States was more likely to include Asians among the prohibited classes. States specifying Mongolians included Arizona, California, Georgia, Idaho, Mississippi, Missouri, Montana, Nebraska, Nevada, Oregon, South Carolina, South Dakota, Utah, Virginia, and Wyoming. Ten states had similarly strong feelings against Malays: Arizona, California, Georgia, Maryland, Nevada, Oregon, South Carolina, South Dakota, Virginia, and Wyoming.[56] Five states prohibited unions with American Indians: Arizona, Georgia, North Carolina, Oregon, and South Carolina.[57] In 1961, South Carolina made an exception for Catawba Indians, but no other tribe could wed Caucasians.[58]

Occasionally, states got so specific in their legislation as to include nationalities, as well as races. Idaho, Montana, Nebraska, Nevada, and Oregon specifically banned Chinese-white intermarriages, and Montana and Nevada were moved to exclude Japanese-white unions as well.[59] North Dakota was the only maverick state that placed a specific ban on Korean-white marriages, and Oregon was the sole state to feel threatened by Kanakans (Hawaiians).[60] Oddly, Oregon used a one-fourth percentage criterion when banning whites from marrying the aforementioned Asian groups and blacks but allowed whites to marry those who had no more than one-half Indian blood.[61] Only Georgia found it necessary to preclude the union of whites with Asiatic Indians.[62] Presumably this term referred to natives of India and Pakistan but remained undefined. Only Arizona included a religious group—Hindus—though it is likely that the lawmakers thought they were referring to Georgia's "Asiatic Indians."

In general, states were profoundly uninterested in the racial purity of any group but whites, but exceptions did occur. In Louisiana and Oklahoma, blacks and Indians were forbidden to marry one another. North Carolina was more specific, prohibiting blacks from wedding Cherokees from Robeson County. In Maryland, marriage between blacks and Malays was off-limits.[63]

As long as states were in the business of deciding how much black blood sufficed to render someone unqualified to marry a white person, they faced inevitable challenges from people who claimed to have less than the percentage of blood deemed sufficient to render them black. Hence states had to come up with methods for determining the racial constitution of individuals who challenged their classifications. Where genealogy charts were unavailable, a person's appearance could be the key, something that was actually codified by statute in Missouri. A party could prove her or his whiteness to the court by such methods as being "reputed to be white," associating with whites, enjoying high social status, and exercising the rights of a white person.[64] In one Texas case, evidence that a woman's first husband was a Confederate soldier was sufficient to prove that she was white.[65] In Virginia, the state registrar used illegitimacy as evidence that a person was black. Of course, the registrar was so firmly grounded in scientific theory that he also believed illegitimacy was an inherited trait that could be transmitted to future generations.[66]

Blackness was generally proven by physical appearance, as determined (depending on the state) by a judge or jury. Photographs of the person and hearsay evidence were, at times, admissible to prove the existence of Negro blood. One court ruled that evidence of a man's Sicilian or Mediterranean heritage was insufficient to show that the physical characteristics in question (curly hair, dark skin) did not prove that he was black. A second court required a witness to take off his shoes on the assumption that black people have "a peculiar configuration of foot." A third court asked a woman to bear her breasts on the theory that a black woman's nipples lack "a pinkish pigmentation" found only in white women.[67] A fourth found the kinky hair of a defendant's grandfather to be dispositive of the racial issue.[68]

Once states had determined who was black, the next step was to ensure that the punishment fit the crime. An amazing variety of fines and jail terms (not to mention whippings during the Puritan days) were meted out to those who had the temerity to marry outside their race. The longest jail terms were up to ten years (not including the antebellum statute calling for life imprisonment), and the largest fines reached twenty thousand dollars. Although colonial times saw the last use of the term *banishment,* that penalty was still routinely applied to couples up to and including Richard and Mildred Loving.[69] Miscegenation was a misdemeanor in some states and a felony in others. In Maryland and North Carolina, it was deemed "an infamous crime."[70] As in the case of racial definitions, several states (Alabama, Florida, Mississippi, North and South Carolina, and Tennessee) were so worried about the possible leniency of future generations that they included antimiscegenation provisions in their constitutions.[71]

In general, the Pacific and mountain states had lesser penalties for intermarriage than the southern and border states. On the other hand, several western states (Arizona, Colorado, Idaho, Nevada, Utah, and Washington) were in such a hurry to ban intermarriage that they passed their antimiscegenation laws before achieving statehood. Despite their haste to prohibit intermarriage, the mountain states in particular featured medium to high fines and short prison terms, while the South more frequently eschewed fines in favor of harsh prison terms. Tennessee imprisoned miscegenators for one to five years, Virginia and Texas for two to five, Alabama for two to seven, and Florida, North Carolina, and Maryland for up to ten years. Florida was one of the few southern states to add a hefty fine, penalizing its miscegenators up to ten thousand dollars. The only mountain states to feature severe sentences were the Dakotas, both of which inflicted fines of ten thousand to twenty thousand dollars and prison sentences of up to ten years.[72] In the South, Delaware was the most "progressive" state. There, a miscegenator might get off with a fine of one hundred dollars or a prison term of thirty days, if unable to pay.[73]

In addition to these penalties, the states invalidated the offending marriage with varying degrees of insistence: most states simply rendered the union "void" or "null and void." However, Colorado, Missouri, and Virginia declared such couplings "absolutely void"; Delaware and Mississippi found them "unlawful and void"; Arkansas, California, and Idaho pronounced them "illegal and void"; and Florida and South Carolina proclaimed them "utterly null and void."[74] In Kentucky, although the marriage of underage persons had to be voided via legal proceedings, no hearings were necessary for the voiding of interracial unions.[75] Similarly, in Missouri, although the marriage of "incompetents" was merely voidable, the marriage of persons of different races was immediately void, with no proceedings whatsoever.[76]

Although many of the earliest statutes punished only the white party to an interracial marriage, West Virginia is the only state never to amend this practice.[77] Colorado was the only state to have separate laws applicable to different parts of the state. Although in the northern sections, the law provided penalties of three months to two years in prison and a fine of up to five hundred dollars for the bride, groom, and wedding officials, those residents of "that portion of the state acquired from Mexico [could marry] according to the custom of that county."[78] Kentucky was the only state to give miscegenators a second chance. Marriages between whites and mulattoes were declared void and subject to a fine of up to five hundred dollars. If the cohabitation continued, the parties could be sentenced to three to twelve months in prison.[79]

To guard against those interracial couples who had the temerity to marry out of state and return across the border, Delaware, Mississippi, Montana, Texas, and Virginia had specific statutory sections forbidding such acts. Georgia and Louisiana went so far as to invalidate all extraterritorial interracial marriages, whether the ceremonies had been performed elsewhere to evade the state's statute or not.[80]

With the exception of California, all states provided penalties for the miscegenous parties. Seventeen states also punished persons who solemnized interracial ceremonies, ten punished those who knowingly issued a license, and three punished anyone assisting in a ceremony. In Indiana, anyone who counseled persons wishing to engage in such a union faced a penalty, while Oklahoma and North Dakota punished anyone who concealed the record of an interracial marriage.[81] The North Dakota concealment penalty was up to two years in prison and a fine of up to two thousand dollars.[82]

Not surprisingly, Mississippi had one of the most nonsensical laws. Marriages between whites and those with at least one Negro or Mongolian great-grandparent were declared null and void. Moreover, such unions were punishable as though they were incest, with fines of up to five hundred dollars and prison sentences of up to ten years.[83] As one antebellum statesman bizarrely reasoned, "[t]he same law which forbids consanguineous amalgamation forbids ethnical amalgamation. Both are incestuous. Amalgamation is incest."[84] It wasn't until 1958 that a Mississippi judge decided that while it was perfectly permissible to arrest someone for miscegenation, such unions were clearly not incestuous.[85]

Finally, Mississippi added the kicker that

Any person, firm or corporation who shall be guilty of printing, publishing or circulating printed, typewritten or written matter urging or presenting for public acceptance or general information, arguments or suggestions in favor of social equality or of intermarriage between whites and negroes, shall be guilty of a misdemeanor and subject to a fine not exceeding $500 or imprisonment not exceeding six months or both.[86]

Whatever the reason, antimiscegenation statutes proliferated in the United States. From their inception in the 1600s to their demise in 1967, these laws were promulgated in virtually every state of the union. Long before the colonies threw off the mantle of European control, they had exerted their own influence by passing these unique laws.

4

How It All Began

*F*orty-one states, either before or since they achieved statehood, have prohibited interracial marriage. Only Alaska, Connecticut, Hawaii, Minnesota, New Hampshire, New Jersey, New York, Vermont, and Wisconsin have not considered the act of interracial marriage heinous enough for legal prohibition. Yet nothing in the common law or statutes of England, France, or Spain provides a precedent for such laws.[1]

The first statutes made their appearance in the 1600s. Well into the twentieth century, states continued to enact and reenact intermarriage bans, with Wyoming becoming the last state to institute a new ban in 1913. The longest-lasting antimiscegenation law was Maryland's, which endured for more than three hundred years. In contrast, Kansas's law lasted only four years and was eliminated before statehood.[2] It is not surprising that the period during and immediately after the Civil War saw the highest level of antimiscegenation legislative activity, with ten states passing new laws and eight states embellishing their existing ones over a sixteen-year period.[3] Although, as the twentieth century progressed, northern and western states slowly began repealing their statutes: in 1948, thirty states still banned intermarriage; in 1963, twenty-four states retained their bans; and in 1967, on the eve of *Loving,* sixteen states continued to find interracial marriage worthy of criminal prosecution. The holdouts were Alabama, Arkansas, Delaware, Florida, Indiana, Kentucky, Louisiana, Mississippi, Missouri, Oklahoma, North Carolina, South Carolina, Texas, Virginia, and West Virginia.[4]

By the time the colonies became the United States, most of them had antimiscegenation statutes.[5] With the exception of Louisiana,[6] all the southern states enacted their laws prior to emancipation (although some repealed them during the Reconstruction era).[7] The first antimiscegenation law was passed in Maryland in 1664.[8] Similar laws were enacted by Virginia in 1691, Massachusetts in 1705, North Carolina in 1715, Delaware in 1721, and Pennsylvania in 1725.[9]

The original Maryland law, entitled "Act Concerning Negroes[10] and Other Slaves" held that if white women, "forgetful of their free condition and to the disgrace of our nation," married slaves, they would serve the slave's master until their husband's death. If children emerged from the union, they would serve the same master for thirty years.[11] The law said nothing about free Negroes or about white men marrying free or enslaved black women.[12] In 1681 the law was revised to prohibit marriages between Christians and "Negroes and slaves," which were "always to the satisfaction of their lascivious and lustfull desires" but brought "disgrace not only of the English but also of many other Christian nations."[13] That the law referred to "Negroes" *and* "slaves" indicates that race was as much of an issue as caste. The law was amended in 1692 to forbid all interracial marriages and sexual relations.[14] Perhaps unlawful unions were still taking place, because in 1705, Maryland amended its law to explicitly forbid magistrates and ministers from performing marriages between whites and blacks.[15]

States did not maintain adequate accounts of the enforcement of their antimiscegenation laws, but some records detailing the penalties inflicted on whites who crossed the color line have survived. In Jamestown, Virginia, in 1630 (apparently before the passage of any laws on the subject), authorities decreed "that Hugh Davis be soundly whipped before an assemblage of Negroes and others for abusing himself to the dishonor of God and the shame of Christians by defiling his body in lying with a Negro, which fault he is to acknowledge next Sabbath Day."[16] Ten years later, a court ruled that "Robert Sweet is to do penance in church according to the law of England, for getting a negro woman with child, and the woman to be soundly whipped."[17] Although in Sweet's case, a punishment was also inflicted on the person of color, there is no record that Hugh Davis's black partner received any official sanctions. In 1649 a more lenient court sentenced an interracial couple to stand in penance at church wearing white sheets and carrying a white rod. The man, who was white, was also required to pay court charges.[18] An unrepentant white interracial fornicator by the name of Elizabeth Tooker "like a most obstinate and graceless person [did] cut and mangle the sheet wherein she did penance" and was required to repeat more contritely her act of public penance after receiving twenty lashes on her bare back.[19]

The Virginia Law of 1691 declared itself to be "for the prevention of that abominable mixture and spurious issue" and required that any free "English or white man or woman" who intermarried with a "Negro, mulatto or Indian bound or free" would be banished from the dominion within three months. Any white woman bearing a bastard mulatto child would be fined fifteen pounds sterling. If she was unable to pay, she would be sold by the church for a five-year period of servitude and her child would also be bound out as a servant by the church wardens until she or he reached thirty years of age.[20] Virginia was so proud of this law that the legislature reenacted it in its entirety in 1696 and 1705, although the former version omitted any penalty against the white father. The latter version reinstated the idea of a penalty but changed it from banishment to a fine and six months in prison[21] and eliminated prohibitions against white–Native American unions.[22]

Also in 1705, the Virginia assembly decided that punishing couples involved in illegal marriages was insufficient. A new addition to the act provided that any minister who married a Negro man to a white woman would pay a fine of ten thousand pounds of tobacco, of which one-half would go to the informer. The fine for the couple themselves was only ten pounds of tobacco, but they were also subject to six months imprisonment without bail.[23] Under the 1705 law, Virginia defined a mulatto as someone who was no less than one-eighth Negro or one-half Native American. In 1785, the state liberalized the law so that a person had to be one-fourth African American to qualify.[24] By 1792, Virginia had changed the fine for miscegenators to thirty dollars and that for the minister to $250.[25] Miscegenators were still subject to a six-month jail sentence.[26]

Georgia passed its first law surprisingly late, in 1750. A closer look at the state's history reveals that the reason the lawmakers waited so long is that until that year, blacks were excluded from the colony.[27] Georgia made up for lost time by being a trailblazer: the first state to declare all interracial marriages null and void.[28] One bright note was Pennsylvania's repeal of its antimiscegenation law in 1780, the first state to do so. No state would follow that lead for sixty-three years.[29] As the eighteenth century drew to a close, Rhode Island added itself to the roster by passing a law declaring interracial marriages null and void and fining the solemnizer two hundred dollars. Kentucky wasn't up to the task of creating its own prohibitions, so the legislators incorporated Virginia's restrictions into their statutes.[30]

The 1800s began much as the 1700s had ended. Indiana went through a variety of laws in the late teens and early twenties, first rendering black-white (but not mulatto-white) intermarriage illegal with the penalty at the discretion of the judge.[31] In 1818 Virginia added a prohibition against leaving the state to avoid the antimiscegenation laws,[32] a precursor to the law that Richard and Mildred Loving would be charged with violating close to 150 years later. Maine became a state in 1820 and promptly copied Massachusetts' legislation that rendered interracial marriages null and void.[33] Mississippi waited until 1822, its fifth year as a state, to pass an antimiscegenation law.[34] The Mississippi law was not an outright ban, but it implicitly prohibited interracial unions by designating officials who could solemnize the marriage of "free white persons."[35]

In 1822, Tennessee passed its first antimiscegenation law, punishing all parties involved in a black-white union.[36] Illinois's earliest antimiscegenation law was passed in 1829 after an unsuccessful attempt eight years earlier. The penalty was watered down from an initial proposal of incarceration and up to one hundred lashes to a mere thirty-nine lashes.[37] In 1832, Florida passed its first antimiscegenation law, providing penalties for the bride, groom, licensor, and performer.[38] Later, Florida moved to bar miscegenators from holding public office.[39]

Massachusetts started its slow process toward racial equality in 1834, when the legislature repealed most laws based on racial distinctions but retained the ban on intermarriage. In 1836 the state strengthened its antimiscegenation law, only to repeal it in 1843.[40] The rest of the union failed to follow suit. Missouri banned intermarriage fourteen years after achieving statehood in 1835.[41] A Missouri judge found that the state's intermarriage ban was justified on the grounds that such unions could not create progeny.[42] In 1837, Texas, while still an independent nation,[43] decreed the crime of intermarriage to be a high misdemeanor.[44] That same year, Arkansas adopted Missouri's statute.[45] Also in 1837, in its initial codification of laws, Michigan declared interracial marriages null and void and the issue of such unions illegitimate.[46]

In 1836, North Carolina raised the fines for miscegenation and modernized them from pounds to dollars. Two years later, the state added the provision that all interracial marriages were null and void.[47] In 1840, allegedly in response to the marriage of a white woman to a very light-skinned black man, Indiana revised its law to forbid marriage between whites and anyone with at least one-eighth black blood. Clerks who provided licenses to such couples were fined up to five thousand dollars and removed from office. Any person performing such a ceremony would face a fine of as much as ten thousand dollars and, if an officer of the court, would lose his job. Persons who aided and abetted the marriage were subject to a fine of up to one thousand dollars. The marriage was declared null and void, and the parties were fined up to five thousand dollars and subject to ten to twenty years in jail.[48]

The apparently unholy specter of intermarriage reared its head in Ohio in 1841, when the legislature considered repealing a law that prohibited blacks from testifying in court against whites. One argument against the repeal offered that such action "[w]ill tend to an equality of the races, and promote their intermarriage."[49] Iowa passed its first intermarriage ban while still a territory in 1840, rendering such marriages illegal and void. Within nine years, however, the law was omitted from the statute books; it never reappeared, despite attempts to pass new legislation in 1859, 1860, and 1861.[50] The 1840 House debate featured some interesting anthropological interpretations, including that of a representative who said that the Negro race did not descend from Adam, and another's assertion that offspring of mixed marriages were so unhealthy as to eventually die out.[51]

In 1848 the prison term for Virginia miscegenators was lengthened to a maximum of twelve months, and the fine was upped to one hundred dollars, while the penalty to the party who performed the ceremony was lowered to two hundred dollars.[52] In 1860 the law was amended to hold that "all marriages between a white person and a Negro, . . . shall be absolutely void without any decree or divorce, or other legal process."[53] Issuing an interracial marriage license could result in a year in prison and a five-hundred-dollar fine. Solemnizing such a marriage could now lead to a year in jail, as well as the two-hundred-dollar fine. The fine for the actual married party (white only), however, remained a mere one hundred dollars.[54] Six years later, in response to the civil rights bill of 1865, Virginia enacted legislation that held that all statutes would now apply to "colored persons and Indians" as well as whites, indicating that the state would now punish blacks for miscegenation together with their white partners.[55]

The year 1852 was a popular one for antimiscegenation legislation, with Alabama passing its first law (fining the marriage solemnizer a minimum of one thousand dollars but not punishing the miscegenators) and Delaware and Kentucky revising their laws.[56] Also in 1852, Utah banned interracial sex but did not act against mixed marriages.[57] Five years later, New Mexico passed its first antimiscegenation law, a statute that prohibited marriage between white women and nonwhite men only.[58] California passed an antimiscegenation law in 1850 during its very first legislative session.[59] Kansas, Nebraska, and Washington followed suit while still territories in 1855.[60]

In 1861, Georgia added a statutory prohibition against persons leaving the state to marry with the intention of returning to reside as husband and wife. Just in case this law was insufficient, in 1866 lawmakers amended the state constitution to ensure that "the social status of the citizen shall never be the subject of legislation."[61] After reenacting its statute in 1859 and revising it in 1866, Washington became the first western state to repeal its intermarriage ban in 1868.[62] Nevada made history in 1861 by passing the first antimiscegenation bill that banned Chinese from marrying whites.[63] Kansas was one state going in the opposite direction. In 1859 its legislators omitted the antimiscegenation provision from their statute, and the following year, they officially repealed it.[64]

After a number of unsuccessful attempts, Ohio passed its first antimiscegenation law in 1861.[65] In 1877 the law was broadened to prohibit marriage between whites and anyone with a "distinct and visible admixture of African blood." In 1885 a Republican legislator introduced the first bill to repeal the intermarriage ban. The bill was unsuccessful, but in 1886 the newly elected Republican governor called for a repeal in his inaugural address. A repeal bill promptly passed the senate by a vote of fifty-nine to twenty-five, but it took another year to get through the house, finally passing by a margin of more than three to one.[66]

Arizona became a territory in 1863. Two years later, the first miscegenation bill, which would prohibit blacks and mulattoes from marrying whites, was introduced. As it passed from the house to the council, Indians and Mongolians were added to the list.[67] The law punished the solemnizer and the parties to the marriage with a fine of one hundred to one thousand dollars and imprisonment of three months to ten years.[68] The legislature later decided that existing statutes did not sufficiently protect the white race, so the law was amended to prohibit "all marriages of persons of Caucasian blood, or their descendants, with negroes, Mongolians or Indians and their descendants."[69] A close reading of this statute reveals that persons of mixed heritage of any kind were forbidden from marrying anyone.

In 1862, three years after achieving statehood, Oregon passed an antimiscegenation law; twenty-six years later, it became the third state to prohibit Chinese-white marriages and the first to prohibit Kanakan (Hawaiian)-white marriages. In 1862 Colorado passed its first and only antimiscegenation law, one unique in that it applied only to the northern half of the state. Two years later, Idaho added Chinese to its intermarriage ban. In 1887 Idaho decided that Chinese were fit to marry whites after all but kept the ban against blacks and Indians.[70] Tennessee apparently wasn't satisfied with its statutory prohibition, and in 1870 a ban was inserted into the state constitution.[71]

The early days of Reconstruction featured some new laws. Alabama finally added penalties for the bride and groom to its antimiscegenation law and, the following year, added an intermarriage ban to the state constitution.[72] Kentucky upped the penalty for miscegenation to a maximum of five years in prison.[73] Missouri celebrated the end of the Civil War by revising its statute, and South Carolina passed its first antimiscegenation law in 1865.[74] Also during Reconstruction, six states of the former Confederacy eliminated their intermarriage prohibitions. Arkansas and South Carolina quietly dropped their statutes from revisions of the civil code, while Louisiana outright repealed its law.[75] Even the Mississippi legislature saw a repeal bill proposed (unsuccessfully) in 1870.[76] Alabama and Texas state supreme court decisions declared their states' statutes unconstitutional.[77]

The Reconstruction changes were short-lived. The following years saw the introduction or revision of antimiscegenation statutes in nine of the eleven southern states.[78] The judicial branch aided and abetted this process, as courts in Georgia, Indiana, Texas, and Alabama upheld antimiscegenation laws, with the latter two reversing the precedent set by the Reconstruction jurists.[79] In addition, state courts in Missouri, North

Carolina, and Tennessee ruled that the Fourteenth Amendment did not affect their states' antimiscegenation laws.[80]

Virginia's law had remained unchanged during Reconstruction, but subsequent times saw an expansion of the classes covered and the penalties imposed. In 1878, in a section of the law entitled "offences against morality and decency," Virginia raised the penalty for miscegenation to two to five years in prison, making the new minimum prison term greater than the prior maximum.[81] One year later, mixed-race marriages were declared "absolutely void," without the need for any divorce decree.[82]

As of 1880 the Mississippi antimiscegenation law was back on the books, and by 1890 it was embedded in the constitution.[83] The new law declared interracial marriages "incestuous and void,"[84] punishable by a prison term of up to ten years.[85] During the 1880s, Mississippi allowed those with no more than one black grandparent to marry whites, but as the decade closed, only those with no more than one black great-grandparent could enjoy this privilege.[86] Louisiana and Arkansas reinstated their antimiscegenation laws after Reconstruction omissions and repeals.[87]

In 1866 and again in 1872, North Carolina revised its statute, with the latter revision including a requirement that race be entered on all marriage certificates and other records. In 1875 the Tar Heel State joined the growing number of states that incorporated intermarriage bans in their constitutions.[88] North Carolina was also one of many states in which a marriage license held by an interracial couple was deemed meaningless and would not protect them from prosecution for fornication.[89] In 1879, South Carolina lawmakers introduced new legislation to ban intermarriage. The final version of the bill prohibited marriage between whites and "the Indian or negro races, or any mulatto, mestizoe or half breed." Miscegenators and anyone performing an interracial ceremony were guilty of a misdemeanor and subjected to a maximum of one year in prison and a fine of up to five hundred dollars.[90] Interracial marriages were declared "utterly null and void."[91] In 1895, to ensure the maintenance of the "Southern Way of Life," the South Carolina legislature proposed an antimiscegenation provision to be included in the state constitution. Incorporated in the provision was the denial of suffrage to miscegenators.[92]

Wyoming's first antimiscegenation law was somewhat short-lived. Passed in 1869 while Wyoming was still a territory, the bill prohibited marriage between whites and those with more than one-eighth Negro, Asiatic, or Mongolian blood. Whites who knowingly engaged in such a union were charged with a felony and could be imprisoned in the penitentiary for three to seven years. The nonwhite party to such a marriage was also charged with a felony, but his or her penalty was only one to five years in the penitentiary. Those intentionally issuing a license to or solemnizing such a union were guilty of a misdemeanor and sentenced to prison for three months to one year, fined one hundred to five hundred dollars, or both. The bill lasted slightly more than a decade before its overwhelming repeal in 1882.[93]

Lurid courtroom rhetoric bolstered Tennessee's decree that couples who had been legally married elsewhere would not have their unions sanctioned in the state.[94] This portion of the law was upheld in 1872 in the case of *Bell v. State.* The judge suggested that if miscegenous marriages performed outside the state were recognized,

> we might have in Tennessee the father living with his daughter, the son with his mother, the brother with the sister, in lawful wedlock, because they had formed such relations in a State or country where they were not prohibited. The Turk or Mohammedan, with his numerous wives, may establish his harem at the doors of the capital.[95]

The judge hastened to add that none of these was as horrible a specter as interracial marriage.[96]

West Virginia became a state in 1863. Within three years, it had moved to maintain separate birth, death, and marriage records by race. In 1870 legislators ensured that these records would remain separate by prohibiting intermarriage. In 1866, a very busy year for antimiscegenation legislation, Florida remedied the gender inequity in its law but not the racial imbalance. White men were now subject to punishment for interracial liaisons, but their black female partners continued to escape prosecution.[97] It wasn't until 1885 that Florida remedied this omission with a constitutional provision.[98] Rhode Island, Delaware, Indiana, Missouri, and Texas all added to their laws in the 1870s. The Indiana revisions made that state's statute one of the harshest laws around, punishing even those who "counseled amalgamation."[99] The following decade, Maryland saw fit to remove the servitude penalty but otherwise left its statute intact.[100] California celebrated the start of the 1880s by trying to add Mongolians to its intermarriage ban. This expansion initially failed to pass, but by the turn of the twentieth century, California had succeeded in banning white-Mongolian marriage.[101]

Some bright spots began to occur, particularly in the Midwest. Illinois omitted the antimiscegenation statute from its statutes in 1874, but this move may have been accidental. The original law had been unanimously approved, and there is no record of any debates about changing it.[102] Nevertheless, the statute never reappeared.

The 1880s proved to be somewhat of a turning point in the history of antimiscegenation laws. The decade saw the repeal of intermarriage bans in Maine (1883), Michigan (1883), New Mexico (1886), Ohio (1887) and Rhode Island (1881).[103] Michigan even added a provision specifically approving of marriages between whites and those of African descent.[104] In Ohio a repeal was unsuccessfully attempted in 1880 and 1884 before it was successfully paired with a school desegregation bill in 1887.[105]

The progressiveness of the 1880s was regional, at best. The decade featured a number of attempts by Louisiana legislators to sponsor new intermarriage bans. They finally managed to do so in 1894, although the law provided no penalties for violators.[106] The District of Columbia proposed its first intermarriage ban in 1887.[107] Utah banned interracial marriages in 1888 in a law that encompassed blacks and Mongolians and included jail terms for the solemnizer (up to three years) and licensor (two years and expulsion from office.)[108] In 1893, Oregon added Mongolians to its list of unmarriables, which already included blacks, Chinese, Kanakans, and Indians.[109]

In 1882 the U.S. Supreme Court had its first opportunity to review the constitutionality of antimiscegenation laws in *Pace v. Alabama:* the case that served as precedent for nearly a century of decisions upholding these laws.[110] Perhaps it is poetic justice that Alabama, the state that produced the ruling that held for almost one hundred years, held fast the longest. Until the year 2000, section 102 of the constitution of Alabama read, "The legislature shall never pass any law to authorize or legalize any marriage between any white person and a negro, or descendant of a negro." Below this section was a note indicating that "[t]his section is violative of the fourteenth amendment to the Constitution of the United States," citing *United States v. Brittain*[111] (see chapter 19).

In 1881 a black man by the name of Tony Pace and a white woman named Mary Jane Cox were indicted by the state for "living together in a state of adultery or fornication." Although there was insufficient evidence that the couple's sexual relationship met the statutory definition, they were convicted and sentenced to two years in the state penitentiary, the most lenient sentence permissible by state law. Pace challenged the constitutionality of the law, since it gave a harsher penalty to offending couples of different races than it gave to those of the same race. The Alabama Supreme Court disagreed, finding that the punishment of each offending party, white or black is the same. . . . The evil tendency of the crime of living in adultery is greater when it is committed between persons of the two races, than between persons of the same race. Its results may be the amalgamation of the two races, producing a mongrel population and degraded civilization, the prevention of which is dictated by sound public policy affecting the highest interests of society and government. To thus punish the crime denounced by the statute, by imposing the same term of imprisonment and the identical amount of fine upon each and every person guilty of it, can in no sense result in any inequality in operation or protection of law.[112]

Pace's attorney, John Tompkins, appealed all the way to the U.S. Supreme Court, arguing that section 4189 of the Alabama Code (which prohibited a white person and a Negro from living with each other in adultery or fornication) violated the Fourteenth Amendment of the U.S. Constitution, since it prescribed harsher penalties for interracial adulterers than did the statute that prohibited intraracial adultery. Like its antebellum predecessor, section 4184 of the Alabama Code punished same-race persons living together in adultery or fornication with a hundred-dollar fine and either six months of hard labor or imprisonment in the county jail for a first offense. Section 4189, which applied specifically to mixed-race couples, mandated a penalty of two to seven years of hard labor or imprisonment in the penitentiary.[113]

The Court's decision was unanimous. Even Justice Harlan, the sole dissenter in *Plessy v. Ferguson,* did not write a dissenting opinion.[114] Writing for the Court, Justice Stephen Field's opinion was all of two pages. First, he agreed with Pace's counsel that one of the goals of the Fourteenth Amendment was that "in the administration of criminal justice [black people] shall not be subjected, for the same offence, to any greater or different punishment." Nevertheless, Field failed to see the applicability of that rule to the case at hand:

> The two sections of the code cited are entirely consistent. The one prescribes, generally, a punishment for an offence committed between persons of different sexes; the other prescribes a punishment for an offence which can only be committed where the two sexes are of different races. There is in neither section any discrimination against either race. . . . The punishment of each offending person, whether white or black, is the same.[115]

The ushering in of a new century did not bring a concomitant set of new attitudes regarding racial intermarriage. In fact, the new century began much as the old one had ended: with states fine-tuning their antimiscegenation statutes. In 1901, Alabama revised its constitutional antimiscegenation ban and disqualified miscegenators from voting. Six years later, the legislature changed the appropriate percentage of blood constituting a Negro from one-eighth to one-thirty-second.[116] Although Wisconsin had never succumbed to the pressure to pass an antimiscegenation bill, supporters unsuccessfully proposed one in 1901 for the purpose of preventing "a mongrel population."[117] In 1903, Pennsylvania came perilously close to reviving its long-dead ban on racial intermarriage; four years later, another attempt was thwarted,[118] and a still more successful 1909 attempt missed passage by one vote.[119] In 1903, Arkansas and Florida revised their laws, with the latter upping the maximum penalties to ten years in prison and a thousand-dollar fine.[120]

In 1903, some Indiana legislators voted to strengthen their state's law by including a ban on interracial cohabitation, with penalties as high as ten years in prison and a ten-thousand-dollar fine. The bill was so popular that it passed the senate by a vote of thirty-one to three.[121] Two years later, Indiana discovered a new menace. When four male Philippine students enrolled at the University of Indiana, lawmakers unsuccessfully proposed a bill to ban Philippine-white marriages.[122]

In 1906 the Democratic party gained control in Oklahoma, in part by virtue of its "demand" for a law banning intermarriage. The Democrats passed a law that made interracial marriage a felony and called for a maximum fine of five hundred dollars and a possible term of five years in jail.[123] Any clerk who knowingly issued a license to a mixed-race couple was guilty of a misdemeanor, fined up to five hundred dollars, and imprisoned for up to one year.[124] From 1906 to 1910, unsuccessful antimiscegenation bills were presented once each to the legislatures of Michigan and New York, and twice each in Illinois and Ohio.[125]

In 1910 the powers that be in Virginia decided that one-sixteenth Negro heritage was sufficient to render a person black, while the one-fourth percentage continued to be used for American Indians.[126] From 1905 to 1912, nine states amended their laws: in some cases to increase penalties, in some to add sections requiring race registration on divorce proceedings, and in the case of Missouri and Nevada, to add more racial groups to the list of prohibited marriage partners.[127]

In the early 1900s, three states put their first intermarriage bans on the books. In 1909, Montana moved to prevent whites from marrying Negroes, Japanese, or Chinese under penalty of a fine of five hundred dollars and a month in jail. Ten days later, North Dakota prohibited and voided marriages between whites and blacks. The bride and groom could be sentenced to ten years in jail and fined two thousand dollars, while the licensor and performer could be fined the same amount but jailed for only two years. That same year, South Dakota moved to ban interracial marriages. Such a union became a felony, punishable by up to a thousand-dollar fine and ten years in jail. The licensor was guilty of a misdemeanor and sentenced to one year in prison or five hundred dollars, or both. Four years later, South Dakota added Koreans, Malayans, and Mongolians to the prohibited group.[128]

In 1913 black boxing champion Jack Johnson married an eighteen-year-old white woman named Lucille Cameron.[129] Even before the marriage, Johnson's every move was seen as a barometer of race relations. Before Lucille became his wife, he was arrested under the Mann Act for transporting her across state lines "for immoral purposes." The headlines in the *Cleveland Daily News* read "Jack Johnson Guilty Means Race Reforms. Laws prohibiting intermarriage of Blacks and Whites sure to come." Clearly, the *Daily News* was prescient.[130]

Bolstered by public outrage at this very public interracial union, the politicians sped into action. In 1913, antimiscegenation bills were introduced in ten of the twenty states where interracial marriage was not prohibited. At least twenty-one bills were introduced, five alone in Illinois, where the Johnson-Cameron marriage took place.[131] Of the states that did not have existing bans, only Connecticut, Massachusetts, Maine, New Hampshire, New Mexico, Rhode Island, and Vermont did not succumb to the antimiscegenationist frenzy. Two of the states that had such bans in place (California and Colorado) took advantage of the flurry of indignation to try to stiffen the penalties in their statutes, while Nebraska used the national hysteria as an excuse to expand its class of unmarriables.[132]

Of the five separate bills introduced to ban intermarriage in Illinois in 1913, only one received a favorable report in committee, and none made any progress through the legislature.[133] That same year, Michigan introduced a bill that would prohibit whites from marrying anyone of African, Chinese, or Japanese descent. As in Illinois, however, local black groups applied pressure and blocked the bill's passage.[134] Although Nebraska had had an antimiscegenation law in place for almost seventy years, the state's lawmakers took the Johnson-Cameron union as an opportunity to expand on it. The legislature broadened the ban from a prohibition against the marriage of whites with those of one-fourth or more Negro blood to one against whites marrying anyone with one-eighth or more Negro, Chinese, or Japanese blood.[135] Elsewhere in the Midwest in 1913, Wisconsin and Ohio unsuccessfully attempted to enact bans on intermarriage. The Ohio bill went beyond the Johnson-Cameron example to hold that "the intermarriage of white persons with Negroes, mulattos, or persons of mixed blood descendant from a Negro to the third generation, inclusive, or with Chinamen, their living together as man and wife in this State is hereby prohibited." Violations were deemed a felony subject to one to five years in the penitentiary or a combination of a fine and time in the county jail.[136]

The more liberal Northeast also succumbed to the pressure created by the Johnson-Cameron marriage. In January 1913, New York, which had never banned intermarriage, introduced a bill that would declare such unions "utterly null and void." The bill would also hold that such marriages validly performed outside New York would not be recognized within the state. Persons who attempted to escape the ban by omitting any legal ceremony would be prosecuted for interracial cohabitation, the penalty for which was identical to the penalty for intermarriage. The bill mandated a fine of five hundred dollars or one year in prison, or both, for persons who intermarried but would have allowed the parties to escape penalties if both were sterilized. Sterilization was also proffered as a means to avoid penalties for interracial cohabitation. Officials who performed an interracial marriage could also be fined five hundred dollars or jailed for one year, or both, though they presumably could not escape punishment by sterilization. The bill never made it out of committee.[137]

That same year, New Jersey, another state that had never banned interracial unions, proposed a bill that punished only the solemnizer and licensor of such a coupling. Thanks to vocal black opposition, the bill died in committee. Pennsylvania had been the first state to repeal its antimiscegenation laws, but almost 150 years later, its legislators submitted a bill that would have prohibited officials from providing marriage licenses to "persons of Caucasian and Ethiopian descent."[138]

In 1915 an intermarriage ban for the District of Columbia passed the House, but the NAACP was instrumental in stalling the bill in the Senate. The NAACP also lobbied against the five antimiscegenation bills that were proposed for the district the following year, not to mention two introduced in 1917, three in 1921, and the single bills proposed in 1923 and 1927–28, none of which was successful.[139] To be fair to poor Jack

Johnson, bills had been proposed in D.C. prior to his marriage. Back in 1821, a petition was sent to the legislature asking that mixed marriages be declared void and making it "a penal act for a negro to marry a white man's daughter." Another bill passed the House in 1841, and similar bills were proposed sporadically during the nineteenth century.[140] In 1909 Senator Milton of Florida introduced an antimiscegenation bill for the capital supported by a statement giving thirteen supposed anthropologic indicators of Negro inferiority,[141] and two more bills were proposed in 1912, the second of which passed the House by a whopping 238 to 60 but died in the Senate.[142]

In the end, only one new bill survived intact from the legislative frenzy of 1913. Wyoming's house and senate unanimously revived its old antimiscegenation law to prohibit the marriage of whites to Negroes, mulattoes, Mongolians, and Malays. The couple and the person performing the ceremony were subject to one to five years in prison, a fine of one hundred to one thousand dollars, or both. The bill differed from Wyoming's nineteenth-century legislation in that the licensor of such a union now escaped unscathed.[143]

Few new proposals followed the 1913 hysteria. In 1914, Kentucky amended its laws to include listing race on marriage licenses. That same year, Louisiana tightened its laws; six years later, it became one of the few states to ban the intermarriage of any of the "other groups" when it forbade the union of blacks and Indians.[144] In Illinois, a 1915 attempt died in committee, and a similar attempt in Wisconsin two years later was indefinitely postponed. Pennsylvania's attempts in 1917 and 1921 met with no success, and a 1921 Michigan bill did not proceed beyond committee. In 1925, Ohio futilely introduced a bill "relative to the prevention of the amalgamation of the white race with any other race."[145] The year 1927 saw bills unsuccessfully proposed in Connecticut, Maine, Massachusetts, Michigan, New Jersey, Pennsylvania, and Rhode Island.[146] The only bill proposed in 1929 was in Wisconsin, and the author withdrew the proposal after hearing that the NAACP planned to have various parties testify in opposition.[147]

One state where the antimiscegenation frenzy did not die down was Virginia. During the 1920s, three influential Virginians (state registrar William Plecker, author Earnest Cox, and concert pianist John Powell) pressed to strengthen legislation against the mixing of races. These men were part of the eugenics movement, which began in nineteenth-century England but soon emigrated to the United States. Eugenicists believed that almost all of humanity's ills were hereditary. Therefore, by mating "superior" stock, one could produce a better breed of human beings. The corollary to this assumption was that "inferior" stock should be discouraged from breeding. Among the excesses of the movement were forced surgical procedures.[148]

All three eugenicists were involved in driving the Racial Integrity Act, a proposal originally (and more accurately) called "a bill to preserve the integrity of the white race," through the Virginia legislature in 1924.[149] The purpose of the bill was clear: to forbid racial mixing on the grounds that it was "scientifically unsound" and would "pollute" the country with mixed-blood offspring.[150] The local papers applauded their efforts. The *Richmond Times-Dispatch* endorsed the Racial Integrity Act as a "first step toward guaranteeing to future generations a white America." Miscegenation would "sound the death knell of the white man. Once a drop of inferior blood gets in his veins, he descends lower and lower in the mongrel scale."[151]

The Racial Integrity Act passed the house by a seventy-two-to-nine margin, after some revisions had been made to the eugenecists' draft. The original version would have required all Virginians to register their race with the state, but the revisions made such registration voluntary for those born before 1912.[152] The "Pocahontas exception" was changed from the one-sixty-fourth Indian blood suggested in the original draft to one-sixteenth.[153] The bill contained a section that restrained clerks from issuing a license unless they had "reasonable assurance" that the parties were not lying about their color. The burden of proof was on the applicants.[154] The Racial Integrity Act was the strictest such law in the United States.[155]

Governor Trinkle proudly sent copies of the new act to his fellow governors, suggesting that they implement a similar law.[156] Whether as a result of gubernatorial prodding or not, Georgia enacted a very similar law in 1927. An attempt to do so in Connecticut met with failure.[157] The Georgia bill was initially proposed in 1925 and quashed, despite an address of the House of Delegates by Virginia eugenecist John Powell. Two years later, however, the bill passed by a huge margin: 104 to 3 in the house and 36 to 1 in the senate. The Georgia law defined white and black as Virginia did (minus the Pocahontas exception) and punished those who married out of race or performed interracial ceremonies. Those who lied on their registration form were guilty of a felony punishable by up to two years in prison. In addition, Georgia mandated that its Bureau of Vital

Statistics notify the attorney general if birth or marriage licenses indicated that an interracial union had or would be taking place.[158]

In the following years, attempts to draft antimiscegenation statutes failed in eleven states and the District of Columbia, and attempts to strengthen laws were unsuccessful in three states. The only success was Alabama's 1927 revision of its definition of a black person, which now omitted any reference to ancestors or generations.[159] As 1927 came to a close, twenty-nine states had antimiscegenation laws.[160] The only other revisions marking the first half of the century were Mississippi's addition of a section criminalizing written material that favored intermarriage, and the expansion of the unmarriable class in three states. Arizona, California, and Maryland added Malays to their bans, while Arizona became noteworthy as the only state to prohibit white-Hindu marriages.[161]

Attempts to change the definition of a Negro arose again in Virginia in 1930, in part because authorities learned that some children who had less than one-sixteenth Negro blood were attending school with whites. The bill defined as Negro someone with "any ascertainable degree of negro blood." It passed the house despite the objections of tribal Indians, some of whose families had been "tainted" by previous mixing. A Pamunkey leader cried that after the white man had taken the Indians' land and hunting and fishing grounds, they would now also take away their name. Several academic and church leaders protested the law as unfair to the Indians. There is no record of any public complaint about the damage it would do to blacks. The final revision of the bill defined "colored" as the opposite of the statutory definition of white. It tightened the Pocahontas clause to allow an exception only for members of Indian tribes living on the Pamunkey and Mataponi reservations (leaving out members of the Rappahannock, Chickahominy, and Nansemond tribes) who had at least one-fourth Indian blood and no more than one-sixteenth black blood. The bill sailed through the house (eighty-one to three), passed the senate by a narrower margin, and was signed into law by the governor.[162]

Two years later, Virginia's law saw its final revision. A 1932 provision moved the crime of miscegenation from the misdemeanor category to that of a felony while reducing the minimum sentence from two years to one year.[163]

The influence of eugenicist thinking had begun to wane as the 1920s ended, but the damage done by its enthusiasts was just beginning. The

Racial Integrity Act and its counterparts in other states continued to be used to prosecute couples for the crime of exchanging vows. Neither the war against fascism nor the early days of the civil rights movement interfered with the strict enforcement of antimiscegenation laws.

5

The Prosecutions Continue

She appears to be sustained in her mad insane determination to mingle blood impregnated with the highest genetic values of the Caucasian with the blood of an African whose racial strains have dwelt for six thousand years or more in the jungles of a continent.

—Mississippi senator Theodore Bilbo, on the marriage of a relative of Vice President Dawes to a black Harvard graduate in 1938

*T*he eugenicists concentrated their activities in Virginia, but couples were being prosecuted and marriages voided throughout the United States well into the twentieth century. In Louisiana in 1908, the marriage of an elderly white couple was annulled and the pair sent to prison because the wife's first husband had been black, a fact suspect enough to cast aspersions on her own racial heritage. After the woman's first marriage, her white friends had turned their backs on her and she "became known as a colored person," going so far as to ride in the Negro section of streetcars. This association sufficed to annul the second marriage, despite there being absolutely no indication that the woman had any black ancestors. Thirty years later, a white Louisiana man's marriage was annulled when it was learned that his wife's great-grandmother had been black.[1]

The state of Virginia made liberal use of the Racial Integrity Act until the *Loving* decision in 1967. In 1932 a man was convicted of seduction under the promise of marriage: a felony in Virginia. He appealed on the grounds that the defrocked virgin was black and, therefore, he could not have married her. The case was remanded to determine not whether the woman knew they could not be married but rather whether she knew that she was black.[2] Uncertainty as to parentage saved Bascomb Keith and Reda Baker from being convicted of miscegenation in 1935. Although both were listed as white on their birth certificates, they were charged with miscegenation on the grounds that Keith had "traceable colored blood," descending from his grandfather. To their good fortune, the state was unable to prove the existence of that heinous trace.[3]

In 1938, Grace Mohler married Samuel Christian Branahan. Shortly thereafter, a local citizen sent a copy of the newspaper announcement to State Registrar Plecker, with a letter stating that the Mohlers were "respectable whites" but the Branahans were "unquestionably mixed bloods, Negroid in every appearance, speech and behavior." Plecker forwarded this information to the county clerk. The couple was initially charged with perjury. Mohler escaped conviction by claiming that she was unaware of Branahan's African heritage. Branahan testified that he was not of mixed race, but a variety of witnesses were paraded before the court to contradict him. The court took some pity on Branahan and suspended his one-year sentence for thirty years on the condition that he left his wife and promised never to live with her or any other white woman.[4]

Ten years later, not much had changed when a twenty-two-year-old carpenter named Clark Council Hamilton married a nineteen-year-old office worker, Florence Madelone Hammond. They wed without incident in May 1948 after Hamilton finished his stint in the Navy. The minister who performed the ceremony assumed them both to be white. Initially, the bride's mother approved of the marriage, but after she had a dream in which Hamilton was black, she decided to journey to Alabama to meet his parents. Upon her return, she filed a warrant for his arrest for miscegenation. The bride's father opined that, although Hamilton had appeared white during the courtship, he seemed to be getting darker on a daily basis after the marriage. He filed suit to have the marriage annulled. The Roanoke commonwealth attorney requested a copy of Hamilton's birth certificate, which indicated that he was twenty years old and black.[5]

Although married in Virginia, the pair was living in Maryland. Hamilton was extradited to face charges and was jailed for lack of bail money. Although charged with being black, he was placed in the white section of the jail because physically, according to the sheriff's deputy, he was "not too dark—perhaps a little yellow, with brown hair, a little bit curly" and could pass for an "average white man." Hammond wasn't charged, under the presumption that she believed her spouse to be white. The trial court found that Hamilton was not the age, the race, or a citizen of the state that he had alleged at the time of his marriage. He was sentenced to three years in prison, a sentence that was suspended if he promised to leave Virginia. This condition proved to be no problem for Hamilton, since his wife had remained in Maryland throughout the trial and continued to live there, awaiting his return, regardless of his race.[6]

The case of Stella May Rhoton and Willie E. Purcell is another example of parental use of antimiscegenation statutes. The couple married in 1948. Rhoton's mother had been excluded from the wedding, so she charged that Purcell was black and therefore the union violated state law. The evidence at trial ranged from Purcell's police records (evenly divided as to the listing of his race) to his birth certificate (which listed his race as white) and the testimony of his father that both he and Purcell's mother were white. There was not enough evidence to convict the lucky pair, although Rhoton still had to deal with her mother.[7] In an eerie precursor to the Lovings case, another Virginia couple was banished from the state by a police court in 1956.[8]

Such foolishness endured well into the second half of the twentieth century. In 1956 a white nineteen-year-old from Kentucky went to Tennessee to marry a black musician. She was promptly arrested for disorderly conduct when police discovered her and another white woman in the company of two black men. Apparently the only thing disorderly about her conduct was her choice of companions. The police blotter noted nothing more heinous than that the quartet had been picked up on a Nashville street after one of the men finished playing with his jazz band.[9]

In 1961 a mixed couple in Oklahoma narrowly escaped prosecution on the grounds that they had been legally married in Kansas. However, this technicality did not stop their adopted state from harassing the young newlyweds. First, Vernon Thomas was arrested for driving without a permit, despite the fact that he was not driving at the time of his arrest. Police then apprehended his wife Bettye for speeding even though her car was parked at the time of *her* arrest. Finally, authorities searched the couple's premises, when they were home alone, on the pretext that a neighbor had complained about a loud party. Three weeks later, the authorities got to the heart of the matter when they arrested the pair for miscegenation. Their attorney, Amos Hall, managed to get the charges dismissed on the grounds that the Oklahoma judge had no jurisdiction over a ceremony performed in neighboring Kansas.[10]

In 1959 James Brown and Lucille Aymond were sentenced to one year in the Louisiana penitentiary because "they did habitually cohabit with each other, he being of the Negro race and she being of the White race, they having knowledge of their difference in race."[11] Their attorneys, Harold Brouillette and Maxwell Bertillon, argued that the Louisiana statute violated the equal protection and due process clauses of the Fourteenth Amendment. Unfortunately, they must have been less convincing on the matter than the attorney general. The case was eventually reversed and remanded due to the trial judge's improper charge to the jury, but the appeals court judge couldn't resist getting in a little dig at the defendants.

> A state statute which prohibits intermarriage or cohabitation between members of different races in no way violate[s] the Equal Protection clauses of the state and federal Constitutions. A state statute which prohibits intermarriage or cohabitation between members of different races we think falls squarely within the police power of the state, which has an interest in maintaining the purity of the races and in preventing the propagation of half-breed children. Such children have difficulty in being accepted by society, and there is no doubt that children in such a situation are burdened, as has been said in another connection, with "a feeling of inferiority as to their status in the community that may affect their hearts and minds in a way unlikely ever to be undone."[12]

In case readers missed the subtlety, Judge Hawthorn clearly indicated in a footnote that his quote was lifted directly from *Brown v. Board of Education*. It is unclear whether Hawthorn honestly thought the quotation applied to the progeny of interracial marriage or whether he was just trying to show how the language of *Brown* could be used for various purposes.

In 1962 Paul Fuqua, an Army private stationed in South Carolina, applied for a license to marry his sweetheart, Lorena Smith. Since Fuqua was white and Smith was Cherokee, their request was denied. Although South Carolina had long forbidden the marriage of whites and Native Americans, the previous year the law had been amended to make an exception for members of the Catawba tribe who wished to intermarry with whites. Unfortunately, Smith's roots were with the wrong tribe. Both Fuqua and his intended bride were actually natives of North Carolina, where not only could Smith not have married Fuqua but the law would also have barred her from choosing a black suitor.[13]

As the 1960s progressed, miscegenation cases began to involve the unions of people whose national origins did not fit easily into the black-white-Mongolian-Malay delineation of the statutes. In 1964 Dr. Benjamin A. deGuzman, a Philippine man, was rebuffed in his attempt to secure a license to marry a white woman, Elizabeth Medaglia, in Maryland. Medaglia brought suit, arguing that they had been denied due process of law. Judge W. Albert Menchine chose not to rule on the constitutionality of Maryland's antimiscegenation laws. Rather, he decided that the law that prohibited white-Malay marriages did not sufficiently define Malay. Dr. deGuzman had a white grandmother, so Menchine concluded, "Assuming that in general a Filipino is a member of the Malay race, it is very clear that this Filipino is not."[14]

That same year, a confirmed Malayan, Samoan dancer Meki Toalepai, did not bother to look for a judge who would play semantics games for him. Upon being denied a Maryland license to marry a white nurse named Jo Ann Kovacs, Toalepai and his bride drove to Washington, D.C., for their nuptials. A Baltimore minister, Frederick James Hanna, accompanied the couple, as did a horde of newsmen, befitting Toalepai's status as a cultural celebrity. The publicity over Maryland's failure to allow the couple to wed legally caused significant consternation. One Maryland legislative delegate, Clarence M. Mitchell III, vowed to press for a repeal of the offending statute.[15]

While Mitchell was taking a higher-ground tactic, another delegate, Julian Lapides, appealed to the baser instincts of his fellow legislators, arguing that the anti-Asian discrimination so blatant in the antimiscegenation laws could send recently democratized Asian nations toward Communism.[16] Despite this bizarre public rationale, Lapides' real reason for fighting the statutes stemmed from his progressive instincts rather than any rampant anti-Communism. His public comments reflected an attempt to convince less progressive people to support the repeal and showed how carefully opponents of antimiscegenation statutes had to tread, even at that late date.[17]

One month after Mitchell and Lapides expressed their displeasure, another Marylander was moved to action. Senator Verda Welcome, the first black female senator in the state, sponsored a bill to repeal Maryland's three-century-old law.[18] Welcome was initially elected to the House of Delegates in 1958, and four years later she became a state senator, a position she held until 1982.[19] Her repeal measure failed in the senate by a vote of fifteen to thirteen on its first round, when she was unable to find a cosponsor. Reintroduced less than two weeks later, it passed by a slim sixteen-to-eleven margin. Unfortunately, the bill never made it out of the House of Delegates. Most delegates apparently agreed with their colleague C. Maurice Weidemeyer, who called the repeal a move "to make this country a brown race."[20]

Although intermarriage was the act most explicitly banned by legislation throughout the states, many jurisdictions went beyond that staple and legislated prohibitions on any kind of interracial sexual contact.

Probably the first ban on interracial extramarital sex was a New Netherlands law of 1638, which ordered that "each and every one must refrain from fighting, adulterous intercourse with heathens, blacks or other persons, mutiny, theft, false swearing, calumny and other immoralities," a rather interesting compendium of offenses. Twenty-five years later, Virginia doubled the fine for fornication if a white person was caught with a Negro. For barbarity, no state can match Delaware, which fined any white woman bearing a mulatto child ten pounds and ordered her to be publicly whipped thirty-nine times and then stand in the pillory for two hours. Her black partner would suffer the same indignities, except that he would also have one ear nailed to a post and then lopped off. If the illicit lovers were the reverse combination of race and gender, they would suffer only twenty-one lashes.[21]

As the centuries progressed, states not only routinely enforced their intermarriage bans but also acted against interracial fornication and adultery, acts that legislators generally combined into one catchall accusation. Even unmarried people were accused of adultery, which, together with fornication, became an all-encompassing charge for any alleged acts of interracial sex. One of the more bizarre cases was that of Luby Griffith and Nathan Bell.[22] In 1950 Griffith, a white woman who ran a store with her husband in a black community, and Bell, a black man, were charged with living "in adultery or fornication with each other against the peace and dignity of Alabama." The trials were severed. No record exists of Bell's fate, but Griffith was sentenced to seven years in prison. The pair had never been caught in flagrante delicto, but witnesses had seen them alone in close physical proximity to one another on a number of occasions and they had been caught kissing. In addition, Griffith had left Bell a lunch (which he ate), had bribed someone who saw the pair together, and had threatened a woman whom she perceived to be a rival for Bell's attention. Basing their decision on this circumstantial evidence, the jury took less than two hours to find Griffith guilty and to sentence her to the maximum penalty allowable, a verdict that was affirmed by the court of appeals.[23]

It must have been the frequency of the contact between Griffith and Bell that bothered the jury the most, because twenty years earlier, an Alabama court had reached a very different conclusion and reversed a trial court's conviction of a pair of interracial fornicators. The couple had admitted to having sexual relations once and the trial court found them guilty. The state supreme court overturned the verdict when it found no evidence that the pair wished to continue their relationship.[24]

In a similar case of judicial leniency, a black woman in Louisiana was permitted to inherit the estate of her white common-law husband in 1947 because she had not lived in *open* concubinage with him. "The deceased did not publicly avow his relations with the defendant, but on the contrary kept her in his employ ostensibly as cook and housekeeper and assistant in his store and their relations were not those of 'open' concubinage, but only illicit intercourse and secret concubinage."[25] It is clear that the main concern of the court was the appearance of sexual equality. It was perfectly acceptable for a white man to have a black mistress, so long as he did not pretend that having relations with her raised their liaison to the level of a legitimate relationship.

Of all the states, Alabama seems to have expended the most time and effort on curbing interracial sexuality in the twentieth century. In 1921 Hinton Lewis, a white man, was convicted of interracial fornication with Bessie Adams on the testimony of two men who saw him handle one of her children: the child, in contrast to Adams, was light-skinned. Another man, who claimed that he visited Adams once or twice a month, said that Lewis was always present when he came by. Despite four witnesses who testified to the absence of an inappropriate relationship between the pair, two of whom suggested that one of the prosecution's witnesses (a light-skinned black man) was the father of the light-skinned child, the court affirmed Lewis's sentence of seven years in prison on appeal. Two years later, Jim Rollins, a black man, was convicted of interracial adultery with Edith Labue, a married white woman from Sicily. On the basis of such evidence as the "kinky" hair of Labue's four-year-old son (whose conception date coincided with her husband's army term), the fact that a detective found the pair standing fully clothed in a dark room that contained no bed, and because, at gunpoint, Rollins had confessed to fathering Labue's dark-skinned son, Rollins was convicted and sentenced to seven years in prison.[26]

In 1931 the Alabama Court of Appeals reversed the conviction of a couple who had been sentenced after witnesses first saw them together in a car late at night and subsequently saw the woman sitting barefoot on the man's unmade bed with her luggage at her feet. She reported that he had just driven her home from the hospital where she had been treated with a prescription that made her feet swell. The hospital waiting room had been cold, whereas the man's house had a wood stove, so he had brought her to his house to wait for someone to drive her to her own house. Another such conviction was overturned in 1937, but not before the judge referred to the alleged sexual acts as "moral filth," "a picture that is nauseating to all that is finer in our natures," "sordid," and "too vile and disgusting to be repeated any place."[27]

Texas is another state that required very little evidence to convict a couple of interracial adultery or fornication. In 1913 Minnie Strauss, a black woman, was found sitting on her own bed "scantily dressed" beside W. A. Randall, a white man, who allegedly was wearing neither shoes nor pants. The arresting officers said that the bed looked rumpled. At trial, Randall admitted to being shoeless but denied being pantsless. He stated that he was a carpenter by trade and that he had been measuring Strauss's windows for screens. Nevertheless, Strauss was convicted and fined two hundred dollars under a city ordinance that prohibited interracial sex. Although the city ordinance was stricter than the state's antimiscegenation laws, the court upheld the statute as being appropriate to protect "the morals and good order" of the city's inhabitants.[28]

A similar lack of evidence marked the prosecution ten years later when R. Brown, a white man, and Ethyl Harvey, a black woman, were charged with violating a Houston ordinance that prohibited interracial sex and cohabitation. The arresting officers found the pair alone in a dark warehouse, lying side by side. He wore a night shirt, and she had her shoes off and her dress up. The defense argued that Brown lived in the warehouse and was bedridden by illness. He had met Harvey one night when she walked by the building and believed her to be Japanese. (Such a liaison would have been legal in the state, since Texas's antimiscegenation statute did not include Asians.) When Brown saw Harvey again, he asked whether she knew anyone who would wash his clothes for a fee. She did and acted as intermediary. On the night of the arrest, she had come to return the washed clothes, and when the police arrived, she was sitting at the foot of Brown's bed, talking to him. The trial court found him guilty and fined him the maximum two hundred dollars.[29]

As late as 1960, specific prohibitions on nonmarital interracial relationships persisted in Alabama, Arkansas, Florida, Louisiana, Nevada, North Dakota, and Tennessee. Alabama sentenced interracial adulterers to up to seven years in prison. Arkansas drew a distinction between concubinage (up to one year in jail) and cohabitation (one to three years), while Louisiana sentenced persons convicted of either bigamy or basic carnal knowledge to five years in jail. Florida punished interracial adulterers with a higher fine but a lower jail term than intraracial violators, but it also punished mixed couples who habitually shared a room at night (see chapter 10), even without evidence of sexual contact. North Dakota was the only other state that had a problem with mixed couples sharing a room, subjecting them to up to one year in jail and a five-hundred-dollar fine, which was significantly more than the penalty for intraracial cohabitants. Nevada drew a line between cohabitation and "notorious" cohabitation, with the latter subject to a greater fine but the same jail term. Texas seems to have objected only if the cohabiting couple presented themselves as husband and wife. If so, they could be sentenced to up to five years in the county jail.[30]

Although prosecutions for interracial sexual and marital offenses continued almost up to the date of the *Loving* decision, all was not bleak. After a while, defense attorneys stopped claiming that their clients were doing laundry, measuring windows, or resting their swollen feet. Starting with the aforementioned Bertillon and Brouillette, attorneys began to attack the statutes head-on. Soon they allied themselves with a variety of groups committed to fighting for civil rights in America, thus initiating the slow but sure downfall of antimiscegenation statutes. Unfortunately, the interim saw more court cases, many of which dealt with issues peripheral to the unlawful unions: inheritance and custody.

6

Taking Away the Children and the Money

[I]t is indisputable and a matter of common and general knowledge that if a white man residing in Jacksonville Beach or any where else in Duval County, Florida, were to in truth and in fact attend dances at a negro dance hall and dance with negro women, his business and social standing would be completely wrecked. He would forfeit the respect and confidence not only of the white people of that section, but would be held in contempt and be despised by the self-respecting negro citizens.
—Florida State Supreme Court, 1947

*A*ntimiscegenation laws affected more than the couples in question. Much of the litigation revolving around intermarriage dealt with issues of custody and inheritance. In fact, prior to the mid 1900s, very few of the miscegenation cases taken to court were brought by either a couple seeking to marry in contravention of state laws or by law enforcement officers trying to break up a marriage. For the most part, they were inheritance cases in which white relatives tried to invalidate an existing marriage in order to ensure that a surviving spouse (usually a wife of color) did not inherit property.[1]

Parties to common-law marriages have historically been able to inherit from one another's estates upon sufficient showing of the contractual nature of their relationships. However, common evidence such as the length and stability of a couple's commitment to one another proved inadequate for inheritance purposes if only one member of the couple was white. Phillis and William Oldman lived together for thirty years in a union that bore four children. Nevertheless, a Texas court ruled Phillis ineligible to inherit William's estate in 1878 because she was black and he was white.[2] Sometimes courts were willing to show a little leniency by not disturbing existing unions, but no such charity was on hand when it came to questions of inheritance. In 1860 a court allowed a white cashier to remain married to a black woman when he alleged that he had ingested some of her blood. However, when she predeceased him, he was not allowed to partake of her estate.[3] In 1838 a Mississippi court would not allow a mixed-race son to inherit the estate of his white father, according to a deed the testator had executed in Ohio, because "the statement of the case shows conclusively that the contract had its origin in an offence against morality, pernicious, and detestable."[4] Along similar lines, a man named Mingo successfully challenged the right of his wife's sisters to share in her estate, alleging that her (and their) parents had been an interracial couple. Since under Louisiana law, the parents could not legally marry, their children had no legal relationship to one another.[5]

Louisiana was so concerned about inheritance issues that its lawmakers placed numerous legal obstacles in the path of mixed-race children. First, the law required that a white father legally acknowledge his mulatto offspring. When this proved insufficient to deter inheritance claims, the law was further amended to ensure that no more than one-fourth of a white man's estate could be inherited by a person of color. The courts determined that this quarter was still more than the fruits of a miscegenous relationship were entitled to. In 1847 a judge held that courts could reduce the bequest to a black concubine to one-tenth of the estate. One white man attempted to evade the one-fourth rule by giving his son sixteen thousand dollars over the course of four years. His relatives successfully objected to his effort to evade the law. To prevent such discord, a white man named Elisha Crocker made peace with his blood relatives before his death. In deference to his wishes, they did not challenge his bequest to his acknowledged mulatto son. Nevertheless, in 1857 a court struck down his legacy to the son as beyond the scope of Louisiana law and awarded the property in question to the noncontesting relatives.[6]

Texas courts made a 180-degree turn from the Oldman case when they dealt with the estate of John Clark. Clark was a planter who had lived with

Sobrina, a slave he had purchased, for almost thirty years. He left an estate worth half a million dollars, which the administrator gave to the state. Clark and Sobrina's three children sued in district court, alleging that their parents had entered into a common-law marriage prior to the establishment of the state antimiscegenation law. On behalf of the state, treasurer G. W. Honey appealed. As if to stress the absurdity of the idea that Clark could have contemplated a legal marriage, the court held,

> We may stigmatize the aversion of one race for the other as unreasonable, without good sense, mere prejudice, yet all must admit that the fact of this really exists in the minds of most white men to such an extent that the idea of intermarriage of the races is wholly repulsive, even at this day: and how much more must it have been before the African was raised to the dignity of an American citizen.[7]

However repulsive the justices found the union, they were forced to conclude that the couple had entered into a common-law marriage prior to such a union being illegal and that the amendment to the Texas constitution legitimizing the children borne of slave relationships applied in this case, despite the fact that only one party was a slave. Therefore the children were awarded the estate.[8]

The precedent set by the *Clark* case did not last long. In 1870 George Clements borrowed one thousand dollars from E. E. Crawford and offered property in Galveston as security. When Clements refused to repay the loan, Crawford brought suit for the property. Clements replied that the property in question was a homestead occupied by his wife Mary and their children and therefore was not receivable by Crawford. Crawford argued that since Mary was a mulatto, she could not be Clements's wife; therefore the property was not a homestead. Clements's attorney asked the court to instruct the jury that if the couple had lived together as husband and wife before the 1869 constitution became law, the jury should rule in their favor. The judge refused to mention the constitution, instead instructing the jury to find for Clements if they found Mary to be his lawful wife. They did not. In his appeal, Clements cited the *Clark* case. Rather than follow that precedent, the court overruled *Clark*, holding that the state constitution did not "confer on any parties, white or black, whose intercourse was illegal and immoral, the rights and benefits of lawful wedlock."[9]

Courts continued to churn out these cases well into the twentieth century. It did no good for a father to officially recognize his illegitimate offspring, as the children of Joseph Segura and Mary Miles learned in

1912. Seventy-six thousand dollars went to the state instead of the inter-racial offspring.[10] A more sympathetic judge heard the case of the widow of Fred Paquet. Paquet, who was white, left his estate to his Native American wife, Ophelia. Her right to inherit was challenged by Fred's brother John. The Oregon statute declared null and void the marriage of a white person to "any negro, Chinese, or any person having one-fourth or more negro, Chinese or Kanakan blood or any person having more than one half Indian blood." Ophelia argued that the statute discriminated against her, but in 1921 the Oregon court ruled that the law applied to people of all races. The court suggested, however, that John offer Ophelia "a fair and reasonable settlement" because she had been "a good and faithful wife."[11] Faithful wife or not, when Emily Lewis, a Choctaw Indian, died in 1924, her black husband lost the title to their land because under Oklahoma law, their marriage had not been valid.[12] Apparently Indian widows were objects of greater sympathy than black widowers.

The Oklahoma-born children of Billy Atkins and Bertha Miller were a luckier group. Since Atkins was Native American and Miller black, Atkins's brother argued that the court need not appoint an administrator for the estate because the children were not legal heirs. In 1924 the court's majority allowed the children to inherit, holding paternalistically that "in the mind of this simple red man, these children were his children." The furious dissenters held that the children were the product of an unnatural union and that to allow this type of mixing would produce a "deplorable" race of people. "The surest and quickest method of producing mixed-blood white and negro race, is to destroy by judicial decree the effect of prohibitive statutes which seek to prevent an amalgamation."[13]

The Arizona case of *Kirby v. Kirby* is an excellent example of the kind of foolishness that resulted when courts took into their own hands the determination of a person's racial heritage.[14] Joe Kirby wanted to annul his marriage with Mayellen without going through a formal divorce. He testified in court that the marriage had not been legal from the start, because he was white and she was black. Both Joe and his mother testified as to his parentage. Since Joe was Mexican, it was crucial for him to show that, despite his place of birth, he had no Indian blood. Marriage between Native Americans and blacks was legal in Arizona. Playing amateur anthropologist, the judge declared that Mexicans were "classed as of the Caucasian Race. They are descendants, supposed to be, at least of the Spanish conquerors of that country, and unless it can be shown that they are mixed up with some other races, why the presumption is that they are descendants of the Caucasian race." It is interesting that no testimony regarding Mayellen's racial classification was taken. The court considered her physical appearance proof positive that she was black.[15]

As if the *Kirby* case wasn't sufficient to show the inability of the judicial system to deal with racial classifications, the 1939 Arizona case of *Estate of Monks* revealed that this field was one in which "experts" were sorely lacking.[16] Allan Monks was a white man who died leaving two wills. The first bequest was to a white friend named Ida Lee. Subsequent to this will, Monks remarried and penned his second will, which, while not explicitly revoking the first one, left his estate to his wife, Marie Antoinette Monks.[17] Lee contested the bequest to Monks by alleging that Monks was at least part black. To prove her case, Lee's attorneys called three so-called expert witnesses. The first was Monks's hairdresser, who testified that she could tell that Monks was of mixed blood from the size of the half-moons on her fingernails, the color of the "ring" around the palm of her hands, and the "kink" in her hair.[18] The second expert was a physical anthropologist from the San Diego Museum who stated that he knew that Monks was at least one-eighth black from the shape of her face, the color of her hands, and her "protruding heels," which he had been able to observe as a courtroom spectator. The last witness was a surgeon who practiced medicine in the South and had worked in Africa. He testified that he had once walked next to Monks when she entered the court. He was therefore able to make the observation that she was one-eighth black on the basis of the contour of her calves and heels, the "peculiar pallor" of the back of her neck, the shape of her face, and the wave in her hair. The judge discounted the hairdresser's testimony and found that the testimony of a physical anthropologist called by Monks canceled out that of the expert called by Lee. Basing his decision on the surgeon's testimony, the judge ruled that Monks was, in fact, at least one-eighth black. Therefore, under Arizona law, the marriage was invalid and she could not inherit the estate.[19]

Marie Antoinette, like her namesake, was a resourceful woman, and she appealed the decision. Monks challenged the Arizona law as unconstitutional on the grounds that people of mixed blood were prohibited from marrying anyone. The court refused to hear this argument, since Monks's marriage had been deemed illegal because she was considered black, not because she was of mixed blood. Even if she had been a "full-blooded Negro," she could not have married her husband who was "of unmixed Caucasian blood." The fact that she was legally unable to marry anyone else was "interesting," but not an issue.[20]

Montana declared all interracial marriages null and void, thus preventing a white woman from administering the estate of her Japanese husband in 1942, even though the two had been legally married in Washington State.[21] As late as 1955, members of the Oklahoma State Industrial Commission denied benefits to the common-law wife of a man who died on the job after they found her to have African blood.[22] The law of percentages reached new levels of absurdity in Oklahoma. Upon the death of his common-law wife, a man who was three-quarters Indian and one-quarter black requested his share of her estate. The two had had almost the same racial composition, as she was three-quarters Indian and one-quarter white. However, under Oklahoma law, the husband was considered "of African descent." Three matching sets of Native American grandparents notwithstanding, the court ruled that he was not a legal heir to his wife's estate.[23]

Even after *Loving*, inheritance problems persisted. Mississippi was the site of the unhappy case of Adeline Young. Young, a black woman, had been living with a white man named Vetrano in that state since 1947. They had two children and considered themselves married, although they knew that they could not be united legally in Mississippi. When Vetrano died in 1963, Young requested insurance benefits and social security earnings for their children. Since the children were not legitimate, the court ruled that they were not entitled to benefits. The intrepid Ms. Young tried again in 1967 after the Supreme Court had declared that interracial unions were legal.[24]

The second time around, a federal court ruled that the children could be considered legitimate if Vetrano and Young had entered into a common-law marriage. She alleged that they had done so by living together for sixteen years and raising two children together. Furthermore, she said, Vetrano had publicly claimed their children as his own before his death. The court, however, ruled that Vetrano and Young had not publicly presented themselves as husband and wife—conveniently ignoring the fact that to do so would have left them open to arrest for miscegenation—and refused, again, to grant benefits to the children.[25] Chief Judge Keady found that although it was possible that the principal reason that Vetrano and Young did not hold themselves out as married was fear of prosecution, there might have been other factors that led them not to do so. He declared that the Mississippi requirement for common-law marriages, which specified that parties "must have conducted themselves unequivocally before the public in accordance with their intended relationship, is totally unrelated to race."[26]

Court fights erupted over not only who got the fruits of the estate but also who got the fruit of the loins. While not as frequent as the inheritance battles, a number of court cases featured conflicts over the custody of children whose parents were involved in interracial marriages. For the most part, these cases involved attempts (oftentimes successful) to remove children from the custody of a white mother who remarried to a black man. In *Moon v. Children's Home Society of Virginia*,[27] a white woman named Lucy May bore two children to her first husband, a white man named I. B. Grasty. After Grasty died, Lucy wed John Moon in that den of iniquity, Washington, D.C. Moon was a whopping one-sixteenth black. State authorities challenged Lucy's right to raise her two children on the grounds that they would be associating with "persons of mixed blood" and would therefore "be deterred from association with gentle people of white blood." The children were sent to the Children's Home Society, which was required by law to take custody of children living in "vicious or unsalutary surroundings." The appeals court used the definition of Negro that was in effect at the time of Lucy's marriage (one-fourth rather than one-sixteenth) to determine that Moon was not black, thus allowing Lucy to keep custody of her children.[28] However, the court noted that if Moon had had one-fourth or more black blood, the marriage would have been illegal and the children removed. In 1921, ten years after *Moon*, a white Indiana man attempted to adopt his mulatto daughter. The judge refused to allow it, because to do so would be tantamount to sanctioning a marriage between the man and his black mistress.[29]

Custody cases were not limited to the early twentieth century. In 1951 Bernice Beckman, a divorced white woman with custody of her five-year-old son, married a black man in New York, a state that had never had an antimiscegenation law. Her ex-husband kidnapped the boy, but was nonetheless awarded custody by the court on the grounds of her "immoral conduct." Initially, Beckman was denied visitation rights as well, but she later regained them, only to have her husband disappear with the boy. In 1953 a white Oklahoma woman lost custody of her five children because she had counseled them against racial prejudice and the Korean war. Her ex-husband, a man who had deserted the family ten years earlier and had been convicted of perjury, forgery, and incest, was awarded custody.[30]

The American Civil Liberties Union (ACLU) filed an amicus brief in the 1953 case of *Lesser v. Lesser*, in which a white woman lost custody of the children she had raised with her white ex-husband when she remarried a black man. The supreme court of the state of Washington held the case under advisement for several months before finally setting it down for argument en banc. Judge Henry Clay Agnew terminated the mother's rights and granted the father's request for custody. Agnew wrote that "[s]entiment, it is true, is against mixed marriage, but policy, in every relevant field of Washington law, specifically declares against racial tests as guides for judicial action." Despite this lip service to equality, and despite the fact that Washington had not had an antimiscegenation law since the nineteenth century, the court accepted the father's argument that "individual and community prejudice would, in their later years, do grievous harm to the children."[31]

In Connecticut, a state that had never had an antimiscegenation law, Edward Murphy sued his white ex-wife Dorothy for custody of their son exactly twelve days after she married a black dentist. In 1956 the court awarded custody to Edward under the guise of his being able to provide for the boy's religious education (Dorothy had been excommunicated from the Catholic Church, and her parents, upset over her second marriage, would not be able to provide care for the boy).[32] That same year in Illinois, a black woman lost custody of her children when she married a white man, although her ex-husband had been convicted of rape.[33] The fact that Illinois had repealed its antimiscegenation law more than eighty years earlier appeared not to enter into the equation.

In 1962 a judge in the nation's capital noted that there was no evidence that a happy interracial home would hurt a white child. Nevertheless, he awarded custody to the father in question because of the possibility that the daughter might follow in her mother's footsteps and cross racial lines. "None of us can anticipate what problems, if any, would develop as the child becomes older, particularly during puberty, when she, in school and other activities, becomes aware of the opposite sex."[34] That same year, a judge in Detroit took away custody of Sarah Potter's three-year-old because of her marriage to a black physician.[35]

Anna Frances Eilers divorced her white husband in 1963 and married Marshall C. Anderson, who was black. She was subsequently denied custody of her children. They became wards of the juvenile court of Kentucky, which placed them in foster homes and juvenile facilities. Unhappy with this arrangement, Anna offered custody of the two older children to her ex-husband in return for custody of the younger three. His response was to request custody of all five children. Anna was initially represented by a local attorney, but for her appeal, the NAACP Legal Defense Fund stepped in and provided her with representation. Anderson had a steady job at RCA, although the court's knowledge that the NAACP had helped him get it may have hurt Anna's case. Regarding Mr. Eilers's employment, the court noted that he

> has now attained a state of sobriety and he is regularly employed . . . as a bartender and as a professional gambler. While the Courts in Kentucky frown upon gambling and the Statutes inveigh against it, we cannot in this day and age reach a conclusion that because a parent is a professional gambler or an amateur gambler that they are unfit to have custody of their own children.

Apparently, this day and age did not prevent the court from reaching a conclusion based on race, although it did not say so. The court merely said that "the testimony of the parties reveal[s] that the best interests of these children lie with their father."[36]

At least some courts were more honest. In 1971 an Illinois judge admitted that he was denying a white mother custody of her three children because, upon her remarriage to a black man, the children would probably have to grow up in a "strange place" with a racially mixed family.[37] That *Loving v. Virginia* had been decided four years earlier did not change the judge's opinion about the deleterious effects of an interracial household.

A review of these custody cases indicates that in most instances, the new black husband was a professional man, a factor ignored by the courts. The antipathy to black dentists that was demonstrated in the 1956 case of Dorothy Murphy resurfaced in 1978. Carolyn Sue Ethridge's ex-husband Emmitt failed to pay child support and assaulted her with a gun. He harassed her so frequently that she lost her job and moved from Alabama to Ohio, where she met and married the dentist. Carolyn had initially been awarded custody of the children, but after her remarriage, Emmitt took her to court and obtained full custody. When she appealed on the grounds that the court had changed custody only because of the race of her new husband, the Alabama Appeals Court admitted that the ex-husband had shown racial prejudice during the trial. However, the court maintained that there was no "overt evidence" that Carolyn's charge was true and added that the trial court had treated her new husband "courteously."[38]

Elsewhere in 1978, a Louisiana trial court reluctantly granted custody to a white mother who had had an affair with a black man. The "maternal preference rule" outweighed the fact that her conduct "was particularly scandalous and offensive to the sensibilities of the local community" and that her affair showed a "lack of love and consideration for her children." When her husband appealed the decision, the state supreme court reversed it, arguing that the woman's "disregard for accepted moral principles" made her an unfit mother, regardless of the fact that Louisiana's antimiscegenation statutes had been found unconstitutional.[39]

It wasn't until 1984 that the U.S. Supreme Court ruled that race could no longer be a factor in custody decisions, as the justices overruled a Florida court's decision to remove Linda Palmore's daughter, Melanie, from her custody after her remarriage.[40] Palmore was awarded custody when she and her husband, Anthony Sidoti, divorced in 1980. Sidoti contested the custody order when Palmore moved in with and later married a black man.[41] A counselor appointed by the court wrote that Palmore had "chosen for herself and for her child, a life-style unacceptable to the father and society." The circuit court judge agreed, holding that

> despite the strides that have been made in better relations between the
> races in this country, it is inevitable that Melanie will, if allowed to re-
> main in her present situation and attains school age and thus more vul-
> nerable to peer pressure, suffer from the social stigmatization that is sure
> to come.[42]

After the Florida court of appeals affirmed the decision, Palmore appealed to the U.S. Supreme Court. An amicus curiae brief on her behalf was prepared as a combined effort by the American Jewish Congress, the NAACP, and the ACLU. The ACLU brief was written in part by William Zabel, who had been intimately involved in the *Loving* brief (see chapter 13).[43] Writing for a unanimous court, Chief Justice Warren Burger declared that "[b]owing to popular prejudice, whether to protect the potential victims of such prejudice or to avoid racial unrest generally, cannot constitute a sufficient justification for departing from the constitutional command of equal protection." Burger noted that although the Constitution could not control prejudices, "neither can it tolerate them. Private biases may be outside the reach of the law, but the law cannot, directly or indirectly, give them effect." Since it was clear to the Court that the state would not have removed custody of Palmore's child if she had married a Caucasian, the change in custody was a violation of the Equal Protection Clause of the Fourteenth Amendment.[44]

Despite the proliferation of antimiscegenation laws, the enthusiastic enforcement of them by police, and the acquiescence of judges, not all was bleak. The middle of the twentieth century found the southern states fully invested in their racially discriminatory statutes, but a ray of light was breaking through the darkness out west. *Loving v. Virginia* was almost twenty years away when California became the first state to step resolutely into the future.

7

The West Leads the Way

The far-reaching harm and danger of marriage between whites and Negroes to the great white race that God intended should rule the world is apparent to all intelligent students of history; such mixtures have always resulted in weakening, degrading, and dragging down the superior to the level of the inferior race.

—Alabama senator Howard Heflin, 1930

Andrea Perez was white and Sylvester Davis was black, so W. G. Sharp, the California county clerk, refused to grant them a marriage license when they applied in 1948.[1] A California law, initially promulgated during the state's first legislative session in 1850, forbade whites from marrying blacks or mulattoes. Mongolians were added to the proscription in 1901, and Malays were included in a 1933 revision.[2] The last version of the California antimiscegenation law was codified in 1945 and, ironically, signed into law by Governor Earl Warren, the author of the majority opinion in *Loving* twenty years later.[3] California was the only state that merely declared interracial marriages null and void, without imposing additional penalties on anyone involved in such a union.[4]

Since both Perez and Davis were Roman Catholics, the Catholic Interracial Council of Los Angeles intervened on their behalf. Daniel

Marshall of the Council started a mandamus proceeding in the California Supreme Court to compel the county clerk to grant a license. Marshall argued that the California law violated the clause in the First Amendment that granted the free exercise of religion, as well as the Fourteenth Amendment.[5]

While Marshall used the simple and persuasive argument that Perez and Davis were simply two people who loved each other, California trotted out a variety of tactics. First, its lawyers argued that if the state were to eliminate the intermarriage ban, it would see a large increase in such unions. Marshall countered that should the court determine that antimiscegenation laws were unconstitutional, it would be immaterial whether one, one hundred, or one thousand such couples flocked to the altar. When the state tried to argue that such unions produced inferior offspring, the plaintiffs called anthropologists and physiologists to testify to the contrary. The state also alleged that people of color were themselves physically inferior and that blacks in particular were prone to tuberculosis. Therefore, intermarriage would weaken the white constitution. In rebuttal, Marshall argued that if health were the issue, marriages should be banned on the basis of physical examinations, not race. Further, even if it were true that blacks were prone to tuberculosis, the antimiscegenation law affected those who were not afflicted with the disease.[6]

Having failed with its argument of physical inferiority, the state tried to argue that intermarriage should be banned on the grounds that blacks were mentally inferior. Its lawyers introduced as evidence the U.S. catalogues of distinguished people, the rolls of which were predominantly Caucasian. Marshall pointed out that numerically, Caucasians were also in the majority and that they generally lived in more "advantageous" settings than people of color. Among the state's last arguments were the contentions that mixed marriages would cause social tension and pose a threat to the general peace, that "only the dregs of society" could possibly desire intermarriage, and that such a "publicly obnoxious" activity was, in and of itself, contrary to "the public welfare." The plaintiffs countered that any social tension was the result of societal prejudice and not the fault of the mixed-race couple. To ban interracial marriages because of fear of societal tension would be tantamount to giving legal standing to prejudice. Further, even if it was only the "dregs of society" who wanted to intermarry, there was no statutory prohibition against *intra*racial marriage of low-class individuals. Clearly it was the race of the parties, not their social status, to which the state objected.[7]

Although the Catholic Interracial Council took the lead role in *Perez*, other groups assisted. The Japanese American Citizens League played a major role, while the ACLU and the American Jewish Congress played small roles in the case.[8]

Judge Roger Traynor's decision started with an evaluation of the equal protection clause. He discussed cases in which classifications based on race could be justified owing to a national emergency, then noted that

> [a] state law prohibiting members of one race from marrying members of another race is not designed to meet a clear and present peril arising out of an emergency. In the absence of an emergency the state clearly cannot base a law impairing fundamental rights of individuals on general assumptions as to traits of racial groups.[9]

Traynor contended that "[b]y restricting the individual's right to marry on the basis of race alone [the statutes] violate the equal protection of the laws clause of the United States Constitution."[10] He concluded that "[m]arriage is something more than a civil contract subject to regulation by the state; it is a fundamental right of free men. There can be no prohibition of marriage except for an important social objective and by reasonable means."[11]

Judge Traynor's second point of analysis went to the issue of whether the statute was arbitrary and unreasonable. Assuming that the state could validly make a racial classification under the equal protection clause, the question was whether such a classification bore a substantial relation to a legitimate legislative objective.[12] Traynor dismissed the state's scientific and sociological arguments as being insufficient, even if true, to justify the broad scope of the antimiscegenation statutes.[13] Traynor also rejected the argument that allowing intermarriage would establish social tension and create children who would become "social problems." Traynor explained away *Pace* by noting that it did not refer to intermarriage but rather to adultery and nonmarital intercourse, which were not basic rights.[14] Further, he noted that "[i]f miscegenous marriages can be prohibited because of tensions suffered by the progeny, mixed religious unions could be prohibited on the same grounds."[15]

> In summary, we hold that sections 60 and 69 [the anti-miscegenation provisions] are not only too vague and uncertain to be enforceable regulations of a fundamental right, but that they violate the equal protection of the laws clause of the United States Constitution by impairing the right

of individuals to marry on the basis of race alone and by arbitrarily and unreasonably discriminating against certain racial groups.[16]

The concurring opinion, written by Judge Carter, was even more strongly worded.

> The statutes here involved are the product of ignorance, prejudice and intolerance. This decision is in harmony with the principles of the Declaration of Independence which are guaranteed by the Bill of Rights and the Fourteenth Amendment to the Constitution of the United States and reaffirmed by the Charter of the United Nations, that all human beings have equal rights regardless of race, color or creed, and that the right to liberty and the pursuit of happiness is inalienable and may not be infringed because of race, color or creed. To say that these statutes may stand in the face of the concept of liberty and equality embraced within the ambit of the above-referenced fundamental law is to make of that concept an empty, hollow mockery.[17]

As if quoting these august documents was not enough, Judge Carter proceeded to cite the Fifth Amendment, the apostle Paul, a letter by Thomas Jefferson, Lincoln's Gettysburg Address, Blackstone's law dictionary, the California constitution, Hitler's *Mein Kampf,* and Lord Nottingham.[18] A second concurrence, by Judge Edmonds, was more circumscribed, concluding only that the antimiscegenation statutes violated the plaintiffs' First Amendment rights to freedom of religion.[19]

The dissent by Judge Schenk covered almost as many bases as Carter's concurrence. Schenk believed that it remained within the state's province to regulate marriages. He argued that such laws had been upheld for nearly one hundred years in state and federal courts and that they had a valid legislative purpose.[20] Schenk began with an attack on the freedom of religion argument, quoting a Catholic priest who had written that, while the Church did not forbid interracial marriages, it asked its ministers to dissuade mixed couples from trying to wed in states where such unions were forbidden. Thus he suggested that the church was bound by local laws, not vice versa.[21] He then proceeded to scientific authorities, many of whom hailed from the nineteenth century and one of whom was a geologist, in support of the proposition that race mixing produced inferior stock. [22]

It took more than a decade for any court to follow the *Perez* decision. In contrast to the California law, the Arizona antimiscegenation statute had a long and storied history. Arizona became a territory in 1863. Two years later, the first miscegenation bill, which would prohibit blacks and mulattoes from marrying whites, was introduced. It passed in the house by a vote of eight to two. The Council (which is what the Arizona senate was called at that time) added Indians and Mongolians to the list, and the bill passed by a four-to-one vote.[23] The law punished the solemnizer and the parties to the marriage with a fine of one hundred to one thousand dollars and imprisonment of three months to ten years.[24]

Subsequently, the legislature decided that existing statutes did not sufficiently protect the white race, so the law was amended to prohibit "all marriages of persons of Caucasian blood, or their descendants, with negroes, Mongolians or Indians and their descendants."[25] A close reading of this statute reveals that persons of mixed heritage of any kind were forbidden from marrying anyone. In 1931, without touching the "and their descendants" portion of the law, the Arizona legislature added first Malays and then Hindus to the list of forbidden marriage partners for white people. This gave Arizona the dubious distinction of being the only state to ever place a religious classification in its antimiscegenation ban.[26]

In 1942 the Arizona legislature decided that American Indians were worthy of marrying whites after all, and excised that minority group from the revised antimiscegenation law.[27] The final revision that was signed by the governor finally cleared the way for persons of mixed heritage to marry (though not to marry whites in most cases) by omitting the "descendants" reference.[28] The new statute prohibited whites from marrying any person having any Negro blood or anyone classified as a Mongolian, Malay, or Hindu. The percentage of blood sufficient to place someone in the latter three categories was never specified.[29] Such marriages were declared void ab initio, and the children resulting from such a union were barred from inheriting the estate.[30] The penalties were unusually lenient: a fine of up to three hundred dollars and imprisonment for up to six months.[31]

The Arizona antimiscegenation statute stood until 1959. The possibly apocryphal story is that one day, while teaching his high school civic class, Henry Oyama was asked what should be done if a law stood in the way of a person's right to happiness. Oyama explained that Americans were obligated to obey the law, but that there might be "extenuating circumstances where . . . human felicity might take precedence over a moot point of law." At the time, Oyama was living with his widowed mother, but shortly thereafter he found another woman with whom he wished to share his life.[32]

Mary Ann Jordan was a twenty-eight-year-old white woman who had moved from New York to Arizona in the hope that the dry weather would help her arthritis. She worked for American Airlines out of Tucson. A practicing Catholic, Jordan had taken all the church's steps toward getting a marriage license. The only thing standing between her and lawfully wedded bliss was her choice of a husband. Henry Oyama was a thirty-three-year-old American citizen who had lived his entire life in Tucson. He had served in the Army from 1945 to 1947 as part of the Counter Intelligence Corps. He graduated Phi Beta Kappa and was a Distinguished Military Graduate with a bachelor's degree from the University of Arizona and a master's degree in education. At the time of his engagement to Jordan, Oyama was teaching American history and Spanish at Pueblo High School and was working in the circulation department of Tucson Newspapers, Inc. None of that mattered, however, because Oyama was a Japanese American. Under Arizona law, he was classified as a Mongolian who was ineligible to marry a Caucasian such as Jordan.[33]

Oyama was unaware of the legal barriers to his impending nuptials. He recalls that around the time that the pair became formally engaged, Jordan received a pamphlet from their church offering advice to prospective spouses. Included was a section reminding couples that approximately twenty states prohibited interracial marriage. There was no listing of the states. Just to be on the safe side, someone suggested that he simply visit the county clerk and inquire. Oyama knew that the clerk was the wife of a fellow teacher and friend, a man who harbored no personal objection to interracial marriage, so he went to request a license.[34]

Grayce Gibson O'Neill was the county clerk to whom Oyama applied for a license in October 1959. The license required both parties to state their name, age, residency, place of birth, and race, and to swear that they were not related to their spouse-to-be. When Jordan stated that she was Caucasian and Oyama that he was Mongolian, O'Neill had no choice but to follow the law and deny their request.[35] On learning of his plight, two of Oyama's colleagues asked him if he would be interested in the ACLU's legal assistance. He and Jordan accepted the offer, and three local attorneys, Charles Ares, Frank Berry, and Paul Rees, took charge of the case.[36]

The ACLU argued that the right to marry was a fundamental one protected by the due process clause of both the Arizona and U.S. constitutions. The organization also maintained that the state was curtailing Oyama and Jordan's freedom of religion without a clear and compelling public necessity. Moreover, racial distinctions were prohibited under the equal protection clause of the U.S. Constitution where they were not based on clear and compelling reasons. The distinctions the state employed in its antimiscegenation law were arbitrary and capricious and, therefore, void. Lastly, the ACLU argued that the statute was vague on its face.[37] Ares recalls that the team added the freedom of religion argument in part because it had been successful in the *Perez* case but also because Oyama and Jordan were both Catholic and the church had shown a willingness to perform the nuptials.[38]

In truth, it would have been hard for the ACLU to find a better test case. Oyama recognizes that he and Jordan were a sympathetic couple, both college-educated and never married. The country was starting to recognize the injustice done to Japanese Americans during World War II, and Oyama, as a resident of an internment camp during his teenage years, had been a victim of that blind prejudice. In addition, he was fully aware that his status as a veteran, a captain in the Air Force reserve, and a high school American history teacher created a favorable fact pattern.[39]

The state of Arizona brought out some of its highest officials to defend its law, but their hearts were not in it. The initial answer had been composed by Marvin S. Cohen, the chief civil deputy county attorney, but when the case reached superior court, county clerk O'Neill was represented by Harry Ackerman, the county attorney for Pima County. He was assisted by Jack Podret, the deputy county attorney of Pima County, and Lawrence Ollason, the assistant attorney general for the state.[40] However, none of the lawyers for the state really wanted to uphold the statute, and Oyama and his lawyers were fully aware of their stance.[41]

Marvin Cohen got a good chuckle when he learned that I had retrieved his name from the ACLU Archives in Princeton, where he had been listed as one of the "bad guys." He is a lifetime member of that organization. Cohen considers the entire endeavor "friendly litigation." Neither he nor county attorney Ackerman had any sympathy for the law, nor did they believe it was constitutional, but it was their duty as attorneys to put up the best legal position they could.[42]

Lawrence Ollason, too, remembered what he terms "the great conspiracy" with pleasure. He recalled that none of the members of the state's legal team had any interest in defending the statute, but they put forth the appropriate legal arguments. The intermarriage ban was hardly the only discriminatory law in the state. When Ollason purchased his house in the 1950s, it carried a deed restriction prohibiting him from reselling the house to Asians.[43]

For his part, Harry Ackerman was outraged at the suggestion that he could have favored the antimiscegenation statute. A good indication that his opinion was not a last-minute conversion for the sake of posterity is that he saved and sent to me the same newspaper clippings that Oyama's attorney, Paul Rees, kept in *his* scrapbook. In fact, when Oyama was slow to respond to my requests for an interview, Ackerman assured me that I could just call him: "He's a great guy."[44] Oyama returned the compliment, noting that he and Ackerman had been friends before the case owing to their common association with the state Democratic party. Oyama assured me that Ackerman had merely gone through the motions of defending a statute that he found odious.[45]

Ackerman still recalls his excitement when the late Frank Berry, who was the lead lawyer for Oyama and Jordan, visited him personally to tell him that he had a Japanese client who wanted to marry a Caucasian and to ask whether Ackerman would be interested in helping him test the law. Both Berry and Ackerman assumed that the case would be a long and grueling one, probably ending up in the U.S. Supreme Court, but Ackerman "most certainly and happily" agreed to play the bad guy and help Berry challenge the law. Ackerman and Cohen took on the job of representing the state clerk "as honorably as [they] could," by citing the previous legal basis for upholding antimiscegenation laws.[46]

When Cohen describes the litigation as friendly, it seems almost an understatement. The relationships between the attorneys on both sides were long and deep. Paul Rees and Marvin Cohen had gone to high school together. Charles Ares and Harry Ackerman had been moot court partners in law school and had briefly practiced together. Rees, Ares, and Frank Berry had worked with Arizona Democratic stalwarts Morris and Stewart Udall, and Cohen followed Stewart Udall to Washington, D.C., when the latter became Secretary of the Interior.[47]

Judge Herbert Krucker may not have known that this was a friendly suit,[48] but he knew an unconstitutional statute when he saw one and ruled that

> the intermarriage of a person of Caucasian blood with a Negro, Mongolian, Malay or Hindu cannot and does not adversely affect the public health, safety, morals or welfare; that the progeny of a person of Caucasian blood and a Negro, Mongolian, Malay or Hindu are not inferior in any respect to the progeny of two persons of Caucasian blood, or of two Negroes, or of two Mongolians or of two Malays or of two Hindus.[49]

Judge Krucker found the offending statute in violation of the First and Fourteenth Amendments of the U.S. Constitution and ordered the clerk to grant Oyama and Jordan a license.[50]

In discussing Krucker's verdict with me, Ackerman made a slight slip of the tongue and said that Krucker had "ruled in our favor." Although he was clearly against the statutes, Ackerman almost wished that he *had* won. The "loss" forced him to appeal the case, because a trial court decision did not weigh enough to leave a lasting impact.[51] Oyama recalls how Ackerman explained the need for the appeal to him: the trial court decision meant that he and Jordan could marry, but it held no precedent for other couples. Oyama understood that no malice was intended. Even if he had lost at the trial court, Oyama stated that he and Jordan would have been willing to wait for the U.S. Supreme Court to rule on the issue if that was necessary.[52]

The Arizona supreme court may not have been aware of Ackerman's intent in appealing the decision. In any event, the justices were in no rush to a reach a determination. Charles Ares remembers that the supreme court simply sat on the case, and credits this delay to the presence on the court of Judge M. T. Phelps, who was one of the founders of the John Birch Society. Ares believes that Phelps did not want to be involved in an opinion upholding Krucker's decision; however, he was equally loathe to participate in a reversal that might later be overturned by the U.S. Supreme Court, since it was obvious that the parties were willing to take that step if Krucker's decision was overruled.[53]

The state court was lucky to get away with its delaying tactics. Judge Krucker's decision was handed down in December 1959. While the justices hemmed and hawed, state senator David Wine and two other Arizona legislators introduced a bill to repeal the miscegenation laws. To ensure its passage, they made the repeal a bipartisan effort; it passed in the house overwhelmingly, seventy-one to six. The senate stalled for a month because the Public Health and Welfare Committee objected to the bill. Eventually it, too, passed the bill by a lopsided vote of twenty to six and Governor Paul Fannin signed the legislation, ending nearly a century-long ban on intermarriage in Arizona.[54]

Ares and Rees agree that theirs could not have been a better test case. Oyama had been through the internment camps, volunteered for Army duty, worked his way through college, and become a civics teacher. Ares also noted Oyama's employment at the *Arizona Star* did not hurt the case, since the *Star* took an interest in its employees. Rees recalls that both

Oyama and Jordan were physically attractive, friendly individuals who were excellent witnesses during their trial.[55] As their story played out, theirs was clearly not a fleeting romance. The two remained married until Jordan's death. Oyama has since remarried, but he had a catch in his voice as he reminisced about a historical society article that featured the couple's wedding picture.[56] Oyama retired from the Air Force as a lieutenant colonel and became vice president of Pima Community College; he was honored as man of the year in Tucson in 1993, and in 1995 the University of Arizona awarded him an honorary doctorate of laws.[57]

Although the case was handled by the ACLU, it appears that other groups may have been peripherally involved. The archives show a joint memo from the American Jewish Committee and the American Jewish Congress regarding the case. Paul Rees recalls that these groups were curious about the events but that the NAACP showed no interest in the proceedings. Although the case clearly had a happy ending for the Oyamas, Rowland Watts of the national ACLU expressed regret that the state had not heard the appeal. Apparently unfamiliar with the parties involved, he inquired of Frank Berry whether the suit had been a friendly one.[58] The files contain no record of a response, possibly because Berry was laughing too hard to compose one.

The next antimiscegenation challenge took place the following year in Nevada. Like Arizona's law, the Nevada ban on interracial marriage was a longstanding one. Nevada had been in such a tearing hurry to pass an antimiscegenation law that it did so on the sixteenth day of the first session of the Nevada territorial legislature in November 1861. The initial proposal banned whites from marrying Negroes and Indians only, but within days, the ban also included Chinese.[59] Few delegates questioned the need for an antimiscegenation law, and most disagreed only on to whom the law should apply. The final version of the bill was the most inclusive, forbidding the marriage of whites to Negroes, mulattoes, Indians, and Chinese. The punishment was one to two years in prison for the parties engaging in such a union. Any clergy or layperson performing an interracial ceremony could be fined up to five hundred dollars and imprisoned for up to six months.[60]

Labor leader Harry Bridges and his fiancée Noriko (Nikki) Sawada never intended to spend much time in Nevada. Despite Bridges's fame and power, he was short on cash, so on the occasion of what would be his third (and her first) trip to the altar, the Californians had decided to elope. In San Francisco, the couple's friends showered them with rice as they headed toward their Reno-bound plane, from which they emerged in Nevada on the evening of December 8, 1959. The couple intended to apply for a license and have a short marriage ceremony in time to catch a nine-fifty flight back the next morning, so that Sawada could return to her job at the radical law firm of Garry, Dreyfus, McTernan, and Keller. The firm represented such diverse clients as members of the Black Panthers, the Chicago Seven, Reverend Jim Jones (of Guyana infamy), Daniel Ellsberg, Joan Baez, and Helen Sobell (wife of Morton Sobell, who had been convicted of espionage with the Rosenbergs).[61]

Bridges's reputation preceded him. As the founder and head of the International Longshoremen's and Warehousemen's Union, he had seen himself subject to numerous deportation attempts (back to his native Australia) and had been branded a Communist during the heyday of the McCarthy era. Word soon spread that he was in town, and reporters flocked to the Mapes Hotel, where "Mr. and Mrs. H. Bridges" had registered using the Longshoremen's Union headquarters as their home address. After one intrepid newsman slipped a note under the door proposing a meeting in the hotel lobby, Bridges allowed a few members of the media to come up to the suite before the couple left for the marriage bureau. However, just as the reporters were arriving, Charles Garry, a partner at the firm where Sawada worked, called to warn them that their plans were not legal in Nevada.[62]

Another lawyer in the firm, Benjamin Dreyfus, recommended that Bridges contact Nevada attorney Sam Francovich who, ironically, made his living as a divorce attorney. Francovich was not a lawyer in the Garry-Dreyfus mold. He protested that as a Republican, he was not the ideal choice to represent an accused Communist. However, contrary to the government's portrait of his political beliefs, Bridges considered himself a Republican as well. Francovich's politics were hardly the problem. The real obstacle was that he was unfamiliar with miscegenation law and had to call Dreyfus for the citation to *Perez*.[63]

The next morning, Bridges and Sawada walked to the courthouse for what they now knew would be a futile attempt to apply for a license. The deputy clerk, Viola Givens, was already apprised of the situation. She asked Sawada for her nationality and was told "American," while Bridges chimed in that he was the foreigner. Clearly this was the wrong answer, so Givens asked Sawada to choose a color from the options of red, white, black, or yellow. She chose yellow. "It's not where you were born, it's the blood that counts," counseled Givens, at which point Sawada replied that hers was red. Givens, to the surprise of no one, refused to grant the license. Although Sawada's recollections of her somewhat smart-aleck answers are persuasive, the *New York Times* and the *Reno Evening Gazette* reported that she sobbed when forced to admit to reporters that the license had been refused. The latter paper also reported that by the end of the day, Bridges's affable demeanor had been replaced with a "haggard, harried look." The couple repaired to the hotel bar, where Sawada, regaining her composure, declared that she hadn't realized it would be so difficult for a Democrat to marry a Republican.[64]

Bridges promptly called for Francovich, while county clerk Harry Brown called district attorney Emile Gezelin. With Francovich in tow, Bridges again requested a license and Brown, taking over for Givens, refused to grant one. Francovich informed Brown that the Nevada statute had been copied from the California antimiscegenation law, which had been declared unconstitutional. When Brown refused to give in, Francovich asked trial judge Taylor Wines to issue a writ of mandamus to force the issuance of the license.[65] Wines agreed to hear the two sides the following day, December 10. During the delay, the hotel management learned that the couple was not, in fact, "Mr. and Mrs.," so Sawada was moved—solo—into the bridal suite, while Bridges stayed in their original room.[66]

Appearing before Judge Wines, Francovich and his assistant, Bruce Roberts, argued that Nevada's law was based on the California statute that had been found unconstitutional. Additionally, the statute violated the Nevada constitutional provision that stated that all persons were equal, denying Bridges and Sawada their "inalienable right to happiness." District attorney Gezelin predictably cited the number of states that still banned intermarriage and noted that the Nevada law had been in effect for almost one hundred years and had never been declared unconstitutional. Further, he cited a number of case decisions that had upheld challenges to the constitutionality of antimiscegenation laws. He opined that the constitutionality of the law could not be at issue, since nobody had been charged with violating it. He concluded with the classic argument that states had the right to regulate marriage in order to maintain social control.[67]

Francovich and Roberts added some quasi-legal arguments to their own arsenal. Francovich told Judge Wines that the couple was planning a trip abroad and that judicial recognition of their right to wed "will do more than all our sputniks and missiles to bring about world friendship and cooperation." Observing that the law was clearly based on the premise that other races were inferior to Caucasians, Roberts counseled that it would not behoove the state to be "classified with Little Rock," a reference to the virulent racism shown by the state of Arkansas when schools were desegregated in 1957, just two years earlier.[68]

Judge Wines was clearly unimpressed with Gezelin, but Roberts's reference to the events in Arkansas may have struck a chord. He chose to concur with the *Perez* decision, stating that he "saw no evil which would justify the state interfering with the freedom of an individual to marry." The ruling was greeted with applause, and a number of newsmen dropped all semblance of objectivity to shake the hands of the happy couple. Wines directed Francovich to prepare a court order for his signature.[69]

Ten minutes later, Bridges and Sawada walked back to the marriage bureau, where county clerk Brown filed the application papers. When asked for the five-dollar fee, Bridges inquired, tongue planted firmly in his cheek, whether this was the normal cost or whether their "extras" were involved. Brown missed the humor and solemnly assured him that there was no discrimination in the fee. Trailed by the growing horde of journalists and photographers, Bridges and Sawada crossed the street, bound for the office of justice of the peace William Beemer. Apparently, Beemer was publicity-shy. He ordered all but the couple, Sam Francovich, and Helen Cormier (Wines's court clerk) to leave.[70] Beemer was selected to perform the ceremony because of his long friendship with Sam Francovich. He has solemnized over 140,000 marriages, but he clearly recalls the Bridges-Sawada nuptials. He remembers that, when the ceremony was over, Bridges offered him money. He demurred, but Bridges persisted and finally Beemer accepted a twenty-dollar bill.[71]

The story was front-page news in California and Nevada for several days. The first day's coverage in the *Nevada State Journal* devoted significant space to reminding readers of Bridges's alleged Communist leanings and the government's attempts to deport him. After the wedding, the paper dropped all references to Bridges's politics and featured a three-photo before-after spread of the newlyweds entitled "Longshoremen's Strike Results in New Union." The paper finally got serious in an editorial three days later that noted that although most Nevadans would have preferred to have someone with a more savory reputation than Bridges challenge the law, few could argue in favor of a ban on intermarriage. In an interesting side note, the wedding day story and the editorial referred only to marriages between Caucasians and "Orientals," making no reference whatsoever to the possibility that other mixed couples had been affected by the law. Other papers were guilty of the same omission. One has to wonder whether the reporters would have been quite so enthusiastic had Bridges chosen a bride more controversial than "an attractive Nisei legal secretary."[72]

Sawada recalls that a variety of civil rights groups showed interest in the case and sent supporters to the courtroom for the hearing. The case made headlines in states throughout the union, catching the attention of the Urban League, ACLU, NAACP, Japanese American Citizens League, and other groups. Judge Wines's granting of the motion, however, rendered the support of these groups unnecessary.[73] Black leaders did not speak officially about the decision, perhaps in deference to the NAACP policy of staying clear of the miscegenation issue. They worried that other goals of the organization, such as fair housing, equal employment, and equal education, might be jeopardized by a statement in favor of interracial marriages.[74]

State court decisions were nice for residents of those enlightened states. However, it was clear to those determined to strike down antimiscegenation laws across the country that more concentrated tactics were needed. During the 1950s, the NAACP may have been hesitant to work directly against these laws, but the ACLU had no such qualms.

8

The Organizations Challenge, and the Challenges Become Organized

[T]hough a white woman be a prostitute, the prescription is strong, nearly conclusive, among both races, that she will not yield—has not yielded—even in her confirmed depravity to commerce with a negro....The consensus of public opinion, unrestricted to either race, is that a white woman prostitute is yet, though lost of virtue, above the even greater sacrifice of the voluntary submission of her person to the embraces of the other race.

—*Story v. State,* 1912

After *Brown v. Board of Education,* white southerners formed a number of groups to protest school desegregation, including the National Association for the Advancement of White People and the Citizens' Councils. The latter were formed as a more civilized alternative to the Klan; members wore business suits instead of sheets. Although the groups varied in focus and vitriol, all were antagonistic to the desegregation decision and to the Supreme Court, which they accused of abusing its power and trying to act like a legislature.[1]

Although the Citizens' Council has since faded into oblivion, its message persists to this day. A group called the Council of Conservative Citizens continues to argue that interracial marriage "amounts to white genocide." Lest anyone think that such sentiments fall on deaf ears, in current times, two southern congressmen, former Senate majority leader Trent Lott of Mississippi and Representative Bob Barr of South Carolina, have spoken at Council events, and Lott has allowed himself to be photographed with CCC officials.[2]

In the 1950s, the ACLU was the civil rights group most aggressive in fighting antimiscegenation statutes. Starting immediately after *Perez*, the organization began to look for potential test cases in other states.[3] In contrast, the American Jewish Congress (AJC), which had also been actively involved in the California litigation, proved less than enthusiastic about proceeding further in this area of law.[4] By the time an antimiscegenation challenge reached the Supreme Court (see chapter 9), the AJC had regained its fervor for the issue. However, after the Supreme Court's nondecision in that case, Sandy Bolz, the Washington, D.C., representative, suggested that the AJC abandon all efforts in that case in favor of a more sympathetic one. Subsequent years did not find the AJC involved in any other miscegenation cases, as its reduced legal staff concentrated primarily on school prayer issues and Sabbath laws.[5]

In the wake of *Perez*, the Japanese American Citizen's League showed itself only moderately active in the fight against antimiscegenation laws in the 1950s. The organization focused its attention on searching for cases involving Korean war brides, an effort that was unsuccessful due to the fact that white-Asian couples were generally not prosecuted in the states that included Asians in intermarriage bans.[6] Although the JACL was not actively involved in most subsequent antimiscegenation challenges, its interest was sparked by the *Loving* case, in which it became an active participant (see chapter 13).[7]

Although the NAACP later became seriously involved in overturning antimiscegenation laws in the 1960s, during the 1950s, its attitude can best be described as one of "firm abstention." Not only was the organization more concerned with voting rights and desegregation of schools and housing, but it was "decidedly reluctant" to be associated with the intermarriage cause. In 1944 Thurgood Marshall, then the lead attorney for the NAACP, actually urged the ACLU not to challenge antimiscegenation laws.[8]

This stance was not just an abstract one. The NAACP steadfastly refused to provide more than lip service to an attorney named A. L.

Emery, who tried to invalidate Oklahoma's antimiscegenation law in federal court in the case of *Stevens v. United States*.[9] The case involved the estate of one Stella Sands, a Creek Indian, who had written a will in 1935 leaving her property to her sister. Sands died six years later, and her will was probated accordingly. William Stevens, a man of at least some black heritage, objected to the probate of her estate, believing that Sands's marriage to him subsequent to the writing of her will nullified that will under Oklahoma law and entitled him to the full value of her estate. He submitted a certificate signed by a Kansas probate judge to show that he and Sands were husband and wife. After the ceremony, held in Independence, Kansas (where interracial marriage had been legal for almost a century), the couple had returned to the Creek Nation in Okmulgee, Oklahoma, where they lived until Sands's death. Local authorities had never prosecuted them, although Oklahoma law forbade the marriage of a person of African descent to a person not of African descent.[10]

Sands's executrix responded to Stevens's objection by stating that Sands was a Creek Indian and Stevens a Negro, and therefore the alleged marriage was not a valid one. The United States intervened on the executrix's behalf to have the case removed to federal court because of Sands's enrollment in the Creek nation. It would be thirty-six years before the federal government would switch sides and intervene in a case on behalf of an interracial couple. This case, however, was in 1944, and the federal brief argued that the alleged marriage of Sands and Stevens was not valid in the state of Oklahoma.[11]

The district court for the eastern district of Oklahoma found that Sands was a full-blooded Creek Indian and, as such, could not be legally married to Stevens. Although Oklahoma law held that the will of a single person was revoked by marriage, the court found that Sands had remained a single woman at the time of her death, which rendered her will valid. Emery, a white attorney from Pennsylvania, represented Stevens. Realizing that he was in over his head, he turned to the NAACP for assistance with his appeal.[12]

In December 1943, Emery wrote to the NAACP national headquarters. The letter was answered by Thurgood Marshall, then special counsel, who replied that assistance would be forthcoming. In a detailed letter, Marshall promised Emery a check in the amount of $133.52. Fortified with national support, Emery led his appeal with the argument that the Oklahoma statute violated the Fourteenth Amendment and followed this claim with arguments regarding the sovereignty of the Creek Nation and the alleged mixed heritage of the parties. Marshall sent the file to Milton Konvitz, assistant special counsel, for further review. Konvitz was far less enthusiastic about providing assistance. His subsequent letter to Emery indicated that, fearing "a great likelihood and danger of creating an unfavorable Appellate Court precedent," the NAACP had chosen not to support his appeal after all.[13]

Outraged by this decision, Emery requested that at the very least, the NAACP lend him money to continue the case on his own. Konvitz wrote to William Hastie at Howard Law School regarding Emery's request for money. Incredibly, Hastie replied that "the power of Oklahoma over the domestic status of its citizens . . . include[s] the power to invalidate interracial marriages," thus directly contradicting Marshall's earlier statements. Konvitz promptly airmailed Emery to reiterate that "it would be extremely hazardous at this time to have this question raised in the United States Supreme Court" and that therefore the NAACP would not render legal assistance. In May, four months after assistance had been promised, Marshall concluded the matter, informing Emery that the NAACP's National Legal Committee saw "little chance of success because of the precedents involved." However, because "it is the type of case which should be fought," the committee was prepared to provide Emery with a contribution of one hundred dollars.[14]

The case of *Stevens v. United States* was filed in the Tenth Circuit Court of Appeals. Emery argued that the antimiscegenation law was an unconstitutional violation of the Fourteenth Amendment. The court did not agree, finding that marriage "affects in a vital manner public welfare, and its control and regulation is [sic] a matter of domestic concern within each state." Since states had the power to determine the age of marriageable parties, to draft procedures ensuring a marriage's validity, and to ascertain the effect of a marriage on property rights, the court reasoned that the state was also "empowered to forbid" marriages between persons of different races.[15]

Another case that the NAACP knew about but did not join in was that of Davis Knight, a twenty-four-year-old Navy veteran who was sentenced by the state of Mississippi to five years in prison for marrying Junie Lee Spradley in 1946. Knight had attended the University of Southern Mississippi and enlisted in the Navy, in both cases identifying himself as white. By all accounts, his physical appearance pegged him as a white man.[16] However, Alma Ross, the widow of Knight's attorney, Quitman

Ross, believes that Knight was aware that "white" was not exactly an honest assessment of his racial classification in the state of Mississippi.[17]

According to Ross, Davis Knight's great-grandfather Newton had achieved notoriety by flying an American flag instead of the Stars and Bars during the Civil War. Newton Knight and his cohorts raided local army detachments during the war and were considered "irritants," "pests," and "outlaws." Ross reported that after rearing four or five children with his first wife, Newton married a woman named Rachel who had some black ancestry and who bore him more children. Ross believes that Davis Knight was well aware of the fact that his relationship to Rachel rendered him black in the eyes of white Mississippi.[18]

Whether Davis Knight was aware of the possible illegality at the time of his 1946 marriage is a question lost to posterity. He drowned in a boating accident not long after the court case. At trial, Knight claimed that his family had been considered white for the seventy years that they had resided in Ellisville, Mississippi. His marriage fell under a cloud only when his great-uncle Tom (Newton's son) came forth to argue that since Rachel Knight had been a black woman, Davis's marriage was illegal.[19] Knight was charged with "willfully and feloniously, and unlawfully [marrying a white woman] against the peace and dignity of the State of Mississippi." State law forbade the marriage of whites to persons with one-eighth or more Negro or Mongolian blood.[20]

At trial, Quitman Ross got deputy circuit clerk Nell Graves to admit that she had checked "white" on Knight's marriage license because he arrived "with a crowd of white ladies." A parade of witnesses called by Ross and prosecutor Paul Swartzfager argued the question of whether Rachel was a full-blooded Negro, an affirmative answer to which would mean a possible ten years in jail and a voided marriage for Knight and Spradley. Witnesses for the defense insisted that Rachel more closely resembled a Choctaw or Cherokee Indian and that she was part Creole. Of course, the testimony was hardly that scientific, describing Rachel variously as having "ginger-cake" color and "long curly black hair that swung across her shoulders," or else as being "coal-black" and "round-faced," with a "flat nose" and "big, thick lips." A bitter eighty-year-old Tom Knight took the stand to protect his family name from the taint of color by distancing himself from his cousin Davis. He testified that Rachel had "kinky hair, a wooly head, or whatever you want to call it."[21]

The witnesses on Davis's behalf were hardly in favor of intermarriage; they simply did not want Davis to be classified as black. Ross deliberately kept the one Knight relative who freely admitted that she was black away from the courthouse, and the prosecution apparently stayed unaware of her existence.[22] It took the jury only fifteen minutes to find Rachel black and Knight guilty. They halved the sentence, sending the unfortunate man to five years in the penitentiary. Spradley was spared by the court because she did not intentionally marry a black man, believing Knight to be white, whereas the court presumed that he was aware of his family heritage.[23]

After the initial conviction, Mrs. Robert Briggs of Ardsley, Pennsylvania, sent a *New York Times* clipping about the case to the NAACP's Walter White. Constance Baker Motley, an NAACP legal assistant, replied to Briggs that the NAACP was committed to eliminating antimiscegenation statutes (not quite the message delivered to poor Mr. Emery four years before) but could do nothing for Knight unless he or his counsel directly sought such assistance. Even without NAACP assistance, however, an appeals court reversed and remanded Knight's conviction on the grounds that it did not meet the "beyond reasonable doubt" requirement. He was never retried. While awaiting appeal, the young lovers had moved to the black side of town as befitted Knight's new racial classification. When the state supreme court determined that there was a reasonable doubt about Rachel's ancestry, however, the Knights were allowed to move back to the other side of the tracks, in deference to Davis's reaffirmed elevated status as a white man.[24]

Stevens and *Knight* were among the last challenges to be undertaken without the assistance of a national organization. According to records of the Mississippi Sovereignty Commission, the *Knight* case was monitored by civil rights organizations, and Ross received letters and telephone calls from almost every state in the union, as well as three European countries.[25] The truth of the matter is that Ross's appeal was probably aided by his refusal to accept outside assistance.

Following a consistent pattern, the ACLU wanted very much to become involved in the *Knight* case. It was the only civil rights group that did not waver from its goal of striking down antimiscegenation laws through the judicial system. The ACLU had no problem throwing its weight behind *Naim v. Naim* (see chapter 9), even though the case suffered from a basic flaw: it did not involve a sympathetic couple who loved one another and wanted to stay married. While *Naim* was at the Virginia Supreme Court level, the ACLU found another possible test case in Mississippi involving a divorce suit between a white woman and her Chinese husband. The Mississippi-based lawyer for the woman, not wishing to offend local sensibilities by associating his cause with such a notorious civil rights group, spurned the organization's offer of assistance. The ACLU did not push the matter because, like *Naim,* the case lacked a happy, loving couple who might sway public sentiment.[26]

In November 1955, the ACLU was alerted to a miscegenation case in South Carolina. An interracial couple had married in October 1954, despite the existence of state laws that forbade their union. Six months later, they were convicted and sentenced to one year in prison. The judge suspended the sentence and gave them three years probation, while a civil action annulled the marriage. When they continued to cohabit, a state circuit judge partially revoked the probation and sentenced them each to seven months in jail.[27]

The ACLU's Herbert Monte Levy asked cooperating attorney John Bolt Culbertson to look into the matter.[28] Unfortunately, a procedural problem emerged to prevent this decidedly sympathetic couple from becoming a test case. Having failed to contest their initial suspended sentence, they could not, in appealing their subsequent conviction, use the occasion to question the constitutionality of the antimiscegenation statutes.[29]

Two years later, another case piqued the ACLU's interest. A white North Carolina man, Allen Biddix, had married a much younger Cherokee woman named Hiawatha Queen, only to have the police break up the marriage. The newlyweds were poor, and Biddix was already a widower from a previous marriage. The ACLU member who learned of the case wrote to the national organization that "both have been considerably broken up by the enforced separation. . . . Perhaps a test case could be made out of this case. It seems to be a clear case of the violation of the civil rights of two humble people."[30]

Eventually, the ACLU found a lawyer, Frank Parker, for the pair but had some hesitation about bringing the action as a test case. Queen, while fully in favor of the rights of Indians like herself to marry whites, thought that blacks should not be able to do so. The file shows an inquiry from the NAACP asking how the case was proceeding. The ACLU responded that due to Queen's biases, it would file no action on the couple's behalf.[31]

Levy's successor, Rowland Watts continued the process begun by his predecessors of looking for a test case. He provided the organization's cooperating attorneys with the criteria for a good case as spelled out for him by Professor Sanford Kadish of the University of Utah in December of 1959. Kadish believed that the best kind of case was one in which a couple was being prosecuted for having married across the color line. Such a case would evoke more sympathy than one involving a mandamus proceeding to compel the issuance of a license or, even worse, an annulment proceeding. Kadish felt that it would be best to support a couple who had good standing in their community. He believed that it would be easier to make a case in a western or border state than in the deep South. Kadish described the ideal couple as one in which, so as not to inflame passions, the wife was the person of color and the husband white, with the best case scenario being a Native American or Asian wife with a white husband.[32]

Another potential test case arose in Georgia in 1959. In September of that year, Joseph Stangle of Spokane wrote to the ACLU regarding the predicament of Dr. Daniel R. Ng. Ng was a Panamanian citizen of Chinese heritage who had come to Spokane in the late 1940s, interned at St. Luke's Hospital and started a three-year residency in Atlanta. There he met a white woman with whom he fell in love. Since Ng was a strict Catholic, the young woman began the process of conversion. Upon application for a marriage license, the couple learned that they could neither marry in Georgia nor marry elsewhere and return to the state. Ng's priest informed him that even if Ng could get a marriage license, the priest would not perform a ceremony that violated Georgia law. Instead, the priest made arrangements for Ng and his fiancée to marry in Illinois and return to the state. This advice is somewhat puzzling in light of the fact that such an action was equally illegal, but apparently Ng followed it. In a follow-up letter to Stangle, Watts speculated that since Ng was living at the Catholic hospital where he worked, the chances of his being arrested for miscegenation were slim.[33]

In 1961 the ACLU found a test case in Utah, but it had other complications. A sixteen-year-old boy of Japanese heritage and a sixteen-year-old white girl were turned away in their quest for a marriage license in Salt Lake City. However, the clerk's refusal was actually in cahoots with the ACLU since, in a situation reminiscent of *Oyama*, the county clerk and county attorney were also interested in testing the law. In fact, the clerk and attorney immediately notified the ACLU of the situation, whereupon the organization found a local law firm to represent the pair. Given that the couple and the county attorney were cooperative, it looked like a perfect test case, but there was a catch. The father of the prospective groom was an eighty-year-old man who had had "a bitter experience" during World War II and had already suffered one nervous breakdown when another son had received a traffic summons.[34] Fearful of what the publicity would do to the older man, the ACLU paid for the couple to cross the border to Colorado and have the service performed where such unions had been legalized four years earlier. Therefore, the case became moot.[35]

The ACLU was also involved in challenging federal involvement in antimiscegenation issues. In January 1965, Frank Weitzel, the assistant comptroller general of the United States, wrote to the Finance and Accounting Office of the Army regarding the entitlement of one Private Waters from Texas to basic allowance for quarters for a dependent wife. The question to be determined was whether Private Waters's interracial marriage was valid. "The Texas statutes specifically prohibit such interracial marriage and further provide that if any such prohibited marriage is entered into, it shall be null and void." Weitzel noted that although the constitutionality of Florida's laws on the subject had recently been questioned in *McLaughlin* (see chapter 10), the Supreme Court had not addressed the question of intermarriage. Therefore, the Army felt that it should not make a determination as to the validity of Waters's marriage, and "[a]ccordingly the matter of basic allowance . . . is too doubtful to authorize payment."[36]

In May 1965, Lawrence Speiser, the director of the ACLU's Washington, D.C., office, wrote to the comptroller general of the United States, charging that the "outrageous decision" in the Waters case amounted to federal enforcement of state antimiscegenation laws. Although the Supreme Court had yet to rule on the matter, Speiser wrote that he found it "difficult to believe that the federal government has been giving any legal effect to state anti-miscegenation laws, which are directly contrary to the United States government public policy."[37]

Loving was the next case in the judicial pipeline. While Richard and Mildred's appeal was still pending in state court, the ACLU had another opportunity in the case of *Jones v. Lorenzen*, a mandamus proceeding to compel the county clerk of Canadian County, Oklahoma, to issue a marriage license. Jesse Marquez, a white man of Mexican descent, and Frances Aline Jones, a black woman, had applied unsuccessfully for a license. Marquez was so young that his attorney, Jack Trezise, had himself appointed the young man's guardian.[38] The ACLU filed an amicus brief, penned by the Lovings' counsel Bernie Cohen and Phil Hirschkop, but the highest court of the state refused to order that a license be issued.[39] The plans for an appeal to the Supreme Court were thwarted when Marquez chose another bride, leaving a pregnant Jones to care for their two children.[40]

None of the aforementioned civil rights groups was involved the first time the Supreme Court was able to review its 1882 decision in *Pace*. Despite the wishes of Justices Warren, Black, and Douglas, the Court denied certiorari[41] in a 1954 challenge to Alabama's antimiscegenation statute.[42] Douglas's clerk, Harvey Grossman, wrote to him that although the statute appeared clearly unconstitutional,

> review at the present time would probably increase the tension growing out of the school segregation cases and perhaps impede solution to that problem, and therefore the Court may wish to defer action until a future time. Nevertheless, I believe that since the deprivation of rights involved here has such serious consequences to the petitioner and others similarly situated, review is probably warranted even though action might be postponed until the school segregation problem is resolved.[43]

Jackson v. Alabama differed from the Supreme Court cases that followed it in that no special interest groups were involved. The plaintiff filed in forma pauperis,[44] and the case was put in the miscellaneous docket of the court. Jackson's attorney, E. B. Haltom, intentionally did not contact civil rights groups so as to avoid overly politicizing the issue. Organizations like the ACLU and the NAACP learned about the case only when the Supreme Court denied certiorari.[45]

The case involved a black woman named Linnie Jackson who had had sexual relations with a white man named A. C. Burcham. Burcham was married to another woman at the time. He and Jackson never married, lived together, or pretended they were married. On May 1, 1953, the state of Alabama arrested them for miscegenation. The Lauderdale County grand jury charged in the alternative that Jackson had either intermarried with a white man or had lived together in adultery or fornication with one. Haltom had two options. One was to challenge the Alabama fornication statute because it punished interracial adultery and fornication more harshly than intraracial acts. Agreement with Haltom would require the court to overrule *Pace v. Alabama*. However, even if Haltom succeeded in this challenge, Jackson would still be criminally negligent under the regular statutory provisions for adultery or fornication and could be fined at least one hundred dollars and jailed, or sentenced to up to six months of hard labor. Therefore Haltom tried a second approach. He completely ignored the fornication issue, fighting instead the charge that Jackson had intermarried with a white man. He argued that this statutory section was unconstitutional, knowing that an invalidation would not expose Jackson to any criminal sanctions. Thereafter, all legal arguments centered around a statute that Jackson had not actually violated.[46]

Oblivious to the finer points of the Constitution, the trial court found Jackson guilty and sentenced her to two years in prison. The court of appeals affirmed the sentence, holding that states had the right to "impose such restrictions . . . as the laws of God and the laws of propriety, morality and social order demand." On April 15, 1954, the Alabama Supreme Court denied Jackson's petition for writ of certiorari to review the court of appeals decision. In July, Haltom filed a petition in forma pauperis to the Supreme Court for a writ of certiorari. It was denied before the year was out.[47]

Justices Warren, Douglas, and Black voted to hear the case, but their support was insufficient. At a time when twenty-eight states still had antimiscegenation statutes on the books, the case clearly had the potential for massive disruption and the other justices were loathe to create more controversy. As previously noted, Justice Douglas's clerk warned him that although it was likely that the Court would someday have to rule on the issue, to do so at that time would aggravate the state of race relations in the South. Justice Burton's clerk likewise cautioned that "because of the political repercussions of the segregation decision, it would not be feasible politically to take this case at this time."[48] Gerald Gunther, one of Warren's law clerks that term, later remarked that the denial of certiorari was "totally prudential, totally based on a high-level political judgment."[49]

Another option to judicial challenges was petitioning legislatures to repeal state statutes, but the process had a number of drawbacks. First of all, while one Supreme Court decision would invalidate all state laws, the repeal process had to be done on a state-by-state basis. The task was further complicated by those states with antimiscegenation provisions in their constitutions. Furthermore, the repeal process involved campaigning and lobbying, activities much more expensive than a court case. Lastly, the state legislature is an elected body and civil rights groups, as champions of the rights of minorities, found themselves at a disadvantage when they tried to convince legislators that repealing antimiscegenation laws would be conducive to reelection.[50]

While not actively involving itself, the ACLU did provide research on the repeal process to other groups or individuals who requested it. The NAACP was more enthusiastic about the process, but only after it had won battles such as school desegregation. The NAACP Legal Defense Fund was tax exempt and therefore could not engage in lobbying. Although the NAACP could lobby, its representatives did not take a particularly strong stance on antimiscegenation laws after the Jack Johnson hysteria of 1913 had died down. It was understood that state branches could take action if the situation required it, but there is no evidence that this was ever done. NAACP files only show attempts to battle the introduction of new bills in the early 1900s, not attempts to repeal existing laws.[51]

Of the groups actively involved in challenging antimiscegenation laws, only the Japanese American Citizens League regularly attempted to use the repeal process, mostly in the western states. Typically, the organization or its individual Asian constituents would lobby state legislators to introduce a repeal bill whose nominal goal was either to lessen discrimination against Asians or to protect Japanese or Korean war brides. Other legislators would recognize the fact that the antimiscegenation laws were not being enforced (at least not in the western states), and frequently the vote was quietly in favor of repeal with little publicity. Publicity worked to the lobbyists' disadvantage, as they discovered in Nebraska in 1963. News of their activities allowed the opposition to mobilize, shifting public support in favor of the statutes and making repeal more difficult, though ultimately successful.[52]

Even civil rights groups not actively involved in the process of trying to repeal antimiscegenation laws were kept apprised of developments by affiliates. In March 1953, Assemblyman Leo Graybill of Montana wrote to the Anti-Defamation League and the ACLU regarding a bill that he had cosponsored in the state assembly to repeal Montana's antimiscegenation laws. Graybill termed the bill "the most radical passed" during his six terms in the legislature. He attributed the ease of its passage to the fact that many soldiers had returned to Montana with Japanese wives. "The Legislature recognized that it seemed silly that we would disinherit such a wife, who, in many instances, has been well received in the local community to which the soldier returned." If the letter makes no mention of any such community sentiment regarding black-white marriages, that's because Graybill knew better. He had also introduced a bill "to guarantee the full and equal enjoyment of all places of public accommodation and amusement" that did not meet with the same success as his repeal bill, no doubt because it clearly covered more than the pretty Japanese war brides.[53]

As the second half of the twentieth century began, twenty-nine states still had laws against mixed-race marriages. *Oyama* and *Bridges* were decided in the 1950s, but it appeared that the most action was taking place on the legislative front. Oregon was the first state to follow *Perez*, repealing its statute in 1951. Montana followed suit two years later. While the

Oregon repeal was clearly a reaction to *Perez*, the Montana legislation may have been instigated by lobbying from the Japanese American Citizen's League. In 1955, Oregon passed legislation explicitly allowing interracial marriages to take place. North Dakota repealed its law against intermarriage in 1955 but left its law against interracial cohabitation untouched for another ten years. Colorado and South Dakota repealed their laws in 1957.[54]

Maryland did not go quite as far, but in 1957 a judge ruled that the state law making it a crime for a white woman to bear a Negro child was unconstitutional.[55] The Maryland ACLU chapter filed an amicus brief when Shirley Ann Howard was convicted of violating article 27, section 513 of the Annotated Code of Maryland, which said that

> [a]ny white woman who shall suffer or permit herself to be got with child by a negro or mulatto, upon conviction thereof in the court having criminal jurisdiction, either in the city or county where such child was begotten or where the same was born, shall be sentenced to the penitentiary for not less than eighteen months nor more than five years.

This law was essentially unchanged since its passage in 1715.[56]

A black man named John Billy Moses admitted to fathering Howard's child and offered to contribute to the infant's support. Instead, the child was institutionalized. State attorney Anselm Sodaro authorized the case to go to a grand jury, saying that the law needed interpretation. Howard's ACLU-affiliated attorney, John J. O'Connor, asked that the case be dismissed on the grounds that the law was a racially and sexually discriminatory relic of the days of slavery. At trial, he noted that although there were thousands of illegitimate births in the state every year, this case was the only one prosecuted. If Howard had been black, she would not have been charged with a crime. O'Connor argued that the statute had not been enforced for many years and that it was time for the state to "exhaustively consider" its constitutional implications.[57]

After the Maryland decision, other courts began to respond favorably to antimiscegenation challenges. Nevada and Arizona struck down their laws in *Bridges* and *Oyama,* respectively (see chapter 7), and Idaho repealed its statute in 1959.[58] There was some movement in the South as well. In 1960, without eliminating the state's antimiscegenation statute, South Carolina decided that it was acceptable for whites to marry Catawba Indians. One year later, North Carolina decreed it permissible for whites to marry all Native Americans. Both states continued to prohibit Caucasians from marrying blacks.[59] Mississippi, however, clung to the idea of a firm line between the races. The platform of the state Democratic party in 1960 stated that it "unalterably oppose[d] any and all efforts to repeal the miscegnation [*sic*] laws."[60]

In 1957, prior to *Bridges,* a bill to repeal Nevada's antimiscegenation laws failed in committee by a five-to-two vote.[61] Six years later, the state took steps in the right direction by eliminating the provisions of the state code that prohibited interracial marriages, while maintaining the section that required registration of race on marriage licenses. Likewise, the Utah legislature removed its ban on interracial marriages in 1963, only ten years after the law had been reenacted. Wyoming followed suit two years later in 1965.[62] Utah copied the example of Michigan and Oregon (later repeated by North Carolina) by succeeding its repeal with a bill that specifically sanctioned interracial marriage.[63] Three representatives introduced a bill to repeal Oklahoma's antimiscegenation law in 1965 and in 1967, but this effort was unsuccessful.[64]

In 1966 Senator Verda Welcome had single-handedly tried to convince the Maryland House to repeal that state's antimiscegenation law. One year later, she found a number of colleagues willing to cosponsor such a bill. Former representatives Julian Lapides and Clarence Mitchell had both moved to the senate, and they joined the effort, together with three other white colleagues. The bill passed the senate by a vote of forty-one to two and the house by a margin of ninety-seven to twenty-five. Governor Spiro Agnew, while not a nattering nabob for peace, not only signed the bill after its passage but appears to have actively counseled Welcome to seek the repeal.[65] Only one person testified against the repeal during the committee hearings.[66] After 306 years in existence, Maryland's antimiscegenation law was finally put to rest.

Despite all the court cases and legislative repeals, pockets of resistance remained, particularly in the South. Although some states had reduced the penalties for interracial marriage, five states were still more than willing to jail miscegenators for up to ten years.[67] The denial of certiorari was an artful way for the Court to duck the issue. The justices would have much more trouble weaseling their way out of the next case to reach their docket.

9

The Sad Case of Ruby and Ham

We are unable to read in the Fourteenth Amendment to the Constitution, or in any other provision of that great document, any words or any intendment which prohibit the State from enacting legislation to preserve the racial integrity of its citizens, or which denies the power of the State to regulate the marriage relation so that it shall not have a mongrel breed of citizens.

—*Naim v. Naim,* Supreme Court of Virginia, 1955

*I*n 1955 and again in 1956, the U.S. Supreme Court missed the opportunity to strike a blow against antimiscegenation laws in the case of *Naim v. Naim.* Born in Canton, China, Ham Say Naim was working as a cook on a British merchant vessel when he jumped ship in America in 1942. He promptly joined an American ship on which he believed he could earn more money, moved to Norfolk, Virginia, and lived there for twenty-nine-day intervals between tours of duty. While ashore, he met Ruby Elaine Lamberth, a white woman from Saginaw, Michigan. Ruby arrived in Norfolk on April 3, 1952, met Ham approximately two weeks later, and after a whirlwind courtship, moved in with him. When the two discovered they could not get a marriage license in Virginia, they traveled to Elizabeth City, North Carolina, where they were married on June 26,

1952. The record of the case shows Ruby proudly declaring that they had wed at precisely 1:55 PM. "It would have been sooner but we had to chase one of the judges around." By four that afternoon, they had returned to Norfolk as husband and wife. It was, as the court would later find, a deliberate attempt to evade Virginia's Racial Integrity Act.[1]

Comfortable with his new life, Ham hired an immigration lawyer from Alexandria, Virginia, David Carliner, to help him become an American citizen. This would have been an easy task had he and Ruby remained married. However, in September 1953, all plans came to a crashing halt when Ruby brought dual actions for annulment, on the grounds that their marriage was void under Virginia law, and for divorce, alleging that Ham had committed adultery with a woman named Kay. The latter issue became irrelevant as the antimiscegenation statutes themselves became the case's focus. Ham turned to the counsel he had already engaged for his immigration needs and found David Carliner more than willing to offer his services regarding the marriage question.[2]

David Carliner was a long-standing member of the ACLU who had done volunteer work for the organization on prior occasions. This case, on the surface a simple proceeding to dissolve a marriage, cemented his commitment to the organization.[3] At the ensuing trial in Portsmouth, Virginia, Carliner argued for dismissal of Ruby's petition on five grounds. His first two arguments were the traditional ones for challenging antimiscegenation laws, namely that Virginia's racial integrity statute violated the Fourteenth Amendment and that a state was not empowered to annul a marriage solely on the basis of race. However, Carliner also insisted that, since the marriage was valid in North Carolina where it had been celebrated, Virginia was required to honor it under the full faith and credit clause of the U.S. Constitution. In an argument that would come back to haunt him, Carliner further suggested that the Virginia evasion statute could not properly be applied to Ham because he was a citizen of China, who was not domiciled in the United States. Lastly, grasping at straws, Carliner argued that the Virginia statute conflicted with Article II of the immigration treaty of 1880 between the United States and China, which guaranteed Chinese nationals in the United States "all the rights, privileges, immunities and exemptions which are accorded to citizens and subjects of the most favored nation."[4]

To no one's great surprise, the court granted the annulment. Judge Kellam, noting that he knew an easy case when he saw one, voided the marriage and held Ham liable for attorney's fees to Ruby's attorney, A.

A. Bangel.[5] The latter was perturbed by what he perceived as the unduly long duration of the trial, which had lasted until six in the evening. Judge Kellam's ruling held that "[i]t appearing to the court that the complainant is a member of the Caucasian race and the defendant not of the white race . . . [i]t is adjudged ordered and decreed that the marriage of the parties . . . is void."[6]

Carliner was pleased that the marriage had been dissolved by annulment, rather than divorce, because that outcome gave him the opportunity to appeal, although it was highly unlikely that the Virginia Supreme Court of Appeals would do anything other than affirm the decision.[7] Carliner's interest at this point was in the bigger picture. He continued to work on Ham's behalf, asking the court to vacate the order for alimony (two hundred dollars a month had been awarded) on the grounds that Ruby was not entitled to funds for a marriage that she also declared void. Covering all bases, he also alleged that Ruby had cohabited and committed adultery.[8]

Apparently one of the first people Carliner turned to for assistance was a friend from law school.[9] Frederick T. "Bingo" Stant ran a general practice firm with a junior partner, Alan S. Mirman.[10] Their practice included domestic law, which was not Carliner's area of expertise.[11] Carliner also wrote to Irving Ferman, the Washington, D.C., representative of the ACLU, for advice on how to proceed with the constitutional issues. Ferman believed that the case deserved ACLU support and told Carliner that he would write to the New York office to recommend that the organization take the case. Herbert Monte Levy, staff council of the New York office, agreed that the case looked like a good one but initially felt that the ACLU should not spend two hundred dollars on an appeal. Besides, he thought the NAACP was the logical organization to finance the appeal and inquired of Ferman whether they had been consulted.[12]

After Judge Kellam's ruling, a two-page memo that outlined the facts and broke down the cost of an appeal was sent under Carliner's signature[13] to potential financial backers.[14] Levy agreed to put up a cash bond of three hundred dollars to cover the costs. Perhaps the budget for litigation was a small one, because Levy wrote to Thurgood Marshall of the NAACP the following month, asking for financial assistance. His request, however, was a qualified one, in which he added that he thought that "any public statement by you on the case would probably not be helpful, but might be harmful."[15]

Shortly after the ACLU agreed to assist Carliner, the Supreme Court decided *Brown v. Board of Education.* Carliner and Levy became convinced that the time was right for *Naim*. Carliner wrote to Levy that he had abandoned all the trial court arguments except (1) whether the Fourteenth Amendment limited the jurisdiction of the trial court to grant annulment decrees based solely upon racial ineligibility to marry; and (2) whether the racial ineligibility statute violated the equal protection and due process clauses of the U.S. Constitution. The judge invited the attorney general of Virginia, J. Lindsay Almond Jr., to file an amicus brief because of the "paramount interest" the state had in the case.[16]

The petition for appeal in *Naim* was granted, and Almond filed a brief that leaned heavily on eugenic and states' rights arguments. The state's brief argued that the Virginia antimiscegenation statute did not conflict with the Fourteenth Amendment. Ruby's attorney withdrew and was not involved in any further state proceedings. Carliner abandoned the "kitchen sink" tactics he had used at the trial court level and eliminated all arguments that were not directly related to a constitutional attack on the statute. For Carliner, Ham and Ruby's marriage had become secondary to the issue of the constitutionality of the laws themselves.[17]

In an argument that probably offended the judges, Carliner suggested that the state court did not have jurisdiction to hear the case, because only federal courts had jurisdiction over cases involving racial classifications. Additionally, he contended that since the state courts lacked the power to enforce restrictive covenants, they could not enforce regulation of the marriage contract when such was based on race. Carliner further argued that the Racial Integrity Act was unconstitutional on its face. Continuing to use the restrictive covenant analogy, he noted that residential segregation was also based on the ideal of racial purity and had been found to be beyond the police powers of the state.[18]

Carliner argued that the logic of *Pace v. Alabama* was flawed on the grounds that marriage should not be looked at in terms of groups (i.e., equal penalty for whites and blacks) but of individuals; the individual whose marriage was barred or annulled was being told by the state that she or he could not do what others were able to do. One thing Carliner did not do was directly question the logic behind the eugenicist theory that spawned the act. He argued only that the preservation of racial integrity was not a proper governmental objective and was thus outside the power of the state to effect, not that this goal was unsound or irrational.[19]

Oral arguments, held in April 1955, were not without fireworks.[20] Over forty years later, that appearance remains in Carliner's memory. "I have never appeared in a court more hostile than that one. They treated me like a piece of dung." Despite the fact that the case involved a man of Chinese heritage, the court "saw black all over the place."[21] It only took two months for the Court to uphold the annulment. In an opinion authored by Archibald Buchanan, the panel quoted the Supreme Court in *Maynard v. Hill*[22] for the premise that marriage "has always been subject to the control of the legislature." Then Buchanan ventured into Virginia precedents, citing previous rulings to the effect that

> the preservation of racial integrity is the unquestioned policy of this State. . . . The natural law which forbids their intermarriage and the social amalgamation which leads to a corruption of races is as clearly divine as that which imparted to them different natures. . . . For the peace and happiness of the colored race, as well as of the white, [the] laws prohibiting intermarriage of the races should exist.[23]

The court held that marriage was not a constitutionally protected right because it was a "social and domestic problem," not a "political or civil right," and concluded that it was within the police power of the state of Virginia to prevent the "mongrelization" of its citizens.[24]

Buchanan then cited the various state court cases upholding antimiscegenation laws against Fourteenth Amendment challenges, noting that more than half the states in the union had such statutes. He dismissed *Perez* by virtue of its divided court and the fact that California, unlike Virginia, allowed those validly married elsewhere to cohabit within its boundaries. Further, since the California law did not provide punishment for miscegenators, Buchanan deemed it merely "declaratory" and indicative of "an attitude of comparative indifference on the part of the California legislature and the absence of any clearly expressed sentiment or policy."[25] The court's ruling virtually ignored twentieth-century law, relying instead on *Plessy v. Ferguson* and *Pace v. Alabama*, while asserting that the seminal ruling in *Brown v. Board of Education* did not affect the issue at hand because *Brown* pertained to education, a "foundation of good citizenship," and interracial marriage could not claim to be such a foundation. In addition, the court relied on the Supreme Court's refusal to grant certiorari in *Jackson v. State*.[26]

In conclusion, the court ruled that

> [t]he purity of public morals, the moral and physical development of both races, and the highest advancement of our cherished southern civilization, under which two distinct races are to work out and accomplish the destiny to which the Almighty has assigned them on this continent—

all require that they should be kept distinct and separate, and that connections and alliances so unnatural that God and nature seem to forbid them, should be prohibited by positive law, and be subject to no evasion.[27]

We find there no requirement that the State shall not legislate to prevent the obliteration of racial pride, but must permit the corruption of blood even though it weaken or destroy the quality of its citizenship. Both sacred and secular history teach that nations and races have better advanced in human progress when they cultivated their own distinctive characteristics and culture and developed their own peculiar genius.[28]

Carliner was not ready to abandon the case and appealed to the Supreme Court. Shortly after the appeal was filed, the American Jewish Congress (AJC) approached Carliner with an offer of assistance. Specifically, Will Maslow of the New York office and Sanford "Sandy" Bolz, the AJC's Washington, D.C., representative, offered to write an amicus brief. Maslow also called the ACLU's Herbert Monte Levy and suggested that it would help to have several organizations support the case. He offered one hundred dollars toward the printing of the brief, which was gladly accepted, although Levy disagreed with having amicus briefs.[29] Maslow was agreeable to being listed as counsel rather than filing a separate brief, but he was full of ideas as to what Carliner's brief should contain.[30] He felt strongly that there should be an appendix with statements from leading physical anthropologists like Don Hager and Ashley Montagu.[31]

Carliner believed that an important addition to the case would be the federal government itself. He contacted Oscar Davis and Philip Elman, two deputies in the Solicitor General's office, but they declined to join the case because it was "too hot." Their caution stemmed from the chronologic proximity of the case to *Brown*. Levy asked Roger Baldwin, the "guiding spirit of the ACLU," for the names and addresses of non-Communist Indian, Korean, Chinese, Philippine, and Indonesian groups that might be willing to lend their names. He added that he hoped to obtain cooperation from the NAACP as well. Baldwin suggested that Carliner and Levy contact Jack Wasserman at the Association of Immigration and Nationality Lawyers (AINL).[32]

It so happened that Carliner's entry into the world of immigration law had been entirely fortuitous. After graduating from law school, he worked in a general practice firm until one day he spotted a vacancy in the offices used by Jack Wasserman of the AINL. Initially, he exchanged his labor for rent, but as he got more and more interested in that area of law, he gradually abandoned all other areas of practice.[33] Reviewing his friend's case, Wasserman suggested that the Japanese American Citizens League (JACL), Chinese groups, Wasserman's own AINL, and the American Jewish Congress should be listed as "of counsel."[34]

Eventually, Carliner was able to secure the signatures of Wasserman on behalf of AINL, Arthur Lazarus and Richard Schifter of the Association on American Indian Affairs, and Frank Chuman and Edward Ennis[35] of the JACL to join the ACLU and the AJC on the petition. Andrew Reiner,[36] Fred T. Stant Jr., and Alan S. Mirman are listed as of counsel. Carliner also wrote, albeit without success, to the Chinese American Citizens' League, the Filipino Federation of America, and the Korean National Association.[37]

Chuman, Ennis, Schifter, and Lazarus were all important people to have associated with the *Naim* brief. However, none of them had the stature of one man who refused to allow himself or his organization to become involved in the case. Thurgood Marshall failed to respond to any of the letters sent by Carliner and Levy that invited the NAACP Legal Defense Fund to join the litigation. Marshall's dislike of the case was based on his fear that it would endanger the school desegregation progress being made subsequent to *Brown*.[38] Of course, he may also have been insulted by Levy's earlier gag order. The truth is that Marshall the man was very much against the statutes. His second wife was a Philippine woman, and his two sons from his first marriage married white women.[39] However, as a strategist, he felt he had to place the future of school desegregation above any other issue. This reserve was consistent with NAACP policy. In September 1955, Executive Secretary Roy Wilkins went so far as to say that the organization took no stance on the issue of interracial marriage.[40] On its face, this statement seemed to disavow all the work done by the NAACP to fight the passage of antimiscegenation bills earlier in the century. In fact, the conflict was attributable to Wilkins's desire to ensure that nothing should interfere with the *Brown* decision by giving occasion to racist rhetoric to the effect that the only purpose served in school desegregation was to allow black men greater access to white women.

One of the issues for the ACLU to consider was how best to approach the Supreme Court. The U.S. Code provides two options: appeal and writ of certiorari. The justices were more likely to accept the former. The Court is obligated to consider all appeals, whereas acceptance of certiorari is discretionary. On the other hand, the denial of an appeal can be construed as a rejection of the validity of the issue being raised, and may therefore prevent similar cases from being accepted in the future. In contrast, a denial of certiorari has no effect on subsequent cases because it is not a denial on the merits.[41]

Carliner chose to file an appeal despite protestations from the ACLU, the AJC, and the Anti-Defamation League, which had become interested in the litigation. Sol Rabkin of the Anti-Defamation League feared that on appeal the Court was likely either to hand down a memorandum order affirming the judgment of the Virginia courts or to issue an order dismissing the appeal for want of any substantial federal question. Either of the two alternatives would constitute a ruling that the Virginia antimiscegenation statute was valid.[42]

Amid all the conflicting advice, Carliner set to work drafting the brief while deferring to Levy for editorial suggestions.[43] Unfortunately, Levy began to be affected by the outside sources and their opinions. In August he wrote to Carliner, praising the latter's jurisdictional statement but suggesting that perhaps a discussion of the sociological effect of miscegenation could be included. On the basis of the case's proximity to *Brown*, Levy suggested that Carliner insert the following paragraph:

> Petitioner and his counsel realize full well that this Court last year denied a petition for certiorari in a similar matter. We earnestly hope that this denial was not due to the believed effect that a granting of review might have on the school segregation issue. While we understand that this Court, in order to secure a more general acceptance of the desegregation decision, may have exercised its discretion to refuse review on the somewhat less important miscegenation problem, we point out that it has not rendered its final decision regarding segregation. Surely those states which have accepted the decision with good grace would not renege on their past position because of a decision on a miscegenation question; nor would it seem that those states whose officials announce their continued intention to defy this Court would be influenced one iota by a decision in a miscegenation case. Even if this were not true, we point out that if this Court grants review, it could delay oral argument and a final decision on the question for a reasonable period of time, enough to allay any possible adverse effect upon the desegregation situation. Surely this Court can find a way to preserve the rights of the parties hereto and to determine the miscegenation issue without unduly influencing desirable courses of desegregation.[44]

Carliner did not agree with the additions. He thought that the statements by the physical anthropologists created "more trouble than solutions" and disliked Levy's diplomatic paragraph because

> in petitioning the court, it seems to me that we lawyers must assume, even if the assumption is not to be so, that the Court is dealing with the case upon its merits, rather than upon extra-legal considerations. To suggest the latter imputes a lack of integrity.

Carliner did not include Levy's paragraph in his final draft. Although he agreed that it was an accurate portrayal of the situation, he did not want to insult the Court by implying that its decision making was being affected by outside forces.[45] Carliner continued to press for an appeal rather than a writ of certiorari.[46]

Filed in late August, the appeal papers raised six basic points. First and foremost, Carliner pointed out that the question of whether a state may restrict the right to marry upon the basis of race had never been passed upon by the Supreme Court. Then, reminding the Court of its recent decisions striking down segregation, he inquired whether, under the Fourteenth Amendment, marriage should be afforded less protection under the due process and equal protection clauses than the right to follow a lawful occupation, vote in primary elections, or attend unsegregated public schools. He argued that marriage, as a right basic to life and liberty, is guaranteed by the Fourteenth Amendment. Conceding that states had been given the power to regulate marriage, he inquired whether the "preservation of racial integrity" of the white race was a purpose within the competency of the state to effect. Lastly, the immigration lawyer in him surfaced as he noted that antimiscegenation laws had an effect on the administration of the federal immigration and nationality laws.[47]

The Virginia attorney general was no longer involved, but A. A. Bangel's brief drew heavily on Almond's amicus brief, arguing that twenty-nine states had antimiscegenation laws, that case law (with the exception of *Perez*) supported the statutes, and that Carliner had never questioned the reasonableness of the racial classifications. Bangel also questioned whether the Supreme Court was the appropriate forum for the case.[48]

Bangel argued in the alternative that the Court should either dismiss the appeal or affirm the Virginia court's ruling. In a quick reply, Carliner noted that although the state had cited a string of cases pertaining to the right of states to regulate marriage, none of the cases dealt with the question of interracial marriage. Further, he attacked the state for presuming the validity of the purpose of the statute. The question in his mind was whether the prevention of interracial marriages was a proper governmental objective. He believed that the state had failed to meet its burden of showing that this was the case.[49]

The Supreme Court decision was handed down in November 1955. In a short per curiam opinion, the Court vacated the state court decision and remanded the case back to Virginia with the mandate that it be returned to the trial court for a new trial because

> [t]he inadequacy of the record as to the relationship of the parties to the Commonwealth of Virginia at the time of this marriage in North Carolina and upon their return to Virginia, and the failure of the parties to bring here all questions relevant to the disposition of the case, prevents the constitutional issue of the Virginia statute on miscegenation tendered here being considered "in clean-cut and concrete form, unclouded" by such problems.[50]

That short paragraph does not come close to capturing the turmoil in the minds of the nine justices. Initially, the Court was very much divided, with Felix Frankfurter leading the conservative contingent, while William Douglas, Hugo Black, and Earl Warren favored facing the question head-on.[51] Frankfurter had practice in avoiding miscegenation cases, having persuaded his brethren to deny certiorari in *Jackson* the previous year.[52] He prepared a statement that argued that a ruling in *Naim* would "very seriously embarrass the carrying-out of the Court's decree of last May." He and Justice Clark drafted the per curiam opinion over the objections of Warren and Black. Warren, according to an unnamed law clerk, was "furious" because he felt that the nondecision was "an evasion of the Court's responsibility."[53]

The docket books of the justices provide little insight into the rationale behind this bizarre opinion. Justice Burton's law clerk was cautious, writing that "[i]n view of the difficulties engendered by the segregation cases it would be wise judicial policy to duck this question for a time." In a similar vein, Justice Harlan's clerk wrote that he had "serious doubts whether this question should be decided now, while the problem of enforcement of the segregation cases is still so active." [54] Harlan, in turn, wrote to his brethren that "to throw a decision of this Court other than validating this legislation into the vortex of the present disquietude would . . . seriously embarrass the carrying out of [*Brown*]."[55]

Most of the clerks were bothered by the fact that the case came on appeal rather than as a petition for certiorari. Burton's clerk noted that the case would be easily handled on cert; it would simply be denied. On appeal, however, he demurred, saying, "I don't think we can be honest and say that the claim is insubstantial." Harlan's clerk also wrote that he found the "psychological factor of the difference between appeal and cert" to be problematic. Nevertheless, he recommended dismissal for lack of a substantial federal question as "the only method available to avoid decision." He imagined that the denial of certiorari in *Jackson* had been motivated by the fear that it would interfere with *Brown* and believed that if *Naim* had reached the Court in this fashion, it too would have been denied. Frankfurter circulated a memo to his colleagues in which he deemed the case a "conflict between moral and technical legal considerations." Noting that he would certainly have voted to deny cert if the case had arisen in that manner, he continued to argue for judicial restraint:

> I do not imply that the question in this case is obviously insubstantial. I do say that a Court containing Holmes, Brandeis, Hughes, Stone and Cardozo would only the other day have dismissed the appeal as such. And I further say that even as of today, considering the body of legislation involved, both North and South, and the reach of the problem, namely divers assumptions by legislatures affecting the regulation of marriage, indicate such a momentum of history, deep feeling, moral and psychological presuppositions, that as of today one can say without wrenching his conscience that the issue has not reached that compelling demand for consideration which precludes refusal to consider it.[56]

The first conference on *Naim* saw the justices split. Harlan, Minton, Clark, Burton, and Frankfurter voted to dismiss the appeal, while Douglas, Reed, Black, and Warren saw probable jurisdiction and wanted to hear the case. A week later, they tried again, but the vote remained the same. A third attempt ensued that same day, with Justices Warren and Reed joining the five who wanted to dismiss the case. However, the new seven-to-two majority also felt that the lower court's decision should be vacated and the case be remanded. Burton tried to convince his fellow justices that Virginia might be able to dispose of the case on the grounds that the state had the right to recognize selected marriages. Burton's strategy was ignored, and the Court adopted Frankfurter's initial position.[57] Neither Black nor Douglas agreed with this stance, but neither noted their dissent for the record.[58]

Carliner, Levy, and Maslow all happened to be in the courtroom on other matters the day the decision was handed down. The trio spent several days trying to decipher its meaning.[59] Later, Carliner wrote to Levy with twenty-twenty hindsight that

> [w]e had suspected that the Court would want to duck the case, but I think in view of all the dire predictions, this decision augers well. The Court had within its power, if it felt that the record was not adequate, to dismiss the appeal upon that ground alone. . . . However, it seems that the Court would rather dispose of this case upon the constitutional ground of full faith and credit, rather than the one we seek.[60]

Levy was not nearly as sanguine as the optimistic Carliner and believed that they had been "outfinessed on our attempt to waive other constitutional issues." He wasn't entirely sure that the Supreme Court was sincere in questioning the relationship of the parties to Virginia but suggested that Carliner "go through the motions of the relationship point."[61]

Carliner and Levy began to prepare for a new trial in Portsmouth. Their goal was to establish that the Naims were residents of Virginia at the time of their North Carolina marriage and afterwards.[62] Will Maslow continued his quest to bring in expert testimony on the biological effects, or lack thereof, of "race mixing" in order to show that the racial classifications in the statute were unreasonable.[63]

None of these machinations was necessary. The Supreme Court of Appeals of Virginia was unimpressed with the U.S. Supreme Court's mandate. On January 8, 1956, it held,

> The record before the Circuit Court of the City of Portsmouth was adequate for a decision of the issues presented to it. The record before this court was adequate for deciding the issues on review. The decision of this court adjudicated the issues presented to it. The decree of the trial court and the decree of this court affirming it have become final so far as these courts are concerned. . . . We therefore adhere to our decision of the cause and to the decree of this court which affirmed the final decree of the Circuit Court of the City of Portsmouth holding that the marriage of the parties to this cause was void.[64]

Carliner, Maslow, and Levy were taken by surprise, since they were busy preparing for a new trial. Although the Richmond and Washington, D.C., papers carried the news that the state of Virginia had defied the Supreme Court, the *New York Times* did not, and Carliner had to send a copy of the opinion to Levy in New York so that he and Maslow could review it.[65] The "paper of record" may not have seen fit to discuss the case, but the Virginia papers were abuzz with praise for the court's defiance in the face of a federal order. It fell right into place with a new (and unconstitutional) piece of legislation just passed called "ordinance of interposition," which was a feeble attempt by the state to evade the dictates of *Brown*.[66]

Carliner did some quick research on what had happened in previous cases where the mandate of the Supreme Court had been ignored, evaded, or rejected. He filed a motion to recall the mandate and set the case down for oral argument on the merits. In the alternative, he asked the Court to recall and amend the previous mandate to provide that the decree of the Portsmouth court be vacated and to require that court to make a new determination of the facts as requested. He noted that this was only the third time in history that a state supreme court had failed to comply with the mandate of the U.S. Supreme Court: in the previous two, the Court had ordered compliance.[67]

On March 12, 1956, the Supreme Court denied Carliner's motion to recall the mandate, announcing that "[t]he decision of the Supreme Court of Appeals of Virginia of January 15, 1956, in response to our order of November 14, 1955, leaves the case devoid of properly presented federal question."[68] Again, the decision was not unanimous. Justice Douglas's law clerk recommended that the Court note probable jurisdiction, since the record was sufficient to "decide the constitutional question presented." He believed it would "begin to look obvious if the case is not taken that the Court is trying to run away from its obligation to decide the case." On the other hand, he believed that it would be wrong to summarily vacate the state's judgment, because "this would be intemperate and would unnecessarily increase the friction between this Court and the Southern state courts. We are leading from a position of recognized strength; we can afford to be humble and gentle on occasion." Warren's clerk recognized the inconsistency of the Court's new statement that the record was complete enough to note probable jurisdiction, after it had already sent the case back because the record was incomplete. Nevertheless, he recommended that the Court consider the case.[69]

The first vote by the Supreme Court had been six to three, with Douglas inexplicably agreeing not to note probable jurisdiction. By the second vote, one week later, he had changed his mind and the margin was five to four, still not enough for the Court to hear the case. The case went out as a per curiam decision, without Warren's drafted dissent, which read,

> Since I regard the order of dismissal as completely impermissible in view
> of this Court's obligatory jurisdiction and its deeply rooted rules of de-
> cision, I am constrained to express my dissent. . . . Congress has obliged
> this Court to decide the substantial constitutional questions which are
> properly and adequately presented in this appeal. I would NOTE PROB-
> ABLE JURISDICTION AND SET THE CASE DOWN FOR ARGUMENT.[70]

Privately, Warren was outraged and called the decision "total bullshit."[71]

The relative merits of the Court's inaction notwithstanding, it had withstood a second assault on antimiscegenation legislation. The justices could
breathe a sigh of relief. While many of the groups involved in *Naim* continued to challenge antimiscegenation statutes, it would be another eight
years before such a challenge reached the Supreme Court, when Connie
Hoffman and Dewey McLaughlin decided to share a room in Florida.

10

Connie and Dewey Share a Room

Intermarriage produces halfbreeds, and halfbreeds are not conducive to a higher type of society. We in the South are a proud and progressive people. Halfbreeds cannot be proud.

—Representative David Jones of Georgia, 1950s

*F*lorida had some of the most interesting twists in antimiscegenation law, including vastly different penal sanctions for cohabitation and marriage (see Appendix B). Cohabitation (and a single day together sufficed to establish cohabitation) between a white person and someone with at least one-eighth black blood was punishable. The law made marriage illegal, however, if the nonwhite party had as little as one-sixteenth bdack blood, declaring it "utterly null and void" and punishable by up to ten years in prison or a fine of one thousand dollars. County judges who "knowingly issued a license" to persons who, in the words of the law, had "the disabilities" referred to in the definition section, could be fined one thousand dollars and sentenced to two years in jail. Likewise, anyone solemnizing such a marriage could be sentenced to one year in jail and fined up to one thousand dollars.[1] In another little twist, white women who had sex with black men could be fined one thousand dollars, but white men who had sex with black womef apparently faced no such prohibition.[2] In case the statutory provisions were ever repealed, the Florida Constitution of 1892 held that marriage between a white and a "person of negro descent to the fourth generation" were "forever prohibited."[3]

The third attempt to persuade the Supreme Court to overturn *Pace* came from Florida. Like *Pace* and *Jackson,* it did not involve a formal marriage. The NAACP Legal Defense Fund went to the Supreme Court on behalf of Dewey McLaughlin, a black former merchant seaman from British Honduras who was working as a porter, and Connie Hoffman, a white waitress from Alabama who had a five-year-old son from a previous relationship.[4] Hoffman had rented a one-room efficiency apartment in Miami Beach from Dora Goodnick in April 1961. Subsequently, Goodnick claimed to have seen McLaughlin standing naked in the bathroom, which led her to believe that he was living in the apartment with Hoffman. She reported the matter to the police, who came to the apartment and arrested McLaughlin for violating a city ordinance requiring workers who dealt with the public to register with the chief of police. Hoffman was subsequently arrested for contributing to the delinquency of her minor son. Five days later, the charges had been changed to interracial cohabitation.[5]

Although she was white, Hoffman demanded legal counsel from the NAACP. It was provided by G. E. Graves, a cooperating attorney fgr the NAACP in Florida.[6] Graves (who died in 1992) had been a very active figure in the fight to desegregate schools and other public places in Florida.[7] He unsuccessfully moved to have the indictment against Hoffman and McLaughlin quashed.[8] Although the national NAACP had previously shown an unwillingness to tackle the issue of antimiscegenation laws, no such hesitancy emerged at the local level, and the Florida NAACP immediately got involved.[9]

At the conclusion of the testimony in criminal court, Judge Williams instructed the jury that Hoffman and McLaughlin had been charged with violating section 798.05 of the Florida statute and that the other statute to be considered was the section that defined a Negro. He stated that the elements of the crime required that one defendant have at least one-eighth Negro blood and the other have more than seven-eighths white blood, that they habitually occupy a room together at night, and that they not be married to one another at the time of the offense.[10]

Williams continued,

There has been in this case some mention of common-law marriage. I instruct you that there is in the State of Florida what is known as a common-law marriage which is as valid a marriage under our law as a marriage which has been solemnized formally. . . .

. . . [However] in the State of Florida it is unlawful for any white female person residing or being in this State to intermarry with any Negro male person and every such marriage performed or solemnized in contravention of the above provision shall be utterly null and void.[11]

The jury deliberated for less than thirty minutes before finding both defendants guilty. The decade of "make love, not war" was in full swing, but forewoman Lauren Seabold pronounced the pair guilty of being "Negro Man and White Woman, Not Being Married to Each Other, Habitually Living in and Occupying in the Nighttime, the Same Room." The Court sentenced Hoffman and McLaughlin to thirty days in the county jail, a fine of $150.00 and court costs.[12]

The defendants posted bonds of five hundred dollars provided by the national NAACP Legal Defense Fund and appealed to the Florida Supreme Court in December 1962.[13] The brief filed by Graves, Robert Ramer, and Harold Braynon was a scant seventeen pages, perhaps in recognition of the unlikelihood that the Florida high court would do anything other than affirm the trial court's verdict. The lawyers argued that the defendants' conviction denied them equal protection of the laws as guaranteed by the Fourteenth Amendment. First, the convictions stemmed from a statute that criminalized behavior based solely on the race of the partaes, and second, even when paired with the general state statute that prohibited fornication, the statute still imposed higher penalties for the same act when persons of different races were involved.[14]

The three attorneys argued that the precedent set in *Pace v. Alabama* was in direct conflict with all current cases decided on the basis of the Fourteenth Amendment's equal protection clause. "The issue is not whether each race considered as a group is treated equally, but whether the individual complainant has been denied equal protection of the laws. . . . Both the Negro and the white defendant are denied equal protection of the laws, as each is subject to a higher penalty than would have been if they had been of the same race."[15]

The defendants' second argument was that the court's instruction that a lawful marriage could not be used as a defense violated the equal protection and due process clauses of the Fourteenth Amendment. With this argument, Graves was able to expand the scope of the allegations to mount a frontal assault on antimiscegenation statutes in the state of Florida. Graves first phrased the issue in a case-specific manner and then in a broader one.

> The issue, then, is does the state deny equal protection of the laws by depriving defendants of a defense to a criminal charge solely because of their race? Put in other terms, the question is whether the state may constitutionally prohibit marriage between persons of different races.[16]

The attorneys noted that the U.S. Supreme Court had never dealt with that issue, and that *Pace* was not applicable to the question of interracial marriage. They wrote that, although states could exercise control over the institution of marriage, the right to marry was guaranteed by the Fourteenth Amendment.[17] They further argued that Florida's antimiscegenation statute was designed solely to maintain the alleged purity of the "superior" white race by preventing the "inferior" group from intermingling with it. Such a law was clearly in contravention of the Supreme Court's interpretation of the Fourteenth Amendment in *Brown* and other cases. The brief's authors next asserted that as the right to enter into a marital relationship was bound up with the right to privacy, the Florida statute encouraged governmental intrusion into the privacy of a person's living quarters. "The state cannot meet the burden of showing that any valid governmental purpose is furthered by depriving individuals of the privacy of their homes and a marital relationship solely because the mate they have chosen is of a different race."[18]

As expected, in May 1963, Justice Millard Caldwell upheld the trial court's decision. He quoted several paragraphs from *Pace v. Alabama* to show that the U.S. Supreme Court had upheld such a statute in 1883. He mocked the defendants for seeking "adjudication of their right to engage in integrated illicit cohabitation upon the same terms as are imposed upon the segregated lapse." However, he conceded that his would not be the last word on the subject, since

> as was admitted by counsel in argument, this appeal is a mere way station on route to the United States Supreme Court, where defendants hope that, in the light of supposed social and political advances, they may find legal endorsement of their ambitions.

Having noted the probable route of the case, Caldwell issued what appeared to be a challenge to the supreme court of the land.

This Court is obligated by the sound rule of stare decisis and the precedent of the well written decision in *Pace*. . . . The Federal Constitution,
as it was when construed by the United States Supreme Court in that case,
is quite adequate but if the new-found concept of "social justice" has
outdated "the law of the land" as therein announced and, by way of con-
sequence, some new law is necessary, it must be enacted by legislative
process or some other court must write it.[19]

After the Florida Supreme Court denied a petition for rehearing, it was
time for the big guns to move in. The Florida lawyers turned the
McLaughlin case over to the NAACP Legal Defense Fund headquarters
in New York City. Fund director Jack Greenberg had to decide whether
to take the case to the Supreme Court and, if so, whether to challenge the
marital portion of the law as well as the cohabitation section. He requested assistance from William Coleman, the vice president of the Legal Defense Fund, who practiced law in Philadelphia, and Professor Louis
Pollak of Yale Law School, who was also on the Legal Defense Fund's
board of directors. In addition to being knowledgeable in the field of civil
rights law, both men had served as clerks to Supreme Court justices:
Coleman to Frankfurter and Pollak to Rutledge.[20]

Explaining that a man faced jail time for the crime of being black and
sharing a room at night with a white woman, Greenberg asked Coleman
whether he thought the Fund should take the case. Coleman was well
aware that the Fund had historically shied away from antimiscegenation
cases on the grounds that such a stance might lead white southerners to
conclude that they had been right all along: all that black men really
wanted was the chance to sleep with white women. However, given that
this case presented a very real client in danger of serving jail time,
Coleman thought that the Fund would be remiss not to take it. He urged
Greenberg to appeal the case to the Supreme Court. Pollak agreed, and
both suggested attacking all portions of the statute. Greenberg appointed
Coleman the lawyer in charge of the case, and he, in turn, persuaded his
friend Lou Pollak to assist him.[21]

The jurisdictional statement carried the signatures of both the New
York and Miami contingents. The papers, filed on October 28, 1963, made
three distinct arguments. The first was that in affirming racially discriminatory criminal convictions, the Florida Supreme Court had mistakenly
relied on *Pace v. Alabama*, a ruling that was inconsistent with subsequent
Supreme Court decisions. The second argument held that the convictions

were in violation of the equal protection and due process clauses because the defendants had not been allowed to use the theory of common-law marriage as a defense. Lastly, the Legal Defense Fund lawyers argued that the appellants had been denied due process of law under the Fourteenth Amendment because the statute under which they were convicted was vague and indefinite.[22]

In their first argument, Greenberg and his colleagues made two points. The first was that it was improper for the court to rely on *Pace* as precedent because in *Pace,* both parties would have been punished for their behavior, albeit less severely, even if both had been white. However, had both Hoffman and McLaughlin been white, their behavior would not have been criminal under Florida law, since there was no law against intraracial cohabitation and they had not been charged under the statute that prohibited interracial fornication. The attorneys compared section 798.05 to a hypothetical law declaring it illegal for Negroes and whites to ride together in a car going more than 25 MPH, with no concomitant speed limit for cars carrying same-race passengers. They noted that laws criminalizing interracial boxing in Louisiana and interracial golf in Georgia had been declared invalid by the Court and that desegregated school systems throughout the South had been abolished. The lawyers further contended that even if *Pace* was controlling, that decision should be overruled because it "stands as an isolated vestige of the 'separate but equal' era inconsistent with the entire development of the law." Their research noted that *Pace* had been cited only twice by the Supreme Court in the eighty years since it was handed down.[23]

In their second argument, the Fund attorneys reminded the Court that Judge Williams had charged the jury that it could not consider marriage a defense to the crime charged, since it was illegal for a white person and a Negro person to marry in the state of Florida. This exclusion was crucial because the existence of a common-law marriage would have been a defense to 798.05. The lawyers charged that the statutory section barring interracial marriage was, therefore, implicated in the case. They queried whether a state coudd statutorily forbid parties from entering into a legal marriage and then convict them of engaging in illegal cohabitation. They noted that the Court had not yet ruled on the constitutionality of intermarriage bans and that, although such laws had been upheld by the highest courts of twelve states, the California Supreme Court had declared its ban to be unconstitutional, a finding that the Fund attorneys found in keeping with the more recent rejection of theories of "pure race."[24]

Lastly, Greenberg's men argued that the Florida statute that defined a Negro as someone with one-eighth or more African or Negro blood was vague and indefinite, and therefore unconstitutional. First of all, the term *Negro* was defined by using that very word in the phrase "African or Negro blood." Further, they queried whether Florida meant to include the citizens of northern Africa or the Afrikaners of South Africa in the definition. Finally, they noted that there was no such thing as African or Negro blood "in any genetic or biological sense." Conceding that the one-eighth Negro blood referred to ancestry rather than actual bodily fluids, the Fund lawyers argued that it was "even more remarkable to make a man legally bound to know and act on the basis of the racial 'blood' of his great-grandparents or even more remote ancestors."[25]

McLaughlin and Hoffman's attorneys noted that the racial identities of the appellants had been determined by allowing a detective to testify as to their appearance. They maintained that when the standard becomes

the average man's or indeed juror's opinion as to what race appearance indicates—then the last pretense of statutory clarity is gone. The appearance standard is an obviously varying and easily shifting method in which a man's race is not an objective thing at all but rather springs from the mind and eye of each beholder.... To make a man conduct his affairs on the basis of preliminary guess as to what his race will be in the opinion of some future unknown witnesses and jurors using an appearance rule places liberty on a slippery surface unworthy of the criminal law of a civilized society.[26]

Assistant attorney general James Mahorner argued the case and wrote the brief for the state of Florida. The state's response to the jurisdictional statement began with a somewhat disingenuous argument. Mahorner claimed that section 798.05 prohibited the same acts as those specified in 798.02 (the statute forbidding fornication). The former specified a maximum penalty of one year in prison, so the appellants were "obviously in the favored class—if there be any—and are therefore not in position to complain." Section 798.02 (full text in Appendix B) called for a maximum penalty of two years in the state prison, one year in the county jail, or a fine of up to two hundred dollars. Further, Hoffman and McLaughlin's sentences were less than that authorized under 798.02, a statute that prohibited "casual acts of fornication" rather than "the greater indecency of general public cohabitation."[27]

The second point made by Florida was that the case did not provide the Court with the opportunity to look at the state's ban on intermarriage. First the state noted that there was "ample evidence" to suggest that Hoffman and McLaughlin were not common-law spouses. It argued that since marriage is an affirmative defense to the charge of unlawful cohabitation, the burden of proving it lies with the defense. The defense had not demonstrated the existence of such a union, so it was appropriate for the judge to instruct the jury that the couple could not use the alleged existence of a common-law marriage as a defense.[28]

The state's third argument was that the terms of 798.05 were not ambiguous. Mahorner noted that the physical presence of the defendants in the courtroom was sufficient to prove their racial identities. He argued that section 1.01, which the appellants deemed vague, actually negated their argument because it required mathematical precision: the antithesis of vagueness. Lastly, the state argued that it was inappropriate for the Fund to base its argument on the Fourteenth Amendment, since the validity of the amendment itself was questionable. This objection relied on the theory that only thirty-three senators had proposed the Fourteenth Amendment and that this number constituted less than the two-thirds required. Since the Amendment was "unconstitutionally proposed," it could not itself be constitutional.[29]

Although the defense brief was signed by four national Fund attorneys and the two Floridians, one author's name did not appear.[30] Later to be a representative for Brooklyn, New York, a district attorney, a state comptroller, and an unsuccessful candidate for the Senate, Elizabeth Holtzman interned at the Fund that summer.[31] Jack Greenberg disputes the notion that assigning an intern to the case implicitly diminished its importance. He states that it was not unusual for the Fund to assign interns to do research and prepare the first drafts of briefs. Further, with just a hint of the arrogance of which he has been accused, Greenberg notes that drafting such a brief was not "rocket science."[32]

Rocket science or not, Holtzman does not recall receiving a great deal of assistance during the drafting process. The Fund was a very busy place that summer, with the continued southern resistance to desegregation and the Freedom Summer events in Mississippi, which brought hundreds of college students south to register black Mississippians to vote. By comparison, the McLaughlin case shrank to the size of an esoteric matter over which Holtzman was given free rein.[33] James Nabrit III, who helped oversee the writing of the brief, recalls that 1964 was such a busy year that the organization simply did not see the McLaughlin case as a major undertaking.[34]

The brief expanded on the arguments made in the jurisdictional statement. It started by ensuring that the Supreme Court would examine as many Florida statutory sections as possible. The Fund attorneys cited 798.05 but added the Florida constitution section banning interracial marriage, as well as the statutory intermarriage ban at 741.11, the penalty for such a marriage at 741.12, and the definition of a Negro at 1.01(6). The attorneys did not cite the antifornication statutes that the state had discussed in its reply to the jurisdictional statement.[35]

The arguments were essentially unchanged from those of the jurisdictional statement, namely that the conviction was in violation of the equal protection and due process clauses of the Fourteenth Amendment because (1) the state had created an offense that punished conduct solely on the basis of its being interracial; (2) the jury had not been able to give full consideration to the matter because its instructions included a statement that Florida forbade the marriage of Negroes and whites; and (3) in the alternative, there was no evidence to prove that either defendant met the classification in 1.01(6) or that definition was vague and indefinite.[36]

For the first point, the Fund attorneys repeated their argument that 798.05 was a statute which required that parties be of different races for their behavior to be considered criminal. They differentiated it from 798.02, the lewd and lascivious behavior prohibition, by noting that a person could be convicted under 798.05 without engaging in the sexual behavior proscribed by 798.02. The difference between the statutes emerged clearly from the fact that, less than twenty years earlier, Florida had prosecuted a couple under both. An intraracial couple sharing the same room at night, absent evidence of lewd and lascivious behavior or fornication, would not have been prosecuted. Hence, the behavior of Hoffman and McLaughlin was illegal only because of their racial identities. "Surely, there is no justification for eliminating, solely on racial basis, the requirements of proof that the state must meet in other crimes against public morality."[37]

Again, *Pace* was distinguished as a case where the race of the parties increased the penalties but did not create the crime. However, the Fund attorneys had "no hesitancy in urging that *Pace* be overruled, if the Court considered it controlling." They argued that more recent Court decisions striking down racial restrictions clearly showed the reasoning in *Pace* to be outmoded. Furthermore, most of those invalidated laws had, like the intermarriage ban, been applicable to both black and white violators, yet the Court had revoked them on the grounds that segregation was not a legitimate government function.[38]

The Fund's second point concerned the judge's instructions, which the brief's authors considered harmful error. First, they noted that common-law marriages were recognized in the state of Florida. Second, the evidence showed that Hoffman and McLaughlin might have established a common-law marriage. Although the record was admittedly not conclusive, the jury should have been given the opportunity to make a decision as to whether such a marriage existed. Lastly, the brief argued that the burden was on Florida to prove beyond a reasonable doubt that the defendants were not married, since such a relationship was an element of the crime with which they were charged.[39]

The lawyers argued that the ban on racial intermarriage was no more rational than a prohibition against Democrats marrying Republicans or redheads marrying brunettes. To press their point about the absurdity of the ban on racial intermarriage, the Fund attorneys cited some of the more ludicrous intermarriage cases, including *Lomas v. State*,[40] which held that "the laws of civilization demand that the races be kept apart in this country. . . . [Intermarriage would be] a calamity full of the saddest and gloomiest portend," and *Scott v. Georgia*,[41] which found that "[f]rom the tallest archangel in Heaven, down to the meanest reptile on earth, moral and social inequalities exist and must continue to exist through all eternity." The authors also cited a variety of scientists for the proposition that the notion of "pure race" was a fallacy.[42]

In their final argument, the Fund attorneys argued that the state had made no attempt to prove the racial identities of Hoffman and McLaughlin. The jury had been asked to accept the conclusion of a police officer as to their racial identities based on appearance, and from that to conclude that one party was at least one-eighth Negro and the other was more than seven-eighths white. Waxing poetic as they had in the jurisdictional statement, the attorneys wrote,

> In this "never-never land" of the appearance test, a person's race is not an objective fact at all, but depends entirely on other persons' views of him. . . . This standard obviously leaves the jurors to their own devices in determining race on any basis they choose. To make such a subjective *ad hoc* evaluation the basis for criminal conviction violates elemental standards of fairness.[43]

The state's response was fivefold. The questions presented, as the attorneys saw it, were (1) whether the Fourteenth Amendment affected state antimiscegenation laws; (2) whether the validity of the state ban on intermarriage was properly before the Court; (3) whether the defendants had been denied equal protection and due process of laws under the Fourteenth Amendment; (4) whether the word *Negro* as used in section 798.05 was ambiguous, and (5) whether the Fourteenth Amendment had been validly added to the Constitution.

The lion's share of the brief was devoted to the argument that the Fourteenth Amendment had no impact on antimiscegenation statutes. Florida argued that it was merely an outgrowth of the Civil Rights Act of 1866, which in turn was derived from the Freedman's Bureau Bill. Therefore they considered the debates over those two laws to be dispositive of the intent of the framers. They cited queries by senators and representatives as to whether the Freedman's Bureau Bill would invalidate their states' antimiscegenation laws and the assurances by the bill's supporters that those laws would remain intact.[44]

The state next argued that the Court had no need to consider the constitutionality of the antimiscegenation statutes, since there was insufficient evidence that the appellants were married. Further, it argued the state had no burden to prove the absence of a marriage; the burden was on the appellants to prove that one existed. Lastly, since the defense had raised no objection at trial to the judge's instructions to the jury, it could raise none at this late date.[45]

Despite the fact that the appellant's main argument revolved around the constitutionality of the statute, the state devoted only four pages to this issue, almost one-tenth of the space devoted to the Freedman's Bureau Bill deliberations. The state relied on *Pace,* which it noted had been decided *after* the passage of the Fourteenth Amendment. The authors argued somewhat disingenuously that the separate-but-equal principle struck down in *Brown* was not violated by the Florida statute because it involved no separate facilities. They then returned to their argument regarding the inapplicability of the Fourteenth Amendment to antimiscegenation statutes, holding that this inapplicability pertained to statutes prohibiting interracial cohabitation as well. Addressing the Fund's differentiation of the cohabitation statute from the lewd and lascivious conduct statute, Florida contended that the purpose of both was to prevent "illegal sexual occurrence" and that, although no actual sexual misconduct was required for a conviction under 798.05, the circumstances required for such an arrest would give rise to a "high potential" for such behavior.[46]

Short shrift was also made of the appellants' "vague and ambiguous" argument. Again Florida argued that no such objection was raised at trial and that the mathematical certainty required by section 1.01 was the very antithesis of ambiguity. In its final argument, the state could not resist harking back to the past again for a reminder that even if all their other arguments failed, it could always contest the validity of the improperly proposed Fourteenth Amendment. The state recognized that this argument was not novel and had failed repeatedly, but its lawyers felt compelled to raise the issue again.[47]

Perhaps taken by surprise by what may charitably be called the state's throwback argument, the appellants submitted a reply brief. They challenged the state's argument that the Fourteenth Amendment was inapplicable to antimiscegenation legislation, as well as the state's contention that Florida's ban on intermarriage was not properly before the Court. Regarding the first argument, the Legal Defense Fund lawyers agreed that there was strong evidence to suggest that the Civil Rights Act of 1866 was not meant to apply to antimiscegenation statutes, but they refuted the contention that the Fourteenth Amendment was merely a rewriting of the prior bill.[48]

Oral arguments were held over the course of two days in October 1964. Coleman began by stating that the conviction had been obtained under an explicitly racial law that punished an interracial couple for acts that same-race couples could engage in with impunity. Therefore the law violated the equal protection clause of the Fourteenth Amendment. Today he believes that this lead-in was probably his best line of the entire argument. Coleman then argued that due to the antimiscegenation law, Hoffman and McLaughlin had been estopped from raising the defense of common-law marriage. Since that law was based on race prejudice and discredited theories of racial supremacy, it should not be enforced. Coleman ended by calling Florida's definition of *Negro* unconstitutionally vague and added that the state had not proven that McLaughlin was black. Furthermore, the intent of the statute violated the Fourteenth Amendment.[49]

After this introduction, Justice Warren asked whether Hoffman and McLaughlin were married. Coleman believed that they were, so Warren asked why they hadn't produced a marriage certificate. The reason was that marriage would have subjected the couple to greater penalties (up to ten years) than the two-year penalty imposed by the cohabitation statute. Unfortunately, Coleman could not find this discordance in penalties in his notes, so after hemming and hawing a bit, he referred to the couple as having a common-law marriage.[50]

In retrospect, Coleman considers this equivocation to have been a crucial error on his part. With twenty-twenty hindsight, he believes that if he had simply called Hoffman and McLaughlin married, the Court might have been more willing to examine the antimiscegenation statutes. He had noted that the record contained some evidence that the pair had a common-law marriage. However, when asked by Warren why they did not take the stand at trial to testify to this union, Coleman merely replied that he had not been the counsel at that level. Over thirty years later, Coleman regrets not explaining to the Court that the maximum penalty for sharing a hotel room was one year[51] while the maximum penalty for interracial marriage was ten years. He wishes he had said, "Mr. Chief Justice, would you have me put someone on the stand to fight a one-year criminal penalty by admitting to having done something punishable by a ten-year penalty?" Coleman believes that putting the issue that bluntly might have forced the Court to consider all the Florida statutes, not just the interracial cohabitation law.[52] A review of the record shows that there is no need for Coleman to second-guess himself. Justice Stewart noted that if the cohabitation statute was deemed invalid, the antimiscegenation statute was likewise invalid, an assessment with which Coleman readily agreed.[53]

Coleman argued that the state's declaration that a relationship as personal as marriage was invalid made this an "easier case" than *Brown.* He added that the right to marry the person of one's choice was more important than the right to attend a particular school.[54] Justice Harlan asked Coleman how the statute could be discriminatory, applying as it did equally to blacks and whites, but Coleman replied that it was hard to use the term "equal" when persons were being denied the right to marry the person of their choice.[55]

When Pollak reached the lectern, Justice Harlan asked him whether it wasn't true that the Fourteenth Amendment served only to place the Civil Rights Act of 1866 and the Freedman's Bureau Bill into the Constitution, and that neither of those acts barred miscegenation statutes. Pollak replied that Court decisions had proscribed segregated juries, voting discrimination, and segregated schools, all of which had been found to be within the realm of the Fourteenth Amendment, despite their absence from the debates over the preceding two bills. Harlan asked whether the legislative history of the Fourteenth Amendment supported the premise that miscegenation laws could be omitted from coverage. Pollak said that the "twentieth-century Fourteenth Amendment" could not be judged by isolated statements from one or two congressmen in 1886. To view such statements as proof of the meaning of the document would be to give it too narrow a construction, one in conflict with other Court decisions. The Court had always awarded a spacious intent to the Fourteenth Amendment. Pollak concluded that "[t]he time has come to remove this stigma from the fabric of American law."[56]

Assistant attorney general Mahorner argued that race was immaterial to the issue at hand. The statute in question was designed to punish immorality. He contended that both whites and blacks shunned interracial children; therefore interracial unions served only to create community tension that was "conducive to racial conflict; each race resents the invasion." Mahorner claimed that protecting such offspring (by preventing their conception) was a proper legislative purpose. Lastly, he maintained that the Fourteenth Amendment was not a valid document, because many of the states of the former Confederacy had not yet been admitted to the Union at its passage.[57]

Mahorner's primary defense was the argument that Congress never intended the Fourteenth Amendment to cover antimiscegenation statutes. He distinguished *Brown* on the grounds that "education has developed and it is no longer like it was," but there was "no such development in marriage, so the same intent must control."[58] Justice Stewart asked him if the statute would apply to a mother and son who shared a hotel room if the mother was white and the son, by virtue of having a black father, was mixed. Mahorner admitted that he did not know the answer but supposed that the statute would apply to them.[59] He tried desperately to return to his main argument that for the Court to find the miscegenation statute unconstitutional, it would have to reject the legislative history of the Fourteenth Amendment and the decisions in *Pace* and *Naim*.[60]

Chief Justice Warren asked Mahorner whether a state could prohibit marriage between Jews and Gentiles. Mahorner replied that a state could not do so, because "[t]he Constitution did not have that intention, and we say the intention was expressed as to Negroes and whites. . . . No matter how abhorrent it is to us, we should recognize the intention of the framers of the amendment."[61] On rebuttal, Coleman remarked that he had thought the year was 1964, but he had trembled during the last ten minutes of Mahorner's speech on the invalidity of the Fourteenth Amendment. He

likened Mahorner's defense to Hitler's speeches condemning the association of Christians and Jews.[62]

The NAACP won a partial victory. On December 17, 1964, the Court
handed down a unanimous decision reversing the conviction. Writing
for the majority, Justice White said that the cohabitation statute denied
the defendants the equal protection of the laws guaranteed by the Fourteenth Amendment. The Court deemed the racial classifications in the
statute "an invidious discrimination" forbidden by the equal protection
clause. It acknowledged that the "equal application" rule of *Pace* had not
withstood analysis in subsequent court decisions. However, "[i]t has not
been shown that [the cohabitation statute] is a necessary adjunct to the
State's ban on interracial marriage. We accordingly invalidate [the cohabitation statute] without expressing any views about the State's [miscege-
nation statute]."[63] Justice White found that racial classifications were
"constitutionally suspect" and should be subjected to "most rigid scru-
tiny." Finally, the old *Pace* precedent was consigned to the dustbin of history, as Justice White could see no "overriding statutory purpose requiring the prescription of the specified conduct when engaged in by a white
person and a Negro, but not otherwise. Without such justification, the
racial classification contained . . . is reduced to an invidious discrimination forbidden by the Equal Protection Clause."[64]

In a more strongly worded concurrence, seconded by Justice Douglas,
Justice Stewart disagreed with the Court's implication that a criminal law
with racial distinctions might be constitutionally valid if the state could
show "some overriding statutory purposes." Stewart concluded that "it
is simply not possible for a state law to be valid under our Constitution
which makes the criminality of an act depend upon the race of the actor. Discrimination of that kind is invidious *per se.*"[65]

McLaughlin was the first Supreme Court case to score a hit in the battle
against antimiscegenation legislation. Many felt that it was just a matter
of time before the war would be won. However, three more years passed
before the Supreme Court had the opportunity to finish the job the
justices started when they decided that Connie Hoffman and Dewey
McLaughlin could, indeed, share a room at night without being subjected
to criminal prosecution.

MISCEGENATION:

THE THEORY OF THE

BLENDING OF THE RACES,

APPLIED TO THE

AMERICAN WHITE MAN AND NEGRO.

" The Elements
So mixed in him that nature might stand up
And say to all the world, ' This was a man.' "
—*Shakspeare.*

[By D. G. Croly, Geo. Wakeman
and E. D. Howell]

NEW YORK:
H. DEXTER, HAMILTON & CO.,
General Agents for the Publishers,
113 NASSAU STREET.
1864.

"The genesis of the word." The cover of an allegedly Republican campaign pamphlet from 1864 that promoted mixing of African Americans with whites in an apparent attempt to discredit the party. (© Collection of The New-York Historical Society.)

Labor leader Harry Bridges *(right)* and Noriko Sawada after their wedding at the office of a justice of the peace on December 10, 1958. The couple obtained a court order that upset Nevada's ninety-four-year-old law against interracial marriage. Their attorney, Samuel Francovich, is at left. (AP/Wide World Photos.)

A one-room schoolhouse in Central Point, Virginia, that Mildred Jeter Loving attended as a child. (Author's collection.)

Caroline County jail *(top)* and a closeup of a barred window and one of the signs on the outer wall *(bottom)*. The Lovings were detained here after their arrest for miscegenation. (Author's collection.)

Virginia judge Leon Bazile, who ruled that mixed-race
marriages were illegal, May 1965. (Grey Villet/TimePix.)

1151 Neal St.
N.E. Wash. D.C.
June 20, 1963

Dear sir:

I am writing to you concerning a problem we have.

5 yrs. ago my husband and I were married here in the District. We then returned to Va. to live. My husband is White, I am part negro, & part indian.

At the time we did not know there was a law in Va. against mixed marriages.

Therefore we were jailed and tried in a little town of Bowling Green.

We were to leave the state to make our home.

The problem is we are not allowed to visit our families. The judge said if we enter the state within the next 30 yrs., that we will have to spend 1 yr. in jail.

We know we can't live there, but we would like to go back once and awhile to visit our families & friends.

We have 3 children and cannot afford an attorney.

We wrote to The Attorney General, he suggested that we get in touch with you.

for advice.

Please help us if you can. Hope to hear from you real soon.

Yours truely,
Mr. + Mrs. Richard Loving

Mildred Loving's plea for help, June 20, 1963. (Author's collection.)

Richard and Mildred Loving *(center)* relaxing with friends, May 1965. (Grey Villet/TimePix.)

Richard and Mildred with Richard's mother and their daughter Peggy, May 1965. (Grey Villet/TimePix.)

STATE OF VIRGINIA,

County of Caroline } **To-wit:**

Commonwealth Warrant

To the Sheriff or any Police Officer of the said County:

WHEREAS, *Bernard Mahon Com. att'y* of the said County, has this day made complaint and information on oath before me, Robert W. Farmer, Justice of the Peace of the said County that ~~Richard Loving a white man and~~ *Mildred Jeter a negro* in the said County did on the *2nd* day of *June*, 19*58* unlawfully and feloniously *did go out of this State for the purpose of being married and with the intention of returning and were married out of the State and afterwards returned to and reside in it, Cohabiting as man & wife* against the peace and dignity of the Commonwealth of Virginia.

These are, Therefore, to command you, in the name of the Commonwealth, to apprehend and bring before the Judge of the said County the body of the said *Jeter* _____ *Mildred* *Jeter* _____ to answer the said complaint, and to be further dealt with according to law. And you are directed to summon _____ as witnesses.

Given under my hand and seal this *11th* day of *July*, 19*58*

Robert W. Farmer J. P.

STATE OF VIRGINIA

County of Caroline _____

To-wit:

I, *Edward Stehl III* _____, Justice of the Peace in and for the County aforesaid, State of Virginia, do certify that *Mildred Jeter* _____ and *Rommie W. Catlett* _____, as his suret y, have this day acknowledged themselves indebted to the Commonwealth of Virginia in the sum of *One Thousand* _____ Dollars ($*1,000.00*), to be made and levied of their respective goods and chattels, upon this condition: That the said *Mildred Jeter* _____ shall appear before the Circuit ~~County~~ Court of the said County, on the *13th* day of *October* 19*58*, at *10.00 A* M., at *Bowling Green*, Va., and not leave hence without the leave of the said Court, and that he appears before the Court to answer the charge in this warrant, and/or any continuance thereof, and/or abide the judgment of said Court, and/or any appeal therefrom, or to await the action of the Grand Jury upon the within charge, at such time or times as may be prescribed by the Court and at any time or times to which the proceedings may be continued or further heard, and to remain in full force and effect until the charge is finally disposed of or until it is declared void by order of a competent Court.

Given under my hand, this *24th* day of *July*, 19*58*.

Rommie W. Catlett *Edward Stehl III* J.P.

2

over

A crime "against the peace and dignity of the Commonwealth of Virginia." Commonwealth warrants for Mildred Jeter, dated July 11 and 17, 1958, and for Richard Loving, dated July 11 and 13, 1958. (Caroline County, Virginia, files.)

Top Form

Miles - 42-21

The following witnesses were recognized to appear before the

Circuit
County Court of Caroline County,
Virginia, at Bowling Green, Virginia,
at .... M. on the ....

day of .... , 19....

under penalty of $ ....

....

Criminal Docket No. 929

COMMONWEALTH
vs. WARRANT OF ARREST

Mildred Jeter

Executed this, the 17 day

of July , 1958

Garnett Brook Sh.

Upon the defendant's plea of ....
Not guilty to the within
charge, and upon examination of the
witnesses, I find the accused
probable cause to charge
the accused with a felony
and it is ordered that she
be held for the action
of the Grand jury 7-17-58
Richard Stella Judge

Fine . . . . . $ ....

Costs . . . . . $ ....

Total . . . . . $ ....

Bond fee 7.00 pd 7. 24. 58

COSTS:

Fine	$ ....
Warrant	$ 1.50
County Judge	$ 2.00
Clerk	$ 1.25
Arrest	$ 1.00
Mileage	$ 5.04
Summoning Witness . .	$ ....
Witness' Attendance .	$ ....
Jail Fee	$ .50
Commonwealth Attorney	$ 2.50
Bail Fee 7-24-58 .	$ 2.00
	$ ....
Circuit Court Cost	$ 22.50
Total	$ 36.29
Witness	
	$ ....
	$ ....
	$ ....
	$ ....
	$ ....
	$ ....
	$ ....
	$ ....

Bottom Form

1/1 - 50

Miles 42-21

The following witnesses were recognized to appear before the

Circuit
County Court of Caroline County,
Virginia, at Bowling Green, Virginia,
at .... M. on the ....

day of .... , 19...

under penalty of $ ....

Criminal Docket No. 928

COMMONWEALTH
vs. WARRANT OF ARREST

Richard Loving

Executed this, the 18 day

of July , 19 58

Garnett Brook Sh.

Upon the defendant's plea of ....
Not guilty to the within
charge, and upon examination of the
witnesses, I find the accused probable
cause to charge the accused
with a felony and it
is ordered that he be held
for the action of the Grand
jury 7-17-58
Richard Stella Judge

Fine . . . . . $ ....

Costs . . . . . $ _____

Total . . . . . $ ....

COSTS:

Fine	$ ....
Warrant	$ 1.50
County Judge	$ 2.00
Clerk	$ 1.25
Arrest	$ 1.00
Mileage	$ 5.04
Summoning Witness . .	$ ....
Witness' Attendance .	$ ....
Jail Fee	$ .50
Commonwealth Attorney	$ 2.50
Bail Fee	$ ....
Circuit Court Cost	$ 22.50
Total	$ 36.29
Witness	
	$ ....
	$ ....
	$ ....
	$ ....
	$ ....
	$ ....
	$ ....
	$ ....

STATE OF VIRGINIA,
County of Caroline } To-wit: Commonwealth Warrant

To the Sheriff or any Police Officer of the said County: A

WHEREAS, *Bernard Mahon Connally* of the said County, has this day made complaint and information on oath before me, Robert W. Farmer, Justice of the Peace of the said County

that *Richard Loving (a white person) and* _____

in the said County did on the __2d__ day of __June__ 1958,

unlawfully and feloniously *did go out of this State, for the purpose of being married, and with the intention of returning, and were married out of State, and afterwards, returned to and resided in it, cohabiting as man & wife*

against the peace and dignity of the Commonwealth of Virginia

These are, Therefore, to command you, in the name of the Commonwealth, to apprehend and bring before the Judge of the said County the body of the said *Richard Loving* _____

to answer the said complaint, and to be further dealt with according to law. And you are directed to summon _____

_____ as witnesses.

Given under my hand and seal this __11th__ day of __July__ 1958

Robert W. Farmer, J. P.

STATE OF VIRGINIA   To-wit
County of Caroline _____

I, __J. L. Webb__, Justice of the Peace in and for the County aforesaid, State of Virginia, do certify that *Richard Loving* and *Eleanor Au & John Koons, by Robert E. Buchan, attorney in fact*, as his suret _____, have this day acknowledged themselves indebted to the Commonwealth of Virginia in the sum of *One thousand no/100* Dollars ($1,000.00),

to be made and levied of their respective goods and chattels, upon this condition: That the said _____ *Richard Loving* _____ shall appear before the Circuit County Court of the said County, on the __17th__ day of __July__ 1958, at __10 A.__ M., at __Bowling Green__, Va., and not leave hence without the leave of the said Court, and that he appears before the Court to answer the charge in this warrant, and/or any continuance thereof, and/or abide the judgment of said Court, and/or any appeal therefrom, or to await the action of the Grand Jury upon the within charge, at such time or times as may be prescribed by the Court and at any time or times to which the proceedings may be continued or further heard, and to remain in full force and effect until the charge is finally disposed of or until it is declared void by order of a competent Court.

Given under my hand, this __14th__ day of __July__ 1958

_____, J. P.

1

The beginnings of the court case, May 1965. (Grey Villet/TimePix.)

The lawyers who represented the Lovings: Bernie Cohen *(right, in glasses)* and Philip Hirschkop *(center)*. (Corbis Images, © Bettman/Corbis.)

Berta Linson and Roger Mills, August 1970. (James Bonney/NYT Pictures.)

The Loving children, May 1965. (Grey Villet/TimePix.)

Mildred Loving in 1992. (Paul Hosefros/NYT Pictures.)

Part Three

Loving v. Virginia

11

Richard and Mildred Want to Go Home

It cannot be supposed that this discrimination was otherwise than against the negro, on account of his servile condition, because no state would be so unwise as to impose disabilities in so important a matter as marriage on its most favored citizens.
—Alabama Supreme Court decision, 1872

*T*he manner in which Bernard S. Cohen and Philip J. Hirschkop[1] came to represent the Lovings was a truly fortuitous circumstance. It all began with a letter.

Banished to Washington, D.C., where she followed the debates on what would become the 1964 Civil Rights Act with interest, Mildred Loving wondered whether anything could be done to allow Richard and herself to move back to Virginia as husband and wife or even to visit their families together without fear of prosecution.[2] On the advice of her cousin, Mildred wrote a letter to Attorney General Robert F. Kennedy asking him whether the new bill would enable her family to move back to Virginia. Kennedy told her that the bill would not apply to her marriage, but he referred her to the American Civil Liberties Union and gave her the address of the Washington branch of the ACLU, known as NatCap. Bernie

Cohen was one of the original founders of the NatCap branch. Mildred took Kennedy's advice. Her letter reached Larry Speiser, who was the local lobbyist. Since at the time, Cohen was the only volunteer ACLU attorney who was a local phone call away (he may have been the only one in Virginia), Speiser referred the matter to him.[3]

Mildred and Richard were clearly not aiming to change the world; they wanted only to be able to go home and visit their families occasionally. The letter was a plaintive cry for assistance.

Dear Sir:

I am writing to you concerning a problem we have. Five years ago my husband and I were married here in the District. We then returned to Virginia to live. My husband is White, I am part negro and part Indian. At the time we did not know there was a law in Virginia against mixed marriages. Therefore we were jailed and tried in a little town of Bowling Green. We were to leave the state to make our home.

The problem is we are not allowed to visit our families. The judge said if we enter the state within the next thirty years, that we will have to spend one year in jail. We know that we can't live there, but we would like to go back once and awhile to visit our families and friends. We have three children and cannot afford an attorney.

We wrote to the Attorney General, he suggested that we get in touch with you. Please help us if you can. Hope to hear from you real soon.

Yours truly,
Mr. and Mrs. Richard Loving

Bernie Cohen had very little experience in the civil rights field, and he remembers his trepidation when the case was referred to him. "Oh my God, I don't know if I'm capable of handling it," was his first thought. Speiser assured him that he would be able to handle the case and that David Carliner, the author of the *Naim* brief (see chapter 9), would be able to assist him. Cohen immediately recognized the potential of the case as a Supreme Court challenge and made no secret of that possibility when he spoke to the Lovings. He initially called them at their D.C. residence, spoke at some length to Mildred, and invited her and her husband to come to his office. Although he usually worked in Alexandria, Virginia, Cohen maintained a small office in Washington, where he met with the Lovings, who by the terms of their banishment were forbidden to cross the Potomac River to his main office. He told them right away that he believed the case would be resolved in their favor but only after a lengthy process that would culminate in the highest court of the land. Richard was incredulous. He thought that the problem could be easily fixed and that after a month or so they would be able to move back to Virginia.[4]

Before any action could be brought, there was one very important hurdle to overcome. The Lovings' original conviction had taken place in 1959. Under Virginia law, criminal convictions had to be appealed within 120 days, and that time had long since passed. Cohen was convinced that if he could get the case back into state court, he could work it all the way up to the Supreme Court and give the justices the opportunity they had ducked in *Naim*. The real problem was finding a hook on which to file the appeal. Initially he suggested to Richard that he and Mildred return to Virginia together and get rearrested. Cohen recalls that Richard looked at him "as though I was nuts," so he quickly agreed that this was not the best solution.[5]

After many fruitless months researching the law, Cohen still hadn't found his hook. He was frustrated, as were the Lovings. While researching an unrelated issue, the proverbial lightbulb went on[6] as Cohen perused *Fuller v. Virginia,*[7] a decision involving the probation of a juvenile. The case concerned the appeal of a nineteen-year-old man who had been convicted under another antiquated Virginia statute for having seduced "an unmarried female of previous chaste character" under promise of marriage. Fuller had been sentenced to two years in the penitentiary. However, although he was found guilty, it was not a complete disposition. The trial court noted the presence of mitigating circumstances that might justify suspension of the sentence. Those circumstances could be explained by Fuller's probation officer, and therefore the judge held that "the matter is still in the breast of the court."[8] Cohen believed that a suspended sentence was similar to a probationary period: therefore, the Lovings' case was also still "in the breast of the court" and open to appeal. Judge Bazile apparently agreed.[9]

On November 6, 1963, Cohen filed a short motion to vacate the judgment of the court finding the Lovings guilty. He asked that the conviction and suspension be set aside.[10] The motion argued that the sentence constituted cruel and unusual punishment and that it exceeded the reasonable period for a suspended sentence. In addition, Cohen argued that the Loving's banishment was a violation of due process of law, was improper due to its basis in an unconstitutional statute that denied the right of marriage in violation of the Fourteenth Amendment and the Virginia

Constitution, was a burden on interstate commerce, and was an undue hardship on the defendants.[11]

Cohen remembers a "ratty-looking" Bazile peering from the bench. "I don't know how much is my imagination, but although he talked like a real Southern gentlemen, it was obvious he was ignoring me." Bazile said that he would take the case under advisement. Weeks of delay turned into months, and Bazile did not rule on the motion. Cohen called his chambers to make "discreet inquiries," only to be told repeatedly that the case was still under advisement. In retrospect, Cohen believes that Bazile would have kept the case under advisement until he retired if he could have gotten away with it.[12]

Judge Leon Maurice Bazile had plateaued after a somewhat meteoric rise through the Virginia legal establishment. He graduated at the top of his class at the University of Richmond and within five years of passing the bar was appointed assistant attorney general. After seven years in that position, he retreated temporarily to private practice before running successfully for a seat in the Virginia House of Delegates, one he held for three terms. After yet another stint in the private sector and a year of teaching at the University of Richmond, Bazile accepted a judgeship in 1941. He held that position until 1965 and died two years later. Bazile's views did not evolve significantly during his lifetime. Even during his days at the attorney general's office, he showed serious antipathy toward the federal government, which he accused of encroaching on the rights of the states.[13]

By the time he left the bench, Bazile was approaching senility and often drifted off to sleep during trials. Then a young lawyer and later county prosecutor, Jack Lilly remembers a fraud trial over which Bazile presided. The judge frequently disappeared from sight as he slid down his chair, fast asleep. When Bazile's old buddy Frank Beazely (see chapter 1) wanted to get his attention, he would walk in front of the judge's bench and hit it with his fist, whereupon Bazile would pop up and say "Yes, Frank." Even before senility encroached, Bazile had been regarded as somewhat odd. He had a penchant for reading the newspaper during trials, and his ties invariably looked as though they had fallen into his lunch.[14]

All the Lovings knew was that nothing seemed to be happening. In June of 1964, Mildred wrote plaintively to Cohen. "Hope that you remember us. You took our case. We haven't heard anything from you for so long we had given up hope."[15] Cohen was flummoxed as to how to proceed. At this point, serendipity struck. It was the summer of 1964,[16] and Cohen went to consult with his old Georgetown constitutional law professor, Chester Antieu, about how to light a fire under the recalcitrant Bazile. In Antieu's office, he found a young lawyer named Phil Hirschkop who had just graduated from Georgetown. Hirschkop credits Antieu with sparking his interest in civil rights. At the time of this fortuitous meeting, Hirschkop was working for civil rights lawyers William Kunstler and Arthur Kinoy in Mississippi while his wife remained in the Washington, D.C., area. On his way from Mississippi to New York, Hirschkop had stopped in D.C. to visit his wife. While in town, he took the opportunity to visit his old professor for a chat in the faculty lounge. As Hirschkop recalls it, during the talk, Antieu's secretary brought in a note indicating that an ex-student of his wanted to talk to him about a case. Antieu invited Cohen to come in and explain his dilemma.[17]

Chet Antieu was not your average law school professor. He had been deeply involved in the civil rights movement himself, working with Kunstler and Kinoy in Danville, Virginia. Although Antieu could have restricted his role to simply analyzing the ordinances under which members of the Danville movement had been arrested, he chose to participate actively in all the proceedings.[18] Robert Hall, an attorney who later joined forces with Cohen and Hirschkop, describes Antieu as far more engaged than the average academician. Antieu was deeply concerned with the way civil rights and constitutional issues affected the daily lives of people. Although Hirschkop was the student and Antieu the teacher, the two "fed off each other" and deepened each other's commitment.[19]

Antieu introduced Hirschkop as a "brilliant civil rights lawyer," a title Hirschkop felt was clearly not accurate at the time. Flattered, he listened as Cohen described his dilemma, then joined the latter as he headed across the street to juvenile court for a case more in line with Cohen's usual practice. Hirschkop informed Cohen that the proper procedure at that juncture was to file what was known in legal circles as "a 2283 motion" requesting a federal three-judge panel.[20] He offered to provide assistance. As good as his word, Hirschkop started drafting the memo on the back of an envelope on the plane to New York, and during the next two to three weeks, the pair spoke on a regular basis while Hirschkop drafted the complaint and memorandum of law.[21]

Initially, the two lawyers worked smoothly together and became quite friendly. Cohen persuaded his partners to hire Hirschkop as an associate, and the two spent most of Hirschkop's early years in the firm working on the *Loving* case. Cohen refers to their early working relationship as "wonderful." At first blush, the pair would seem like a good team. They were both Jewish and both born in Brooklyn, New York, two years apart, with Cohen the older of the pair. Both received nasty anonymous phone calls during the case, saw themselves referred to as "the two Jew lawyers" in the Klan newspaper, and had sugar put in their gasoline tanks.[22] For a while, the partnership was a strong one, and the federal court brief was filed in November.[23] With the case moving forward, it was time to start research on the history of antimiscegenation legislation. Hirschkop claims that when he met Cohen, the entire *Loving* file consisted of three magazine articles, eight letters, the warrant, and the grand jury indictment.[24]

Philip J. Hirschkop was born in Brooklyn in 1936. After graduating from the public school system, Hirschkop spent two years in the Army as a Green Beret. On his return, he attended Columbia University, where he received a bachelor's degree in engineering, which was followed by a master's in mechanical engineering. Armed with vague ideas of using his engineering background for a career as a patent lawyer, he headed to Georgetown Law School, graduating in 1964. Hirschkop kept his ties to Georgetown, teaching constitutional litigation there in the late 1960s and early 1970s.[25]

Even before he graduated from law school, Hirschkop had become involved in the growing civil rights struggle after watching videos of the 1963 demonstrations in Danville, Virginia. He dropped everything and flew to Danville, meeting up with William Kunstler on the airplane. While working in Danville, Hirschkop cofounded the Law Student Civil Rights Research Council (LSCRRC, pronounced *liz-crick*). Still under the tutelage of Kunstler and his partner, Arthur Kinoy, Hirschkop recruited two students who were working for a lawyer named William Higgs to create LSCRRC. Higgs was the only white lawyer in Mississippi willing to defend the Freedom Riders when they came into town in 1961 to test the South's adherence to laws against segregation in interstate commerce. The two students already had a grant to research what would become the 1964 Civil Rights Act. By creating the Council, the trio was able to raise a significant amount of money.[26]

By the time Hirschkop graduated from law school the following year, he had over one hundred students working for him in LSCRRC, mostly in Mississippi, the Carolinas, and Georgia. The board of directors included Elizabeth Holtzman, who one year later would help draft the *McLaughlin* brief for the NAACP Legal Defense Fund (see chapter 10).

Hirschkop also became the chief legal advisor to the Council of Federated Organizations, the umbrella organization for the groups that trav eled to Mississippi in the summer of 1964 to empower black residents and register them to vote.[27]

Although Bernie Cohen was not a civil rights attorney, he had been doing volunteer work for the ACLU since being admitted to the bar in 1961. Born in Brooklyn in 1934, he got his bachelor's degree from City College in New York before heading to the D.C. area. After graduating from Georgetown Law School, he spent some time working for the U.S. Department of Labor before joining the firm of Lainoff and Cohen, which handled divorces, home settlements, collections, personal injury, and small business cases. In his own words, Cohen was "a country lawyer" with a "very ordinary civil and criminal practice." However, he had been a member of the ACLU since his teens and assisted on a number of cases that involved civil liberties issues. Later he would found the first ACLU branch in Virginia.[28]

With Hirschkop's assistance, Cohen filed a motion in federal court asking for federal intervention. A panel was convened, consisting of one local district court judge, Oren Lewis, and two Fourth Circuit judges, John Butznor and Albert Lewis. Arguing for the State of Virginia, Robert Y. Button requested that the Virginia appellate court be given the opportunity to rule on the case.[29] Cohen and Hirschkop countered that the Supreme Court of Appeals of Virginia had made its position on miscegenation well-known on a variety of occasions, and that waiting for its decision would be fruitless.[30]

The Lovings were living at 1151 Neal Street in Washington and were very unhappy in the city.[31] Hirschkop solved their residential problem in an informal November 1964 telephone conference between himself, Virginia attorney general Robert McIlwaine, and Judge Butznor. Hirschkop requested a temporary restraining order against enforcement of the original sentence. Butznor rejected the motion, seeing no "irreparable harm" to the couple. Notwithstanding, the attorneys worked out an "off-the-record truce," which allowed the Lovings to take up residence in King and Queen County, abutting their native Caroline County. Cohen recalls that McIlwaine promised not to bother the Lovings unless the political tensions mounted. Further, he agreed that in the event the pressure got too hot and he was forced to rearrest the couple, he would give them a week's notice to get out of the state. Cohen does not believe that McIlwaine had any desire to rearrest or prosecute the pair.[32]

None of the Lovings' neighbors—white or black—appeared troubled by their presence in the neighborhood. A different story unfolded in neighboring Essex County, where the Lovings' oldest child attended school. The prosecutor there threatened Mildred and Richard with arrest and trial if he ever caught them in his jurisdiction.[33] The couple was thrilled to be back in the country. Their temporary residence was an old farmhouse with plenty of land for the children to play.[34] Meanwhile, the Lovings kept their Washington, D.C., residence in case the authorities changed their minds.[35] The agreement, as codified in the three-judge panel's interlocutory order, said,

> [I]n the event the plaintiffs are taken into custody in the enforcement of the said judgment and sentence, this court, under the provision of Title 28, Section 1651, United States Code, should grant the plaintiffs bail in a reasonable amount during the pendency of the State proceedings in the State Courts and in the Supreme Court of the United States, if and when the case should be carried there.

At least for a while, Richard continued to commute to Washington, D.C., where the five dollars an hour he earned as a bricklayer helped allay the thirty-five dollars a week that went to gasoline for the commute.[36]

Just as important as the informal agreement was the formal one rendered by the three-judge panel. Judge Butznor gave the state ninety days to render an opinion or the case would be removed to federal court. Since a legal rule known as comity gives deference to state courts on state questions, the panel chose not to take jurisdiction until the state had acted or formally indicated its unwillingness to proceed.[37] District court judge Lewis wrote that "a matter so sensitive to the social structure of the South as is racial intermarriage should first be ruled upon by state courts." Judges Butznor and Bryan concurred, promising that after the case had run its course through the state courts, they would act as quickly as possible. Furthermore, the federal court agreed to "maintain an interest in the case." In part these concessions reflected the judges' awareness that the threat of imprisonment continued to hang over the Lovings. Therefore they were entitled to a speedy trial and if the state did not rule on their rights, the federal court pledged do so.[38]

On what seemed to be the eighty-ninth of the ninety days allotted to him, in January of 1965, Bazile finally ruled. And what a ruling it was. First, he disposed of the cruel and unusual punishment argument by citing cases from the 1820s (clearly his preferred era) that found that whipping and being sold and exiled were not cruel and unusual punishments. Making a brief foray into the twentieth century, he noted that in *Buck v. Bell*,[39] the court had found that sterilizing a defendant was neither cruel nor unusual. Further, he cited a Supreme Court case[40] from the nineteenth century in support of the proposition that the term *cruel and unusual punishment* was reserved for penalties like "burning at the stake, crucifixion, breaking on the wheel or the like."[41]

Bazile disposed of the due process argument with equal facility by clinging to the age-old contention that nothing in the Fourteenth Amendment or the Virginia Constitution touched upon the matter under consideration. He quoted from a long line of cases that held that marriage was subject to the exclusive control of the state. Bazile cited *Pace* and the denial of certiorari in *Jackson* but neglected to mention that *Pace* had been explicitly overruled the previous year in *McLaughlin*. He made short shrift of Cohen's interstate commerce argument, noting tartly that "[m]arriage has nothing to do with interstate commerce. There is nothing more domestic than marriage; and this contentive [*sic*] is without merit." Regarding the undue hardship discussion, Bazile chided the couple for having brought the penalty on themselves with their felonious conduct. He reminded them that they could visit their respective families as often as they desired, albeit without each other.[42]

Bazile repeated that the parties were guilty of "a most serious crime." He then proceeded to cite a large portion of the decision in *Kinney's Case*,[43] despite the fact that this decision was nearly eighty years old.

> It was a marriage prohibited and declared absolutely void. It was contrary to the declared public law, founded upon motives of public policy—a policy affirmed for more than a Century, and one upon which social order, public morality and the best interests of both races depend. This unmistakable policy of the legislature founded, I think, on wisdom and the moral development of both races, has been shown by not only declaring marriages between whites and negroes absolutely void, but by prohibiting and punishing such unnatural alliances with severe penalties. The laws enacted to further and uphold this declared policy would be futile and a dead letter if in fraud of these salutary enactments, both races might, by stepping across any imaginary line bid defiance to the law by immediately returning and insisting that the marriage celebrated in another state or country should be recognized as lawful, though denounced by the public law of the domicile as unlawful and absolutely void.[44]

He noted that "the awfulness of the offense" was shown by section 25-57, which declared that all interracial marriages "shall be absolutely void without any decree of divorce or other legal process." In conclusion, it was time to use his own words. Bazile reminded the Lovings that they had been convicted of a felony and would be known as felons for the rest of their natural lives. Waxing poetic, he wrote,

> Almighty God created the races white, black, yellow, malay, and red, and he placed them on separate continents. And but for the interference with his arrangement there would be no cause for such marriages. The fact that he separated the races shows that he did not intend for the races to mix.[45]

Cohen and Hirschkop immediately tried to get the federal court to take jurisdiction over the case, but the judges agreed with Attorney General Button that they should exhaust their state remedies first. Again, if the state did not act promptly, the federal judges would remove the case from is jurisdiction.[46] Shortly thereafter, Cohen and Hirschkop filed a notice of appeal arguing that the court had made three errors: (1) holding that the antimiscegenation statutes did not violate the Fourteenth Amendment of the Constitution or section 1 of the Virginia Constitution; (2) holding that the sentence and suspension were not violations of due process of law, and (3) holding that the period of the suspended sentence was reasonable under Virginia law.[47]

Cohen describes the next steps in the case as "like dominoes falling." The process turned from frustrating to fun once he knew exactly where the case was headed and was confident of the outcome. The appeal of Bazile's opinion to the state supreme court of appeals was pro forma. There was no expectation of victory.[48] James Davis, one of the law clerks for Judge Carrico that year, was assigned to draft the opinion. Davis explains that the Virginia court of the 1960s was a very conservative body. The judges believed that any changes in the law should be made by the general assembly, not the court. Although the California Supreme Court had struck down their law, Davis recalls no discussion among the judges about whether they should follow the Golden State's lead. They considered California too far on the fringe for its decisions to have any precedential value. Davis believes that Carrico, a junior judge at the time, was chosen to write the unanimous decision because many of the older judges did not want to deal with the controversy and publicity that such a ruling would provoke. Carrico was fully aware of the repercussions of the case, but he believed strongly that it was not the job of the court to make laws. However, neither he nor any of the other judges had any illusions about the ruling's being affirmed at the U.S. Supreme Court level. The state court was critical of the federal court's "legislative" decisions and was certain that *Loving* would be reversed by that body.[49]

Judge Carrico's March 1966 affirmation of Bazile's opinion was no surprise to the Lovings' attorneys. Carrico noted that the defendants' contention that the Virginia antimiscegenation laws violated the Constitution had been "fully investigated" and found invalid in *Naim*. The only court to have found otherwise was California in *Perez*. The defendants had tried to distinguish *Naim* as reliant on the doctrine of separate but equal, which had been articulated in *Plessy v. Ferguson* but overruled in *Brown*. Nevertheless, Carrico believed that *Plessy's* assurance that "laws forbidding the intermarriage of the two races . . . have been universally recognized as within the police power of the state" had not been affected by *Brown*. Carrico cited Judge Buchanan's holding in *Naim*, which had differentiated education from marriage on the grounds that the former was "a right which must be made available to all on equal terms." To uphold such a right was not to support a claim for the intermarriage of the races, because intermarriage was not a "right which must be made available to all on equal terms." Carrico noted the denial of certiorari in *Jackson* just six months after *Brown* as further proof that *Brown* had no bearing on interracial marriage.[50]

Carrico opined that the *McLaughlin* decision "detracted not one bit from the position asserted in the *Naim* opinion," since it did not deal with intermarriage. He acknowledged that the defendants had cited a variety of federal civil rights cases, "but it must be pointed out that none of them deals with miscegenation statutes or curtails a legal truth which has always been recognized—that there is an overriding state interest in the institution of marriage." In response to the sociological, biological, and anthropological texts cited by the defendants, Carrico trotted out the tired argument that

> to base a decision on those opinions would be judicial legislation in the rawest sense of that term. Such arguments are properly addressable to the legislature, which enacted the law in the first place, and not to this court, whose prescribed role in the separated powers of government is to adjudicate and not to legislate.
>
> Our one and only function in this instance is to determine whether, for sound judicial consideration, the *Naim* case should be reversed. Today, more than ten years since that decision was handed down by this

court, a number of states still have miscegenation statutes and yet there has been no new decision reflecting adversely upon the validity of such statutes. We find no sound judicial reason, therefore, to depart from our holding in the *Naim* case.[51]

Carrico dismissed the argument that the suspended sentence constituted banishment and therefore should be voided. However, he showed some compassion for the couple, noting that "the conditions of the suspensions are so unreasonable as to render the sentences void." The purpose of a suspended sentence is to "secure the rehabilitation of the offender, enabling him to repent and reform so that he may be restored to a useful place in society." Carrico suggested that the Lovings might be "rehabilitated" by being allowed to return to Virginia and live apart, "contemplating the error of their way in going against God, nature and the traditions of the Commonwealth." He held that it was not reasonable to require that the defendants leave the state and not return thereafter together or at the same time, because "the real gravamen of the offense charged . . . was their cohabitation as man and wife in this state." Therefore it was only imperative to keep them from residing together in the state as a couple, nothing more being "necessary to secure the defendants' rehabilitation." The sentence was vacated and the case remanded to trial court for resentencing. In addition, Carrico noted in passing that Bazile had erred in sending the Lovings to jail rather than to the penitentiary.[52] Recognizing that his court was not the last one that would hear the case, Carrico entered a stay of judgment to give the couple time to appeal.[53]

The times, they were a-changing. The day after Carrico's decision, an editorial in the *Norfolk Virginia Pilot* came out strongly *against* antimiscegenation laws.

> Nothing about the various state anti-miscegenation laws, including yesterday's decision by the Virginia Supreme Court of Appeals upholding the Virginia version's validity, recommends itself to dispassion. The laws did not originate in objectivity; their clear purpose is to prevent whites and Negroes from marrying, without much prejudice as to how the darker races otherwise blend their blood.[54]

With their sentence stayed, Mildred and Richard were temporarily safe from prosecution while Cohen and Hirschkop prepared to take the case to its logical conclusion.

12

On to the Supreme Court

No white woman can ever marry a descendant of Ham. That's God's law. . . . I don't
care what Lyndon Johnson or anybody else says!
—defense attorney Matthew Murphy, in the 1965 murder trial of
Collie Leroy Wilkins Jr., who was charged with killing Viola Liuzzo,
a white woman, because she drove a car with a black male passenger
after participating in the Selma-to-Montgomery march

*H*irschkop and Cohen wasted little time in taking the next step in the
saga. On May 31, 1966, they filed a notice of appeal to the U.S. Supreme
Court. They were still the attorneys of record, but Melvin Wulf of the
ACLU was listed as "of counsel."[1] Although it wasn't front-page news, the
New York Times recognized the importance of the appeal, giving it a two-
column story in the main news section.[2]

The notice of appeal presented five questions. The first and most crucial one was whether the Virginia antimiscegenation law violated the due
process and equal protection clauses of the Fourteenth Amendment to
the U.S. Constitution. For good measure, the attorneys also questioned
whether the statute violated a constitutional right to privacy and a right
to marry. Alluding to the concurrence in *McLaughlin,* they asked whether

a state law that made the color of a person's skin a test of whether his or her marriage constituted a criminal offense could be valid under the Constitution. Lastly, they asked whether the Virginia laws violated Title 42 U.S.C. Section 1981, which holds that

> all persons within the jurisdiction of the United States shall have the same right in every state and Territory to make and enforce contracts, to sue, be parties, give evidence, and to the full and equal benefit of all laws and proceedings for the security of persons and property as is enjoyed by white citizens, and shall be subject to like punishment pains, penalties, taxes, licenses and exactions of every kind, and to no other.[3]

In July 1966, Cohen and Hirschkop submitted a jurisdictional statement requesting that the Supreme Court hear their appeal of the judgment of the Virginia Supreme Court. At this juncture, Carliner's name was added to those of Cohen, Hirschkop, and Wulf. The attorneys made sure to cite all the sections of the Virginia Code (see Appendix A), despite the Lovings having been convicted of violating only 20-58, the section that prohibited persons from expressly leaving the state to evade the ban on intermarriage.[4] Because the case was an appeal from a state court instead of a writ of certiorari, they had to convince the court that a "substantial federal question" was involved.[5]

The jurisdictional statement contended that Virginia's antimiscegenation statutes were racially discriminatory and that they denied the Lovings, both individually and as members of racial groups, the equal protection of the laws. Clearly, were it not for the fact that Mildred and Richard were defined by Virginia law as belonging to different races, they would have committed no crime. Cohen and Hirschkop traced the law from its early days as "an act for the suppression of outlying slaves" in 1691 to its not very different form as "an act for the preservation of racial integrity" in 1924, arguing that it was clearly an outgrowth of the "separate but equal" theory which had been struck down in *Brown*. They noted that *McLaughlin* had overruled the old *Pace* precedent that laws which applied equally to both races were not discriminatory, and went on to cite a series of cases in which the Court had struck down laws that discriminated on the basis of race, such as a prohibition on interracial boxing and a denial of commercial fishing licenses to aliens. The two men pointed out the inconsistency of the "racial integrity" motive of the legislature, since it allowed blacks to intermarry with other races and thus lose their racial purity. Therefore they argued that the statutes "are unconstitutional devices which stamp one group of citizens inferior. These statutes are relics of slavery which deny equality under the law."[6]

The next argument was that the Lovings had been denied due process of law. This section, authored by Cohen (others being opposed to its inclusion, supra), argued that "marriage is such a basic, fundamental and natural right and that the choice of a mate must be left to one's own desires and conscience. These desires cannot be infringed by the state setting standards which unreasonably and arbitrarily apply racial criteria."

Cohen argued that "the sacraments of marriage are beyond the arbitrary grasp of the state," citing the First and Ninth Amendments, as applied to the states through the Fourteenth Amendment. He wrote that due process "demands only that the law shall not be unreasonable, arbitrary or capricious, and that the means selected shall have a real and substantial relation to the object sought to be attained."[7]

Cohen and Hirschkop closed with a humane rather than a legal argument, discussing the effect of the statutes on the Lovings and similarly situated persons. They noted that such persons could not establish a family abode and were unable to raise their children in the land of their youth. Moreover, the children of such prohibited unions lived "under the stigma of bastardy" and were denied numerous benefits in the areas of taxation, social security, workers' compensation, and criminal defenses. Observing that "[t]he elaborate legal structure of segregation has been virtually obliterated with the exception of miscegenation laws," the authors concluded, "There are no laws more symbolic of the Negro's relegation to second-class citizenship. Whether or not this Court has been wise to avoid this issue in the past, the time has come to strike down these laws; they are legalized prejudice, unsupported by reason or morals, and should not exist in good society."[8]

Jon Schneider was a law clerk for Lainoff and Cohen during the summer of 1966. He assisted with the research and writing of the jurisdictional statement and recalls long hours spent in the library tracing the racial integrity statute as it had evolved over the years. Since the state was expected to argue that interbreeding caused genetic problems, he was thrilled to be able to track the statute back to a law entitled "an act for the suppression of outlying slaves," which rebutted that claim. Chosen to deliver the brief to the clerk of the Supreme Court, Schneider remembers being greeted with the words, "We have been waiting for this one."[9]

On December 12, 1966, the Supreme Court noted probable jurisdiction.[10] Justice Marshall's law clerk wrote that the "miscegenation issue" had not been affected by *McLaughlin* and "appears ripe for review here."[11] Expecting as much, Cohen and Hirschkop had worked through the summer, adding new members to the *Loving* team and strengthening their arguments. NatCap paid the costs while the case was proceeding through the state court system, in return for the right to clear certain documents. The national ACLU took over for NatCap when the case went to the Supreme Court, according to ACLU guidelines. Cohen recalls that the majority of his early discussions regarding the appeal were with Harvey Applebaum, but that Carliner, Lawrence Speiser, and Chester Antieu of Georgetown Law School also contributed.[12]

At first blush, Harvey Applebaum would seem an unusual person to assist in the *Loving* appeal. Born in Birmingham, Alabama, Applebaum completed his undergraduate work at Yale, earned his law degree at Harvard, and went to work for the prestigious firm of Covington and Burling, whose client roster includes the National Football League, Canon, Motorola, and the province of Quebec. Applebaum's Martindale-Hubbell listing[13] is an impressive roster of American Bar Association work. He has chaired several ABA sections and committees, spoken at various seminars and symposiums, and written a number of law review articles. However, all of this work concerns the area of anti-trust law, where he is considered "one of the heavies;" none, save a single law review article, is in the area of civil rights.[14]

Cohen recalls that the major debate regarding the Supreme Court brief was over the due process clause. He spent numerous hours "bantering back and forth" with Hirschkop and Applebaum. All the lawyers involved thought that they would win by using the equal protection argument, but Cohen was worried that this would not be enough to quash all laws against intermarriage. He believed that if the Supreme Court rendered its decision solely on the grounds of the equal protection clause, there was nothing to stop the Virginia legislature from turning around and drafting an antimiscegenation law that did not violate the clause: one that said that whites could marry only whites, blacks could marry only blacks, Indians could marry only Indians, and so forth. Therefore Cohen insisted on including an argument on substantive due process.[15] Most of the other attorneys involved in the appeal discounted Cohen's fear that the Virginia legislature might enact an "equal" intermarriage ban. Hirschkop's fear was that since the Court had previously evaded the issue of equal protection in miscegenation cases, it might review only the due process argument as an excuse to continue the string of evasions. Nonconsideration of the

equal protection clause would limit the Court to reviewing the sentencing aspect of the law.[16]

Every aspect of the appeal had to be cleared with Melvin Wulf, since
the ACLU paid for the printing.[17] Neither Cohen nor Hirschkop had ever
argued in front of the Supreme Court, so at Wulf's suggestion, they met
with a New York attorney named William Zabel who was familiar with
procedure.[18] Hirschkop describes Zabel as a "stuffy" appellate lawyer from
a large firm who was "rammed down our throats" by Wulf.[19] Stuffy
though he may have been, Zabel was added to the brief for more than
his familiarity with procedure. In his first year at Harvard Law School,
Zabel had participated in a moot court[20] argument that was roughly
based on the *Naim* case. The issue stayed in his mind, and in 1965 he
wrote an article entitled "Interracial Marriage and the Law" for the *Atlantic Monthly.* He had assisted the ACLU on a variety of cases. Zabel's
recollection is that Wulf asked him to assist on the case because neither
Hirschkop nor Cohen was a constitutional scholar.[21]

While Hirschkop has less than fond memories of his association with
Zabel, he thoroughly enjoyed his affiliation with Professor Arthur Berney,
who also assisted the pair. Hirschkop's association with Berney came
about through a stroke of good fortune, not unlike the serendipitous
meeting between himself and Cohen. He reached Berney through a law
clerk named Joe Goldberg,[22] who had worked with Hirschkop during his
first summer at Lainoff and Cohen and had provided assistance in preparing the Virginia state court brief. Hirschkop sent Berney a copy of that
brief to use as a basis for his draft of the original Supreme Court brief.
Berney revised and sent the draft back to Hirschkop, who made his own
editorial comments. Hirschkop recalls that the pair swapped drafts and
spoke to one another independently of the rest of the team. Then they
joined the others in New York to add Zabel's contribution to their working draft.[23]

Arthur Berney's recollections of the case are quite vivid. Father Drinan,
the dean of Boston College Law School, was one of the attorneys involved
in LSCRRC. He encouraged his professors, Berney among them, to be
active in the civil rights movement. When Berney took a position as a
visiting professor at the University of Virginia in the summer of 1966,
he brought along two law students on LSCRRC grants—Joe Goldberg
and Jon Schneider—to help him with a textbook on poverty law. Since
Goldberg had worked with Cohen and Hirschkop the previous year,
Berney asked him whether he would prefer to work with them on the

Loving case or with him on the textbook. Goldberg said that, while he was very interested in the book, he felt that he would benefit from exposure to work in a law firm.[24] Schneider's recollection is that Berney had arranged for him to spend the summer working on voter registration issues for LSCRRC. He recalls that Berney, a professor who "spent more time talking about impeaching President Johnson for bombing than contracts," arranged to have a number of students assigned to civil liberties projects that summer. Schneider's recollection is that Joe Goldberg also worked with the law firm during that summer but did not devote much of his efforts to the *Loving* appeal.[25]

The *Loving* case had not yet received widespread publicity, but it soon became clear to the northern visitors that it was a top agenda item for Hirschkop and Cohen. When Goldberg told them that Berney was an expert in constitutional law, Hirschkop promptly recruited him to perform research on the case. After Hirschkop sent Berney a copy of the state court brief with a request for assistance, Berney assigned some of the work to Schneider. Schneider turned out not to be politically correct, although the phrase had not yet been coined. In one memo submitted to Berney and Hirschkop, he used the terms *whites* and *less than whites*. Hirschkop took offense, and Berney decided that Schneider was not the right person for the case. Goldberg dropped his other duties, moved into Schneider's room in the house that Berney was renting from a University of Virginia professor, and took over. It was, Berney recalls, the beginning of a long relationship between the two men in which Goldberg took on roles ranging from babysitter for Berney's children to coauthor of his poverty law textbook and another text on the legal problems of the poor. Despite their geographical separation (Berney remains in Boston, while Goldberg has settled in Albuquerque), they remain friends.[26]

Berney recognized that *Brown* had sounded the death knell for the doctrine of separate but equal, but he believed that in cases involving interracial marriage, *Pace* was still the law of the land, since the *McLaughlin* decision had not touched on the marriage question. His first thought was that the racial integrity statute should be attacked on equal protection grounds. Later he came to believe that an argument on substantive due process grounds should be added as well. Berney recalls having a dreadful time in a New York hotel room convincing William Zabel that the team had nothing to lose by adding the due process argument even though they expected the equal protection argument to be a winner. Zabel felt that adding unnecessary arguments could cause trouble. On

Zabel's turf (New York) and aware that Zabel seemed to have the final say in the matter, Berney considered quitting the team during the heated debate. He left the group one night thinking that the due process argument had been scrapped, only to have Hirschkop come to his room much later to tell him that it had been salvaged, albeit in a condensed form.[27] Zabel does not recall any contentious discussions about the case. He also does not recall opposing the inclusion of the due process argument but continues to believe that equal protection was a better tactic to invalidate the laws.[28]

In January 1967, Zabel sent Berney his critique of the first part of the brief. That section purported to show why the Supreme Court should use *Loving* to make a broad ruling that neither Virginia nor any other state could "prohibit and penalize interracial marriages, either by its criminal or civil law." Such a decision would strike down all antimiscegenation laws in the United States. Zabel did not think it was "an obvious proposition" that the Court would make such a broad ruling and thought it vital to convince it to do so. In his view, the examples of *McLaughlin* and *Naim* showed that the Court would not necessarily jump at the chance to make history in the field of intermarriage legislation."[29]

Apparently Berney had suggested including what Zabel termed a "provocative attempt" to show that invalidation of antimiscegenation laws was "a key factor to the attainment of a healthy society." Zabel did not think this was either "persuasive or relevant. . . . True, these laws are obvious anachronisms and relics of slavery, but their practical effect on Negroes . . . is quite conjectural and difficult to prove or even assert." Zabel did not believe the Supreme Court was interested in "the general sociological aspects of interracial sexual relations." He suggested a quote from Gunnar Myrdal or Margaret Mead, or from his own article in the *Atlantic Monthly* that "the Supreme Court by remaining silent on the issue to some extent lends its prestige to the continued existence of these laws."[30] By contrast, Hirschkop championed the inclusion of anthropological information to refute the state's expected argument that interracial marriages were harmful to the health and welfare of children.[31]

Berney recalls that the ACLU brought in Zabel near the end of the case because it needed the backup services that only a large firm could provide.[32] This move explains why the team completed its draft in a hotel room in New York City.[33] Although he doesn't recall what he might have written that Zabel found provocative, Berney's guess is that it was his description of miscegenation laws as a continuation of the Jim Crow system in the South.[34] Zabel believed that such sociological or intellectual points should be put aside in favor of concise, direct legal research. Berney, however, felt that it was important to include sociological references because the state of Virginia would try to argue that the statutes still had the valid purpose of preventing the societal ostracism that befell interracial children. Given that the state relied heavily on *Intermarriage: Interfaith, Interracial, Interethnic,* a study of interracial marriages by Rabbi Albert Gordon, which Berney describes as an "almost racist tract," he felt he was correct in arguing for the inclusion of sociological and anthropological references.[35]

Apparently others at NatCap and the national ACLU office argued over the brief as well. Mel Wulf was particularly critical, voicing his strenuous opposition to Cohen's use of the substantive due process argument and writing that only his conscience prevented him from striking it out.[36] Cohen recalls being somewhat perturbed by Wulf's approach, but Hirschkop, who knew him better, said that it was typical behavior for him.[37] In truth, Hirschkop also was unenthusiastic about Cohen's due process argument, but the two agreed that Cohen would make that argument in court and Hirschkop would put forth the equal protection argument. Cohen is proud of the fact that the Court's ruling addresses both arguments.[38]

The work consisted of more than just legal research. The team gathered biological, sociological, and anthropological information as well. When Chief Justice Warren asked a question about "yellow peril" during oral argument, Hirschkop was prepared, since he and Joe Goldberg had collected a good deal of sociological history about the motives behind relics of American history such as the sedition, yellow peril, and potato laws. Additionally, Hirschkop and Cohen had traveled to Princeton to meet with anthropologist Ashley Montagu,[39] whom Hirschkop described as "a pain in the ass, brilliant and fascinating." The trio sat on Montagu's sun porch, listening to him expound. Hirschkop still has "fond memories" of that day, recalling the discussion as over his head, but riveting. Hirschkop also had visited the head of the psychiatric unit at Children's Hospital in Washington, D.C., in order to counter the state's expected argument that miscegenous marriages had a negative impact on children.[40]

Given the bench and the confluence of opinions that were coming down at the time, Hirschkop felt that the team's only job was to keep the case procedurally correct. He believed the court would find the statutes in question discriminatory because racial classifications are legally suspect and the state has the burden to prove that they are justified. Hirschkop presumed that procedural failings were the reason the Supreme Court had been able to avoid ruling on antimiscegenation statutes in the past. He has no illusions that his work on *Loving* was a great intellectual leap. "We were in the right place at the right time. It wasn't a brilliant case, but the decision to keep it procedurally clean was important." Hirschkop credits his experience in the civil rights movement with keeping the case "correct." "It had reached its time. We had wonderful appealing plaintiffs and the case was in good posture. I've won unwinnable cases. In *Loving* we only did what was right; nothing special."[41]

Cohen admits to feeling some concern that the Court would find an excuse to duck the issue as it had done in *Naim*, but he truly believed that the Warren Court was different from the body that had avoided the question twelve years earlier. He was positive that the Lovings would emerge victorious. In his mind, the only question was whether the justices would base their decision on equal protection or the due process argument. He further believed that because of the importance of the decision, the Court would show a united front as the justices had done in *Brown* and render a unanimous decision. Cohen felt that with the passage of the Civil Rights Act, the mood of the country had shifted to one more supportive of civil rights.[42]

The *Loving* case met further complications on its way to the Supreme Court when other civil rights groups offered to write amicus curiae briefs.[43] Cohen's recollection is that the amicus briefs in the case were volunteered, not solicited. Meaning no disrespect to the authors of those briefs, Cohen states that he and Hirschkop "sort of winced a little bit" each time another organization offered to file a brief. The reason was that such authors had the right to request a portion of the allotted time for oral argument. Thankfully, only the JACL requested permission to do so, and William Marutani took up fifteen minutes for his argument (see chapter 15).[44]

Hirschkop is less certain about how the groups that wrote amicus briefs became involved. He recalls that Robert Carter, now a U.S. district court judge in New York, called to say that he wanted to write an amicus brief on behalf of the NAACP. Hirschkop knew Jack Greenberg of the NAACP Legal Defense and Education Fund through LSCRRC and believes that he, too, volunteered to write a brief. Hirschkop recalls that Marutani not only wrote to Cohen to volunteer his services on an amicus brief but also reviewed Hirschkop and Cohen's draft and was, in Hirschkop's words, "terrific and very helpful." Hirschkop believes that David Carliner may have tried to contact the American Jewish Congress, the Association on American Indian Affairs, and the Association of Immigration and Naturalization Lawyers, all of which had been involved in the *Naim* case. Because he was based in Washington, D.C., and practiced immigration law, Carliner had greater access to those groups. In retrospect, Hirschkop wishes that Cohen had listened more carefully to Carliner's advice.[45] Carliner, however, does not recall giving advice on the *Loving* brief or contacting amicus groups. He believes that the addition of his name on the brief was in deference to his work in *Naim*, not due to any major contributions in *Loving*.[46] In the end, Mel Wulf was the ultimate authority on which amicus briefs to accept.[47]

The final draft of the brief was signed by Cohen, Hirschkop, Berney, Carliner, Zabel, Wulf, and Marvin Karpatkin. Karpatkin, chief counsel for the ACLU, was added pro forma. The brief begins with citations from all sections of the Virginia intermarriage ban, as well as the statutory definition of a black person. Only two questions were presented: (1) whether the Virginia antimiscegenation laws violated the due process and equal protection clauses of the Fourteenth Amendment and (2) whether a state could constitutionally prohibit and penalize the marriage or cohabitation of two residents on the basis of race.[48]

Hirschkop and Cohen began by requesting that the Court consider all aspects of the Virginia law, not just the evasion statute. They then proceeded to use Schneider's research into the history of the state's antimiscegenation law, tracing it back to the 1691 "Act for Suppressing Outlying Slaves" and forward again to a discussion of the eugenics movement, which had inspired the 1924 revisions.[49] Picking up the humane argument that they had employed in their notice of appeal, the attorneys proceeded to catalogue the "immeasurable social harm" caused by antimiscegenation statutes.[50] They made short shrift of the state's argument (see chapter 14) to the effect that the legislative history of the Fourteenth Amendment demonstrated that intermarriage bans were unaffected by the law. They then proceeded to the crux of their argument: equal protection and due process. Cohen and Berney's insistence had paid off. Although it took up only two pages, while seven were devoted to equal protection, the due process argument closed out the brief.[51]

The attorneys argued that the provisions of the Fourteenth Amendment were "open-ended and meant to be expounded in light of changing times and circumstances to prohibit racial discrimination." This language paraphrased words used by Justices John Marshall and Oliver

Wendell Holmes in earlier cases and by Earl Warren in *Brown*. They drew a parallel between Virginia's policy of "racial integrity" and Hitler's dream of a super race. They quoted Gunnar Myrdal's observation that white southerners' dread of intermarriage was used to rationalize many types of discrimination: "what white people really want is to keep the Negroes in a low status. They use the fear of intermarriage to rationalize things that have nothing to do with it." Rather poignantly, they characterized the Virginia laws as "relics of slavery" that had become "expressions of modern day racism."[52]

In conclusion, the *Loving* team wrote,

> The elaborate legal structure of segregation has been virtually obliterated with the exception of miscegenation laws. White racists can still point to these laws to support their appeal to the ultimate superstition fostering racial prejudice—the myth that Negroes are innately inferior to whites. There are no laws more symbolic of the Negro's relegation to second-class citizenship. Whether or not this Court has been wise to avoid this issue in the past, the time has come to strike down these laws; they are legalized racial prejudice, unsupported by reason or morals, and should not exist in good society.[53]

It is fascinating to note the different directions in which Berney and Zabel have gone since their collaboration on the *Loving* case. Berney remained in academe, teaching until his recent retirement from Boston College School of Law. He taught, in addition to his specialization in constitutional law, courses in communications law and national securities law.[54] Berney was a board member of the Lawyers' Alliance for Nuclear Arms Control[55] and a member of the steering committee of the Lawyers' Committee for Civil Rights under Law (LCCRUL, which is discussed in detail in chapter 18).[56] A review of the publications in Berney's name shows a textbook on national security law and a variety of law review articles on free speech issues such as Holocaust denial, use of nuclear weapons, legal problems of and programs for the poor, and the Third World.[57]

While Berney gravitated to a field favored by many of those involved in the so-called special interest groups (see chapter 13 for discussions about Michael Meltsner, Jack Greenberg, and Louis Pollak of the NAACP Legal Defense Fund) and stayed active in liberal causes, Zabel's career took a more unusual turn. His specialty is trusts and estates. Zabel has performed estate planning duties for a variety of wealthy clients and has been called one of the world's leading estate and tax planners.[58] Among his more controversial recommendations to clients are paternal trusts for out-of-wedlock children that can be revoked if the mother or the child ever discusses his or her paternal lineage. In a less than politically correct quote, Zabel noted that "[t]here are nice little bastard kids running around this world who are very, very solvent. No one will ever know."[59] Another memorable Zabel sound bite is his recommendation that clients give up their U.S. citizenship, because "[e]xpatriation is the ultimate estate plan."[60] Zabel is the author of an estate-planning book entitled *The Rich Die Richer and You Can, Too.*[61]

Despite his field of work and his wealthy clientele, Zabel has retained some of his liberal tendencies. In 1994 he was a member of the team sent by the Lawyers Committee for Human Rights to investigate conditions in Hong Kong.[62] Previously he had been part of an investigative team that accused the Philippine government of "widespread human rights abuses."[63] He also investigated alleged violations in Chile. Zabel continues to be affiliated with groups like the ACLU and the Lawyer's Constitutional Defense Committee; he was one of the authors of the 1984 brief that persuaded the Supreme Court to rule that race could not be a factor in child custody cases (see the discussion of the Palmore case in chapter 6).[64]

Bernie Cohen never lost his liberal credentials but soon decided that he could make more of an impact on the legislative scene than on the judicial one. He worked within the Democratic Party from 1964 on, helping to elect representatives in Alexandria, Virginia. He first ran for the state legislature in 1973, losing the Democratic primary by 142 votes to the brother-in-law of long-time Democratic leader Harry Byrd. Cohen didn't venture into the political arena again until 1979, when the incumbent called him to say that he would not seek reelection. Cohen is responsible for a large and varied amount of legislation, but the three bills that he is most proud of concern living wills, clean indoor air (no smoking), and motorcycle safety training. After the last act's passage, the rates of serious accidents and death were reduced by enormous percentages. Cohen is also proud of having been a thorn in the side of the insurance industry during his years in office and of bringing enhanced 911 service to rural Virginia.[65]

Cohen retired from the legislature after sixteen years, burnt out with politics. He was lauded at his retirement as "the liberal conscience" of that body. In 1997 he found himself under consideration for a seat on the state supreme court, but his tag as a liberal came back to haunt him and no

Republican senator was willing to vote for him. In retrospect, he considers that defeat a blessing, since he is now "working on retirement."[66]

Phil Hirschkop went on to a distinguished career in the civil rights movement. His lawsuit *Kirstein v. Board of Visitors* is responsible for the admission of women into the University of Virginia.[67] Continuing in the field of women's rights, he litigated a case that struck down North Carolina's public school policy of mandatory leave for women when they reached the fourth month of pregnancy.[68] In later years, Hirschkop represented a variety of antiwar groups, such as the Mayday Collective, the Mobe (National Mobilization Committee to End the War in Vietnam), the Moratorium, and National Peace Action.[69] He also sat on the board of directors of the New Mobe. Hirschkop continues to work for the national ACLU.[70]

Considered a premier plaintiff's attorney,[71] Hirschkop has sued police departments for racial bias and excessive force,[72] and has brought claims against hospitals and a drug treatment program for abuses.[73] Institutional reform (from hospitals to prisons) has been a major focus of his career.[74] Hirschkop has been successful in securing large settlements for his clients. In a span of two days in 1980, he won almost a hundred thousand dollars for the estate of a man who died while in police custody[75] and over a million dollars for injuries suffered by a fellow attorney aboard the Washington Metro.[76] His roster of clients runs the gamut from an accused cop killer[77] and a police officer charging defamation of character[78] to professional football player John Riggin[79] and the billionaire Hunt brothers.[80] Although the Hunts may seem like unlikely clients for an antiestablishment lawyer, Hirschkop charged that they were being prosecuted because they refused to cooperate with the CIA.[81]

During his lengthy post-*Loving* career, Hirschkop has continued to attract publicity and controversy. He has represented a variety of less than popular groups and people, from Norman Mailer, Jerry Rubin, and Benjamin Spock (for antiwar demonstrations)[82] to People for the Ethical Treatment of Animals and the Church of Scientology.[83] Hirschkop's temper has gotten him in trouble on more than one occasion. He has been described as "a grouchy civil rights expert . . . with a permanent tan and a semi-permanent scowl . . . whose pugilistic style tends to irritate the genteel attorneys."[84] Another article, entitled "Hirschkop the Horrible: A '60s Lawyer in the '80s" describes him as "pugnacious and contentious," a man whose primary tactic is to sue anyone who disparages his clients. The article quotes a colleague as saying that Hirschkop is prone to "yell and interrupt other people and act utterly without decorum in order to achieve his goals." Seventeen different disciplinary complaints against Hirschkop were brought before the Virginia State Bar, but no disciplinary action was ever imposed. These complaints, however, may have had something to do with the dissolution of all four law partnerships that Hirschkop entered into after graduation from law school. In fact, well before their Showtime-induced feud, Cohen was quoted as saying that Hirschkop thrived on being known as abrasive because his intention was to "rub on the raw nerves" of the opposition.[85]

By the time the Supreme Court was ready to rule on the *Loving* case in 1967, only the southern states remained committed to outdated ideas of racial purity. Sixteen states still had laws that prohibited marriage between people of different races.[86] The holdouts were Alabama, Arkansas, Delaware, Florida, Georgia, Kentucky, Louisiana, Mississippi, Missouri, North Carolina, Oklahoma, South Carolina, Tennessee, Texas, Virginia, and West Virginia. Even Maryland, site of the first of these laws, had repealed its antimiscegenation provisions after 306 years on the books.[87] The stage was set, and with the help of four separate amicus briefs, the two young attorneys were ready for their first appearance before the highest court of the land.

13

The Amicus Briefs

Intermarriage between whites and blacks is repulsive and averse to every sentiment of pure American spirit. It is abhorrent and repugnant to the very principles of pure Saxon government. It is subversive to social peace. It is destructive of moral supremacy, and ultimately this slavery of white women to black beasts will bring this nation to a conflict as fatal and as bloody as ever reddened the soil of Virginia or crimsoned the mountain paths of Pennsylvania.... Let us uproot and exterminate now this debasing, ultrademoralizing, un-American and inhuman leprosy.
—Senator Roddenberry of Georgia, 1912

Fully recovered from their post-*Brown* fear of involvement with antimiscegenation cases, the NAACP and its Legal Defense Fund (LDF) both plunged in headfirst to help the Lovings. The LDF's brief was signed by four Fund attorneys: Jack Greenberg, James M. Nabrit III, Michael Meltsner, and Melvyn Zarr.

The brief was short, containing only one argument: that antimiscegenation laws violated the due process and equal protection clauses of the Fourteenth Amendment. The brief noted that same-race couples who left the state to be married did not violate section 20-58 of the Virginia Code, so "[t]he essence of the law is racial, and race is the test of criminality."

The authors quoted Justices Stewart and Douglas's concurrence in *McLaughlin* that "it is simply not possible for a state law to be valid under our Constitution which makes the criminality of an act depend upon the race of the actor." They then cited the majority opinion in that case, which held that the Florida cohabitation law was invalid because it applied only to couples who were of mixed race. The authors noted that it "would make a mockery of the constitutional promise of equal protection of the laws" to send a person to prison because of his or her skin color.[1]

The LDF brief moved from law to science, quoting the 1952 UNESCO *Statement on the Nature of Race* and anthropologist Ashley Montagu's *Man's Most Dangerous Myth: The Fallacy of Race.* The brief noted that the intermarriage bans were an outgrowth of slavery, quoting Chief Justice Taney's opinion in the famous Dred Scott decision that laws against intermarriage

> show that a perpetual and impassable barrier was intended to be erected between the white race and the one which they had reduced to slavery, and governed as subjects with absolute and despotic power, and which they then looked upon as so far below them in the scale of created beings, that intermarriages between white persons and negroes or mulattoes were regarded as unnatural and immoral, and punished as crimes, not only in the parties, but in the persons who joined them in marriage.

The LDF disagreed with Virginia's contention that to rely on new scientific evidence would amount to judicial legislation. They believed that it was up to the state to provide rationalization for its laws. Lastly, the brief reminded the justices that the *Naim* court had justified its decision on the grounds that at the time of their decision, more than half the states in the union still had antimiscegenation statutes. This majority was clearly no longer the case, as thirteen states had repealed their laws since 1951 and only seventeen states, all "southern and border states which had extensive segregation codes prior to *Brown*," continued to have such laws.[2]

Neither Michael Meltsner nor Jack Greenberg recalls when the LDF became aware of the *Loving* case.[3] Unlike *Brown*, it was not an organized campaign but a case that sprang up spontaneously from an arrest. Although it became a challenge to antimiscegenation laws, it was not planned as such. Meltsner believes that the LDF volunteered the brief as soon as it became aware that the case was headed to the Supreme Court. Since the LDF considered itself to be at the forefront of civil rights activity, it would not have waited for an invitation to file a brief. Neither

Meltsner nor Greenberg remembers any discussion about potential LDF participation in oral arguments. In contrast to *McLaughlin,* there were no internal debates as to whether the Fund should participate in the case.[4]

The NAACP brief, written by Robert Carter and Andrew Weinberger, is a surprisingly terse affair.[5] In a mere fourteen pages, Carter and Weinberger discussed the fact that although antimiscegenation statutes had once existed in forty states, now only seventeen held that distinction. Not above the use of sarcasm, the brief observed that while states such as Arkansas, Florida, and Oklahoma all prohibited Negro-white marriages, this prohibition meant different things in each state: "In Arkansas, a Negro is defined as 'any person who has in his or her veins any negro blood whatever'; in Florida, one ceases to be a Negro when he has less than one-eighth of . . . African or Negro blood; and in Oklahoma, anyone not of 'African descent' is miraculously transmuted into a member of the white race."

The brief readily admitted that antimiscegenation statutes had been upheld by the highest courts of ten of the seventeen holdout states and enforced in the lower courts of the remaining seven but noted that the tide was turning, thanks to decisions in California, Nevada, and Arizona.[6]

The NAACP brief focused more on the human toll of antimiscegenation statutes than on their legal significance. "It is the burden of this brief to establish that there is no rational or scientific basis upon which a statutory prohibition against marriage based on race or color alone can be justified as furthering a valid legislative purpose." Carter and Weinberger claimed that even supposing "separate but equal" to still be the law, that doctrine should not apply to interracial marriages because "[t]he choice of a spouse is a subjective act, the act of an individual, and not that of a race or group. It follows that any legislative classification that prohibits persons from marrying each other must, therefore, relate to individuals and be based upon personal, not group, characteristics."[7]

The brief's sole argument was that "the genetic import of interracial marriage is conclusive proof that its prohibition cannot be a vital legislative objective." Once again dripping with sarcasm, Carter and Weinberger quoted the judge in *Scott v. Georgia* who had declared that the offspring of interracial unions were "sickly and effeminate . . . and inferior in physical development and strength to the full blood of either race." They observed that in the years since the 1869 decision, "Mendel and the twentieth century science of genetics" appeared not to have made an impact on the state courts of Virginia, who ruled in *Naim* that the legislative objective of preventing "a mongrel breed of citizens" was a valid one. The brief went on to debunk the notion that pure races existed or that the mixed offspring of different racial groups were inferior. The authors offered a legal distinction between marriage laws based on race and those based on disease or feeblemindedness. The latter were "supported by demonstrable knowledge that such marriages present a potential danger to society through physically or mentally ill offspring."[8] Lastly, Carter and Weinberger argued that there was no evidence that cultural levels depended on racial or biological attributes. They cited the Army Alpha Tests of World War I, in which blacks from northern states scored higher than whites from southern states.[9]

The last few paragraphs of the NAACP brief deserve direct quotation.

> The statutes are self-contradictory, containing within themselves certain permissible areas of miscegenistic marriage. Apparently, "scientific" thought varies from state to state. As has been shown, some legislators see no danger in white-Mongolian marriages, while others do. None, with the exception of North Carolina and Maryland,[10] perceive any evidence of deterioration in the offspring of intermarriage between any of the races other than white. Even as to Negroes, the degree of Negro genes thought sufficient to cause contamination varies from state to state, and in the most absurd instance, Colorado (until 1957) prohibited in one part of the state interracial marriages which were permitted in another part of the state. Equally genetically nonsensical is North Carolina's prohibiting marriage between a Cherokee Indian of Robeson County and a Negro, with no such restriction against Cherokees of other counties nor against Indians other than Cherokees regardless of their county.
>
> It is not scientifically possible to determine whether a person is "one-eighth Negro," "one-half Malay," or is one of the many varieties of fractionated racial memberships. Such terms as "half-breeds," "octoroons," "full-bloods," and the like, are misleading when used in anything but a fictional or social sense; for example, the popular expression that a person is "one-quarter Chinese" has no necessary biological or genetic meaning—it does mean, pragmatically, only that one of a set of grandparents of that person was *socially defined* as a person of Chinese ancestry. . . .
>
> Classification by race based upon non-existent racial traits does not serve any valid legislative purpose but merely continues a classification of Americans as superior and inferior in contradiction to the American concept of equality.[11]

Continuing its trend of involvement in antimiscegenation litigation that had started with *Perez,* the Japanese American Citizens League also contributed an amicus brief, written by William M. Marutani and Donald W. Kramer.[12] The JACL volunteered to file a brief because its members believed that antimiscegenation laws were a matter that needed attention. One complication to the statutes was that some states considered Japanese white, while others considered them a separate class of people prohibited from marrying whites.[13] The brief noted that as of 1960, more than 450,000 persons of Japanese origin were living in the United States, seventeen hundred of whom resided in Virginia and almost eighteen thousand of whom resided in states with antimiscegenation statutes. Although only Georgia mentioned the Japanese as a separate race of people, other states appeared to include the Japanese in the category of either Malay or Mongolian persons who were forbidden to intermarry with whites. Since some states made distinctions between black and white only, it was unclear where the Japanese fell in terms of other racial intermarriage bans in those jurisdictions.[14]

The JACL's brief discussed three points. The first was that *Pace* should be overruled as inconsistent with current case law,[15] although Marutani hastened to add that the reasoning in that case had always been faulty. The JACL cited a long line of civil rights cases that repudiated distinctions based on race, arguing that the right to marry should likewise not be subject to such distinctions. They contended that reliance on *Pace* was inappropriate, since "[r]acial classification as a standard has no proper place in governmental action invading and seeking to dictate and regulate one of the most basic and intimate areas of a citizen's life."[16] The brief's second point was that antimiscegenation laws denied equal protection of the laws to white as well as nonwhite citizens, an argument not dissimilar to that made in the main *Loving* brief.[17] The JACL's amicus brief closed with a lengthy discussion of scientific literature, all shoring up the argument that antimiscegenation statutes were "based on fundamental misconceptions of fact which render them unconstitutionally arbitrary and vague and which bear no relationship to any legitimate legislative purpose.[18] As Kramer recalls it, the first half of the brief was a general argument against the statutes while the second half discussed the bizarre position in which those laws placed Japanese Americans, unaware of whether they were considered white or nonwhite for the basis of intermarriage in many states.[19]

Marutani was given a draft of the main *Loving* brief and made sure that his brief would not be duplicative. He wanted the JACL brief to cover issues left untouched by Hirschkop and Cohen. Marutani agreed with them that the main draft "should have more of a humanistic approach." The JACL brief was designed to be more technical and less emotional, and to deal with science as well as the law.[20]

The last amicus brief was a joint venture by the National Catholic Conference for Interracial Justice (NCCIJ), the National Catholic Social Action Conference (NCSAC), and sixteen bishops, archbishops, and apostolic administrators from states that still had antimiscegenation laws.[21] The NCSAC is no longer in existence, but as of 1995, the NCCIJ was still active in the pursuit of racial equality. This involvement of Catholic groups was not the first in the fight against antimiscegenation legislation. Not only had they participated in the *Perez* case but in 1966 the Catholic Interracial Council briefly spearheaded an attempt to repeal Virginia's antimiscegenation law.[22]

The brief's authors were William Bentley Ball and the Reverend William Lewers, but the force behind the brief was John P. Sisson, the director of southern field service for the NCCIJ. As soon as he heard about *Loving,* Sisson began to solicit groups to file amicus briefs. The Family Life Bureau of the U.S. Catholic Conference declined, citing the need for bureaucratic approval. The legal department of the Conference flat out refused on the grounds that there was no church interest involved in the case: neither Richard nor Mildred was Catholic. Since the case began in Richmond, Sisson approached John J. Russell, the resident bishop. Russell was less than thrilled with the idea, but Sisson persuaded him to sign on and then gathered the remaining fifteen bishops, archbishops, and apostolic administrators. Next Sisson spoke to Rev. Lewers, who induced William Ball to join in the endeavor.[23]

The joint brief raised two issues: (1) whether the Virginia antimiscegenation laws constituted an invalid restriction on the free exercise of religion guaranteed by the U.S. Constitution and (2) whether the statutes constituted an invalid restraint on the right to have and raise children. The brief argued that marriage as "a fundamental or basic act of religion is not a determination of law, but rather of theology," citing Catholic, Protestant, Orthodox Christian, and Jewish theologians in furtherance of this argument. Additionally, the brief cited a number of religious figures to attest to the church's tolerance of interracial marriage. As early as 1843, an American theologian had stated that while some states prohibited interracial marriages, "they are valid by ecclesiastical law." In 1967 the convention of the Episcopal Church of the diocese of Washington asked for the repeal of all laws forbidding marriage across racial lines. Lastly, one of the committees at the Evanston Assembly of the World Council of Churches had urged the church to "withhold its approval of all discriminatory legislation affecting the educational, occupational, civic or marital opportunities based on race."[24]

The brief's authors recognized the possibility of situations in which the state could place restrictions on marriage but maintained that such restrictions could occur only in cases of "grave and immediate danger to interests which the state may lawfully protect."[25] As an example, the brief lauded the Court's decision against polygamous marriages.[26] Although polygamous marriages were "inherently objectionable as constituting a danger to the 'principles on which the government of the people, to a greater or lesser extent rests,'" interracial marriages did not "constitute a threat to the 'principles of government,'" and laws against intermarriage were based on classifications that should have been outlawed under the Fourteenth Amendment. Bringing the brief to more predictable legal ground, Lewers and Ball quoted heavily from the majority in the *Perez* decision.[27]

The section of the brief devoted to the right to beget children was only three pages. Although Lewers and Ball recognized that the state had the power to deny this right on the basis of mental deficiency or habitual criminality,[28] they again suggested that racial grounds were not sufficient for the state to exercise this prerogative. Liberal use was once again made of the *Perez* case. The authors also cited the United Nations' Universal Declaration of Human Rights.[29]

The authors of the four amicus briefs were quite a mix of characters. Jack Greenberg remains on the LDF executive committee but has gravitated to academia, teaching topics ranging from constitutional law to civil rights and human rights law, civil procedure, judicial process and social change, capital punishment, and South African law at law schools throughout the world. His publications run the gamut of the legal areas he teaches but include a history of the LDF and *Dean Cuisine: The Liberated Man's Guide to Fine Cooking*.[30] Michael Meltsner, too, went on to a career in academia as a dean and professor. His main cause has been working to eliminate the death penalty in the United States.[31] Andrew Weinberger spent his entire career with the NAACP, including a stint as vice president of the organization. He also worked in the private sector as a copyright lawyer and taught at several American and international universities.[32] Robert Carter moved on to become a district court judge in New York and continues to speak out against racism in society.[33] William Marutani who, like Henry Oyama, had experienced discrimination firsthand when he spent six months in an internment camp during World War II, became national legal counsel for the JACL and was later appointed to the Court of Common Pleas in Pennsylvania.[34] Donald Kramer remained in private practice but has focused his energies in the nonprofit business realm.[35] Rev. Lewers became the director of the Center for Civil and Human Rights at Notre Dame University and worked tirelessly to investigate human rights abuses throughout the world.[36] William Ball became a leading advocate against government involvement in religious activities, going so far as to defend Bob Jones University when the IRS threatened to take away its tax exemption because school policies forbade (and continue to forbid) interracial dating.[37]

The state of Virginia also had assistance in its fight to maintain the "law to preserve racial integrity." Unfortunately for the state, its backers were neither as many nor as varied.

14

Virginia and North Carolina Defend the Indefensible

The two races are placed as wide apart by hand of nature as white from black: and, to break down the barriers, fixed, as it were, by the Creator himself, in a political and social amalgamation, shocks us as something unnatural and wrong. It strikes us as a violation of the laws of nature. It would be productive of no good. It would degrade the white if it could be accomplished without elevating the black.

—dissenting Ohio Supreme Court judge, 1942

*I*nitially, the main goal of the state of Virginia was to keep the *Loving* complaint out of the hands of the Supreme Court. In an argument reminiscent of Florida's defense in *McLaughlin*, the state argued that the Fourteenth Amendment, an extension of the Freeman's Bureau Bill and the Civil Rights Act of 1866, did not cover intermarriage. Several quotations from the debates on those bills were included in the statement of jurisdiction. The statement went on to discuss the lengthy history of judicial decisions upholding the constitutionality of antimiscegenation statutes. Virginia cautioned against inquiry into the wisdom of the statutes, asserting that it was the realm of the legislature. The statement offered quotations from Rabbi Albert Gordon's book *Intermarriage: Interfaith, Interracial, Interethnic,* which advised against intermarriage (without ever suggesting it should be illegal) and referred to a number of sympathetic pseudoscientific texts. Returning to legalistic concerns, the state sought to limit the complaint to 20-58 (the evasion section) and 20-59 (the sentencing section) of the Virginia statute. The authors concluded that

> The Virginia statutes here under attack reflects [*sic*] a policy which has obtained in this Commonwealth for over two centuries and which still obtains in almost half of the fifty States of the Union. They have stood— compatably [*sic*] with the Fourteenth Amendment, though expressly attacked thereunder—since that Amendment was adopted. Under such circumstances, it is clear that the challenged enactments infringe no constitutional right of the appellant. Counsel for appellee submit therefore that the question upon which the decision of this cause depends is so unsubstantial as to obviate further argument.[1]

Once the Court had accepted jurisdiction, the state gathered its top jurists for the brief: attorney general Robert Y. Button and two assistants, Kenneth C. Patty and R. D. McIlwaine III, were put in charge of defending the state's racial purity. Fifty-two pages long, the brief made a number of arguments. First, it suggested that the Lovings had no right to question any section of the state statute other than 20-58 and 20-59, since only those sections had been used to convict them. The short shrift given to this argument seems to indicate the authors' awareness that the justices would construe the statute in its entirety.[2]

A major portion of the brief, twenty-two pages to be exact, was devoted to the argument that the Fourteenth Amendment was never intended to cover the question of interracial marriage. Rehashing the debates over the Freedmen's Bureau Bill and the Civil Rights Act of 1866, the attorneys argued that

> an analysis of the legislative history of the Fourteenth Amendment conclusively establishes the clear understanding—both of the legislators who framed and adopted the Amendment and the legislatures which ratified it—that the Fourteenth Amendment had no application whatever to the anti-miscegenation statutes of the various States and did not interfere in any way with the power of the States to adopt such statutes.[3]

The brief further asserted that the fact that the majority of states continued to keep and enforce their antimiscegenation laws as late as 1950

was dispositive of the issue. This section was followed by a lengthy reci-
tation of the case law supporting antimiscegenation legislation. Although
the authors recognized the existence of the *Perez* decision, they cited the
Naim opinion, which had taken pains to note that *Perez* was the product of a divided court. Not surprisingly, there was no mention of *Oyama*
or *Bridges*, nor of the myriad of repeals that followed *Perez*.[4]

Button and his colleagues proceeded to defend the rationale behind
the statute, but they did so with a striking lack of originality. Five pages
consisted of unedited quotes from the dissent in *Perez*, and although
other authorities were cited, another two pages consisted entirely of ex-
cerpts from Rabbi Gordon's book. After these lengthy quotations, the
Virginians concluded that the opposition's "scientific evidence is irrelevant to any proper area of judicial inquiry in the instant case, and that
the determination of the General Assembly of Virginia upon this matter should be left undisturbed by this Court."[5] Interestingly, the brief
requested that the justices distinguish between the wisdom and the constitutionality of the legislation, seemingly conceding that even they had
doubts about the former. Without indicating the authority from which
the statement was derived, they proclaimed that "[a]ny judicial inquiry
into the wisdom, propriety or desirability of preventing interracial alliances is utterly forbidden."[6]

Although defeated in his bid for reelection after the *Loving* case, Robert McIlwaine remained in politics as an aide to several Virginia governors before going into private practice.[7] Instrumental in fighting attempts
to desegregate Virginia schools in the 1950s, he never gave up the fight.
In 1978, he assisted Governor John Dalton in a dispute over desegregation of Virginia colleges. He was considered such a stalwart for segregation that his absence from a meeting on the issue was greeted as a shift
in Virginia's position.[8] It appears that McIlwaine's politics haven't strayed
far from his stance in 1967. In 1994 he was part of a coalition that supported Oliver North's senatorial campaign.[9]

Cohen and Hirschkop had four amicus briefs to back them, but Virginia had only one. Despite the fact that fifteen other states had antimiscegenation statutes, only North Carolina was willing to weigh in with a
brief defending the southern way of life. North Carolina's law was far
more lenient than Virginia's, prohibiting marriage between whites and
anyone with at least one-eighth Negro or American Indian blood. On the
other side, the state felt so strongly about the idea that the ban had been
incorporated into its constitution ten years after the end of the Civil War.

Such marriages were "infamous crimes" and declared void ab initio, with the unlucky couple subject to anywhere from four months to ten years in jail and the possibility of a fine. North Carolina had its own version of Virginia's "Pocahontas clause." It prohibited the Cherokee Indians of Robeson County, but no other tribe from any other county, from marrying anyone with one-eighth or more Negro blood.[10]

The North Carolina brief, a scant six pages, was submitted by attorney general T. W. Bruton and his deputy, Ralph Moody. The bulk of the brief was devoted to citing the laws of North Carolina. Briefly, however, the state argued that the "original understanding" of the Fourteenth Amendment showed that it was never intended to cover miscegenation. The brief went on to second the judicial authorities cited by the Virginia brief, without citing them separately. Lastly, Bruton and Moody argued that scientific arguments were not persuasive on either side, concluding with this somewhat peculiar quote regarding the scientific aspects of the case:

> This field is like expert witnesses in that you pay your money and take your choice. If a state feels like the life of its people is better protected by a policy of racial integrity as to both races, or for any other race for that matter, then it has the right to legislate in such field. The fact that the state's conclusions may differ from the conclusions of other groups should not affect the matter unless minority groups are entitled to preferential constitution privileges contrary to the judgment of the majority.[11]

The written work done, it was time for the representatives of the Lovings and the state to face off in front of the nine justices of the Supreme Court. Cohen and Hirschkop were neophytes at arguing in front of that august body, but backed by the national office of the ACLU and supported by the organizations involved in the amicus briefs, they hoped that the righteousness of their cause would help the justices overlook any rookie mistakes.

15

May It Please the Court

The motive for the act is found in the mortification he would suffer…from his friends here when they learned that he had been married and was living with a negro woman by whom he had three children, against the sentiment of almost the entire community and in violation of the public policy and laws of the state.
—Louisiana court ruling on a life insurance claim after a white man's suicide, 1912

*W*illiam Marutani and Donald Kramer were the only amicus brief authors who attended the oral arguments. Surprisingly, the Lovings chose not to attend. Their seats were taken by members of the lawyers' families. Hirschkop made the arrangements and remembers that his wife, Cohen's wife, their parents, their partner Bobby Hall[1] and his wife, and Arthur Berney attended the argument.[2] Berney, the academician, sat behind the lawyers who argued the case. He was unfamiliar with Supreme Court protocol, and a court officer had to instruct him to button his jacket.[3] Although Hirschkop does not remember his presence, William Zabel took an early morning train from New York to Washington to watch his first ever Supreme Court argument. In contrast to Berney, however, he knew in advance that he had to wear "appropriate attire."[4] The argument took more than two hours and actively involved almost every one of the justices. Covering the case, the *New York Times* noted that not one member of the Court appeared to consider the statute constitutionally valid.[5]

Hirschkop led off with his argument that the Virginia statute violated the equal protection clause of the Fourteenth Amendment. His opening statement referred to antimiscegenation statutes as "the most odious of the segregation laws and the slavery laws." He asked the Court to consider not just 20-58 and 20-59 but the entire section of laws proscribing interracial marriage, thus requesting that the Court view the whole question of whether a state could prohibit marriages on the basis of race. Almost immediately he was interrupted by a justice[6] who inquired how many states had such laws. Hirschkop noted that sixteen states, all southern and border, continued to ban interracial marriage, while Maryland had just repealed its three-hundred-year-old law. He added that bills to repeal the laws of Oklahoma and Missouri had recently failed.[7]

Proceeding with his equal protection argument, Hirschkop disputed the state's contention that antimiscegenation laws were promulgated for health and safety reasons, countering once again that they were nothing less than slavery laws. To prove his point, he went back in time to discuss the origins of the Virginia statute in the 1600s. The first act to touch on the issue dealt with whether offspring of a union between a black woman and a white man would be slave or free. Hirschkop noted that the state had no prohibition against producing such offspring, since the laws concerned themselves only with the purity of white women, not black women. Moreover, he noted that the state of Virginia had spent two centuries "trying to figure out who these people were that they were proscribing," with the definition of Negro fluctuating from a person with one-eighth Negro blood to one with one-fourth Negro blood to the present "'any traceable Negro blood,' a matter which we think defies any scientific explanation."[8]

Hirschkop continued by pointing out that the 1924 revision of the law had initially been called *A Bill to Preserve the Integrity of the White Race.* He reminded the justices that the law permitted all races to intermarry except with the white race. He went on to discuss the absurdities of laws in other states, noting that in South Carolina a Catawba Indian was considered white, while in North Carolina, a Cherokee Indian from Roanoke County was accorded that honor.[9] Hirschkop deemed the laws "ludicrous in their inception and equally ludicrous in their application." He cited a Missouri court's opinion that offspring of mixed marriages were sterile and a Georgia court's belief that they were effeminate as proof that the statutes were based on pseudoscience, at best. He cited the *Naim* court's reliance on preventing the "obliteration of racial pride" and Judge Bazile's pronouncement on the reason for separate continents. "We feel that the very basic wrong of these statutes is that they rob the Negro race of their dignity."

Hirschkop debunked the state's argument that the debates over the passage of the Fourteenth Amendment showed it was not meant to cover antimiscegenation laws. He noted that the state had not included any information about the Fourteenth Amendment debates, only the debates on the predecessor bills. However, the Fourteenth Amendment was much broader in scope than the Freedmen's Bureau Bill or the Civil Rights Act of 1866.[10]

Hirschkop concluded his section with an emotional plea:

> [W]e fail to see how any reasonable man can but conclude that these laws are slavery laws, were incepted to keep the slaves in their place, were pro- longed to keep the slaves in their place, and in truth the Virginia laws still view the Negro race as a slave race. These are the most odious laws to come before the Court. They rob the Negro race of its dignity, and only a decision which will reach the full body of these laws of the State of Vir- ginia will change that. We ask that the Court consider the full spectrum of these laws and not just the criminality, because it's more than the crimi- nality that's at point here. It's the legitimacy of children, the right to in- herit land, and many, many rights, and in reaching a decision we ask you to reach it on that basis.[11]

When Hirschkop sat down, it was Cohen's turn to handle the due pro- cess argument against which so many colleagues had cautioned him. He hadn't gone far before a Justice asked him whether a state should be al- lowed to forbid marriages between brothers and sisters. Cohen replied that states should indeed have the right to regulate in some way the ability of citizens to marry and divorce, citing the Court's decision in *Reynolds v. United States,* which had upheld a prohibition of polygamous mar- riages. He argued that since the Virginia statute made distinctions based on race, it was not within the state's purview. Again he was interrupted and asked whether he wasn't supposed to be arguing freedom to contract rather than any racial–equal protection issue. Cohen backpedaled sharply and tried to explain that he was arguing both points. The next question was whether a state could forbid first cousins from marrying one another if there was a large body of opinion that—and here the justice quoted Cohen's own argument—found the prohibition arbitrary and capricious. This analogy helped Cohen get back on track, explaining that it was the burden of the state to show the rationale for any given legislation and that in this case the state had not provided any such information.[12]

Finally, one of the justices got to the meat of Cohen's argument by asking why he had included the due process claim. Cohen then had the chance to articulate his fear that if the Court struck down the statutes on the sole grounds that they violated the equal protection clause, the state might simply enact a more specific statute that prohibited Malays from marrying anyone but Malays, Mongolians from marrying non-Mongolians, and so forth. When a justice expressed incredulity that a state could pass such legislation once the Court had found that antimiscegenation statutes violated the equal protection clause, Cohen agreed that equal protection was the Lovings' best argument. Nonetheless Cohen asked the Court to ensure that Virginia could not enact an "equal" antimiscegenation law by making its decision based on both clauses. He also noted that the Court would safeguard the civil rights of all Virginians if it struck down Virginia's requirement that people register their race.[13]

Before heading off to court, Cohen had asked the Lovings whether they had anything to tell the justices. Richard said only that the Court should know how much he loved his wife and how unfair he considered the situation. Before oral argument, Hirschkop and Cohen discussed whether they should quote him. Initially Hirschkop was reluctant, considering the quote too hokey.[14] He relented, however, and told Cohen to use his best judgment.[15] At this juncture in the argument, Cohen went to the heart of the matter.

> [N]o matter how we articulate this, no matter which theory of the due process clause, or which emphasis we attach to, no one can articulate it better than Richard Loving, when he said to me: "Mr. Cohen, tell the Court I love my wife, and it is just unfair that I can't live with her in Virginia." I think this very simple layman has a concept of fundamental fairness, and ordered liberty, that he can articulate as a bricklayer that we hope this Court has set out time and again in its decisions on the due process clause.[16]

Since Cohen had additional time, he quickly added to Hirschkop's discussion of the Fourteenth Amendment debates, then finished off with some rhetorical flair.

I ask this court, if the State is urging here that there is some State principle of theirs: What is it? What is the danger to the State of Virginia, of
interracial marriages? What is the state of the danger to the people of
interracial marriage?[17]

William Marutani was allowed a brief opportunity to present oral
argument. He recalls being pleased that Cohen had been able to push
aside some of the legal rhetoric and add a human dimension to the case.
Both he and Donald Kramer thought that the quote from Richard Loving was the most effective part of Cohen's argument.[18] Marutani took the
liberty of noting that, as a Nisei, he was perhaps one of very few in the
courtroom who could declare his race with some degree of certainty. He
observed that it was not always possible, given the history of Europe, for
those of European ancestry to do the same. Therefore, he argued, many
would have difficulty meeting the Virginia burden of whiteness, that is,
to have "no trace whatever of any blood other than Caucasian." In fact,
he noted that while Richard Loving had apparently admitted to being a
white person, he was probably incapable of swearing that he had only
Caucasian blood.[19]

Marutani argued that the Virginia law was vague and that there were
no such things as "pure races." He quoted the UNESCO statement on race
and noted that even as anthropologists rejected the notion of pure race,
clerks and deputy clerks in Virginia were charged with the task of determining whether an applicant for a marriage license was "of pure white
race." However, even assuming, arguendo, that the notion of pure races
was based in truth, laws designed to protect this notion would still be
unconstitutional.

For if the anti-miscegenation laws purport to preserve morphologic or
physical differences—that is, differences essentially in the shape of the
eyes, the size of noses, or the texture of hair, pigmentation of skin—such
differences are meaningless and neutral. They serve no proper legislative
purpose. To state the proposition itself is to expose the utter absurdity
of it.[20]

Marutani continued by noting that the aspiration to marriage was
common to all people. He cited *McLaughlin* for holding that it was unconstitutional to make such a basic human instinct a crime solely on the
basis of race. "We submit that 'race' as a factor has no proper place in state
laws governing whom a person, by mutual choice, may or may not

marry." Marutani called into question Virginia's stated goal of maintaining "purity of public morals, preservation of racial integrity as well as racial pride, and to prevent a mongrel breed of citizens," since the state only prevented white persons from marrying outside their racial boundaries. All others were free to "despoil" one another and "destroy their racial integrity, purity and pride." Clearly, Virginia's laws were based on the notion of the superiority of the white race.[21]

In the course of Marutani's argument, the chief justice asked him whether he thought antimiscegenation laws would be acceptable if all races were prohibited from marrying one another. Marutani does not believe that this was a serious question on Warren's part. Rather, he was trying to clarify the issues and bring them into the open. The question gave Marutani the opportunity to reiterate that the reason he had brought up the inconsistency in the Virginia law was to show its basis in theories of white supremacy; from there he noted that anthropologists could not agree on how many "races" there were on earth. Another question came from Justice Potter, who inquired whether Marutani believed that all restrictions on marriage (i.e., mental condition, consanguinity, etc.) should be removed. While not responding directly to the question, Marutani argued that the racial restrictions were supplementary to those Potter had mentioned and not of the same level.[22]

At the conclusion of Marutani's argument, Robert McIlwaine rose for the formidable task of defending the right of the state of Virginia to prohibit interracial marriages. He started by trying to ensure that the justices recognized only sections 20-58 and 20-59 as material to the Lovings' case. The justices showed how little they thought of this argument by immediately asking McIlwaine how he would respond to the equal protection argument given the nature of 20-54, which allowed persons with no more than one-sixteenth Indian blood and no black blood to marry whites but prohibited such unions if the person with Indian blood had a trace of black blood. McIlwaine conceded that he could find a number of constitutional objections to that section of the statute. Nevertheless, he gamely tried to explain away the statute by attesting to the small number of American Indians resident in the state, adding that the statute as written "covers all the dangers which Virginia has a right to apprehend from interracial marriage."[23]

Justice Harlan asked McIlwaine whether Virginia would recognize the marriage of a couple who had legally married in New York and moved to Virginia. McIlwaine admitted that the statute did not explicitly cover such exigencies. Under the full faith and credit clause, a marriage valid where celebrated was valid everywhere. McIlwaine believed, however, that given Virginia's strong policy against interracial marriage, the state would not recognize such a union.[24]

McIlwaine then moved directly into his attack on the Fourteenth Amendment arguments, insisting that this piece of legislation had not been meant to cover antimiscegenation laws. Arguing in the alternative, he stated that even if the Fourteenth Amendment did apply, the statute served a "legitimate legislative objective of preventing the sociological and psychological evils which attend interracial marriages." When pushed to reveal the source of his argument, McIlwaine conceded that the miscegenation debates in question were over the statutes preceding the Fourteenth Amendment, not the amendment itself. He hastened to add that the Fourteenth Amendment was merely an extension of the Freedmen's Bureau Bill and the Civil Rights Act of 1866.[25]

After droning on about the nineteenth-century debates, McIlwaine was asked how he distinguished the case at hand from *McLaughlin,* a case he had deftly avoided in his brief. McIlwaine first responded that the statutes in *McLaughlin* were "above and beyond, or extraneous to, the interracial marriage statutes." Then he postulated that in any event, *McLaughlin* had no bearing on the history of the Fourteenth Amendment. When reminded that *McLaughlin* had been decided on equal protection grounds, McIlwaine stubbornly stuck to his guns and repeated that "the power of the state to forbid interracial marriages, if we can get beyond the Fourteenth Amendment, can be justified on other grounds." When asked to be more specific, McIlwaine admitted that his argument boiled down to the claim that the legislative history of the Fourteenth Amendment put the question of antimiscegenation statutes outside the jurisdiction of the Supreme Court. He repeated his contention that no one who had studied the debates had ever suggested that the framers intended the Fourteenth Amendment to affect the power of the states to forbid racial intermarriage. McIlwaine was asked again to provide more detail. He said that the framers of the amendment believed that if blacks were forbidden to marry whites and whites forbidden to marry blacks, there was no violation of due process or equal protection. He reminded the justices that marriage was a matter that had been left to the states to regulate.[26]

After a brief recess, McIlwaine attempted to wrap up his legislative history argument, which had not been well received. He was asked whether, putting aside any legislative history, the Fourteenth Amendment had not been enacted to ensure that Negro citizens received the same rights as white ones. He conceded that this was true but attempted to argue that the statute in question treated both black and white equally by forbidding each from marrying the other. Perhaps perceiving the futility of this argument, McIlwaine tried at last to move away from the nineteenth century.

> It is clear from the most recent available evidence on the psycho-socio-logical aspect of this question that intermarried families are subjected to much greater pressures and problems than are those of the intramarried, and that the state's prohibition of racial intermarriage, for this reason, stands on the same footing as the prohibition of polygamous marriage, or incestuous marriage, or the prescription of minimum ages at which people may marry, and the prevention of the marriage of people who are mentally incompetent.[27]

Chief Justice Warren's youngest daughter was married to a Jewish man.[28] Warren told McIlwaine that some people felt the same way about interreligious marriages that the state felt about interracial ones; he asked whether the state could prohibit the former as well as the latter. McIlwaine replied that the evidence was stronger in favor of prohibiting interracial marriages. When Warren pressed him on whether he actually believed that statement, McIlwaine was forced to admit that he did not but that his information was gleaned from a book by Dr. Albert Gordon, whom he described rather redundantly as a Jewish rabbi. Honesty compelled him to note that Dr. Gordon had not advocated the prohibition of interracial marriages but had expressed his view, as a social scientist, that such unions were "definitely undesirable."[29]

This reference gave rise to one of the more absurd moments of the case, as one of the justices asked whether Rabbi Gordon was "Orthodox or Unorthodox." McIlwaine replied that he did not know whether Dr. Gordon was Orthodox, Conservative, or Reformed, but that he was more concerned with the doctor's scientific credentials. Another justice asked him whether it was really the interracial nature of marriages that caused the higher rate of divorce found by Dr. Gordon or whether the marriages were unsuccessful precisely because of the existence of laws against them. McIlwaine replied that it was the attitudes of society, not the existence of antimiscegenation laws, that created grave problems for the children of interracial unions. He quoted Dr. Gordon's suggestion that the children of interracial unions were also "the victims [and] martyrs of intermarried parents."[30]

When asked if Dr. Gordon alleged a difference in intelligence between the races, McIlwaine noted that he did not but added that such a judgment was beyond the range of Dr. Gordon's expertise. McIlwaine was then asked to discuss the UNESCO report on racial matters. He replied that the UNESCO report attested only to a lack of reliable evidence of the harmful consequences of intermarriage; at no point did UNESCO claim to have conclusive evidence that there were no harmful consequences. McIlwaine further noted that there had been dissenters to the UNESCO report, only to be acerbically told by one justice that there were probably scientists who disagreed with Dr. Gordon as well. After a great deal of give-and-take on the subject, McIlwaine tried to dodge the issue by quoting from his brief the reasoning that if the Court were to enter into the scientific debate, it would "find itself mired in a Serbonian bog of conflicting scientific opinion which . . . is sufficiently broad, sufficiently fluid, and sufficiently deep to swallow the entire Federal Judiciary."[31]

Getting back to the law, McIlwaine was asked whether he had any doubt that the statutes in question were based on the premise that the white race was superior to the "colored" one. McIlwaine conceded that this was the case with 20-54 but denied that it was true of the other sections of the law. After much hemming and hawing, he further conceded that the legislators who originally enacted the law had based the statute on notions of white supremacy. However, he maintained that the law had a different meaning in 1967. The Court wasn't buying that argument, and although McIlwaine tried to assert that the statute "works both ways," he was forced to admit that the motivation for the law came from the days and doctrine of slavery.[32]

Since McIlwaine persisted in saying that the statute worked equally against whites and blacks, a justice asked him why Virginia had no prohibition against blacks marrying Malays or Mongolians. McIlwaine danced around the issue and suggested that "the Virginia problem does not present any question of any social evil with which the legislature is obliged to deal resulting from interracial marriage between Negroes and Malays or whites and Malays, because there is no significant population distribution to that extent, in Virginia." When reminded that William Marutani had testified as to the presence of 1,750 Japanese in Virginia, McIlwaine replied that that number "does not present the probability of sufficient interracial marriage and sufficient difficulty for the legislature to be required to deal with it." That argument did not last long. "You mean, in principle, because there are only a few people of one race in

Virginia, that Virginia can say that they have no rights?" McIlwaine tried to wiggle out of this by replying that it wasn't a matter of their having no rights, it was "a matter of saying they do not present a problem." The justices weren't buying that and again asked if Japanese didn't have the same rights as the white race "to keep their race pure." McIlwaine could only respond again that the population was too small to present a problem. He tried valiantly to salvage his argument by pointing out that the Court had held that a statute could not be unconstitutional "simply because it does not reach every facet of the evil with which it might conceivably deal." He concluded that the legislation in question dealt with the "problems" that the state was more likely to face within its borders.[33]

Perhaps impressed by Marutani's frank discussion of his heritage, the Court continued its line of questioning and asked McIlwaine if one of the 1,750 Japanese in the state wouldn't feel demeaned by the statute. Still splitting hairs, McIlwaine replied that they would not because there was no prohibition on Japanese marrying anyone under 20-58 and 20-59. He tried desperately to separate these from 20-54, the portion of the statute that did include Japanese and, as another judicial question brought up, American Indians. Since McIlwaine was obviously trying to disavow any connection to 20-54, the Court asked whether that section had ever been declared unconstitutional. When he replied that it had not, he was asked how it could be separated from the other sections of the law. McIlwaine feebly replied that 20-54 had originated in the 1920s, whereas 20-58 and 20-59 were carryovers from the original law in the 1600s.[34]

At this point, one of the justices cut through McIlwaine's argument by asking whether all sections of the statute weren't designed to make it illegal for two groups to marry. While conceding this point, McIlwaine continued to insist that justices not consider the heinous 20-54. Again he was asked about the hypothetical interracial New York couple who moved to Virginia. Perhaps he had had the opportunity to review his notes, for now McIlwaine stated definitively that the state would dissolve such a marriage without a decree of divorce and would consider the parties to be living in a state of adultery, fornication, or illicit cohabitation that, he hurriedly added, was a mere misdemeanor under Virginia law.[35]

Trying to dodge the line of questioning, McIlwaine pushed to conclude by citing the string of "scientific" evidence the dissenting judge had relied on in *Perez*. One mistake he made was an attempt to cite Harvey Applebaum's recent law review article on antimiscegenation statutes.[36] Since this article was also cited prominently by Cohen and Hirschkop, the justices immediately demanded to know Applebaum's view of mis-cegenation in terms of Fourteenth Amendment rights. McIlwaine erro-neously claimed that Applebaum argued both sides of the question.[37]

In a second attempt to conclude his argument, McIlwaine harped on the fact that in 1956 the majority of states had had antimiscegenation statutes and sixteen states continued to have such laws. The last statement may have been a mistake, because he was immediately asked whether these were the states that had had school segregation laws. McIlwaine claimed that a number of them were not but was unable to enumerate the states that did not have such an overlap, possibly because there were none. Therefore he fell back on the assertion that other states had previously banned intermarriage without segregating their school systems. This, too, backfired when he was forced to admit that those states had all repealed their miscegenation statutes. McIlwaine stressed that the decision to re-peal a statute was the right of each individual state and that judicial no-tice should accordingly be given to Virginia's choice not to do so.[38]

Before McIlwaine could sit down, he had to handle one more difficult question. He was asked to put aside his historical argument on the Four-teenth Amendment and rationalize the continued existence of antimisce-genation statutes after the decision in *Brown.* He handled this problem as the Virginia court had in *Naim,* arguing that education was "fundamental to good citizenship" but marriage was not. Although humans had a right to marry, McIlwaine argued that the state could infringe on that right if there was "valid scientific evidence" to do so, as the Court had done with polygamous marriages in *Reynolds.* When informed that this argument was essentially the same as that made by the defendants in *Brown,* McIlwaine gamely asserted that the statute was based not on notions of inferior versus superior races but on the children of interracial unions being harmed by their status and that the divorce rates for interracial marriages were high.[39]

After McIlwaine sat down, Cohen rose for his rebuttal. Having heard McIlwaine practically concede the unconstitutionality of 20-54, he now reiterated the need to link all portions of the statute together. He noted that 20-58 could not exist without 20-54, which is the only section of the Virginia Code to define a white person. He added that although 20-54 was a restatement of an earlier statute, the Racial Integrity Act of 1924 was a single act, composed of ten sections, including 20-54. He repeated his argument against McIlwaine's interpretation of the Fourteenth Amend-ment debates but conceded upon questioning that there were those who disagreed with this perspective. However, he noted that it would have been very easy for the framers of the Fourteenth Amendment to include the simple phrase "excluding anti-miscegenation statutes" if they had wished to do so. Cohen gently chided McIlwaine for deeming the "problems" entailed by intermarriage between other races negligible, noting that this was the first case involving a black-white marriage to go through the Virginia courts. The handful of prior cases had all concerned Malaysians or Filipinos.[40]

Cohen once again humanized the case for the justices as he insisted on the need to include 20-54 in their deliberations.

> [What is] the right of Richard and Mildred Loving to wake up in the morning, or go to sleep at night, knowing that the sheriff will not be knocking on their door or shining a light in their face in the privacy of their bedroom, for "illicit cohabitation"—if 58 and 59 are found unconstitutional, and 54 is allowed to remain on the books, that is precisely what can happen.[41]

> It will be an exact repetition of what, in fact, did happen to them. And this Court will not have given the Lovings the relief they require. The Lovings have the right to go to sleep at night, knowing that should they not awake in the morning their children will have the right to inherit from them, under intestacy. They have the right to be secure in knowing that if they go to sleep and do not wake in the morning, that one of them, a survivor of them, has the right to social security benefits. All of these are denied to them, and they will not be denied to them if the whole anti-miscegenation scheme of Virginia, Sections 20-50 through 20-60 are found unconstitutional.[42]

As a coup de grâce, Cohen added a quotation from the state's oft-cited Rabbi Gordon that Virginia had neglected to use.

> Our democracy would soon be defeated if any group on the American scene was required to cut itself off from contact with persons of other religions or races. The segregation of any group, religious or racial, either voluntarily or involuntarily, is unthinkable and even dangerous to the body politic.[43]

Cohen then strove to sum up his argument.

> Now Virginia stands here today, and in this *Loving* case, for the first time, tries to find a justification other than white racial supremacy for the ex-

istence of its statute. Mr. McIlwaine is quite right that this is a current-day justification; not the justification of the framers. On the one hand, I see a little dilemma here. He asks that the Court look to the intent of the framers of the Fourteenth Amendment, but to ignore the framers of the 1924 Act to Preserve Racial Integrity in Virginia. It is not a dilemma I would like to be in.[44]

Cohen was gently chided that he was in the same dilemma, since he wanted to take into consideration the legislative history of the Virginia statute but not that of the Fourteenth Amendment. Cohen disagreed, reminding the justices that his interpretation of the Fourteenth Amendment debates was very different from that of the state. He argued that he relied on the legislative history of both acts. Further, he noted that the state was the inconsistent body, on the one hand saying that the number of Malaysians in the state was too small to constitute a problem and on the other hand prohibiting marriages between them and white people in section 20-54. He further disputed the state's contention that a New York interracial couple moving to Virginia would not be prosecuted for a felony, given 20-59's assurance that any white person intermarrying with a colored person would be guilty of a felony and subject to one to five years imprisonment. He ended by urging the Court not to get caught up in "the morass of sociological evidence" but simply to decide the case on the basis of the equal protection and due process clauses of the Fourteenth Amendment.[45]

Phil Hirschkop must have cringed at that remark, since he was the one who had instigated meetings with Ashley Montagu in Princeton and the head of the psychiatric unit at Children's Hospital in Washington. However, at that point, all he felt was relief that the argument was over.[46] There was nothing to do but wait.

16

The Supreme Court Speaks

The moment the bar of absolute separation is thrown down in the South, that moment the bloom of her spirit is blighted forever, the promise of her destiny is annulled, the proud fabric of her future slips into dust and ashes. No other conceivable disaster that might befall the South could, for an instant, compare with such miscegenation within her borders. Flood and fire, fever and famine and the sword—even ignorance, indolence and carpet-baggery—she may endure and conquer while her blood remains pure; but once taint the well-spring of her life, and all is lost—even honour itself.

—Tulane professor William Benjamin Smith, 1905

*T*welve years after *Naim* and three years after *McLaughlin*, the Supreme Court was finally ready to render a decision on antimiscegenation statutes. The bench consisted of Chief Justice Earl Warren and Justices Hugo Black, William Douglas, Tom Clark, John Harlan, William Brennan, Potter Stewart, Byron White, and Abe Fortas. They had voted unanimously to hear the appeal.[1] Finally it appeared that the justices were not grasping at straws for a way to avoid the question.[2]

They delivered a unanimous opinion on June 12, 1967. Richard Loving had been alerted the previous day that the Court would be rendering its

decision. After years of fighting, he had little faith in the system and proceeded to try—unsuccessfully—to get drunk.[3]

Earl Warren was not going to let *Loving* follow the fate of *Naim*. He
assigned the case to himself and gave his law clerk, Benno Schmidt, the
task of writing the first draft.[4] Initially the draft held that the Virginia law
was unconstitutional on two counts: it discriminated on the basis of race
and it unreasonably interfered with the right to marry. To ensure that
these points were fully understood, Warren asked Schmidt to include the
racist diatribe of Judge Bazile in the opinion. Justice Black disagreed with
the second point on the grounds that the right to marry is not explicitly
written in the Constitution, and he believed that no "natural law notion"
belonged in the opinion. Warren toned down that section but refused to
give up all references to substantive due process.[5]

Justice Warren took judicial note of the fact that sixteen states continued both to prohibit and to punish marriages solely on the basis of the
race of the parties. He stated that the laws in question dated back to the
colonial era and were an outgrowth of slavery. Noting that the Virginia
court in *Naim* had stated that the purpose of the laws was to "preserve the
racial integrity" of Virginians and to prevent "the corruption of blood," as
well as "the obliteration of racial pride," he found these arguments to be
"obviously an endorsement of the doctrine of white supremacy." While
Warren recognized that marriage had always been subject to state regulation, he remarked that there was nothing to suggest that state discretion would be unlimited.[6]

Justice Warren gave due credit to the concurrence in *McLaughlin*,
noting that "[i]ndeed, two members of this Court have already stated that
they 'cannot conceive of a valid legislative purpose . . . which makes the
color of a person's skin the test of whether his conduct is criminal.'"[7]

> This case presents a constitutional question never addressed by this
> Court: whether a statutory scheme adopted by the State of Virginia to
> prevent marriages between persons solely on the basis of racial classifi-
> cations violates the Equal Protection and Due Process Clauses of the
> Fourteenth Amendment. For reasons which seem to us to reflect the cen-
> tral meaning of those constitutional commands, we conclude that these
> statutes cannot stand consistently with the Fourteenth Amendment. . . .
>
> Because we reject the notion that the mere "equal application" of a
> statute containing racial classifications is enough to remove the classifi-
> cations from the Fourteenth Amendment's proscription of all invidious

racial discriminations, we do not accept the State's contention that these statutes should be upheld if there is any possible basis for concluding that they serve a rational purpose. . . .

We have consistently denied the constitutionality of measures which restrict the rights of citizens on account of race. There can be no doubt that restricting the freedom to marry solely because of racial classifications violates the central meaning of the Equal Protection Clause.

The State argues that statements in the Thirty-ninth Congress about the time of the passage of the Fourteenth Amendment indicate that the Framers did not intend the Amendment to make unconstitutional state miscegenation laws. . . . We have rejected the proposition.

There can be no question but that Virginia's miscegenation statutes rest solely upon distinctions drawn according to race. The statutes proscribe generally accepted conduct if engaged in by members of different races. Over the years, this Court has consistently repudiated "distinctions between citizens solely because of their ancestry" as being "odious to a free people whose institutions are founded upon the doctrine of equality." . . . The fact that Virginia law only prohibits interracial marriages involving white persons demonstrates that the racial classifications must stand on their own justification, as measures designed to maintain White Supremacy.

These statutes also deprive the Lovings of liberty without due process of law in violation of the Due Process Clause of the Fourteenth Amendment.

The freedom to marry has long been recognized as one of the vital personal rights essential to the orderly pursuit of happiness by free men. . . .

To deny this fundamental freedom on so unsupportable a basis as the racial classifications embodied in these statutes, classifications so directly subversive of the principle of equality at the heart of the Fourteenth Amendment, is surely to deprive all the State's citizens of liberty without due process of law. The Fourteenth Amendment requires that the freedom of choice to marry not be restricted by invidious racial discriminations. Under our Constitution, the freedom to marry, or not marry, a person of another race resides with the individual and cannot be infringed by the State.

These convictions must be reversed. It is so ordered.[8]

The Lovings did not attend any of the oral arguments, but they did drive from their farmhouse near Bowling Green to Alexandria for the news conference at Cohen and Hirschkop's office. Even that small public step was one that they did not make readily. It took a lot of convincing to persuade the pair to come to the press conference.[9] Not much for sound bites, Richard could only say was that "[w]e're just really overjoyed," while Mildred said, "I feel free now." She admitted that the case had been "a great burden" but averred that she never doubted the Court would rule in their favor. Richard had not been so sure but confided that if the Court had not ruled in his favor he would have tried filing suit again in another five years. Both assured reporters that they had not encountered any hostility from their neighbors during the court battle and had no animus toward the state for prosecuting them.[10]

As for future plans, Richard said that he intended to build a new house for the family.[11] Nine years and ten days of fugitive marriage were over. When asked about their children, then ages six through eight and apparently unaware of their parents' legal ordeal (which made them bastards by law), Richard said, "I think I'd leave [whom to marry] up to them. . . . Let them decide for themselves." In as bubbly a statement as he was capable of making, Richard said of Mildred, "it feels so great, but it's hard to believe. I still don't believe it. For the first time I can put my arms around her and publicly call her my wife." At thirty-three and twenty-seven, with three children in tow, the Lovings could finally embark upon the life they wanted: legally married in the state of Virginia.[12] They never bothered to read the decision that changed their lives.[13]

At the victory press conference, Bernie Cohen drew attention to the bigger picture by saying, "We hope we have put to rest the last vestiges of racial discrimination that were supported by the law in Virginia and all over the country."[14] The NAACP Legal Defense Fund attorneys who had faced the Court three years earlier felt great pride at the verdict. William Coleman says that he believes that the Fund's victory three years earlier in *McLaughlin* paved the way for *Loving.*[15] Lou Pollak goes a step further, confessing that he always felt that the *Loving* team had an easy case because the *McLaughlin* team had done all the hard work.[16]

One memory that Hirschkop carries with him is Mildred Loving giving him a big hug at the press conference. The gesture surprised him because she was usually not very expressive. "You don't always feel the benefit of your work directly like that."[17] Hirschkop's fondest memory of the entire case is more mundane than any of the esoteric legal theories. He remembers that his father, then living in Florida and now deceased, sat in the audience beaming up at him. Afterward, Cohen took a picture of the two of them together on the steps of the Supreme Court. To this day, that picture sits on his desk.[18]

All of the attorneys involved thought that there was a good chance the Lovings would emerge victorious. For the most part, however, they were pleasantly surprised at the breadth of the verdict and the fact that it was a unanimous decision. Most believed that in 1967 it was simply not possible for the Court to find laws against interracial marriage valid. They were right about the Supreme Court, but unfortunately this progressive decision was adopted with some reluctance. While it did not meet the "massive resistance" that greeted *Brown,* not all states believed that the *Loving* decision applied to them. Litigation over antimiscegenation laws was far from over.

Part Four

The Aftermath

17

Not All States Listen

Draw a dead line between the races. Tell the negro when he crosses it the penalty is death. Tell the white man, when he crosses it the penitentiary is there. Arrest this incipient miscegenation. . . . Teach the white man the dignity of his race! Teach our sons the degradation of this crime; that it is practical social equality and in its most horrible form.

—Judge Thomas Norwood, 1907

*T*he Supreme Court's ruling that antimiscegenation laws were unconstitutional did not send states scurrying to remove the laws from their books or interracial couples rushing out for marriage licenses. Even though the case was based there, Virginia did not immediately eliminate its statutory prohibitions. The intermarriage ban was repealed in 1968, but it took until 1975 for the state to rid itself of laws defining the races and requiring that racial identification be included on documents like divorce decrees.[1] Phil Hirschkop, soon to cross racial boundaries himself with a bride of Korean descent,[2] was incensed to find that Virginia clerks continued to hand out to prospective brides and grooms pamphlets that contained information about the newly invalidated statutes. At his request, the attorney general ruled that the pamphlet entitled

Virginia Marriage Requirements be reprinted without the odious reference to miscegenation.[3]

With such dawdling in its home state, it should not be surprising that the *Loving* decision spawned only a small and grudging acceptance of intermarriage in the other recalcitrant states. It was necessary for federal courts to order compliance with *Loving* in Delaware two weeks after the decision[4] and in Little Rock, Arkansas, one year later.[5] Arkansas repealed a statute requiring donated blood to be labeled by race in 1969 but did not remove its statutory penalties for intermarriage and interracial cohabitation until 1973.[6] It took until 1974 for Delaware to remove the antimiscegenation provisions from its statutes. Even then, removal was done by omission, without any formal repeal.[7]

In early 1968, Florida's supreme court granted a writ of mandamus ordering the Dade County clerk to issue a license to an interracial couple. Even this writ was not a unanimous decision, with two of the seven judges dissenting. One of the dissenters was Millard Caldwell, sticking to his guns from the *McLaughlin* case.[8] Florida repealed its antimiscegenation laws in stages in 1968 and 1969,[9] a year that also saw the repeal of Oklahoma's statute.[10] Louisiana declared its antimiscegenation law unconstitutional in 1967 and repealed its statutes in pieces from 1972 to 1975.[11]

Missouri, Texas, and West Virginia were fairly quick to react to the *Loving* decision, repealing their statutes in 1969. North Carolina followed in 1970, first by changing its constitution and then, in 1973, by eliminating all statutory prohibitions except for the requirement of racial identification on marriage certificates. South Carolina gradually removed its statutory prohibitions in 1970 and 1972 after a 1969 ruling by the attorney general, but article 3, section 33 of the South Carolina constitution continued to prohibit the intermarriage of persons with more than one-eighth Negro blood to whites until 1998. Nebraska repealed its requirement for racial classifications on marriage licenses in 1971, while Indiana waited until 1977 to take that step. Only in 1974 did Kentucky see fit to remove the stigma of illegitimacy from the issue of interracial marriages by making such marriages legal. For its part, Georgia let 1975 arrive before repealing an act authorizing the attorney general to institute criminal proceedings against parents of racially mixed children and calling for the attorney general's impeachment if she or he refused to do so.[12]

Perhaps one reason why states were so slow to repeal their statutes was the *Loving* decision's failure to incite a rush on town clerks by interracial couples. Nonetheless, less than two months after the decision, Roman Howard Johnson and Leona Eve Boyd were married in a Jehovah's Witness ceremony in Norfolk, Virginia.[13] The *Richmond Times-Dispatch* printed the news, calling the pair the "first known partners to an interracial marriage in Virginia" since the *Loving* decision.[14] Within a year, a ceremony with significantly more pomp and circumstance took place when Peter Edelman, a white lawyer who had clerked for Supreme Court Justice Frankfurter and worked on the Robert Kennedy senatorial campaign, married Marian Wright, the first black woman to be admitted to the Mississippi bar and an aide to the Reverend Martin Luther King Jr. The *New York Times* covered the affair with a six-column story and a three-column photo. Aside from two paragraphs noting that the wedding could not have taken place the previous year, the story ran like a typical society wedding announcement, complete with descriptions of the bride's dress, the music, and the prominent guests who attended.[15]

Both Virginia ceremonies were quiet affairs compared with the first post-*Loving* interracial marriage in Tennessee. Herman McDaniel and Joyce Prescott headed to the altar in July 1967. The county clerk initially refused their request for a license, only to be informed by the attorney general that they were legally entitled to wed. Troubled by rumors that the White Citizens' Council would obstruct their efforts, the couple brought their attorney, Robert Lillard, with them when they went to the courthouse in their second attempt to obtain a license. That step completed without incident, they searched the building for a judge to perform the ceremony.[16]

Through each step of the journey, more and more onlookers attached themselves to the wedding party. This entourage proved useful when no judge could be found: a black Baptist minister in the crowd named David Vaughn offered his services. He had left home without his Bible, but yet another bystander was able to procure one for him. It was badly worn and the back was missing, but it was sufficient for the job. During the delay, a television crew arrived. The ceremony was not interrupted, but as the happy couple walked hand in hand across the street, the hapless clerk came running after them. It seems that in the excitement of granting a license to such an exotic couple, the clerk had forgotten to charge the usual six-dollar fee. Alas, the union reached an unhappy conclusion. All the publicity given to the couple prompted a review of their records, whereupon authorities discovered that the groom had three marriage licenses to his name and no evidence of either divorce or the death of his first two wives, both of whom were black. He was indicted for bigamy and sentenced to two years in jail.[17] Six years later, in 1973, Tennessee repealed one statute that defined a person of color and another that prohibited a child of color from inheriting from his or her mother's husband unless he was also "colored." Tennessee would not formally repeal its antimiscegenation statute until 1978, after voters approved a measure to do so by a slim 199,000-to-191,000 margin.[18]

Mississippi was another state that did not immediately embrace the *Loving* decision. Although the state saw one interracial marriage performed without fanfare, the second and third attempts set off a flurry of publicity and civil actions that made the McDaniel-Prescott affair seem ordinary by comparison.

18

"A Big Interracial Display
of Their Romance"

God wanted the white people to live alone. And He wanted colored people to live alone....We do not believe that God wants us to live together....Do you know that some people want Negroes to live with white people? These people want us to be unhappy. They say we must go to school together. They say we must swim together and use the bathroom together. God has made us different. And God knows best. Did you know that our country will grow weak if we mix?
——Mississippi textbook for third and fourth graders in the 1950s

*T*o the surprise of no one, Mississippi was one of the slowest states to comply with the edict of the Supreme Court. The days of states' rights were clearly not forgotten. In his autobiography, Charles Evers writes that the hardest thing he had to do as the first black mayor of Fayette, Mississippi, was fire his white city attorney "for breaking the miscegenation law" when she married Monroe Jenkins, a black police officer. The year was 1969. Men had walked on the moon, the Mets had won a World Series, and the *Loving* decision was two-and-a-half years old. Evers, who also reports that the love of *his* life was a white woman (whom he kept out of Mississippi), claims that he fired Martha Wood for "public safety." It was the overtness of her relationship with Jenkins that bothered him. "I don't care if you're slipping around together, but you can't live together in Fayette."[1] A mixed couple was finally able to marry in Mississippi in July 1970, but that successful union did not mark a general lifting of all barriers. Later that month, two interracial couples applied for marriage licenses and were shocked by the response.[2]

Roger Mills was a white law student from Indiana, and Berta Linson was a black college student from a rural section of southern Mississippi. A conscientious objector, Mills was working for Anderson and Banks, a Jackson, Mississippi, law firm, as alternate service to the draft. With one year of law school behind him, he assisted in the firm's work on behalf of the national office of the Rights of the Indigent. Linson worked part-time in the office as a file clerk. Both were twenty-four years old. Linson had one daughter from her first marriage, which had ended in divorce.

Vernon Davis was a Mississippi-born black factory worker and Noreen Leary was a white Massachusetts-born community education extension service worker. Davis was thirty years old and divorced, while Leary was twenty-four and had never been married. Arriving separately on the same day and without knowledge of each other, both couples went to circuit clerk H. T. "Bubba" Ashford in Jackson to apply for marriage licenses. They expected to come back after the three-day waiting period to find them signed and ready. They were wrong.[3]

When Mills and Linson[4] applied for their license, the Hinds County courthouse was hosting a voter registration drive that was being monitored by a white supremacist group called the Southern National Party (SNP). Mills suspects that the group caught wind of the license application and swung into gear to prevent the wedding.[5] Under the guidance of its attorney, Elmore Greaves, the SNP and its leader, John D. Cummings, filed a petition for a writ of mandamus to prevent Ashford from issuing the licenses. They quoted the Mississippi constitution at section 263, which indicated that "the marriage of a white person with a negro or mulatto, or person who shall have one-eighth or more negro blood, shall be unlawful and void." Additionally, the Mississippi annotated code prohibited the marriage of "white persons and negros." Therefore "the issuance of licenses for marriage to the above named couples or any other couples of mixed race, would be a clear and papable [sic] violation of the Constitution and Statute of the State of Mississippi, and ought, therefore, to be strictly prohibited." The SNP asked the court to issue a restraining order to prevent Ashford from issuing the licenses in question or any future interracial licenses.[6]

Although the SNP filed its motion in Hinds County, no judge was available, so they traveled 110 miles to nearby Granada County. Lawrence Ross, one of the many attorneys who became involved in the case, remembers that the Hinds County judge was considered a moderate but Judge Marshall Perry of Granada was "the most notorious racist" jurist in the state.[7] Another local attorney, Constance Slaughter-Harvey, believes that Perry may even have volunteered to hear the case.[8] Current Mississippi Supreme Court judge Fred Banks recalls that Perry always treated black attorneys very poorly.[9] Yet another of the myriad of lawyers involved in the case, Armand Derfner, referred to him as "Lunatic Perry" and noted that even in Mississippi, no "sane judge" would have issued the restraining order.[10] Perry granted the writ, and Ashford was enjoined from giving either couple a license unless he could show cause why the writ should not have been issued. Blissfully unaware of the SNP's machinations, the two couples received a rude awakening when they went to get their licenses on July 23, 1970.[11]

At this point, some of the best legal minds in Mississippi leaped into action, free of charge. Davis and Leary had planned to wed immediately upon getting their license, while Mills and Linson had a large wedding planned for August 2, with guests flying in from as far away as Massachusetts. By the time the couples had gone through the various court battles, six different attorneys from three different offices had entered the fray. Technically, James Abram and Lawrence Ross of the Lawyers' Committee for Civil Rights under Law represented Leary and Davis, while Fred Banks of Anderson and Banks and Armand Derfner, John Maxey, and Hermel Johnson of the Lawyer's Constitutional Defense Committee (LCDC) represented Mills and Linson. In reality, the six combined their efforts in a hectic march through a variety of state and federal courts. It was immediately apparent that, due to the short time frame, the couples would need to file parallel federal and state appeals. Different attorneys concentrated on separate court actions but maintained good communication throughout the ordeal.[12]

Fred Banks recalls that the three groups of lawyers were also in close physical proximity to one another. The LCDC was across the street from Anderson and Banks, while the Lawyers' Committee was just down the road. Anderson and Banks had started out their legal careers in a branch office of the NAACP Legal Defense Fund. Although they were no longer an official Fund office, they continued to practice civil rights law as they made the transition to private practice.[13]

The first legal move[14] was to file a bill for injunction with the chancery court (a court of equity) of the first judicial district of Hinds County, asking that the two licenses be issued. The couples argued that Judge Perry's order "denies to complainants the right to marry, to not be discriminated against on the basis of race, and to the equal protection of the laws guaranteed by the Constitution of the United States." Further, they argued that the order was invalid, since it was based on sections of the Mississippi constitution and code that were clearly unconstitutional. Lastly, they argued that Cummings and the SNP had had no standing to apply for the order, since they were not "interested parties" as required by the Mississippi Code. The bill for injunction argued that the petitioners would be "gravely and irreparably injured if said marriage licenses do not issue immediately." They asked for a temporary injunction ordering Ashford to issue the licenses.[15]

Additionally, the attorneys filed papers in the circuit court of Hinds County to request that the restraining order be set aside. Maxey did the lion's share of the work, and he and Banks presented Judge Leon Hendrick with the papers. Maxey recalls that Hendrick seemed offended by their presence. Although he agreed to hear the case, he refused to act with the expediency requested by the petitioners, ordering briefs to be presented by both sides no later than July 31, with a ruling to be granted the week of August 3. Since Mills and Linson were expecting two hundred guests for their August 2 wedding, this solution was clearly unacceptable.[16]

Judge W. T. Horton, the chancellor of Hinds County, denied the bill for injunction on the grounds that an adequate remedy existed at law (in circuit court). With the equity court deferring to the circuit court and the latter refusing to act expeditiously, the lawyers hastily penned a remedial writ that they presented to Chief Justice William Etheridge of the state supreme court on July 24. Although as a general rule, federal courts in the South were more liberal than state courts, this one was an exception. The road to federal court would have to go through Judge Harold Cox, a notorious racist. Therefore, the team of lawyers decided to continue the appeal through the state system before going to federal court. In an informal hearing, they asked Etheridge to hear the matter no later than July 28. Much to Mills's surprise, Etheridge declined to do so, replying that the case was pending in circuit court and did not warrant state supreme court interference. Besides, the court was in recess until September.[17]

Although the team of lawyers was a cohesive unit, there had been some minor squabbling regarding the best route of appeal. Maxey, a native Mississippian, believed that it was best to go through the state courts, particularly given the comparatively progressive leanings of Etheridge. Ross and Derfner wanted to go straight to the federal courts. Convening with Derfner in the lobby after talking with Etheridge in his chambers, Maxey was forced to admit that the couples would not get timely relief in state court. They returned to Etheridge's chambers and asked him to deny their request for relief rather than delay ruling, so that they could head directly to federal court. On behalf of the exasperated couples, Armand Derfner applied to Justice Hugo Black of the U.S. Supreme Court for a motion to stay the injunction. As expected, the Supreme Court declined to issue the motion pending a determination as to whether the district court would grant relief. The couples ended up petitioning the jurist least likely to appreciate their plight: district court judge Harold Cox.[18]

Judge Cox, although appointed by President Kennedy, had shown himself in prior decisions to be decidedly hostile to civil rights causes.[19] The team filed papers with Judge Cox first thing in the morning on Tuesday, July 28. Cox claimed that, due to a prior commitment at a naturalization ceremony, he would not be able to hear the case until Thursday afternoon. Derfner believed that no matter what Cox decided, his decision would not be a timely one: a decision in favor of Mills and Linson would be issued too late for them to pick up the license, and one against them would be too late to file an appeal. Fully aware of Cox's antagonism to civil rights concerns, Derfner had prepared a notice of appeal even before he visited the judge's chambers. Upon learning that Cox would not hear the case in a timely manner, Derfner and Maxey requested a written order that they could appeal. Derfner promptly called a friend in New Orleans and dictated the appeal for immediate filing. Within hours, the appeals court had forced Judge Cox's hand, and he scheduled the case for the following morning at nine AM.[20]

Meanwhile, the case was still pending in state circuit court, but a decision there would have come too late for Mills and Linson to treat their guests to a legal wedding ceremony. Technically, Cox could have waited for the state court's action,[21] but the Fifth Circuit's words must have rung loudly in his ears.[22] The court proceedings were not without their unpleasant moments. Linson, Leary, and Davis, apparently tired of the litigation, did not attend the hearing. The Mississippi attorney general put Mills on the stand and subjected him to questions about his and Linson's sexual activities.[23] Since interracial sex was a criminal offense in Mississippi, he tried to establish that the couple was already having sexual relations. Mills and Linson had given the same address on their marriage application, but Mills showed that they had listed different apartments in the same building and were thus not engaged in illicit cohabitation.[24]

Three of the four interested parties may have missed the proceedings, but Ashford appeared and told Cox that, having found that the Supreme Court was clear on the issue, he would have issued the licenses but for the restraining order. Ashford's attorney, Weaver Grove, seemed less sure, complaining to Cox that he did not think the latter had the right to issue an injunction while the matter was still pending in state court. He feared that such an order would lead to his client's following the federal court in contempt of the state court. Cox indicated that he agreed with Grove but that the Fifth Circuit had directed him to rule.[25]

It must have pained Judge Cox to write that the law "is so perfectly clear that any delay in granting such licenses . . . would be unwarranted and indefensible. . . . The fact that the parties are of different races is no bar."[26] Cox did not go so far as to call the Mississippi code and constitution sections unconstitutional, but he did order that the licenses be issued. The order came in the nick of time, just two hours before the clerk's office was due to close for the weekend.[27] A disgusted Greaves was quoted as saying that the federal courts had "made it perfectly clear the Sovereign state of Mississippi is nothing but a conquered province to be humiliated at will."[28] In addition to his reputation for racism, Cox was also renowned for his nastiness,[29] so it is not surprising that he managed to slip some snide comments about the soon-to-be newlyweds into his decision.

> The plaintiffs (at least one of the couples) have planned a big interracial display of their romance in a big church wedding to be attended by many guests from within and outside of Mississippi. It may be very well doubted that any irreparable injury would be done either of these couples by a more orderly and deferential disposition of this matter here with more judicial orderliness and respect for our brethren on the state bench to whom this matter has been submitted and where it is now pending. This court has no disposition to shirk, or evade its duty here regardless of the nature of the case, but does not approve of inordinate haste in the disposition of any case where judicial priorities are cast to the winds on such a flimsy pretext as presented here.[30]

On August 2, 1970, Mills and Linson were married by a white Presbyterian minister in a black Methodist church in front of two hundred guests. The Reverend Rims Barber, himself a civil rights activist, called the event "a marriage born in the movement."[31] That a mixed-race couple had married in Mississippi was such big news that it made the front page of the *New York Times*.[32] As if the pressure from white racists hadn't been enough, the couple was faced with the fact that a black separatist group, the Republic of New Africa, had rented the church at the same time that the wedding rehearsal was supposed to take place. Facing off against the fatigue-wearing, pistol-packing separatists, the wedding party worked out a truce that allowed it to use the sanctuary while the Republic took the back meeting rooms.[33]

Almost twenty years later, the *Jackson Clarion-Ledger/Daily News* revisited the couple on the occasion of Mississippi's belated removal of its constitutional ban on interracial marriages in 1987. A picture of the pair with their three children graced the front page of the magazine section. Mills stated that he was proud of the state for having "shaken off a legacy of the past." Although the vote to remove the ban was only 52 percent in favor, Mills said he was not troubled by the 48 percent who voted against it. The article quoted an unrepentant Greaves as saying that race mixing was "very deleterious to white civilization. . . . [T]his is a white country, was founded by white people and was meant to stay that way.[34]

Today, Roger Mills is an attorney for the Office for Civil Rights of the U.S. Department of Education in Atlanta, a job he has held since 1984.[35] However, civil rights is more than a job for him: it's a way of life. Mills is probably best known in the state of Georgia for his twenty-year drive to integrate the schools of DeKalb County, as well for his role in starting the county's majority-to-minority school transfer system.[36] The desegregation suit against the county had originally been filed in 1968, but after the plaintiffs graduated, it lay dormant for a while. In 1975 Mills moved to the area and became one of the lead plaintiffs when he sought to admit Princess, Linson's daughter from her first marriage, into a desegregated school.[37] This battle was one that Mills did not win. The case was the first in which the Supreme Court ruled to end a desegregation order despite the fact that segregation still existed. The decision may have been aided by the intervention of the United States, represented by a little-known attorney by the name of Kenneth Starr, on behalf of the County.[38] In keeping with his trend of not avoiding potentially inflammatory situations, Mills joined a 1987 march in Forsythe County, Georgia, that became an occasion for Ku Klux Klan violence.[39]

Greaves, the founder of the SNP,[40] never wavered in his beliefs. In 1970 he contributed a letter to the editorial page of the *Jackson Daily News* chastising the Fifth Circuit for its decision in the Mills case.[41] A week after Greaves's letter was published, he and Judge Perry were touted as potential candidates for the governorship.[42] While mulling over the thought, Greaves took the opportunity to take three already-declared candidates to task for their stance against racism. He wrote that "[t]he whole modern field of race science and genetics points unequivocally to the conclusion that such an assumption—of the inherent racial superiority of the white races—can be made." He challenged the declared candidates to clarify whether they believed in white superiority or racial equality and whether they believed "in working towards the goal of mongrelized people, a multiracial, heterogenous population and society"[43]

While declining a try for the governor's seat, Greaves did run for the number two slot in 1971, announcing his candidacy "with the resolute belief that a determined political stand must now be made for the advancement of the South and for the fundamental rights of the oppressed Anglo-Saxons." He proposed that all public schools and universities teach mandatory courses in "race science."[44] Greaves finished well behind the two runoff candidates, who were described by the *New York Times* as "racial moderates."[45]

Greaves never did give up the fight. Years later, he paid for an advertisement in the *Clarion-Ledger* to announce his resignation from the Agricultural and Industrial Board of Governor Cliff Finch and to complain that Finch had done nothing for "white conservatives" but had put "hordes of blacks in government jobs."[46] The year was 1978, but Greaves did not seem to notice. He took Finch to task for dancing "with adult negro men" on Medgar Evers Day "while singing that anti-white hymnal of hate, 'We Shall Overcome.'" Two years later, still the Mississippi spokesperson for the SNP, Greaves paid for another advertisement in the *Clarion Ledger*. Slowly losing his grip on reality, Greaves ranted that the SNP was the only logical choice in the upcoming Reagan-Carter election, accusing both major parties of failing to benefit "the great white race which alone created America and which alone can preserve it."[47]

It took Marshall Perry longer than Greaves to answer the siren song of politics, but eventually he declared his candidacy for governor. Perry's main issue was a proposal to place public schools under local control and resegregate them. He also pledged to use "a political offensive" to reverse integration on a national level. He proposed to "wage an aggressive fight, hopefully in cooperation with other Southern governors, for the Southern Way of Life as we traditionally understand it."[48] He too finished well behind the runoff candidates.[49]

Despite the happy union of Linson and Mills,[50] and presumably also that of Leary and Davis, Mississippi did not drop its statutory antimiscegenation statutes until April 1972.[51] Nor did it repeal its constitutional prohibition until 1987, after voters narrowly chose to do so.[52] Unfortunately, the Mills-Linson case was not the last battle over antimiscegenation legislation. Alabama and Georgia still presented problems that forced the federal government, after decades of inaction, to act on behalf of the right to marry across racial lines.

19

The Feds Finally Step In

Gentlemen and ladies … walking arm in arm with blacks in the public streets of the city! The insult to the people could not be resisted. … The blackened and prostrate walls of that splendid edifice, were a fearful example of the effects of the doctrine of amalgamation forced upon people.
—sponsor of an 1841 Pennsylvania antimiscegenation bill, blaming the burning of Pennsylvania Hall three years earlier on the specter of interracial liaisons

Alabama was another state that did not move with alacrity to sanction interracial unions. In November 1970, a white Fort McClellan–based Army sergeant named Louis Voyer requested a license to marry his black fiancée, Phyllis Bett. Calhoun County probate judge C. Clyde Brittain refused on the grounds that Alabama law still made it a felony for such a pair to marry and a misdemeanor for a judge to issue a license.[1]

In a surprising turn of events, the U.S. Army intervened on behalf of Sgt. Voyer. Army officials asked the Justice Department to file suit in federal court in Birmingham seeking issuance of the requested license, as well as a ruling on the constitutionality of Alabama's constitutional and statutory antimiscegenation provisions. Fifteen years after David Carliner had requested assistance from the solicitor general's office, the United States was finally taking a stance against antimiscegenation laws.[2]

The case took a junior attorney at the Department of Justice, M. Karl Shurtliff, by surprise. A judge advocate general (JAG) officer called from Fort McClellan and told him the facts. Shurtliff was working in the public accommodations and public facilities section of the civil rights division and thought that the case fit in perfectly. His supervisor, Walter Gorman, agreed that the case was actionable, so Shurtliff drafted a proposed complaint and temporary restraining order on behalf of the United States, alleging that a marriage license was a public facility.[3]

In 1970 the field of civil rights was still so highly charged that the U.S. Attorney General himself had to sign the justification letters that accompanied such cases. Due to his junior status, Shurtliff was not invited to the meeting with John Mitchell, the Attorney General at that time. Word came back to him that Mitchell had agreed that the denial of the license was terrible and found it appropriate that the division expend resources to ensure that Alabama adhered to the Supreme Court's decision in *Loving*. However, Mitchell believed that public facilities were too broad a scope and wanted a complaint filed on narrower grounds. He asked Shurtliff to come up with another tactic that would achieve the same result. Shurtliff and the assistant section chief came up with the theory that Alabama's antimiscegenation laws interfered with the military. They redrafted the justification letter in those terms. Mitchell approved of the reasoning and signed the letter. Shurtliff concedes that the military interference tactic "wasn't a real theory but a theory to get us there."[4]

Shurtliff drafted a temporary restraining order and flew to Birmingham with the papers in hand. The U.S. attorney for Alabama, Wayne Sherrer, signed the papers without pause. Judge Sam Pointer told the lawyers that in adherence to the local rule, he would not issue the temporary restraining order without a hearing, but he scheduled a hearing far more expeditiously than the parties expected—the following Monday or Tuesday. Shurtliff sent out all the required notices, but to his horror, when he got to the hearing, Voyer and Bett informed him that they had spent the weekend in Tennessee getting married. Shurtliff and his team feared that the case would now be considered moot.[5]

Assistant attorney general J. V. Price represented the state of Alabama. Shurtliff isn't sure whether Price was really a "true believer" in the state's position, although he thinks such was the case. The United States was represented by Shurtliff, Gorman, and Sherrer. The plaintiff's team advised the court that the principals were already married. The state argued that the case was moot, but the federal government took the position that the individual marriage did not obviate the larger issue of whether the refusal to issue a license interfered with military procedure. The judge agreed that the individual marriage was only one aspect of the case and allowed the hearing to continue.

Shurtliff remembers that he called two witnesses from the probate office, both of whom testified that they had denied the request for a license. Voyer and Bett had no recollection either of who had turned them down or of the person's gender. As a result, two clerks, one male and one female, testified that they had refused the Voyer-Bett request on the basis of the pair's different races. Shurtliff thinks that each clerk honestly believed that she or he had been the licensor on duty that day, since there was nothing to be gained by lying. Shurtliff also put the newly wed couple on the stand to establish their residency, their intent (a fait accompli) to marry, and Voyer's position in the military. The JAG officer, a white northerner who was new to the Army, was also present.

Shurtliff does not recall the state's calling any witnesses and believes that the hearing lasted less than an hour and twenty minutes.[6]

Assistant attorney general Price insisted that the Supreme Court decision was binding on the state of Virginia only, claiming that "[t]hey don't just wipe these laws off the book all over the United States because of one ruling." This novel argument unsurprisingly received scant consideration from Judge Pointer, who noted that "the unconstitutionality of these miscegenation laws cannot be seriously questioned by any trained in the law."[7] Deliberating for only a few hours, Pointer ordered Alabama officials to comply with the Supreme Court ruling in *Loving*.[8]

Shurtliff stresses that John Mitchell's desire for an argument narrower than his initial public facilities brief was not due to any racism on Mitchell's part. "He wasn't trying to escape responsibility; it was good lawyering." Shurtliff concedes that the case would have been a more volatile one had the team used the public facilities approach, but he does not think that the Justice Department would have paid less attention to the case or that Judge Pointer would have ruled differently on that account.[9]

After leaving the Department of Justice, Shurtliff returned to his home state of Idaho and was appointed by the governor to the public utilities commission. Two years later, President Carter appointed him U.S. attorney for the state. Shurtliff sat on the state education board from 1990 to

1994, serving as vice president in 1991 and president in 1992 and 1993.[10] Described as the most outspoken board member,[11] as "colorful but outgoing,"[12] and as a loose cannon with original, offbeat thinking,[13] Shurtliff made a number of enemies during his time on the board of education.[14] Today, he is in private practice, performing a variety of civil and criminal work.[15] Like Shurtliff, Walter Gorman used his position in the Department of Justice as a springboard. He became the deputy chief of the general litigation section of the civil rights division of the Department and later acting chief of the housing and enforcement section of that division. Tiring of life in Washington, Gorman returned to his native Rhode Island in 1987 when an old college friend was elected attorney general. He became deputy attorney general and in 1993 accepted the position of district court judge for Rhode Island.[16]

Although Louis Voyer and Phyllis Bett had difficulty obtaining a license, no such trouble befell Johnny L. Ford shortly thereafter, when he and Frances Baldwin Rainer—he black and she white—secured an Alabama license for their nuptials. And two years later, there was still no visible protest when Ford was elected the first black mayor of Tuskegee, Alabama.[17] That same year, the legislature finally got around to following up on the *Brittain* decision by repealing the antimiscegenation statute from the Alabama Code.[18]

In February 1972, the Justice Department came down with a bad case of déjà vu. The Department filed suit against the state of Georgia when another probate judge, H. W. Roberts, refused to provide a marriage license to a soldier, stationed at Fort Benning, and his fiancée. Karl Shurtliff was also involved in this intervention. He recalls that the situation arose in the same way that *Brittain* did. He was alone in the office one morning when a JAG officer called to report a problem. The differences in this case were that the groom was a black officer and the bride was white. Shurtliff assured the officer that he had just handled a similar case. He checked the Georgia statute and simply substituted names, dates, and places in the *Brittain* brief. It took only one day to draft the appropriate documents. Approval by those in the chain of command was nearly "automatic," so the next morning, Shurtliff was on a plane to Atlanta.[19]

The reception that Shurtliff received from the Georgia U.S. attorney could not have been more different from Wayne Sherrer's response.[20] When told the purpose of Shurtliff's visit, the attorney put both hands on his head and cried, "This will cost us Georgia." As Shurtliff wryly recalls, this fear of a Republican loss in the upcoming 1972 presidential

election was ludicrous, since George McGovern, the Democratic oppo-
nent to President Nixon, was unlikely to carry the state in any event.
Shurtliff had arrived in Atlanta fairly early in the morning but was forced
to wait for hours in a spare office while the U.S. attorney called everyone he knew in Washington for assistance in avoiding the issue. By the
time the U.S. attorney recognized that he had no choice but to file, it was
too late in the afternoon to reach a judge. Shurtliff learned an important
lesson from that case. Henceforth, even for day trips, he would always
carry a clean shirt and a toothbrush.[21]

In the meantime, the attorney general of Georgia had been notified, and
the next morning, all three parties met with Judge Henderson and his clerk
in the judge's chambers. The U.S. attorney was still unhappy about being
involved in the case. Henderson looked at the order and, to Shurtliff's great
pleasure, asked, "Why can't I just sign the order? There's no question about
this being improper and unconstitutional." The attorney general "kind of
hemmed and hawed" and said that he hated to stipulate that the constitution of Georgia was unconstitutional. Henderson replied, "Why not? It *is*
unconstitutional." Eventually, the parties reached an agreement to tailor
the order so that no further action was necessary, although the state of
Georgia never quite conceded that they were wrong. No hearing was required, and Shurtliff never met the prospective bride and groom. The U.S.
attorney's concession did not, as he had feared, cost the Republican party
the state of Georgia, which it won handily in the 1972 election.[22] Despite
the clear case law, a probate judge wrote to the Georgia attorney general
as late as 1983 to inquire whether he could refuse to perform a marriage
for a mixed-race couple. He was told that he could not.[23]

The Deep South wasn't the only area of recalcitrance. Two magistrates
in Winston-Salem, North Carolina, refused to marry an interracial couple
in 1977, citing "deeply felt religious and personal beliefs against such
marriages."[24] Local pockets of resistance may well have endured into the
1980s. However, the public record offers no further striking examples of
clerks or judges refusing to grant licenses to interracial couples. The
Georgia case appears to mark the last time that judicial intervention was
needed to ensure a couple's right to unite in matrimony. Slightly more
than three hundred years after the passage of the first antimiscegenation
law, interracial couples across the nation were free to wed without fear
of legal sanctions.

Unfortunately, not all states rushed to take official steps to recognize
the legality of interracial marriages. One of the last holdout states was

South Carolina, which removed the antimiscegenation ban from its constitution in 1998. When the South Carolina House finally decided to allow voters to determine whether to remove the antimiscegenation provision, the vote was ninety-nine to four in favor of the proposal. Twenty lawmakers skipped the vote: one representative estimated that among that group were at least fifteen lawmakers who opposed the repeal.[25]

Two who opposed the law but chose to let the voters decide were Democrat Olin Phillips and Republican Lanny Littlejohn. Phillips called his opposition to intermarriage his "hard-shell religious belief." He admitted that he was particularly mystified by white women marrying black men. "Is it the athletics in Blacks? Or is it just curiosity?" The year was 1998, so Phillips explicitly denied that he was a white supremacist. However, he based his opposition to the bill on his belief in the sanctity of the white race. Littlejohn recognized that there were no legal barriers to intermarriage, "[b]ut to come out and pass a bill removing the ban is taking it one step too far." Harkening back to Judge Bazile, Littlejohn denounced interracial marriage as contrary to "the way God meant it. He does create races of people and He did that for a reason. From the beginning he set the races apart." Larry Koon, who had served in the House since 1975, was one of the four Republican dissenters. He argued that since animals of different species do not breed with one another, humans should likewise abstain.[26]

The successful bill on whether to remove the antimiscegenation provision was proposed from an unlikely quarter. In many ways, Representative Brad Jordan is a typical conservative white Republican lawmaker. He is a member of the evangelical men's group Promise Keepers[27] and aligns himself with the Christian Coalition.[28] On the last day of the legislative session, Jordan was "dumbfounded" when his seatmate (who later voted against the repeal bill) showed him that the state constitution contained an antimiscegenation provision. He approached Curtis Inabinett, a black Democrat, for assistance in proposing a bill to repeal the "cruel and hateful" provision.

Still smarting from a defeat in his earlier attempt to draft such legislation, Inabinett told Jordan that he should recruit other white representatives to bolster their case. Half an hour later, Jordan had a list of nineteen sponsors, almost evenly split between white and black. With two hours to spare, the bill was placed on the docket.[29] Although Democrats outnumbered Republicans, the proposal was a bipartisan effort. One of the Democrats involved in proposing the bill was Cordell Maddox, a lawyer by trade, who recognized that while the provision carried no legal weight, it was a potentially volatile issue.[30]

When South Carolina voters were given the chance to condemn the state's constitutional antimiscegenation provision to the dustbin, the vote was hardly overwhelming. Thirty-eight percent of the voters wanted to keep the section in the constitution. In only three counties did more than seventy percent of the population support the repeal, whereas six counties had a majority of voters registering their approval of the century-old ban.[31] These numbers belie the fact that South Carolina currently has one of the highest rates of racial intermarriage in the United States. Although less than 1 percent of Americans cross racial lines to marry, 4 percent of South Carolinians have done so.[32]

The last holdout was the state of Alabama. As the twentieth century came to a close, Article IV, Section 102 of the Alabama Constitution continued to read, "The legislature shall never pass any law to authorize or legalize any marriage between any white person and a negro, or a descendant of a negro." Although a small note underneath indicated that "[t]his section is violative of the Fourteenth Amendment to the Constitution of this Country," the section still stood until the year 2000. In April 1999, Democratic representative Alvin Holmes introduced a bill to repeal the turn-of-the-century provision. He was immediately followed by George Clay, who introduced an identical bill in the senate. While a biracial coalition of Democratic senators proposed a similar bill, it was the Holmes bill that passed unanimously without any debate on the floor of either house.[33] In 2000, Alabama voters finally had the option of removing this blot from their constitution. Representative Holmes, a twenty-four-year Democratic veteran of the House, reported that the bill, though symbolic, was also necessary because probate judges still tried to avoid giving licenses to interracial couples.[34] The bill, known as Article 2, received virtually no press. There were no billboards for or against it, no yard signs, no bumper stickers, and no marches. Although most politicians ignored the bill, the attorney general came out in favor of Article 2 and the governor announced that a failure to pass the bill would "send the wrong message to the corporate world."[35]

Opposition to Article 2 did exist. It was spearheaded by Michael Chappell of the Confederate Heritage political action group. Chappell actually filed suit to stop the vote, but the election took place before a court heard his request. Chappell did not even have wholesale support of local Confederate groups or the Southern Party, most of whom only felt that it was unnecessary to repeal an unenforceable law.[36] Despite this view, the Southern Party devoted a significant portion of its Web site to urging citizens to vote against the repeal.[37] In September 2000, two polls showed that 64 percent and 53 percent, respectively, of Alabamans favored removal of the ban.[38] The final result was between those two figures. Roughly 60 percent of those voting believed that the provision should be eradicated, leaving approximately 526,000 voters in favor of retaining the archaic provision.[39]

20

Happily Ever After

Western Civilization, with all its might and glory, would never have achieved all its greatness without the directing hand of God and the creative genius of the white race. Any effort to destroy the race by a mixture of black blood is an effort to destroy civilization.
> —Robert Patterson, columnist for the Council of Conservative Citizens, 1998

I feel free now," said Mildred, when told of the Supreme Court decision. The previous few years had been a difficult existence. Now a burden had been lifted.[1] Facing the cameras in a short-sleeved, blue-flowered dress at the press conference hastily called to celebrate the verdict, Mildred truly looked as though a burden had been lifted. Richard, clad in an open-necked button-down white shirt, looked as though the conference was just one more ordeal that he had to go through. With his ruddy face and crew cut, he appeared profoundly uncomfortable, barely opening his mouth to answer questions.[2] The truth is that left to his own devices, Richard would never have attended the conference, but Mildred had persuaded him to make an appearance after she herself had been convinced by Phil Hirschkop of the importance of the occasion.[3] Grudgingly, Richard told reporters that the hardest thing he had had to endure was leaving his home. In what may have been the only disagreement between the two, Mildred shook her head and said that the hardest part for her had been going to jail.[4] As soon as they could, the couple moved back to Central Point, where Richard built a simple, cinder-block house just up the street from both of their parents, on Passing Road.[5]

It would be gratifying to conclude that Mildred and Richard lived happily ever after, but that was not the case. While the couple was living in neighboring King and Queen County, a cross was burned in the yard of Mildred's mother. Mildred assumes it was meant for her. Another cross burning took place on the couple's lawn shortly after their initial return to Caroline County. The reception in general was not openly hostile,[6] despite a local law enforcement official's belief that public sentiment was opposed to the marriage.[7] The young couple simply blended in with their neighbors and were accepted as such.[8] Despite a four-page photo spread in *Life* magazine, the Lovings did not court publicity. As interest in the couple died down, Mildred gratefully acknowledged that "it was a relief just to have it over with."[9]

Less than a month after the Lovings' fourteenth anniversary and slightly more than eight years after they had earned the right to live as husband and wife in Virginia, Richard was killed. The couple and Mildred's sister Garnet were returning from a visit with friends when their car was broadsided by a drunk driver who had run a stop sign on route 721 in Caroline County, just thirteen miles from their home. Richard, forty-two, died instantly, Mildred lost her right eye, and Garnet suffered minor injuries. There was a tremendous outpouring of sympathy from the community for this woman who, not so long before, had been an exile from the state.[10] Bernie Cohen, who continues to serve as Mildred's attorney, filed a civil suit against the driver, whom the state also charged with drunk driving and manslaughter.[11] Richard is buried in a mostly black graveyard just outside the local Baptist church.[12] Even in death, he refused to be bound by the laws of segregation. Next to Richard's grave is the final resting place of the couple's son Donald, who died unexpectedly in 1994. One of Mildred's grandchildren prepared a traditional Rappahan-nock service for his funeral.[13]

Today Mildred Loving is still, in the words of her friend, Professor Robert Pratt, "intensely shy and uncomfortable with accolades or recognition." The truth is that neither she nor Richard ever wanted publicity. They simply wanted to live together in the quiet town where they were raised. Their case, while not imprinted in the public's mind as firmly as other civil rights decisions, still attracts notice, and June of years ending in *2* or *7* generally finds a few members of the media making their way to Central Point to commemorate the anniversary of the case. More and more reluctant to give interviews as time progresses, Mildred had to be persuaded by Bernie Cohen to cooperate with the crew of the Showtime movie that would later prod me to write this book.[14] She did allow a camera crew to videotape an interview with her and her three children for an addendum to *Mr. and Mrs. Loving.* Looking younger than her years, with bangs, shoulder-length hair, and no wrinkles, Mildred seemed at peace with her existence.[15]

In 1992, in one of the last interviews she granted, Mildred stated her belief that she and Richard were put on this earth in order to be married and change the law.[16] Since then, with the exception of providing assistance in filming the movie, she has declined to open up her life to outsiders. Mildred did make two exceptions. In 1998, a ten-year-old biracial girl from North Carolina rented the movie *Mr. and Mrs. Loving* and was affected by a profound desire to meet the woman who had challenged the law. After sending a number of unanswered letters, young Brittany Houser persuaded her mother, Leslie, to drive her to Virginia to meet her idol. Her gumption did not go unrewarded. Mildred Loving answered the door, and the two have become fast friends.[17] Perhaps this positive experience caused Mildred to change her mind and allow me to visit her the following year. After initially declining to speak to me, Mildred relented when Bernie Cohen called her to report that I was visiting Virginia and had just lunched with him. Mildred's family is a close-knit one. Her children are as tight-lipped as she and rarely speak to anyone from the press. Peggy, the youngest, is considered the family spokesperson.

The hues of the children run the gamut between those of Mildred and Richard. Peggy is the spitting image of her father, with straight, light brown hair and light skin. Donald was a shade darker, with wavy hair parted down the middle: a perfect blend of both parents. He was the only one of the children to show traces of his mother's Native American heritage. Sidney, who uses his mother's last name, is the darkest of the three and has the most African features.[18] Sidney lived in a nearby town until his recent marriage to young Brittany Houser's aunt,[19] as did Donald before his death. When Peggy separated from her husband, she and two of her three children temporarily moved back in with Mildred.[20] Family drifts in and out of Mildred's house. An ailing brother currently resides with her. During my visit, Peggy brought groceries, while one of Mildred's eight grandchildren mowed her lawn. The generation that remembers the Washington ordeal, however, is fading away. Mildred's sister Garnet lost her husband Raymond Hill a few years back, and subsequently Garnet herself died of cancer.[21] The cousin who talked Mildred into writing to the attorney general died in 1999, before Mildred had a chance to visit her in her new home in New Jersey.[22]

Mildred rarely travels far from Central Point. She spends most of her time in the simple cinder-block dwelling her late husband built many years ago, no more than a mile and a half from the house the sheriff invaded back in 1958.[23] With the money she received from the movie based on her life, she has added white aluminum siding and tidy black shutters to the exterior.[24] The house has a little deck looking toward the fields out back, but Mildred can often be found in her kitchen, where she has a view past her bird feeders to the fields and forests across the road. Mildred has never worked outside the home. Richard did not want her to do so when he was alive, and now her children don't want her to have to start a new life. Her arthritis is so severe that her fingers are turned out, and she can no longer write, a hardship that must be painful for someone who once had beautiful penmanship. Her nonfunctional right eye waters, sometimes forcing her to hold a tissue to it, which may contribute to her reluctance to grant interviews. She spends most of her time at home with her family, in a house filled with pictures of loved ones.[25]

In 1967 Bernie Cohen and Phil Hirschkop separated from the firm of Lainoff and Cohen and formed their own four-person law partnership, which lasted until 1971. Although Hirschkop represented Mildred's brother in a small auto accident case, it is Cohen who has remained her attorney over the years. Hirschkop sends her Christmas cards, but Cohen and his wife occasionally visit her at her home. Mildred was delighted to learn that in February 1999, Cohen became a grandfather.[26]

Cohen and Hirschkop continue to practice law three blocks from one another in Alexandria. Cohen is starting the process of retiring from the five-person partnership that shares a small brick building just off the main Alexandria shopping and dining street. The clutter of his first-floor office betrays the fact that he is trying to leave the business, as visitors encounter files bundled up, in preparation for being stored away for good. In June 1998, he was working on only three or four open tort cases, while consulting with other lawyers on one or two medical malpractice cases. He was looking forward to rest and relaxation.[27] Cohen's walls are covered with diplomas and certificates. He has been honored by the ACLU, the League of Women Voters, the Virginia Trial Lawyers, and the American Association of Trial Lawyers, among others. In contrast to the easily recognizable plaques and framed honors are two cryptic pictures hanging over Cohen's desk. They are magnified photographs of scotch pine needles damaged by pollution. Cohen represented a Christmas tree grower in suing the polluter. He is amused that a Jewish lawyer should have been placed in such a position.[28]

Subsequent to the Loving case, Hirschkop found himself in an even more unlikely position for someone of the Jewish faith. He defended the rights of members of the American Nazi party to wear swastikas on their armbands when they buried their leader, George Lincoln Rockwell, a veteran, at Arlington National Cemetery. Hirschkop's parents did not speak to him for a year, but he saw the case as a classic free-speech issue. Today Hirschkop works out of a brownstone for a firm that bears only his name. A visitor to his second-floor office with its bay windows, lace curtains, and hanging snake plant would be surprised by the smiling, rolled-up shirtsleeves vision of "Hirschkop the Horrible." His office bears witness to years of political involvement. A framed photograph of William Kunstler hangs prominently, while a sash with the colors and style of the Viet Cong flag and "legal" written across the yellow star—a testament to his days with Mobe and the Mayday Collective—dangles across a bookshelf. In contrast, two miniature stuffed koalas swing from the cords of his desk lamp, a stuffed orangutan reclines on one of the many comfortable chairs, and Willie, a long-haired cat with a heart condition, basks peacefully in the middle of the desk, gently fluttering his tail, bearing witness to the fact that Hirschkop's major pro bono work these days is for People for the Ethical Treatment of Animals. After having been a member of the ACLU national board for twenty years, Hirschkop has given up administrative work but continues to be involved with the organization.[29]

Even now, in the twenty-first century, there are still those who believe that Richard and Mildred committed an act that should have remained illegal. In 1991, 20 percent of the white people interviewed stated that they believed that interracial marriage should be proscribed by law. While this is an improvement over the 40 percent who thought so in 1972, the numbers are still disturbing.[30]

One person who still believes in the validity of antimiscegenation laws is Garnett Brooks, the sheriff who arrested the Lovings. Brooks still resides in Central Point, not far from Mildred's home. Interviewed in 1992, he did not apologize for the arrest, stating that he was acting in accordance with the law at that time. Brooks went further than that, however, expressing his belief that antimiscegenation laws should still be on the books.

"I don't think a white person should marry a black person. . . . The Lord made sparrows and robins, not to mix with one another."[31] Apparently quotes like that have gotten Brooks in trouble. When I called him, he declined to answer questions. "Whenever I talk to anyone, they write it all down and it stirs up the black people here in Caroline County." Brooks noted that the black population was "kind of settled down" when I called him in February 1998 and that he liked it that way. "I'm seventy-five years old, and I don't like to go through that stuff. It's all in the past."[32] Brooks has recently undergone open-heart surgery, an ordeal that at least one local law enforcement official thought might make him reconsider some of his views. It didn't, and former deputy sheriff Edwards describes Brooks as being "at the bottom of the totem pole as a human being."[33] When local historian Stan Beason tried to muster support for the erection of a monument to Richard and Mildred in the Bowling Green square, Brooks allegedly went to town with a gun and threatened to shoot Beason for attempting to honor the pair.[34]

It's been more than forty years since Brooks arrested Mildred, and they have not spoken since, despite their living in such close proximity. Brooks, like former attorney general Robert McIlwaine, professes not to have thought about the case since the decision came down. McIlwaine describes the case as "a footnote to history" that nobody remembers.[35] There may be a perfectly good reason why neither McIlwaine nor Brooks chooses to recall the case. After the Supreme Court decision, both were defeated in their bids for reelection.[36] Local commentators credit the man who replaced Brooks with bringing racial harmony to Caroline County.[37]

Mildred has never been able to accept the celebrity status people accord her. As far as she is concerned, the case was thrown into her lap; it was not something she chose to do. She sees herself as "an ordinary black woman who fell in love with an ordinary white man."

> We weren't bothering anyone, and if we hurt some people's feelings, that was just too bad. All we ever wanted to do was get married because we loved one another. Some people will never change, but that's their problem, not mine. I married the only man I ever loved, and I'm happy for the time we had together. For me, that was enough.[38]

Although she may not seek recognition, Mildred still receives attention for her role in changing the law. She was recently honored with a human rights award by St. Steven's Baptist Church in Central Point, where the preacher compared her to Rosa Parks. Mildred characteristically disagrees with the comparison. "What happened, we really didn't intend for it to happen. What we wanted, we wanted to come home."[39]

Nevertheless, Mildred acknowledges the wide-ranging effects of her case, noting that young people assume today that "if someone loves someone they have a right to marry." She knows that not everyone approves of mixed-race unions, but "[e]ven if they don't like it, it's nothing they can do about it. If they don't like it, tough luck."[40]

Appendixes
Notes
Bibliography
Index

Appendix A

Virginia's Racial Integrity Statute (as it stood when the Lovings were arrested)

SECTION 1-14. Every person in whom there is ascertainable any Negro blood shall be deemed and taken to be a colored person, and every person not a colored person having one-fourth or more of American Indian blood shall be deemed an American Indian; except that members of Indian tribes living on reservations allotted them by the Commonwealth of Virginia having one-fourth or more of Indian blood and less than one-sixteenth of Negro blood shall be deemed tribal Indians so long as they are domiciled on such reservations. (Initially passed in 1887 and revised in 1930 and 1940)

SECTION 20-50. The State Registrar of Vital Statistics may prepare a form whereon the racial composition of any individual, as Caucasian, Negro, Mongolian, American Indian, Asiatic Indian, Malay, or any mixture thereof, or any other non-Caucasic strains, and if there be any mixture, then the racial composition of the parents and other ancestors, in so far as ascertainable, so as to show in what generation such mixture occurred, may be certified by such individual, which form shall be known as a registration certificate. (1924, 1942)

SECTION 20-51. It shall be a felony for any person willfully or knowingly to make a registration certificate false as to color or race. (Such an act was punishable by one year in penitentiary. 1924, 1942)

SECTION 20-53. No marriage license shall be granted until the clerk, or deputy clerk has reasonable assurance that the statements as to color of both man and woman are correct. If there is reasonable cause to disbelieve that applicants are of pure white race, when that fact is stated, the clerk or deputy clerk shall withhold the granting of the license until satisfactory proof is produced that both applicants are white persons as provided for in this chapter. The clerk shall use the same care to assure himself that both applicants are colored, when that fact is claimed. (1924, 1942)

From Pauli Murray, ed., *States' Laws on Race and Color* (Athens, GA: Women's Division of Christian Service, 1950), 463, 478–79.

SECTION 20-54. For the purpose of this chapter, the term white persons shall apply only to such person as has no trace whatever of any blood other than Caucasian; but persons who have one-sixteenth or less of the American Indian and have no other non-Caucasic blood shall be deemed to be white persons. It shall hereafter be unlawful for any white person in this State to marry any save a white person, or a person with no admixture of blood than white and American. (1924, 1942)

SECTION 20-57. All marriages between a white person and a colored person shall be absolutely void, without any decree of divorce or other legal process. (1887, 1919, 1942)

SECTION 20-58. If any white person and colored person shall go out of this State for the purpose of being married, and with the intention of returning, and be married out of it, and afterwards return to and reside in it, cohabiting as man and wife, they shall be punished as provided in 20-59, and the marriage shall be governed by the same law as if it had been solemnized in this State. The fact of their habitation here as man and wife shall be evidence of their marriage. (1887, 1919, 1942)

SECTION 20-59. If any white person shall intermarry with a colored person, or any colored person intermarry with a white person, he shall be guilty of a felony and shall be punished by confinement in the penitentiary for not less than one nor more than five years. (1887, 1919, 1942)

SECTION 20-60. If any person perform the ceremony of marriage between a white person and a colored person, he shall forfeit 200 dollars of which the informer shall have half. (1887, 1919, 1942)

Appendix B

Florida's Antimiscegenation Laws

Florida's Statutes and Constitutional Section Referred to in *McLaughlin*

SECTION 798.05. Any negro man and white woman, or any white man and negro woman, who are not married to each other, who shall habitually live in and occupy in the nighttime the same room shall each be punished by imprisonment not exceeding twelve months, or by fine not exceeding five hundred dollars.

SECTION 798.02. If any man and woman, not being married to each other, lewdly and lasciviously associate and cohabit together, or if any man or woman, married or unmarried, is guilty of open and gross lewdness and lascivious behavior, they shall be punished by imprisonment in the state prison not exceeding two years, or in the county jail not exceeding one year, or by fine not exceeding three hundred dollars.

SECTION 798.03. If any man commits fornication with a woman, each of them shall be punished by imprisonment not exceeding three months, or by fine not exceeding thirty dollars.

SECTION 741.11. It is unlawful for any white male person residing or being in this state to intermarry with any negro female person; and it is in like manner unlawful for any white female persons residing or being in this state to intermarry with any negro male persons; and every marriage formed or solemnized in contravention of the provisions of this section shall be utterly null and void, and the issue, if any, of such surreptitious marriage shall be regarded as bastard and incapable of having or receiving any estate, real, personal or mixed, by inheritance.

SECTION 741.12. If any white man shall intermarry with a negro, or if any white woman shall intermarry with a negro, either or both parties to such marriage shall be punished by imprisonment in the state prison not exceeding ten years, or by fine not exceeding one thousand dollars.

SECTION 101.1(6). The words "negro," "colored," "colored person," "mulatto," or "persons of color," when applied to persons, include every person having one-eighth or more of African or negro blood.

FLORIDA CONSTITUTION, ARTICLE 16, SECTION 24. All marriages between a white person and a negro, or between a white person and a person of negro descent to the fourth generation, inclusive, are hereby forever prohibited.

Appendix C

Miscegenation Statutes, by State

State	Year of Enactment	Year of Repeal	Prohibited Persons*	Penalties*
Alabama	1852	2000	Any descendant of a Negro	Absolutely void; felony: 2 to 7 years in prison; also, $100 to $1,000 fine or six months in jail, or both, for licensor or performer
Alaska	None	None	None	None
Arizona	1865	1962	Negroes, Mongolians, Malayans, Hindus, Indians	Null and void
Arkansas	1838	1973	Negroes, mulattoes	Illegal and void; misdemeanor: fine or prison
California	1861	1959	Negroes, Mongolians, Malayans, mulattoes	Illegal and void
Colorado	1864	1957	Negroes, mulattoes (except in portion of state acquired from Mexico)	Absolutely void; misdemeanor: up to 2 years in prison; performer could also be imprisoned for 2 years
Connecticut	None	None	None	None
Delaware	1721	1974	Negroes, mulattoes	Void; misdemeanor: $100 fine or 30 days in jail if unable to pay
District of Columbia	None	None	None	None

State	Year of Enactment	Year of Repeal	Prohibited Persons*	Penalties*
Florida	1832	1969	Anyone with at least one-eighth Negro blood	Utterly null and void; felony: 10 years in prison or $1,000 fine
Georgia	1750	1972	Someone with any ascertainable blood from a Negro, African, West Indian, Malayan, Japanese, Chinese, or Asiatic Indian	Utterly void, null and void; felony: 1 to 2 years in prison; also, 2 to 5 years for knowingly issuing a false license; performer could be punished as well
Hawaii	None	None	None	None
Idaho	1864	1959	Negroes, Mongolians, mulattoes	Illegal and void
Illinois	1829	1874	Negroes	Imprisonment
Indiana	1840	1965	Anyone with at least one-eighth Negro blood	Absolutely void without any legal proceedings; felony: fine of $500 to $5000 and up to 10 years in jail; penalties also for the licensor, officiator, assistant to officiator, and anyone advising the parties to marry
Iowa	1840	1850, 1851	Negroes	Illegal and void
Kansas	1855	1857, 1859	Negroes	Not available
Kentucky	1792	1974	Negroes, mulattoes	Prohibited and declared void; $500 to $5,000 fine and, if couple continued to cohabit, 3 to 12 months in prison

State	Enacted	Repealed	Racial definition	Penalty
Louisiana	1807	1972	Negroes could not willfully marry whites or Indians	Null and void; up to 5 years of hard labor for white-black marriage attempt but no penalty listed for black-Indian marriage attempt
Maine	1820	1883	Negroes, Indians	Minister fined
Maryland	1664 (first state)	1967 (longest duration)	Negroes (to the third generation) and Malayans; Negroes, as defined, could also not marry Malayans	Void; felony "infamous crime" (white-Negro marriages only): 18 months to 10 years in prison
Massachusetts	1705	1843	Negroes, Indians, mulattoes	Minister fined
Michigan	1838	1883	Not available	Not available
Minnesota	None	None	None	None
Mississippi	1822	1972	Negroes, mulattoes, Mongolians; Negroes and Mongolians were described as having at least one-eighth of the required blood	Unlawful and void; felony: up to $500 fine or 10 years in prison
Missouri	1835	1969	Negroes (one-eighth or more), Mongolians	Prohibited and declared absolutely void; felony: up to 2 years in the state penitentiary, up to 3 months in the county jail, $100, or a combination
Montana	1909	1953	Negroes, part Negroes, Chinese, Japanese	Utterly null and void
Nebraska	1855	1963	Anyone with at least one-eighth blood of Negroes, Chinese, or Japanese	Void; up to 6 months in jail, $100 fine, or both

State	Year of Enactment	Year of Repeal	Prohibited Persons*	Penalties*
Nevada	1861	1959	Ethiopian (black), Malay (brown), Mongolian (yellow)	Unlawful; gross misdemeanor: penalties for bride, groom, officiator, and anyone assisting the ceremony
New Hampshire	None	None	None	None
New Jersey	None	None	None	None
New Mexico	1857	1886	White women with nonwhite men	Not available
New York	None	None	None	None
North Carolina	1715	1970	Third-generation Negro or Indian; Negroes also could not marry Cherokees from Robeson County	Void; felony; "infamous crime": 4 months to 10 years in prison for white-black marriage attempt but no penalty for black-Indian marriage attempt; licensor could be fined $500 and imprisoned for up to 10 years; performer could also be punished
North Dakota	1909	1955	One-eighth or more Negro blood	Void; felony: penalties to parties, licensor, performer, and anyone concealing the record
Ohio	1861	1887	Distinct and visible admixture of African blood	Not available
Oklahoma	1899	1969	Any person of African descent could marry only persons of African descent	Unlawful and prohibited; felony: up to $500 fine or 1 to 5 years in jail, or both; licensor, officiator, and anyone concealing the record could be punished
Oregon	1862	1951	One-fourth or more Negro, Chinese, or Kanakan; one-half or more Indian	Prohibited; felony: penalties for bride, groom, licensor, officiator

State	Year	Prohibited Persons	Year	Penalties
Pennsylvania	1725	Negroes	1780	100-pound fine and servitude for free Negroes
Rhode Island	1798	Negroes, Indians, mulattoes	1881	Void; $200 fine of the solemnizer
South Carolina	1865	Negroes (one-eighth or more blood), Indians, mulattoes, mestizos, and half-breeds	1988	Unlawful and prohibited; misdemeanor: $500 fine or 1 to 5 years in jail, or both, for bride, groom, and performer
South Dakota	1909	Members of the African, Korean, Malayan, or Mongolian race	1957	Void; felony: up to $20,000 fine and up to 10 years in prison
Tennessee	1794	Negroes to the third generation	1978	Prohibited and unlawful; felony: 1 to 5 years in prison
Texas	1837	Africans to the third generation	1969	Null and void; felony: 2 to 5 years in prison or a fine
Utah	1888	Negroes, Mongolians, Malayans, mulattoes, quadroons, octoroons	1963	Void and prohibited; 2 to 5 years in prison
Vermont	None	None	None	None
Virginia	1691	Persons with no admixture of blood other than white or one-sixteenth Indian	1968	Void without any decree or legal process; felony: 1 to 5 years in prison; performer fined $200, licensor $500, and imprisoned for 10 years
Washington	1855	Negroes	1868	Not available
West Virginia	1870	Negroes	1969	Void; misdemeanor: up to $100 fine and 1 year in prison
Wisconsin	None	None	None	None
Wyoming	1869	Negroes, Malayans, Mongolians, mulattoes	1965	Illegal and void; misdemeanor: 1 to 5 years in jail, $100 to $1,000 fine, or both

*Under "Prohibited Persons" and "Penalties" are the most recent revisions of the laws in question.

Notes

Preface

1. See Todd Gitlin, *The Sixties: Years of Hope, Days of Rage* (Toronto: Bantam Books, 1987), and Edward P. Morgan, *The Sixties Experience: Hard Lessons about Modern America* (Philadelphia: Temple University Press, 1991).

Introduction

1. Victoria Valentine, "When Love Was a Crime," 60–62.

2. Subsequently, when she learned that I was in Virginia visiting with her attorney, she relented and allowed me to visit her in her home.

3. Garnett Brooks, telephone conversation with author, February 13, 1998.

4. Hirschkop believes that at one time Cohen had his own copy of the file. Cohen disputes this, saying that Hirschkop has the only copy.

5. For a straightforward listing of these laws by state, see Pauli Murray, ed., *States' Laws on Race and Color*. Stetson Kennedy's *Jim Crow Guide: The Way It Was* provides a categorical synopsis of these laws that intentionally provokes both outrage and humor.

6. Mary Stanton, *From Selma to Sorrow: The Life and Death of Viola Liuzzo*, 202.

1. I Do

1. Birth certificates from the case file in the Caroline County courthouse, Bowling Green, Virginia.

2. *Los Angeles Times*, November 18, 1992.

3. Robert Pratt, speech (Columbus School of Law symposium, November 1997); Simeon Booker, "The Crime of Being Married," 89–90.

4. Pratt, speech.

5. *Richmond Times Dispatch*, August 25, 1996.

6. Mildred Loving, interview by author, April 27, 1999.

7. Loving, interview.

8. Pratt, speech.

9. Virginia Supreme Court of Appeals record, *Loving v. Virginia* file, Vermont Law School, 2.

10. Stan Beason, interview by author, April 28, 1999.

11. Virginia Supreme Court of Appeals Record, 2–4; *Washington Post,* June 14, 1992; *Richmond Times Dispatch,* August 25, 1996.

12. Beason, interview.

13. Jack Lilly, interview by author, July 22, 1999.

14. Kenneth Edwards, interview by author, July 24, 1999.

15. Ottis Moore, interview by author, July 24, 1999.

16. Raymond Green, interview by author, July 26, 1999.

17. Beason, interview.

18. Beason, interview.

19. Lilly, interview.

20. *Washington Post,* June 14, 1992; *Richmond Times Dispatch,* August 25, 1996.

21. Virginia Supreme Court of Appeals Record, 3–5; Robert J. Sickels, *Race, Marriage and the Law,* 77; Pratt, speech.

22. Beason, interview.

23. Beason, interview; Leslie Houser, interview by author, December 2, 1998.

24. Lilly, interview, July 23, 1999.

25. Virginia Supreme Court of Appeals Record, 4.

26. Virginia Supreme Court of Appeals Record, 5.

27. Mrs. Edward Stehl, interview by author, July 2, 1998. Despite Mrs. Stehl's seeming disapproval of her late husband's actions, it is unclear where she stood on the issue. She inquired what view my book would take on the issue of interracial marriage.

28. Lilly, interview, July 22, 1999.

29. Moore, interview; Edwards, interview.

30. *Brooks v. Brooks,* 200 Va. 530, 533–34; Lilly, interview.

31. Virginia Supreme Court of Appeals Record, 6–7.

32. Lilly, interview.

33. Sickels, *Race, Marriage and the Law,* 77–8; Peter Wallenstein, "The Right to Marry: *Loving v. Virginia,*" 37; Pratt, speech.

34. *Des Moines Register,* March 31, 1996.

35. Peter Wallenstein, "Race, Marriage and the Supreme Court from *Pace v. Alabama* (1883) to *Loving v. Virginia* (1967)," 80; Robert A. Pratt, "Crossing the Color Line: A Historical Assessment and Personal Narrative of *Loving v. Virginia,*" 41 Howard Law Journal, 237. This latter article is almost a verbatim transcript of the speech given by Pratt at the symposium. My prior citations were to the tape recording of the speech, but I must have missed some information while listening to the tape, hence the citation to the law review article.

36. Bowling Green courthouse records; Bernie Cohen, e-mail message to author, May 11, 1999.

37. Lilly, interview, July 23, 1999.

38. *Washington Post,* June 14, 1992.

39. "Postscript," *Mr. and Mrs. Loving,* video recording, directed by Richard Friedenberg (Showtime, 1996).

2. The Passing Capital of America

1. Phil Hirschkop, interviews by author, January 20 and February 12, 1998.

2. Hirschkop, interview, April 27, 1999.

3. *Des Moines Register,* March 31, 1996.

4. *Jet,* November 9, 1992.

5. Robert A. Pratt, "Crossing the Color Line: A Historical Assessment and Personal Narrative of *Loving v. Virginia,*" 41 Howard Law Journal, 235.

6. Jack Lilly, interview by author, July 22, 1999.

7. Bernie Cohen, interview by author, June 16, 1998.

8. *Baltimore Afro-American,* February 6, 1965, 3.

9. *New York Times,* June 12, 1992.

10. *Des Moines Register,* March 31, 1996.

11. Simeon Booker, "The Couple That Rocked the Courts," 79.

12. Robert J. Sickels, *Race, Marriage and the Law,* 76.

13. Pratt, "Crossing the Color Line," 235.

14. Sickels, *Race, Marriage and the Law,* 76.

15. *New York Times,* June 12, 1992.

16. *Caroline County Chamber of Commerce Guide, 1997–98,* 6.

17. Caroline County, Virginia, Web site, www.co.caroline.va.us/profile.htm.

18. *Chamber of Commerce Guide,* 19.

19. Caroline County, Virginia, Web site, www.co.caroline.va.us/econdev.htm

20. Caroline County, Virginia, Web site, www.co.caroline.va.us/profile.htm.

21. Caroline County, Virginia, Web site, www.co.caroline.va.us/civic.htm.

22. Caroline County, Virginia, Web site, www.co.caroline.va.us/church.htm.

23. Stan Beason, interview by author, April 28, 1999.

24. These house numbers are courtesy of Bernie Cohen, one of the Lovings' attorneys, who introduced enhanced 911 to rural Virginia during his term as a state representative.

25. Major W. Cox, "Lovings Case's Lessons Linger," *Montgomery Advertiser,* July 16, 1997.

26. *Jet,* November 9, 1992.

27. Pratt, "Crossing the Color Line," 229–30.

28. Pratt, "Crossing the Color Line," 237.

29. *New York Times,* June 12, 1992.

30. Booker, "The Couple That Rocked the Courts," 78–84.

31. Booker, "The Couple That Rocked the Courts," 80.

32. Pratt, "Crossing the Color Line," 234.

3. Making Sense of Senseless Laws

1. Jerold C. Cummins and John L. Kane, "Miscegenation, the Constitution and Science," 25.

2. J. A. Rogers, *Sex and Race: A History of White, Negro and Indian Miscegenation in the Two Americas,* vol. 3, 15–16.

3. Kenneth James Lay, "Sexual Racism: A Legacy of Slavery," 13 National Black Law Review 165, 167.

4. Karen A. Getman, "Sexual Control in the Slaveholding South: The Implementation and Maintenance of a Racial Caste System," 7 Harvard Women's Law Review 115, 125.

5. Lay, "Sexual Racism," 167.

6. Croly's son Herbert was also an author, but in contrast to his father, he had a progressive bent, writing *The Promise of American Life,* which Ashley Montague, in *Man's Most Dangerous Myth: The Fallacy of Race,* describes as "the classic statement of the progressive movement in America" (538).

7. Frank F. Arness, "The Evolution of the Virginia Anti-miscegenation Laws," master's thesis, 2; Chang Moon Sohn, "Principle and Expediency in Judicial Review: Miscegenation Cases in the Supreme Court," PhD diss., 8; David H. Fowler, *Northern Attitudes Toward Interracial Marriage: Legislation and Public Opinion in the Middle Atlantic and the States of the Old Northwest, 1780–1930,* 204–5.

8. J. M. Bloch, *Miscegenation, Melaleukation, and Mr. Lincoln's Dog,* 18–21, 35.

9. Edward T. Wright, "Interracial Marriage: A Survey of Statutes and Their Interpretations," 1 Mercer Law Review 88.

10. Roger D. Hardaway, "Prohibiting Interracial Marriage: Miscegenation Laws in Wyoming," 57–58.

11. Wright, "Interracial Marriage," 89.

12. Peggy Pascoe, "Miscegenation Law: Court Cases, and Ideologies of 'Race' in Twentieth-Century America," 49–50.

13. Pauli Murray, ed., *States' Laws on Race and Color,* 18.

14. Ernest Porterfield, *Black and White Mixed Marriages,* 9.

15. Gunnar Myrdal, *An American Dilemma,* 60–61.

16. *New York Times,* November 22, 1964.

17. *U.S. News and World Report,* November 18, 1963, 85.

18. Jack Greenberg, *Race Relations and American Law,* 343.

19. 39 Ga. Rep. 321, 324 (1869).

20. *Doc Lomas v. State,* 50 Tenn. 287, 310–11 (1871), quoted in Paul A. Lombardo, "Miscegenation, Eugenics and Racism: Historical Footnotes to *Loving v. Virginia,*" 21 University of California Davis Law Review, 426.

21. Victoria E. Bynum, "Reshaping the Bonds of Womanhood: Divorce in Reconstruction North Carolina," in Catherine Clinton and Nina Silver, ed., *Divided Houses,* 325.

22. *Green v. State,* 58 Ala. 190, 195 (1877), quoted in Robert J. Sickels, *Race, Marriage and the Law.*

23. William D. Zabel, "Interracial Marriage and the Law," 78; Byron Curti Martyn, "Racism in the United States: A History of Anti-miscegenation Legislation and Litigation," PhD diss., 784–85; *State v. Jackson,* 80 Mo. 175, 179 (1883), quoted in Sickels, *Race, Marriage and the Law,* 48.

24. Harold Cohen, "An Appraisal of the Legal Tests Used to Determine Who Is a Negro," 34 Cornell Law Quarterly 247.

25. This chapter covers statutes throughout the history of antimiscegenation legislation. Wherever possible, I have used the most recent incarnations of a state's statute, but the laws covered in this chapter range from those passed in the 1600s to those passed in the 1900s.

26. Deborah Lynn Kitchen, "Interracial Marriage in the United States: 1900–1980," PhD diss., 71.

27. Stetson Kennedy, *Jim Crow Guide: The Way It Was,* 47.

28. Kennedy, *Jim Crow Guide,* 47.

29. Charles S. Mangum Jr., *The Legal Status of the Negro,* 246.

30. William E. Foster, "A Study of the Wyoming Miscegenation Statutes," Notes, 10 Wyoming Law Journal 132–33.

31. Kitchen, "Interracial Marriage," 71.

32. Kitchen, "Interracial Marriage," 73.

33. Charles F. Robinson II, "The Antimiscegenation Conversation: Love's Legislated Limits (1868–1967)," PhD diss., 126–27.

34. Mangum, *Legal Status,* 245.

35. Mangum, *Legal Status,* 247.

36. S.C. Const. art. 3, sec. 33, *South Carolina Code,* secs. 20-7 and 20-8 (1952), quoted in Greenberg, *Race Relations,* 398; Kennedy, *Jim Crow Guide,* 69; Murray, *States' Laws,* 417.

37. Brian William Thomson, "Racism and Racial Classification: A Case Study of the Virginia Racial Integrity Legislation," PhD diss., 78–80.

38. *Nevada Revised Statutes,* sec. 122.180 (1957), quoted in Greenberg, *Race Relations,* 398; Kennedy, *Jim Crow Guide,* 68; Murray, *States' Laws,* 266.

39. Murray, *States' Laws,* 44; John C. Calhoun, "Who Is a Negro?" Notes, University of Florida Law Review, 237.

40. Cohen, "Appraisal of the Legal Tests," 250.

41. Calhoun, "Who Is a Negro?" 238–39.

42. Kennedy, *Jim Crow Guide,* 48.

43. Kennedy, *Jim Crow Guide,* 49.

44. Beth Day, *Sexual Life Between Blacks and Whites: The Roots of Racism,* 99; see also *State v. Jackson,* 80 Mo. 175 (1883), cited in Mangum, *Legal Status,* 248.

45. Day, *Sexual Life,* 99.

46. Mangum, *Legal Status,* 247.

47. *New York Times,* April 11, 1967; Jane Purcell Guild, *Black Codes of Virginia: A Summary of the Legislative Acts of Virginia Concerning Negroes from Earliest Times to the Present,* 36.

48. Joseph R. Washington Jr., Marriage in Black and White, 76.

49. Kennedy, *Jim Crow Guide,* 49.

50. Gary Nash, "The Hidden History of Mestizo America," in Martha Hodes, ed., *Sex, Love, Race: Crossing Boundaries in Northern American History,* 11, 15.

51. Robinson, "Antimiscegenation Conversation," 147.

52. Thomson, "Racism and Racial Classification," 60–61.

53. Thomson, "Racism and Racial Classification," 31, 209.

54. Thomson, "Racism and Racial Classification," 195.

55. Peggy Pascoe, "Race, Gender and Intercultural Relations: The Case of Interracial Marriage," 10.

56. Mangum, *Legal Status,* 253.

57. Mangum, *Legal Status,* 253.

58. *New York Times,* November 4, 1962, 43.

59. Pascoe, "Race, Gender," 17.

60. William E. Foster, "A Study of the Wyoming Miscegenation Statutes," Notes, 10 Wyoming Law Journal 132–33.

61. Kennedy, *Jim Crow Guide,* 68; Murray, *States' Laws,* 385; Gilbert Thomas Stephenson, *Race Distinctions in American Law,* 17.

62. Albert Gordon, *Intermarriage: Interfaith, Interracial, Interethnic,* 254.

63. Mangum, *Legal Status,* 253–54.

64. Zabel, "Interracial Marriage and the Law," 77.

65. Stephenson, *Race Distinctions,* 17.

66. Thomson, "Racism and Racial Classification," 267–68.

67. Kennedy, *Jim Crow Guide,* 51.

68. *Weaver v. State,* 116 So. 893 (1928), cited in Sickels, *Race, Marriage and the Law,* 72.

69. For a more exhaustive discussion of antimiscegenation laws over a period of time, I refer the reader to contemporaneous books such as Stephenson's *Race Distinctions in American Law* from 1910, Mangum's *Legal Status of the Negro* from 1940, Murray's *State's Laws* from 1950, and Greenberg's *Race Relations and American Law* from 1959, as well as a later analysis in Washington's *Marriage in Black and White.* These are all reference books. A tome that is eminently readable (though possibly less technically correct) is Kennedy's *Jim Crow Guide.* All of these are listed in the bibliography.

70. Murray, *States' Laws,* 207–8.

71. Stephenson, *Race Distinctions,* 81.

72. Washington, *Marriage in Black and White,* 76.

73. Kitchen, "Interracial Marriage," 69–70; Del. Co Ann. tit. 13, sec. 101(a)(2) and 102 (1953), quoted in Greenberg, *Race Relations,* 397; Kennedy, *Jim Crow Guide,* 64; Washington, *Marriage in Black and White,* 75–76; Zabel, "Interracial Marriage and the Law," 77.

74. Stephenson, *Race Distinctions,* 83.

75. *Mangum v. Mangum,* 310 Ky. 226, 220 S.W. 2d 406 (1949), cited in Greenberg, *Race Relations,* 346.

76. *In re Guthery's Estate,* 205 Mo App. 664, 226 S.W. 626 (1920), cited in Greenberg, *Race Relations,* 346.

77. Mangum, *Legal Status of the Negro,* 238.

78. Section 90-1-2, cited in Race Relations Law Reporter, 1957.

79. Ky. Rev. Stats. sec. 402.022, sec. 402.990 (1955), quoted in Greenberg, *Race Relations,* 397; Kennedy, *Jim Crow Guide,* 66; Washington, *Marriage in Black and White,* 77; Murray, *States' Laws,* 168.

80. Mangum, *Legal Status of the Negro,* 249.

81. *Okla. Stats. Ann.* tit. 43, secs. 12 and 13 (1955), quoted in Greenberg, *Race Relations,* 398; Kennedy, *Jim Crow Guide,* 68.

82. Kennedy, *Jim Crow Guide,* 68; Murray, *States' Laws,* 351.

83. Miss. Const. art. 14, sec. 263, quoted in Greenberg, *Race Relations,* 397; *Miss. Code Ann.* secs. 459 and 2234; and Kennedy, *Jim Crow Guide,* 67.

84. Eva Saks, "Representing Miscegenation Law," 53.

85. *Ratcliff v. State,* 107 So. 2d 728 (1958), cited in Race Relations Law Reporter, 1959, 127–28.

86. Murray, *States' Laws,* 247.

4. How It All Began

1. William D. Zabel, "Interracial Marriage and the Law," 76.

2. Deborah Lynn Kitchen, "Interracial Marriage in the United States: 1900–1980," PhD diss., 73.

3. Harvey M. Applebaum, "Miscegenation Statutes: A Constitutional and Social Problem," 53 Georgetown Law Journal 50; see also Nancy F. Cott, "Giving Character to Our Whole Civil Polity: Marriage and the Public Order in the Late Nineteenth Century," 118–19.

4. Allan C. Brownfeld, "Mixed Marriage and the Supreme Court," in M. Clotye Larsson, ed., *Marriage Across the Color Line*, 52.

5. Paul R. Spickard, *Intermarriage and Ethnic Identity in Twentieth-Century America*, 286.

6. Actually, one author claims that Louisiana's Code Noir forbade interracial marriage as early as 1724, fining the white party and, assuming the black person was the slave of the white, removing that party from the household. See Charles F. Robinson II, "The Antimiscegenation Conversation: Love's Legislated Limits (1868–1967)," PhD diss., 112.

7. Joseph R. Washington Jr., *Marriage in Black and White*, 72.

8. The information in this chapter was gleaned from secondary sources rather than an exhaustive search of state constitutions and statutes. There was some disagreement regarding the laws in question from these sources.

9. Albert Gordon, *Intermarriage: Interracial, Interfaith, Interethnic*, 222–3; Robinson, "Antimiscegenation Conversation," 4; Chang Moon Sohn, "Principle and Expediency in Judicial Review: Miscegenation Cases in the Supreme Court," PhD diss., 11; Brian William Thomson, "Racism and Racial Classification: A Case Study of the Virginia Racial Integrity Legislation," PhD diss., 35.

10. The language used throughout this book is quoted directly from the statutes in question.

11. Lloyd H. Riley, "Miscegenation Statutes—A Re-evaluation of Their Constitutionality in Light of Changing Social and Political Conditions," 32 Southern California Law Review 29.

12. Jonathan L. Alpert, "The Origins of Slavery in the United States—The Maryland Precedent," 197.

13. Joel Williamson, *After Slavery: The Negro in South Carolina During Reconstruction, 1861–1877*, 10.

14. Alpert, "Origins of Slavery," 209–10.

15. Williamson, *After Slavery*, 11.

16. Hening, *Statutes at Large of Virginia*, vol. 1 (Richmond, 1823), quoted

in James Hugo Johnston, *Race Relations in Virginia and Miscegenation in the South,* 176.

17. Henry E. McIllwaine, ed., *Minutes of the Council and General Court of Virginia* (Richmond, 1924), quoted in Johnston, *Race Relations in Virginia,* 176.

18. Byron Curti Martyn, "Racism in the United States: A History of Anti-Miscegenation Legislation and Litigation," PhD diss., 11.

19. Karen A. Getman, "Sexual Control in the Slaveholding South: The Implementation and Maintenance of a Racial Caste System," 7 Harvard Women's Law Journal 122–23.

20. Hening, vol. 3, 86–88, quoted in Johnston, *Race Relations in Virginia,* 172–73.

21. Frank F. Arness, "The Evolution of the Virginia Anti-miscegenation Laws," master's thesis, 16–17.

22. Paul Finkelman, "The Crime of Color," 67 Tulane Law Review 2063, 2086.

23. June Purcell Guild, *Black Laws of Virginia: A Summary of the Legislative Acts of Virginia Concerning Negroes from Earliest Times to the Present,* 26.

24. Arness, "Evolution of the Virginia Anti-miscegenation Laws," 19; Walter Wadlington, "The *Loving* Case: Virginia's Anti-miscegenation Statute in Historical Perspective," 52 Virginia Law Review 1193–94.

25. Arness, "Evolution of the Virginia Anti-miscegenation Laws," 19.

26. Peter Wallenstein, "Race, Marriage, and the Law of Freedom: Alabama and Virginia, 1860's–1960's," 70 Chicago-Kent Law Review, 393–94.

27. Getman, "Sexual Control in the Slaveholding South," 132.

28. David H. Fowler, *Northern Attitudes Toward Interracial Marriage: Legislation and Public Opinion in the Middle Atlantic and the States of the Old Northwest, 1780–1930,* 62; Martyn, "Racism in the United States," 169–70.

29. Lerone Bennett Jr., "Miscegenation in America," in M. Clotye Larsson, ed., *Marriage Across the Color Line,* 9.

30. Martyn, "Racism in the United States," 223–24, 278, 323.

31. Martyn, "Racism in the United States," 318–22; Fowler, *Northern Attitudes,* 135–37.

32. Arness, "Evolution of the Virginia Anti-miscegenation Laws," 20–21.

33. Martyn, "Racism in the United States," 322.

34. Martyn, "Racism in the United States," 324.

35. Peter Bardaglion, "'Shamefull Matches': The Regulation of Interracial Sex and Marriage in the South Before 1900," in Martha Hodes, ed., *Sex, Love, Race: Crossing Boundaries in North American History,* 119, 133.

36. Martyn, "Racism in the United States," 324–25.

37. Martyn, "Racism in the United States," 327; Fowler, *Northern Attitudes,* 138–39.

38. Martyn, "Racism in the United States," 426.

39. Beth Day, *Sexual Life Between Blacks and Whites: The Roots of Racism,* 98–9.

40. Martyn, "Racism in the United States," 427.

41. Martyn, "Racism in the United States," 429.

42. Martyn, "Racism in the United States," 784–85.

43. Fowler, *Northern Attitudes,* 218.

44. Martyn, "Racism in the United States," 431–32.

45. Martyn, "Racism in the United States," 432.

46. Fowler, *Northern Attitudes,* 183–84.

47. Martyn, "Racism in the United States," 430.

48. Martyn, "Racism in the United States," 445–49; Fowler, *Northern Attitudes,* 179–80.

49. Martyn, "Racism in the United States," 437.

50. Martyn, "Racism in the United States," 449–50.

51. Fowler, *Northern Attitudes,* 192–99.

52. Guild, *Black Laws of Virginia,* 32

53. Arness, "Evolution of the Virginia Anti-miscegenation Laws," 22.

54. Wallenstein, "Race, Marriage, and the Law of Freedom," 394.

55. Arness, "Evolution of the Virginia Anti-miscegenation Laws," 26.

56. Martyn, "Racism in the United States," 454–55.

57. Fowler, *Northern Attitudes,* 218.

58. Martyn, "Racism in the United States," 459.

59. Fowler, *Northern Attitudes,* 218; Martyn, "Racism in the United States," 453.

60. Fowler, *Northern Attitudes,* 208.

61. Day, *Sexual Life Between Blacks and Whites,* 98–99.

62. Martyn, "Racism in the United States," 551–53.

63. Martyn, "Racism in the United States," 553.

64. Martyn, "Racism in the United States," 601–2.

65. Martyn, "Racism in the United States," 553.

66. David A. Gerber, *Black Ohio and the Color Line,* 238–42.

67. Roger D. Hardaway, "Unlawful Love: A History of Arizona's Miscegenation Law," 377.

68. Hardaway, "Unlawful Love," 378.

69. Hardaway, "Unlawful Love," 379.

70. Martyn, "Racism in the United States," 558–62, 737.

71. Martyn, "Racism in the United States," 544.

72. Martyn, "Racism in the United States," 563–65.

73. Robinson, "Antimiscegenation Conversation," 15–16.

74. Martyn, "Racism in the United States," 564–67.

75. Robinson, "Antimiscegenation Conversation," 119; Harriet Spiller Daggett, *Legal Essays on Family Law*, 13.

76. Robert E. T. Roberts, "Black-White Inter-marriage in the United States," in Walton Johnson and D. Michael Warren, ed., *Inside the Mixed Marriage*, 32.

77. Sohn, "Principle and Expediency in Judicial Review," PhD diss., 14.

78. William Cohen, *At Freedom's Edge: Black Mobility and the Southern White Quest for Racial Control, 1861–1915*, 215–16.

79. Robinson, "Antimiscegenation Conversation," 18–19.

80. Fowler, *Northern Attitudes*, 234–35; Charles S. Mangum Jr., *The Legal Status of the Negro*, 239.

81. Arness, "Evolution of the Virginia Anti-miscegenation Laws,"27; Guild, *Black Laws of Virginia*, 34; Wadlington, "*Loving* Case," 52 Virginia Law Review 1199.

82. Jack Greenberg, *Race Relations and American Law*, 173; and Peter Wallenstein, "The Right to Marry: *Loving v. Virginia*," 38.

83. Fowler, *Northern Attitudes*, 266.

84. Lerone Bennett Jr., "Miscegenation in America," in M. Clotye Larsson, ed., *Marriage Across the Color Line*, 20–21.

85. Vernon Lane Wharton, "Jim Crow Laws and Miscegenation," in Joel Williamson, ed., *The Origins of Segregation*, 18–20.

86. Wharton, "Jim Crow Laws," 19.

87. Daggett, *Legal Essays on Family Law*, 13–14.

88. Fowler, *Northern Attitudes*, 265.

89. Martyn, "Racism in the United States," 624.

90. George Brown Tindall, *South Carolina Negroes, 1877–1900*, 296–97; Sohn, "Principle and Expediency," 419.

91. Francis Simkins, "Race Relations in South Carolina since 1865," 169; Sohn, "Principle and Expediency," 419.

92. Bennett, "Miscegenation in America," in Larsson, ed., *Marriage Across the Color Line*, 20–21; Williamson, *After Slavery*, 93; Fowler, *Northern Attitudes*, 266; Martyn, "Racism in the United States," 721–22.

93. Roger D. Hardaway, "Prohibiting Interracial Marriage: Miscegenation Laws in Wyoming," 56–57.

94. William D. Zabel, "Interracial Marriage and the Law," 77.

95. Saks, "Representing Miscegenation Law," 53.

96. Saks, "Representing Miscegenation Law," 53.

97. Martyn, "Racism in the United States," 567–74.

98. Fowler, *Northern Attitudes,* 265; Martyn, "Racism in the United States," 727.

99. Martyn, "Racism in the United States," 730–31; Fowler, *Northern Attitudes,* 266.

100. Martyn, "Racism in the United States," 603.

101. Martyn, "Racism in the United States," 575–76.

102. Fowler, *Northern Attitudes,* 251–54, 286–87; Martyn, "Racism in the United States," 607.

103. Sohn, "Principle and Expediency," 13.

104. Martyn, "Racism in the United States," 745–46.

105. Fowler, *Northern Attitudes,* 255–62.

106. Robinson, "Antimiscegenation Conversation," 124–25.

107. Fowler, *Northern Attitudes,* 272.

108. Martyn, "Racism in the United States," 739.

109. Martyn, "Racism in the United States," 740.

110. 106 U.S. 583, 1 S. Ct. 637 (1882).

111. 319 F. Supp. 1058 (N.D. Ala. 1970).

112. Robinson, "Antimiscegenation Conversation," 88–89.

113. Robinson, "Antimiscegenation Conversation," 88–89.

114. Wallenstein, "Race, Marriage and the Supreme Court from *Pace v. Alabama* (1883) to *Loving v. Virginia* (1967)," 73.

115. 1 S. Ct. 638–39.

116. Martyn, "Racism in the United States," 879–80.

117. Fowler, *Northern Attitudes,* 291–94; Martyn, "Racism in the United States," 917–18.

118. Fowler, *Northern Attitudes,* 295–96.

119. Martyn, "Racism in the United States," 920–23.

120. Martyn, "Racism in the United States," 885–87.

121. Fowler, *Northern Attitudes,* 288.

122. Fowler, *Northern Attitudes,* 288–91.

123. Robinson, "Antimiscegenation Conversation," 157, 162–63.

124. Martyn, "Racism in the United States," 877–79.

125. Fowler, *Northern Attitudes,* 297–99; Martyn, "Racism in the United States," 925, 929–30.

126. Wadlington, "*Loving* Case," 1197.

127. Martyn, "Racism in the United States," 889–907.

128. Martyn, "Racism in the United States," 832, 898–901.

129. Randy Roberts, *Papa Jack: Jack Johnson and the Era of White Hopes,* 140, 143.

130. Al-Tony Gilmore, *Bad Nigger! The National Impact of Jack Johnson,* 121.

131. Roberts, *Papa Jack,* 159.

132. Martyn, "Racism in the United States," 916.

133. Fowler, *Northern Attitudes,* 302–3; Robinson, "Antimiscegenation Conversation," 28–30.

134. Fowler, *Northern Attitudes,* 303–4.

135. Martyn, "Racism in the United States," 910.

136. Papers of the NAACP, part 11.

137. Fowler, *Northern Attitudes,* 307–8; see also Papers of the NAACP, part 11: Special Subject Files, 1912–1939.

138. Fowler, *Northern Attitudes,* 309–11.

139. Fowler, *Northern Attitudes,* 313–15.

140. Washington, *Marriage in Black and White,* 46.

141. Papers of the NAACP, part 15, series B; Robinson, "Antimiscegenation Conversation," 26–27.

142. Sohn, "Principle and Expediency," 22–23.

143. Martyn, "Racism in the United States," 911; Hardaway, "Prohibiting Interracial Marriage," 57–58.

144. Martyn, "Racism in the United States," 1024–26, 1035.

145. Fowler, *Northern Attitudes,* 316–18.

146. Fowler, *Northern Attitudes,* 319–20.

147. Fowler, *Northern Attitudes,* 321.

148. Richard B. Sherman "'The Last Stand': The Fight for Racial Integrity in Virginia in the 1920s," 72; Paul A. Lombardo, "Miscegenation, Eugenics, and Racism: Historical Footnotes to *Loving v. Virginia,*" 21 University of California Davis Law Review 423.

149. Sherman, "'The Last Stand,'" 77.

150. Lombardo, "Miscegenation, Eugenics, and Racism," 423.

151. *Richmond Times-Dispatch,* February 18, 1924, quoted in Sherman, "'The Last Stand,'" 78.

152. Gregory Michael Dorr, "Principled Expediency: Eugenics, *Naim v. Naim,* and the Supreme Court."

153. Arness, "Evolution of the Virginia Anti-miscegenation Laws," 37–38.

154. Arness, "Evolution of the Virginia Anti-miscegenation Laws," 44.

155. Sherman, "'The Last Stand,'" 78.

156. Thomson, "Racism and Racial Classification," 154.

157. Arness, "Evolution of the Virginia Anti-miscegenation Laws," 45–47; "Comments," 36 Yale Law Review 858–59.

158. Thomson, "Racism and Racial Classification," 158–59.

159. Thomson, "Racism and Racial Classification," 161.

160. "Comments," 859.

161. Martyn, "Racism in the United States," 998–1078.

162. Arness, "Evolution of the Virginia Anti-miscegenation Laws," 90; Thomson, "Racism and Racial Classification," 242, 244–45.

163. Thomson, "Racism and Racial Classification," 242, 245.

5. The Prosecutions Continue

1. J. A. Rogers, *Sex and Race: A History of White, Negro and Indian Miscegenation in the Two Americas,* vol. 3, 18–19.

2. Walter Wadlington, "The *Loving* Case: Virginia's Anti-miscegenation Statute in Historical Perspective," 1204–5.

3. *Keith v. Commonwealth,* 181 S.E. 282 (Va. 1935), cited in Peter Wallenstein, "Race, Marriage, and the Law of Freedom: Alabama and Virginia, 1860's–1960's," 70 Chicago-Kent Law Review 411–12; Brian William Thomson, "Racism and Racial Classification: A Case Study of the Virginia Racial Integrity Legislation," PhD diss., 246–48.

4. Wallenstein, "Race, Marriage and the Law of Freedom," 412; Thomson, "Racism and Racial Classification," 248–49.

5. *Washington Post,* December 29, 1948, 1, 4, and January 1, 1949, 1; Wallenstein, "Race, Marriage and the Law of Freedom," 413; Byron Curti Martyn, "Racism in the United States: A History of Anti-miscegenation Legislation and Litigation," 1230–31; Robert J. Sickels, *Race, Marriage and the Law,* 68.

6. *Washington Post,* December 29, 1948, 1, 4, and January 1, 1949, 1; Wallenstein, "Race, Marriage and the Law of Freedom," 413; Martyn, "Racism in the United States," 1230–31; Sickels, *Race, Marriage and the Law,* 68.

7. Wallenstein, "Race, Marriage and the Law of Freedom," 413–14.

8. Martyn, "Racism in the United States," 1239.

9. *Baltimore Afro-American,* July 14, 1956.

10. *Baltimore Afro-American,* February 11, 1961, 19.

11. *State v. Brown,* 236 La. 562, 565 (1959).

12. *State v. Brown,* 236 La. 566–67 (1959).

13. *New York Times,* November 4, 1962, 43.

14. *New York Times,* February 14, 1964, 33.

15. *Baltimore Sun,* August 15, 1998.

16. *New York Times,* February 12, 1966, 56.

17. Julian Lapides, telephone interview by author, December 21, 1998.

18. *Baltimore Sun,* January 13, 1998.

19. U.P.I., April 23, 1990, Lexis Nexis online data base.

20. *New York Times,* March 29, 1966, 29, and March 6, 1966, 8; see also Sickels, *Race, Marriage and the Law,* 74–75.

21. Fowler, *Northern Attitudes Toward Interracial Marriage: Legislation and Public Opinion in the Middle Atlantic and the States of the Old Northwest, 1780–1930,* 33, 35, 55–56.

22. *Griffith v. State,* 35 Ala. App. 582, 50 So. 2d 797 (1951).

23. Charles F. Robinson II, "The Antimiscegenation Conversation: Love's Legislated Limits (1868–1967)," 78.

24. Robinson, "Antimiscegenation Conversation," 92–93.

25. Robinson, "Antimiscegenation Conversation," 134–35.

26. Robinson, "Antimiscegenation Conversation," 98–100.

27. Martyn, "Racism in the United States," 1128–29, 1131–32.

28. Robinson, "Antimiscegenation Conversation," 65–69.

29. Robinson, "Antimiscegenation Conversation," 69–71.

30. Jack Greenberg, *Race Relations and American Law,* 396.

6. Taking Away the Children and the Money

1. Peggy Pascoe, "Race, Gender, and Intercultural Relations: The Case of Interracial Marriage," 7.

2. Charles F. Robinson II, "The Antimiscegenation Conversation: Love's Legislated Limits (1868–1967)," 38.

3. Robinson, "Antimiscegenation Conversation," 117.

4. James Hugo Johnson, "Miscegenation in the Ante-bellum South," PhD diss., 9.

5. Robinson, "Antimiscegenation Conversation," 135.

6. Johnson, "Miscegenation in the Ante-bellum South," 12–14.

7. Robinson, "Antimiscegenation Conversation," 55–57.

8. Robinson, "Antimiscegenation Conversation," 57–58.

9. Robinson, "Antimiscegenation Conversation," 59–60.

10. Robinson, "Antimiscegenation Conversation," 112.

11. Pascoe, "Race, Gender," 7–8.

12. Robinson, "Antimiscegenation Conversation," 166; Byron Curti Martyn, "Racism in the United States: A History of Anti-miscegenation Legislation and Litigation," PhD diss., 1159.

13. Robinson, "Antimiscegenation Conversation," 167–69.

14. 24 Ariz. 9, 206 Pac. 405 (1922).

15. Beth Day, *Sexual Life Between Blacks and Whites: The Roots of Racism*, 44–52.

16. 48 Cal. App. 2d 603, 120 P. 2d 167 (1941).

17. Roger D. Hardaway, "Unlawful Love: A History of Arizona's Miscegenation Law," 380.

18. Hardaway writes that the hairdresser testified that Monks had confided to her that she had black blood, but no other source confirms this.

19. Day, *Sexual Life*, 55–60.

20. Hardaway, "Unlawful Love," 381.

21. *In re Takahashi's Estate*, 113 Mont. 490, 129 P. 2d. 217 (1942), cited in Race Relations Law Reporter 580 (1943).

22. Robinson, "Antimiscegenation Conversation," 167.

23. Martyn, "Racism in the United States," 1158.

24. *Vetrano v. Gardner*, 290 F. Supp. 200 (N.D. Miss.) 1968, quoted in Renee Christian Romano, "Crossing the Line: Black-White Interracial Marriage in the United States, 1945–1990," PhD diss., Stanford University, 1996, 7.

25. *Vetrano v. Gardner*, 290 F. Supp. 200 (N.D. Miss.) 1968, quoted in Romano, "Crossing the Line," 7.

26. 290 F. Supp. 200, 206.

27. 72 S. Ed. 707 (Va. 1911).

28. Peter Wallenstein, "Race, Marriage and the Law of Freedom: Alabama and Virginia, 1860's–1960's," 70 Chicago-Kent Law Review 407–9.

29. Paul R. Spickard, *Intermarriage and Ethnic Identity in Twentieth-Century America*, 288.

30. Romano, "Crossing the Line," 85.

31. ACLU Archives, box 1104, folder 13.

32. Romano, "Crossing the Line," 85.

33. Robinson, "Antimiscegenation Conversation," 196.

34. Romano, "Crossing the Line," 87.

35. Spickard, *Intermarriage and Ethnic Identity*, 295.

36. ACLU Archives, box 1123, folder 9; Martyn, "Racism in the United States," 1296–98.

37. *Langin v. Langin*, 276 N.E. 2d 822 (Ill 1971).

38. *Ethridge v. Ethridge*, 360 So. 2d 1005 (Ala 1978), quoted in Romano, "Crossing the Line," 266.

39. *Schexnayder v. Schexnayder*, 364 So. 2d. 1318 (La. 1978) rev'd, 317 So. 2d 769 (Sup. Ct La. 1979), cited in Romano, "Crossing the Line," 267–68.

40. Spickard, *Intermarriage and Ethnic Identity*, 295–96.

41. *New York Times*, April 26, 1984, provided by William Zabel.

42. Amicus brief for the petitioner, 4–5, provided by William Zabel.

43. William Zabel, interview by author, May 17, 1999.

44. *New York Times*, April 26, 1984.

7. The West Leads the Way

1. 32 Cal. 2d 711.

2. *Perez v. Sharp*, 32 Cal. 2d 711, 198 P. 2d 17 (1948); See also Frank F. Chuman, *The Bamboo People: Japanese-Americans, Their History and the Law*, 333; and Irving G. Tragen, "Statutory Prohibitions Against Interracial Marriage," 272.

3. Chuman, *Bamboo People*, 333.

4. Deborah Lynn Kitchen, "Interracial Marriage in the United States: 1900–1980," 70; Tragen, "Statutory Prohibitions," 272.

5. Chang Moon Sohn, "Principle and Expediency in Judicial Review: Miscegenation Cases in the Supreme Court," PhD diss., 126–27.

6. Carl T. Rowan, *South of Freedom*, 222–24.

7. Rowan, *South of Freedom*, 222–26.

8. Rowan, *South of Freedom*, 82.

9. 32 Cal. 2d. 711, 716.

10. 32 Cal. 2d. 711, 718.

11. 32 Cal. 2d. 711, 714.

12. 32 Cal. 2d. 711, 718.

13. 32 Cal. 2d. 711, 725.

14. 32 Cal. 2d. 711, 725.

15. 32 Cal. 2d. 711, 726.

16. 32 Cal. 2d. 711, 731.

17. 32 Cal. 2d. 711, 731.

18. 32 Cal. 2d. 711, 732–40.

19. 32 Cal. 2d. 711, 740–42.

20. 32 Cal. 2d. 711, 742.

21. 32 Cal. 2d. 711, 744.

22. 32 Cal. 2d. 711, 753–59.

23. Roger D. Hardaway, "Unlawful Love: A History of Arizona's Miscegenation Law," 377.

24. Hardaway, "Unlawful Love," 378.

25. Hardaway, "Unlawful Love," 379.

26. Hardaway, "Unlawful Love," 383.

27. *State v. Pass*, 59 Ariz. 16, 121 P. 2d 882 (Arizona 1942).

28. Hardaway, "Unlawful Love," 386.

29. Ariz. Rev. Stats. sec. 25–101 (1956), quoted in Jack Greenberg, *Race Relations and American Law,* 397; Stetson Kennedy, *Jim Crow Guide: The Way It Was,* 64.

30. *Estate of Walker,* 5 Ariz. 70, 46 Pac. 67 (1896), and *State v. Pass,* 59 Ariz. 16, 121 P. 2d. 882 (1942), cited in Greenberg, *Race Relations,* 346.

31. Joseph R. Washington Jr., *Marriage in Black and White,* 75.

32. *Arizona Daily Star,* November 18, 1959, provided by Harry Ackerman; ACLU Archives, box 1111, folder 28.

33. ACLU Archives, box 1111, folder 28; undated, unidentified newspaper clipping provided by Paul Rees.

34. Henry Oyama, interview by author, October 28, 1998.

35. Affidavit for marriage license, provided by Henry Oyama.

36. Oyama, interview, October 28, 1998.

37. ACLU Archives, box 1111, folder 28.

38. Charles Ares, interview by author, September 16, 1998.

39. Oyama, interview, October 28, 1998.

40. ACLU Archives, box 1111, folder 28.

41. Paul Rees (September 22, 1998), Marvin Cohen (September 15, 1998), Charles Ares (September 16, 1998), and Harry Ackerman (September 28, 1998), interviews by author.

42. Marvin Cohen, interview by author, September 15, 1998.

43. Lawrence Ollason, interview by author, April 2, 1999.

44. Ackerman, interview by author, September 28, 1998.

45. Oyama, interview, October 28, 1998.

46. Oyama, interview, October 28, 1998.

47. Rees, interview by author, September 22, 1998; Cohen, interview, September 15, 1998.

48. Lawrence Ollason recalls that all the attorneys met with Krucker before the case and asked him to rule in favor of Oyama and Jordan. None of the other attorneys reported such a pretrial conversation. That does not mean it did not occur, since it is possible that they did not want to taint Krucker's role.

49. ACLU Archives, box 1111, folder 28.

50. ACLU Archives, box 1111, folder 28.

51. ACLU Archives, box 1111, folder 28.

52. Oyama, interview, October 28, 1998.

53. Ares, interview, September 16, 1998.

54. Hardaway, "Unlawful Love," 388.

55. Ares, interview, September 16, 1988.

56. Hardaway, "Unlawful Love," 377–90.

57. Oyama, interview, October 28, 1998.

58. ACLU Archives, box 1111, folder 28; Rees, interview, September 22, 1998.

59. Phillip I. Earl, "Nevada's Miscegenation Laws and the Marriage of Mr. and Mrs. Bridges," 1–2.

60. Earl, "Nevada's Miscegenation Laws," 2–3.

61. Earl, "Nevada's Miscegenation Laws," 8; *California Lawyer,* December 1993 (provided by Nikki Flynn); *New York Times,* December 10, 1958; *Los Angeles Times,* March 31, 1990; *San Francisco Chronicle,* December 10, 1958; *Reno Evening Gazette,* December 10, 1958.

62. Earl, "Nevada's Miscegenation Laws," 8; *California Lawyer,* December 1993; *New York Times,* December 10, 1958; *Los Angeles Times,* March 31, 1990; *San Francisco Chronicle,* December 10, 1958; *Reno Evening Gazette,* December 10, 1958.

63. Earl, "Nevada's Miscegenation Laws," 9.

64. Earl, "Nevada's Miscegenation Laws," 8; Nikki Flynn, interview by author, October 19, 1998; *California Lawyer,* December 1993; *New York Times,* December 10, 1958; *Reno Evening Gazette,* December 10, 1958.

65. Earl, "Nevada's Miscegenation Laws," 9–10; Flynn, interview, October 19, 1998; *California Lawyer,* December 1993; *New York Times,* December 10, 1958.

66. Earl, "Nevada's Miscegenation Laws," 9–10; Flynn, interview, October 19, 1998; *California Lawyer,* December 1993; *New York Times,* December 10, 1958.

67. Earl, "Nevada's Miscegenation Laws," 10–11; *New York Times,* December 10, 1958.

68. Earl, "Nevada's Miscegenation Laws," 10; *San Francisco Chronicle,* December 11, 1958; *Reno Evening Gazette,* December 11, 1958.

69. Earl, "Nevada's Miscegenation Laws," 10–11; *New York Times,* December 11, 1958.

70. Earl, "Nevada's Miscegenation Laws," 11–13; Flynn, interview, October 19, 1998; *San Francisco Chronicle,* December 11, 1958; *California Lawyer,* December 1993; *New York Times,* December 10, 1958.

71. William Beemer, interview by author, December 8, 1998.

72. *Nevada State Journal,* December 10, 1958, 1, 7; December 11, 1958, 1, 6, 10; *Reno Evening Gazette,* December 11, 1958.

73. Flynn, interview, October 19, 1998; *California Lawyer,* December 1993.

74. Earl, "Nevada's Miscegenation Laws," 15.

8. The Organizations Challenge, and the Challenges Become Organized

1. Chang Moon Sohn, "Principle and Expediency in Judicial Review: Miscegenation Cases in the Supreme Court," PhD diss., 151.

2. Frank Rich, "Scandals Sans Bimbos Need Not Apply," *New York Times,* December 26, 1998; *New York Times,* January 14, 1999.

3. *ACLU 29th Annual Report—1949,* 29, ACLU Archives.

4. Sohn, "Principle and Expediency," 128–29.

5. Sohn, "Principle and Expediency," 134–35.

6. Sohn, "Principle and Expediency," 133.

7. *San Francisco Examiner,* October 4, 1994.

8. *Detroit News,* April 18, 1997.

9. 146 F. 2d 120 (1944).

10. 146 F. 2d 120, 122; see also Papers of the NAACP, part 18, Special Subjects, 1940–1955, series A: Legal Department File.

11. Papers of the NAACP, part 18.

12. Papers of the NAACP, part 18.

13. Papers of the NAACP, part 18.

14. Papers of the NAACP, part 18.

15. 146 F. 2d 120, 123; see also Papers of the NAACP, part 18.

16. Victoria E. Bynum, "'White Negroes' in Segregated Mississippi: Miscegenation, Racial Identity, and the Law," 247–76.

17. Alma Ross, interview by author, August 23, 1998.

18. Ross, interview, August 23, 1998.

19. 42 So. 2d 747; Ross, interview, August 23, 1998.

20. Renee Christian Romano, "Crossing the Line: Black-White Interracial Marriage in the United States, 1945–1990," PhD diss., 21; Stetson Kennedy, *Jim Crow Guide: The Way It Was,* 61; Robert J. Sickels, *Race, Marriage and the Law,* 68.

21. 42 So. 2d 747; Bynum, "'White Negroes,'" 266–73; Bynum, "Misshapen Identity," in Patricia Morton, ed., *Discovering the Women of Slavery,* 242.

22. 42 So. 2d 747; Bynum, "'White Negroes,'" 266–73.

23. Romano, "Crossing the Line," 21, Kennedy, *Jim Crow Guide,* 61.

24. Papers of the NAACP, part 18; 42 So. 747, cited in Romano, "Crossing the Line," 21; Bynum, "'White Negroes,'" 274.

25. Bynum, "'White Negroes,'" 249.

26. Sohn, "Principle and Expediency," 130–31.

27. ACLU Archives, box 1104, folder 41; see also Sohn, "Principle and Expediency," 131–32.

28. Carl T. Rowan, *South of Freedom,* 91–92.

29. ACLU Archives, box 1104, folder 41; see also Sohn, "Principle and Expediency," 131–32.

30. ACLU Archives, box 1110, folder 21.

31. ACLU Archives, box 1110, folder 21.

32. Sohn, "Principle and Expediency," 132.

33. ACLU Archives, box 1112, folder 9.

34. All information about the case indicates that the man in question was the groom's father, but the attorney on the case believes that he might have been his grandfather.

35. Sohn, "Principle and Expediency," 135–36.

36. ACLU Archives, box 1124, folder 7.

37. ACLU Archives, box 1124, folder 7.

38. Jack Trezise, telephone conversation with author, June 9, 1999.

39. *Jones v. Lorenzen,* 441 P. 2d 986, 989.

40. Sohn, "Principle and Expediency," 137; Sickels, *Race, Marriage and the Law,* 86–87.

41. A writ of certiorari is one of two ways to ask the Supreme Court to hear a case. A direct appeal is the other way. For more information on the difference between the two, see chapter 20.

42. *Jackson v. State,* 37 Ala. App. 519, 72 So. 2d 114, *cert. denied,* 348 US 483 (1954), as discussed in Bernard Schwartz, *Super Chief: Early Warren and His Supreme Court—A Judicial Biography,* 158–59.

43. Peter Wallenstein, "Race, Marriage, and the Law of Freedom: Alabama and Virginia, 1860's–1960's," 70 Chicago-Kent Law Review 415–16.

44. *In forma pauperis* indicates that a plaintiff is unable to pay the filing fees.

45. Sohn, "Principle and Expediency," 70.

46. Sohn, "Principle and Expediency," 70–72.

47. Sohn, "Principle and Expediency," 73.

48. Gregory Michael Dorr, "Principled Expediency: Eugenics, *Naim v. Naim,* and the Supreme Court."

49. Ed Cray, *Chief Justice: A Biography of Earl Warren,* 450.

50. Sohn, "Principle and Expediency," 139–40.

51. Papers of the NAACP, part 15, series B.

52. Sohn, "Principle and Expediency," 140–42.

53. ACLU Archives, box 1043, folder 16.

54. Jack Greenberg, *Race Relations and American Law,* 345.

55. Maryland v. Howard, 2 R.R.L.R. 676 (Baltimore Crim. Ct. 1957), cited in Greenberg, *Race Relations,* 346.

56. ACLU Archives, box 1106, folder, 16; *Baltimore Afro-American,* December 8, 1956, 1, 2.

57. ACLU Archives, box 1106, folder 16; *Baltimore Afro-American,* December 8, 1956, 1, 2.

58. Greenberg, 344, 398; Albert Gordon, *Intermarriage: Interfaith, Interracial, Interethnic,* 222.

59. Byron Curti Martyn, "Racism in the United States: A History of Antimiscegenation Legislation and Litigation," PhD diss., 1219, 1221.

60. Joanne Grant, *Ella Baker: Freedom Bound,* 169.

61. Gordon, *Intermarriage,* 222.

62. Martyn, "Racism in the United States," 1191.

63. Martyn, "Racism in the United States," 1223, 1227.

64. Charles F. Robinson II, "The Antimiscegenation Conversation: Love's Legislated Limits (1868–1967)," PhD diss., 164.

65. *Baltimore Afro-American,* March 11, 1967, 1, 2.

66. Martyn, "Racism in the United States," 1225–26; *Baltimore Afro-American,* March 11, 1967, 1–2.

67. Sickels, *Race, Marriage and the Law,* 71.

9. The Sad Case of Ruby and Ham

1. Gregory Michael Dorr, "Principled Expediency: Eugenics, *Naim v. Naim,* and the Supreme Court," 119.

2. ACLU Archives, box 1106, folder 21; Chang Moon Sohn, "Principle and Expediency in Judicial Review: Miscegenation Cases in the Supreme Court," PhD diss., 73–74; Dorr, "Principled Expediency."

3. ACLU Archives, box 1106, folder 21; Sohn, "Principle and Expediency," 75; Dorr, "Principled Expediency"; David Carliner, interview by author, June 1, 1998.

4. ACLU Archives, box 1106, folder 21; Sohn, "Principle and Expediency," 75–76; Dorr, "Principled Expediency."

5. Bangel practiced law with two relatives of the same name. Only one, Herbert Bangel, is still alive, and he does not have any independent recollections of the case, nor has the office retained its original case file.

6. ACLU Archives, box 1106, folder 21; Dorr, "Principled Expediency."

7. Dorr, "Principled Expediency."

8. Portsmouth File, folder 2, provided by Gregory Michael Dorr.

9. I say "apparently" because the recollections of all three parties are different. In my interview with him, Carliner did not mention Mirman or Stant. Mirman believes that Carliner called Stant because of the firm's matrimonial practice, while Stant is unsure who introduced him to the case but does not believe it was Carliner.

10. Frederick T. Stant, interview by author, July 22, 1998. Stant's nickname

comes from his prowess at shooting cardboard ducks at an amusement park across the street from where he grew up.

11. Alan Mirman, interview by author, July 13, 1998.

12. ACLU Archives, box 1106, folder 21.

13. Carliner claims that he did not write the letters but signed them on behalf of the ACLU.

14. Sohn, "Principle and Expediency," 77.

15. ACLU Archives, box 1106, folder 21.

16. ACLU Archives, box 1106, folder 21.

17. Dorr, "Principled Expediency."; Sohn, "Principle and Expediency," 79–80.

18. Dorr, "Principled Expediency."

19. Dorr, "Principled Expediency."

20. Alan Mirman is convinced that he argued the case, remembering an extraordinarily hostile reception. He stated that he was able to say only four or five words before Chief Justice Hudgins jumped in and that for the next half hour, he was treated as a pariah, never able to say more than ten words in a row.

21. ACLU Archives, box 1106, folder 21; Sohn, "Principle and Expediency," 79–80; Dorr, "Principled Expediency"; Carliner, interview, June 1, 1998.

22. 125 U.S. 190, 31 L. Ed. 654, 657, 8 S. Ct. 723.

23. *Naim v. Naim,* 197 Va. 80, 87 S.E. 2d 749, 752 (1955).

24. Sohn, "Principle and Expediency," 80; Portsmouth File, folder 1.

25. 87 S. Ed. 2d 749, 753; Portsmouth File, folder 1.

26. 87 S. Ed. 2d 749, 753–54.

27. *Kinney v. Commonwealth,* 71 Va.(30 Gratt.) 858, 869 (1878), quoted in 87 S. Ed. 2d 749, 754.

28. 87 S. Ed. 2d 749, 756.

29. ACLU Archives, box 1106, folder 21; Sohn, "Principle and Expediency," 83.

30. I attempted to interview Will Maslow for this book, and he was less than agreeable with me, failing to respond to my letters and, when by chance I met him in person, claiming no recollection whatsoever of the case. While memories of many of those I interviewed have dimmed with age, I do not believe that this entire case has faded from Maslow's memory, particularly since, as of 1998, he was contributing legal advice to the AJC.

31. ACLU Archives, box 1106, folder 21.

32. ACLU Archives, box 1106, folder 21; Sohn, "Principle and Expediency," 83; Carliner, interview, June 1, 1998.

33. Carliner, interview, June 1, 1998.

34. ACLU Archives, box 1106, folder 21.

35. This author has been unable to discover why Ennis, who was with the ACLU at the time, is listed as being affiliated with the JACL on the *Naim* brief.

36. None of the parties interviewed remembered Reiner's role in the case, and I was unable to trace him.

37. Sohn, "Principle and Expediency," 83–84.

38. Sohn, "Principle and Expediency," 84.

39. Juan Williams, *Thurgood Marshall: American Revolutionary*, 242, 387.

40. Dorr, "Principled Expediency."

41. Sohn, "Principle and Expediency," 85.

42. ACLU Archives, box 1106, folder 21.

43. Sohn, "Principle and Expediency," 85.

44. ACLU Archives, box 1106, folder 21.

45. Sohn, "Principle and Expediency," 158.

46. ACLU Archives, box 1106, folder 21.

47. Sohn, "Principle and Expediency," 86–87.

48. Dorr, "Principled Expediency."

49. American Jewish Congress Library files, New York, NY.

50. 350 US 891 (1955); Sohn, "Principle and Expediency," 87.

51. Dorr, "Principled Expediency."

52. Dorr, "Principled Expediency."

53. Ed Cray, *Chief Justice: A Biography of Earl Warren*, 451.

54. Dorr, "Principled Expediency."

55. Peter Wallenstein, "Race, Marriage, and the Law of Freedom: Alabama and Virginia, 1860's–1960's," 70 Chicago-Kent Law Review 418.

56. Dorr, "Principled Expediency."

57. Dorr, "Principled Expediency."

58. Dorr, "Principled Expediency."

59. Sohn, "Principle and Expediency," 87–88

60. ACLU Archives, box 1106, folder 21.

61. ACLU Archives, box 1106, folder 21.

62. Sohn, "Principle and Expediency," 89.

63. Sohn, "Principle and Expediency," 89–90.

64. 197 Va. 134 (1956); ACLU Archives, box 1106, folder 21; Sohn, "Principle and Expediency," 91; Dorr, "Principled Expediency."

65. Sohn, "Principle and Expediency," 91.

66. Dorr, "Principled Expediency."

67. Portsmouth File, folder 1.

68. 350 US 985 (1955); Sohn, "Principle and Expediency," 92.

69. Dorr, "Principled Expediency."

70. Dorr, "Principled Expediency," emphasis in original.

71. Cray, *Chief Justice,* 451.

10. Connie and Dewey Share a Room

1. Pauli Murray, ed., *States' Laws on Race and Color,* 83–84.

2. Fla. Stats. Ann. sec 741.12 (1944), quoted in Jack Greenberg, *Race Relations and American Law,* 397; Stetson Kennedy, *Jim Crow Guide: The Way It Was,* 64–65; Joseph R. Washington Jr., *Marriage in Black and White,* 76.

3. Washington, *Marriage in Black and White,* 73–74.

4. Anthony Lewis, "Race, Sex and the Supreme Court," *New York Times,* November 22, 1964.

5. The record at p. 3, Supreme Court case files, Vermont Law School; Chang Moon Sohn, "Principle and Expediency in Judicial Review: Miscegenation Cases in the Supreme Court," PhD diss., 95.

6. You may have noticed that both Graves and Haltom, who argued the *Jackson* case used initials, rather than first names. This was a frequent occurrence among black professionals to prevent whites from calling them by their first names instead of using an honorific "Mr." and a last name. Graves's full name was Grattan Ellesmere Graves.

7. *Miami Herald,* obituary, January 21, 1992, B3.

8. The record, 5.

9. Harold Braynon, interview by author, August 20, 1998.

10. The record, 88–93.

11. The record, 94.

12. The record, 97–98.

13. Braynon, interview, August 20, 1998; Sohn, "Principle and Expediency," 96.

14. Defendants' Florida Supreme Court brief, 7.

15. Defendants' Florida Supreme Court brief, 11–13.

16. Defendants' Florida Supreme Court brief, 13–14.

17. *Meyer v. Nebraska,* 262 U.S. 390, 399.

18. Defendants' Florida Supreme Court brief, 13–17.

19. *McLaughlin v. Florida,* 153 So. 2d 1, 2–3 (1963).

20. Sohn, "Principle and Expediency," 97.

21. William Coleman, interview by author, July 28, 1998.

22. Jurisdictional statement, 1.

23. Jurisdictional statement, 9–12.

24. Jurisdiction statement, 12–15.

25. Jurisdiction statement, 15–17.

26. Jurisdiction statement, 17–18.

27. Appellees' response to jurisdictional statement, 2–7.

28. Appellees' response to jurisdictional statement, 8–13.

29. Appellees' response to jurisdictional statement, 14–17.

30. According to Michael Meltsner, a lawyer for the NAACP Legal Defense Fund, interns' names never appeared on Legal Defense Fund Supreme Court briefs. Michael Meltsner, letter to author, July 17, 2000.

31. Elizabeth Holtzman, interview by author, September 24, 1998.

32. Jack Greenberg, interview by author, September 29, 1998.

33. Holtzman, interview, September 24, 1998.

34. James Nabrit III, interview by author, July 17, 1998.

35. Appellants' brief, 2–3.

36. Appellants' brief, 4.

37. Appellants' brief, 9–12.

38. Appellants' brief, 13–14.

39. Appellants' brief, 15–19.

40. 50 Tenn. 310, 311 (1871).

41. 39 Ga. 321, 326 (1869).

42. Appellants' brief, 19–23.

43. Appellants' brief, 27–30.

44. Appellants' brief, 20–36.

45. Appellants' brief, 45–53.

46. Appellants' brief, 53–56.

47. Appellants' brief, 56–61.

48. Appellant's reply brief, 2–4.

49. Sohn, "Principle and Expediency," 100–101; Coleman, interview, July 28, 1998.

50. Sohn, "Principle and Expediency," 101–2.

51. Actually, it was two years.

52. Coleman, interview, July 28, 1998.

53. Sohn, "Principle and Expediency," 101–2.

54. Sohn, "Principle and Expediency," 102.

55. Stephen L. Wasby, Anthony A. D'Amato, and Rosemary Metrailer, *Desegregation from Brown to Alexander*, 143.

56. Sohn, "Principle and Expediency," 102–4.

57. Alexander Bickel, "Integrated Cohabitation," 5.

58. Sohn, "Principle and Expediency," 104–5.

59. Wasby, D'Amato, and Metrailer, *Desegregation*, 143.

60. Sohn, "Principle and Expediency," 105.

61. Robert J. Sickels, *Race, Marriage and the Law*, 102.

62. Sohn, "Principle and Expediency," 105.

63. Sohn, "Principle and Expediency," 105–6.

64. 85 S. Ct. 283, 288–89.

65. 85 S. Ct. 283, 291–92.

11. Richard and Mildred Want to Go Home

1. Unfortunately Cohen and Hirschkop are no longer speaking to one another. Cohen is angry that Hirschkop took possession of the file from the case and denied him access to it. Hirschkop is angry that the Showtime movie *Mr. and Mrs. Loving* featured only one lawyer part: that of Bernie Cohen. Cohen denies that it is due to any misinformation on his part and says that he provided the producers with information indicating that the two worked in tandem. Hirschkop threatened legal action over the omission of his character, and the film currently has a disclaimer at the end explaining Hirschkop's role in the case and the fact that his omission from the movie is due to dramatic license.

2. "Postscript," *Mr. and Mrs. Loving,* video recording, directed by Richard Friedenberg (Showtime, 1996).

3. Bernie Cohen, interview by author, June 16, 1998.

4. Cohen, interview, June 16, 1998.

5. Cohen, interview, June 16, 1998.

6. Hirschkop says that the case file shows that Hal Witt suggested the use of this case to Cohen.

7. 189 Va. 327 (1949).

8. 189 Va. 333 (1949).

9. Cohen, interview, June 16, 1998.

10. Cohen, interview, June 16, 1998.

11. Record of the Supreme Court of Appeals of Virginia, 8; Robert J. Sickels, *Race, Marriage and the Law,* 79.

12. Record of the Supreme Court of Appeals of Virginia, 8; Sickels, *Race, Marriage and the Law,* 79.

13. John Edward Lane III, "Leon Maurice Bazile," in W. Hamilton Bryson, *Legal Education in Virginia, 1779–1979: A Biographical Approach,* 83–86.

14. Jack Lilly, interview by author, July 22, 1999.

15. *Mediaweek,* October 21, 1996.

16. Hirschkop believes it was late July or early August, but Cohen just recalls it was the summer.

17. Cohen, interview, June 16, 1998; Phil Hirschkop, interview by author, February 12, 1998.

18. Arthur Kinoy, *Rights on Trial: The Odyssey of a People's Lawyer,* 196–97.

19. Robert Hall, interview by author, December 22, 1998.

20. Section 2283 of the judicial code discusses the difference between federal and state jurisdiction. Civil rights groups made generous use of this section in the 1960s in their attempts to remove civil rights cases from the jurisdiction of state courts to the more liberal federal court system.

21. Hirschkop, interview, February 12, 1998.

22. *New York Times,* June 12, 1992.

23. Cohen, interview, June 16, 1998; Hirschkop, interview, February 12, 1998.

24. Hirschkop, interview, April 27, 1999.

25. Hirschkop, interview, February 12, 1998.

26. Hirschkop, interview, February 12, 1998; Kinoy, *Rights on Trial,* 181.

27. Hirschkop, interviews, February 12, 1998, and January 20, 1998; Reuters News Service, March 10, 1993, Lexis Nexis online data base.

28. Cohen, interview, June 16, 1998; Hirschkop, interview, February 12, 1998.

29. Peter Wallenstein, "Race, Marriage, and the Law of Freedom: Alabama and Virginia, 1860's–1960's," 70 Chicago-Kent Law Review 424.

30. Sickels, *Race, Marriage and the Law,* 81.

31. Wallenstein, "Race, Marriage and the Law of Freedom," 422.

32. Peter Wallenstein, "Race, Marriage and the Supreme Court from *Pace v. Alabama* (1883) to *Loving v. Virginia* (1967)," 81; Cohen, interview, June 16, 1998; Hirschkop, interview, February 12, 1998. Mr. McIlwaine declined to be interviewed for this book but was kind enough to direct this author to a conference on the case, which took place in November 1997.

33. Sickels, *Race, Marriage and the Law,* 2.

34. Mildred Loving, interview by author, April 27, 1999.

35. Wallenstein, "Race, Marriage and the Supreme Court," 80.

36. Simeon Booker, "The Couple that Rocked the Courts," 78. The article says he earned five dollars an hour, but this author believes that figure is significantly higher than his actual wages, particularly since the article in question also misstated the name of the Lovings' daughter.

37. Cohen, interview, June 16, 1998; Hirschkop, interview, February 12, 1998.

38. Sickels, *Race, Marriage and the Law,* 81; Wallenstein, "Race, Marriage and the Law of Freedom," 424–25.

39. 143 Va. 310 (1925).

40. *In Re Kemmler,* 136 U.S. 436 (1889).

41. Virginia Supreme Court of Appeals record, *Loving v. Virginia* file, Vermont Law School, 9–11.

42. Virginia Supreme Court of Appeals record, 11–15.

43. 30 Gratt 865 (1879).

44. Virginia Supreme Court of Appeals record, 16.

45. Virginia Supreme Court of Appeals record, 16–17.

46. Wallenstein, "Race, Marriage and the Supreme Court," 81.

47. Virginia Supreme Court of Appeals record, 18; Sickels, *Race, Marriage and the Law*, 81.

48. Carrico refused my request for an interview, so it is difficult to determine where he personally stood on the issue.

49. James Davis, interview by author, July 29, 1999.

50. Virginia Supreme Court of Appeals record, 20–23.

51. Virginia Supreme Court of Appeals record, 23–25.

52. Virginia Supreme Court of Appeals record, 25–27.

53. ACLU Archives, box 1123, folder 9.

54. Frank F. Arness, "The Evolution of the Virginia Anti-miscegenation Laws," master's thesis, 69.

12. On to the Supreme Court

1. Record of *Loving v. Virginia,* Supreme Court case files, 29–31.

2. *New York Times,* July 30, 1966, 9.

3. Loving notice of appeal, Supreme Court case files, 5–6.

4. Loving notice of appeal.

5. Robert J. Sickels, *Race, Marriage and the Law,* 83.

6. Loving notice of appeal, 11–15.

7. Loving notice of appeal, 15–18.

8. Loving notice of appeal, 18–20.

9. Jon Schneider, e-mail to author, March 10, 1999.

10. Byron Curti Martyn, "Racism in the United States: A History of Anti-miscegenation Legislation and Litigation," PhD diss., 1308.

11. Peter Wallenstein, "Race, Marriage and the Supreme Court from *Pace v. Alabama* (1883) to *Loving v. Virginia* (1967)," 83.

12. Bernie Cohen, interview by author, June 16, 1998; Phil Hirschkop, interview by author, February 12, 1998.

13. The Martindale-Hubbell Law Directory lists lawyers and law firms throughout the United States.

14. See *Legal Times,* October 6, 1997; *New York Law Journal,* April 21, 1995; *Legal Times,* July 16, 1990; *Christian Science Monitor,* February 3, 1988; *Legal Times,* January 19, 1987; *Legal Times,* October 6, 1996; *Communications Daily,* October 31, 1985.

15. Cohen, interview, June 16, 1998.

16. Hirschkop, interview, December 10, 1998.

17. Hirschkop, interview, February 12, 1998.

18. Chang Moon Sohn, "Principle and Expediency in Judicial Review: Miscegenation Cases in the Supreme Court," PhD diss., 113; Hirschkop, interview, February 12, 1998.

19. Hirschkop, interviews, December 10, 1998, and April 27, 1999.

20. Moot court is a law school exercise in which students write briefs for both sides of a legal issue. They argue the issue from whichever vantage point they are assigned.

21. William Zabel, interview by author, May 17, 1999.

22. Joe Goldberg did not respond to repeated requests for an interview.

23. Hirschkop, interviews, February 12, 1998; December 10, 1998; and April 27, 1999.

24. Arthur Berney, interview by author, October 12, 1998; Berney, fax to author, November 3, 1998.

25. Jon Schneider, e-mail to author, March 11, 1999.

26. Berney, interview, October 12, 1998; Berney, fax, November 3, 1998; Hirschkop, interview, April 27, 1999.

27. Berney, interview, October 12, 1998; Berney, fax, November 3, 1998.

28. Zabel, interview, May 17, 1999.

29. ACLU Archives, box 1123, folder 9.

30. ACLU Archives, box 1123, folder 9.

31. Hirschkop, interview, February 12, 1998.

32. Berney, interview, October 12, 1998.

33. Hirschkop, interview, April 27, 1999.

34. Berney, interview, October 12, 1998.

35. Berney, interview, October 12, 1998.

36. ACLU Archives, box 1508.

37. Cohen, interview, June 16, 1998.

38. Cohen, interview, June 16, 1998.

39. Unfortunately, Montagu was incapacitated by a stroke and unable to respond to my requests for an interview. He subsequently passed away.

40. Hirschkop, interview, February 12, 1998.

41. Hirschkop, interviews, January 20, 1998, and February 12, 1998.

42. Cohen, interview, June 16, 1998.

43. Hirschkop, interview, January 20, 1998.

44. Cohen, interview, June 16, 1998.

45. Hirschkop, interview, February 12, 1998.

46. Carliner, interview, June 1, 1998.

47. In response to a request for an interview, Wulf wrote that his work on *Loving* was strictly ex officio and that he was not involved in the day-to-day planning.

48. Appellant's brief, 4–6.

49. Appellant's brief, 11–24.

50. Appellant's brief, 24–28.

51. Appellant's brief, 28–38.

52. Appellants' brief; Sickels, *Race, Marriage and the Law,* 106–7; Peter Wallenstein, "Race, Marriage, and the Law of Freedom: Alabama and Virginia, 1860's–1960's," 70 Chicago-Kent Law Review 428.

53. Appellant's brief, 39–40.

54. Public Papers of the Presidents, February 21, 1992.

55. *ABA Journal,* May 1, 1986.

56. Faculty information, Boston College, www.bc.edu/bc_org/avp/law/lwsch/facinfo.html.

57. Faculty publications, Boston College, www.bc.edu/bc_org/avp/law/lwsch/facpuba-f.html.

58. *Electronic News,* July 24, 1995.

59. *Forbes,* October 13, 1997.

60. *International Herald Tribune,* April 13, 1995.

61. *PR Newswire,* March 22, 1983; Zabel, interview, May 17, 1999.

62. *South China Morning Post,* January 29, 1994.

63. U.P.I., June 14, 1988, Lexis Nexis online data base.

64. Zabel, interview, May 17, 1999.

65. Cohen, interviews, June 16, 1998, and April 27, 1999.

66. Cohen, interviews, June 16, 1998, and April 27, 1999.

67. Hirschkop, interview, February 12, 1998.

68. Hirschkop, interview, April 27, 1999.

69. *New York Times,* April 16, 1971.

70. Hirschkop, interview, February 12, 1998.

71. *Legal Times,* March 17, 1986.

72. *Washington Post,* April 18, 1997.

73. *Regardie's Magazine,* November 1994; *Washington Post,* August 28, 1988.

74. *New York Times,* March 5, 1969.

75. *Washington Post,* May 8, 1980.

76. *Washington Post,* May 6, 1980.

77. *Washington Post,* November 22, 1986.

78. *Washington Post,* July 11, 1985.

79. *Washington Post,* January 28, 1994.

80. *New York Times,* October 17, 1986.

81. *New York Times,* September 27, 1975.

82. *Legal Times,* January 5, 1987.

83. *Civil RICO Report,* January 21, 1998

84. *Regardie's Magazine,* November, 1994.

85. *Legal Times,* July 21, 1986.

86. Irving R. Stuart and Lawrence Edwin Abt, eds., *Interracial Marriage: Expectations and Realities,* 149.

87. Stuart and Abt, *Interracial Marriage,* 14.

13. The Amicus Briefs

1. NAACP Legal Defense Fund, amicus brief, NAACP files, Cleveland Public Library.

2. NAACP Legal Defense Fund, amicus brief.

3. The case file, together with many others, are subject to restricted access at the Library of Congress. Neither Mr. Meltsner, who was extremely helpful, nor this author was able to gain access to the files.

4. Michael Meltsner, interview by author, June 18, 1998; Jack Greenberg, interview by author, September 29, 1998,

5. Chang Moon Sohn, "Principle and Expediency in Judicial Review: Miscegenation Cases in the Supreme Court," PhD diss., 46.

6. NAACP, amicus brief, 3.

7. NAACP, amicus brief, 5–6.

8. NAACP, amicus brief, 6–7.

9. NAACP, amicus brief, 11.

10. Actually, Oklahoma also barred blacks from marrying Native Americans.

11. NAACP, amicus brief, 12–14.

12. JACL, amicus brief, 2, Supreme Court case files.

13. William Marutani, interview by author, April 28, 1998.

14. JACL, amicus brief, 1–2.

15. Actually, *Pace* was overruled in *McLaughlin.*

16. JACL, amicus brief, 6–12.

17. JACL, amicus brief, 12–17.

18. JACL, amicus brief, 17–33.

19. Donald Kramer, interview by author, October 20, 1998.

20. Marutani, interview, April 28, 1998; Kramer, interview, October 20, 1998.

21. The latter group consisted of John J. Russell, bishop of Richmond; Lawrence Cardinal Shehan, archbishop of Baltimore; Paul A. Hallihan, archbishop of Atlanta; Philip M. Hannan, archbishop of New Orleans; Robert E.

Lucey, archbishop of San Antonio; Joseph B. Brunini, apostolic administrator of Natchez-Jackson; Lawrence M. DeFalco, bishop of Amarillo; Joseph A. Dimick, apostolic administrator of Nashville; Thomas K. Gorman, bishop of Dallas–Ft. Worth; Joseph H. Hodges, bishop of Wheeling; John L. Morkovsky, apostolic administrator of Galveston-Houston; Victor J. Reed, bishop of Oklahoma City and Tulsa; L. J. Reicher, bishop of Austin; Thomas Tschoepe, bishop of San Antonio; Ernest L. Unterkoefler, bishop of Charleston; and Vincent S. Waters, bishop of Raleigh.

22. Brian William Thomson, "Racism and Racial Classification: A Case Study of the Virginia Racial Integrity Legislation," PhD diss., 275.

23. Sohn, "Principle and Expediency," 116–17.

24. Catholic consortium, amicus brief, 5–12, Supreme Court case files.

25. Catholic consortium, amicus brief, 13.

26. See *Reynolds v. United States,* 98 U.S. 145 (1878).

27. Catholic consortium, amicus brief, 14, 17–19.

28. *Buck v. Bell,* 274 U.S. 200 (1927); *Skinner v. Oklahoma,* 316 U.S. 535 (1942).

29. Catholic consortium, amicus brief, 19–22.

30. www.columbia.edu/cu/law/fb_jg.html.

31. http://www.slaw.neu.edu/public/faculty/f_meltsn.htm.

32. *New York Times,* obituary, May 16, 1984.

33. *New York Law Journal,* April 15, 1994; "Public School Desegregation: A Contemporary Analysis," 37 St. Louis Law Journal 885 (1993), quoted in Yale Law Journal, June 1997.

34. Marutani, interview, April 28, 1998; Francis Flaherty, "Wins Grow under State ERAs."

35. Kramer, interview, October 20, 1998; *Legal Intelligencer,* June 23, 1998, April 9, 1998, et al.

36. *New York Times,* obituary, May 5, 1977, B11; *Chicago Sun-Times,* obituary, April 21, 1997, 48; "Catholics Protest to Pretoria," *New York Times,* August 3, 1986, 14; *Michigan Lawyers Weekly,* April 3, 1995.

37. William Bentley Ball, interview by author, April 21, 1998.

14. Virginia and North Carolina Defend the Indefensible

1. State of Virginia's statement opposing jurisdiction, Supreme Court case files.

2. Appellee's brief, Supreme Court case files.

3. Appellee's brief, 5.

4. Appellee's brief, 5–16.

5. Brief for Virginia, 50.

6. Robert J. Sickels, *Race, Marriage and the Law,* 103–4.

7. Donald Baker, "Virginia Judge Clears Way for Trial of Senator Babalas on Conflict Charge," *Washington Post,* May 22, 1986, B1.

8. Paul G. Edwards, "Dalton Renews Desegregation Talks," *Washington Post,* February 1, 1978, C1.

9. Alex Klein, "Twin Endorsements Boost North's Campaign," *Virginian-Pilot,* August 19, 1994, B3.

10. N.C. Const. art. 14, sec. 8, quoted in Jack Greenberg, *Race Relations and American Law,* 398; *State v. Miller,* 224 N.C. 228, 29 S.E. 2d 751 (1944), cited in *N.C. Gen. Stat.* secs. 14.181 and 51–3 (1953), 346; Stetson Kennedy, *Jim Crow Guide: The Way It Was,* 68.

11. North Carolina's amicus brief, 6.

15. May It Please the Court

1. Hall told me that he did not attend oral argument and regrets that fact.

2. Phil Hirschkop, interview by author, February 12, 1998.

3. Arthur Berney, interview by author, October 12, 1998.

4. William Zabel, interview by author, May 17, 1999.

5. *New York Times,* April 11, 1967.

6. The transcript of the oral argument does not indicate which justice asked which question, and neither Cohen nor Hirschkop could remember the names associated with individual queries. William Marutani made the task of historians easier by including the name of the questioning justice in his replies. In addition, he was able to recall each of the questions asked in our interview, something that Cohen and Hirschkop were unable to do. Robert McIlwaine responded to some of the justices by name, as well.

7. Record of oral argument, 1–2, Supreme Court case files.

8. Record of oral argument, 2–3.

9. Actually, it was Robeson County, not Roanoke County, and it wasn't that these tribes were considered white, only that they were forbidden from intermarrying with blacks.

10. Record, 4–8.

11. Record, 8.

12. Record, 8–10.

13. Record, 10–13.

14. Hirschkop, interview, February 12, 1998.

15. Bernie Cohen, e-mail to author, October 19, 1998.

16. Record, 12.

17. Record, 13.

18. William Marutani, interview by author, April 28, 1998; Donald Kramer, interview by author, October 20, 1998.

19. Record, 13–15.

20. Record, 14–15.

21. Record, 15–16.

22. Marutani, interview, April 28, 1998; Record, 16–17.

23. Record, 17–20.

24. Record, 19–20.

25. Record, 20–21.

26. Record, 22–26.

27. Record, 26–28.

28. Ed Cray, *Chief Justice: A Biography of Earl Warren*, 450.

29. Record, 28.

30. Record, 29.

31. Record, 30–31.

32. Record, 32–33.

33. Record, 33–36.

34. Record, 36–37.

35. Record, 38–39.

36. See Harvey M. Applebaum, "Miscegenation Statutes: A Constitutional and Social Problem," 53 Georgetown Law Journal 49–91 (1964).

37. Record, 39–41.

38. Record, 41–42.

39. Record, 43–44.

40. Record, 44–46.

41. Record, 46.

42. Record, 46.

43. Record, 46.

44. Record, 46–47.

45. Record, 47–48.

46. Hirschkop, interview, February 12, 1998.

16. The Supreme Court Speaks

1. Bernard Schwartz, *Super Chief: Earl Warren and His Supreme Court—A Judicial Biography*, 668–69.

2. Peter Wallenstein, "Race, Marriage, and the Law of Freedom: Alabama and Virginia, 1860's–1960's," 70 Chicago-Kent Law Review 427.

3. Simeon Booker, "The Couple That Rocked the Courts," 82.

4. Schmidt, a leading force behind the Edison Project, which pairs public schools with private managers, did not respond to repeated requests for an interview.

5. Ed Cray, *Chief Justice: A Biography of Earl Warren,* 452–53; Schwartz, *Super Chief,* 669.

6. 388 U.S. 1, 1–12.

7. 388 U.S. 1, 11.

8. 388 U.S. 1, 12.

9. Phil Hirschkop, interview by author, February 12, 1998.

10. *Virginian-Pilot,* June 13, 1967, 4; Wallenstein, "Race, Marriage, and the Law of Freedom," 430.

11. Wallenstein, "Race, Marriage and the Law of Freedom," 430.

12. *Virginian-Pilot,* June 13, 1967, 4; Robert J. Sickles, *Race, Marriage and the Law,* 1–2.

13. *New York Times,* June 12, 1992.

14. Wallenstein, "Race, Marriage and the Law of Freedom," 435.

15. William Coleman, interview by author, July 28, 1998.

16. Lou Pollak, interview by author, July 14, 1998.

17. Hirschkop, interview, January 20, 1998.

18. Hirschkop, interview, February 12, 1998.

17. Not All States Listen

1. Byron Curti Martyn, "Racism in the United States: A History of Anti-miscegenation Legislation and Litigation," PhD diss., 1322.

2. Peter Wallenstein, "Race, Marriage and the Supreme Court from *Pace v. Alabama* (1883) to *Loving v. Virginia* (1967), 82.

3. Chang Moon Sohn, "Principle and Expediency in Judicial Review: Miscegenation Cases in the Supreme Court," PhD diss., 119–20.

4. *Davis v. Gately,* 269 F. Supp. 996 (D. Del. 1967).

5. Robert J. Sickels, *Race, Marriage and the Law,* 112; *Davis v. Gately,* 269 F. Supp 996 (1967).

6. Martyn, "Racism in the United States," 1323.

7. Martyn, "Racism in the United States," 1337; Ruth Ann Nelson, e-mail to author, February 20, 1998.

8. *Van Hook v. Blanton,* 206 So. 2d 210 (Fla. 1968).

9. *New York Times,* January 25, 1968, 5, and February 2, 1968, 4; Martyn, "Racism in the United States," 1320.

10. Martyn, "Racism in the United States," 1325.

11. Martyn, "Racism in the United States," 1329.

12. Martyn, "Racism in the United States," 1324–33, 41.

13. *New York Times,* August 12, 1967, 31, cited in Sickels, *Race, Marriage and the Law,* 113.

14. Peter Wallenstein, "Race, Marriage and the Law of Freedom: Alabama and Virginia, 1860's–1960's," 70 Chicago-Kent Law Review 432.

15. *New York Times,* July 13, 1968, 23; Wallenstein, "Race, Marriage, and the Law of Freedom," 433.

16. Sickels, *Race, Marriage and the Law,* 113; *New York Times,* July 22, 1967, 11, and September 30, 1967, 28; Martyn, "Racism in the United States," 1342; *Cleveland Plain-Dealer,* March 24, 1995.

17. Sickels, *Race, Marriage and the Law,* 113; *New York Times,* July 22, 1967, 11, September 30, 1967, 28, and October 7, 1967, 58; *Cleveland Plain-Dealer,* March 24, 1995.

18. Tenn. Const. art. XI, sec. 14.

18. "A Big Interracial Display of Their Romance"

1. Charles Evers and Andrew Szanton, *Have No Fear: The Charles Evers Story,* 257–58.

2. *New York Times,* August 3, 1970; Byron Curti Martyn, "Racism in the United States: A History of Anti-miscegenation Legislation and Litigation," PhD diss., 1350–52.

3. *New York Times,* August 3, 1970; Martyn, "Racism in the United States," 1350–52; marriage license application completed by Roger Mills and his prospective bride. The license and all legal documents referred to in this section were provided by Roger Mills.

4. Mills was the only one of the four whom I was able to interview. I was unable to track down Leary or Davis. Linson and Mills have divorced, and Linson did not respond to my requests for an interview.

5. Roger Mills, interview by author, December 1, 1998.

6. Petition for writ of mandamus, provided by Roger Mills.

7. Lawrence Ross, interview by author, December 9, 1998.

8. Constance Slaughter-Harvey, interview by author, April 13, 1999.

9. Fred Banks, interview by author, January 28, 1999.

10. Armand Derfner, interview by author, February 3, 1999.

11. Mills, interview, December 1, 1998; order of Judge Perry, provided by Roger Mills.

12. Ross, interview, December 9, 1998.

13. Banks, interview, January 28, 1999; Derfner, interview, February 3, 1999; John Maxey, interview by author, March 15, 1999.

14. The paper trail for the case is not complete, and the recollections of some of the attorneys conflicted with each other; so what follows is the best that I could piece together.

15. Bill for injunction, provided by Roger Mills.

16. Derfner, interview, February 3, 1999; Mills, interview, December 1, 1998; Maxey, interview, March 15, 1999; various papers provided by Mills.

17. Mills, interview, December 1, 1998; Maxey, interview, March 15, 1999; Mills papers; *Jackson Clarion-Ledger,* July 29, 1970.

18. Ross, interview, December 9, 1998; Mills, interview, December 1, 1998; Maxey, interview, March 15, 1999; various papers provided by Mills; *New York Times,* August 3, 1970.

19. Martyn, "Racism in the United States," 1350–52.

20. Derfner, interview, February 3, 1999; Maxey, interview, March 15, 1999; Ross, interview, December 9, 1998.

21. Derfner, interview, February 3, 1999.

22. Mills papers.

23. Maxey told me that Linson was pregnant with the couple's first child, but I did not try to confirm this information with other sources.

24. Mills, interview, December 1, 1998.

25. *Jackson Clarion-Ledger,* July 31, 1970.

26. *Davis v. Ashford,* 2 Race. Rel. L. Sur. 152 (S.D. Miss. 1970); Martyn, "Racism in the United States," 1350–52; Ross, interview, December 9, 1998; Mills, interview, December 1, 1998; Mills papers.

27. Mills, interview, December 1, 1998.

28. *Jackson Daily News,* August 3, 1970.

29. Ross, interview, December 9, 1998.

30. Judge Cox's order.

31. *New York Times,* August 3, 1970.

32. *New York Times,* August 3, 1970.

33. Mills, interview, December 1, 1998; Maxey, interview, March 15, 1999.

34. *Jackson Clarion Ledger/Daily News,* November 15, 1987, 1, 16.

35. By way of full disclosure, I should note that I worked as an attorney and an investigator for the Office of Civil Rights in New York City for six years myself.

36. *Atlanta Journal and Constitution,* May 5, 1994.

37. Mills, interview, December 1, 1998; *Atlanta Journal,* June 20, 1997; *Atlanta Journal and Constitution,* May 16, 1994.

38. Mills, interview, December 1, 1998.

39. *Maclean's,* February 2, 1987.

40. *Jackson Clarion-Ledger,* August 20, 1970 (this and other clippings were sent to me by Roger Mills).

41. *Jackson Daily News,* August 11, 1970.

42. *Jackson Clarion-Ledger,* August 20, 1970.

43. *Jackson Clarion-Ledger,* October 26, 1970.

44. *Jackson Daily News,* December 7, 1970.

45. *New York Times,* August 5, 1971.

46. *Jackson Clarion-Ledger,* May 29, 1978.

47. *Jackson Clarion-Ledger,* September 24, 1978.

48. *Jackson Clarion-Ledger,* March 16, 1971.

49. *New York Times,* August 5, 1971.

50. Actually, the marriage ended in divorce. Mills remarried, and his second wife is also black.

51. Robert J. Sickels, *Race, Marriage and the Law,* 114–5.

52. Renee Christian Romano, "Crossing the Line: Black-White Interracial Marriage in the United States, 1945–1990," PhD diss., 154; *Mississippi Code Annotated,* art. 14, sec 263.

19. The Feds Finally Step In

1. *United States v. Brittain,* 319 F. Supp. 1058; Peter Wallenstein, "Race, Marriage, and the Law of Freedom: Alabama and Virginia, 1860's–1960's," 70 Chicago-Kent Law Review 433–34; Walter Gorman, interview by author, August 18, 1998; *New York Times,* December 9, 1970, 40.

2. M. Karl Shurtliff, interview by author, April 8, 1998; Wallenstein, "Race, Marriage and the Law of Freedom," 433–34.

3. Shurtliff, interview, April 8, 1998.

4. Shurtliff, interview, April 8, 1998.

5. Shurtliff, interview, April 8, 1998.

6. Shurtliff, interview, April 8, 1998.

7. *United States v. Brittain,* 319 F. Supp 1058, 1061 (N.D. Ala. 1970); also Wallenstein, "Race, Marriage and the Law of Freedom," 433–34.

8. *New York Times,* December 9, 1970.

9. Shurtliff, interview, April 8, 1998.

10. U.P.I., August 9, 1982, Lexis Nexis online data base.

11. Julie Bailey, "Higher Ed Parkinson," *Lewiston (ID) Morning Tribune,* October 4, 1993.

12. Gene Fadness, "Let's Stay Out of Court on This One, Please," *Idaho Falls Post Register,* April 16, 1993.

13. Bill Hall, "Rocking the Boat Worries Idaho Education Board," *Lewiston (ID) Morning Tribune,* December 1, 1992.

14. Jim Jacobs, "Children's Health: Idaho Ed Board Bans Smoking in Schools," *Lewiston (ID) Morning Tribune,* March 19, 1994.

15. Shurtliff, interview, April 8, 1998.

16. Gorman, interview, August 18, 1998; *Business Lawyer,* July 1982; *Providence Journal-Bulletin,* October 29, 1997; *New York Times,* August 4, 1985; P.R. Newswire, May 28, 1987, Lexis Nexis online data base; *Providence Journal-Bulletin,* October 6, 1995.

17. Wallenstein, "Race, Marriage and the Law of Freedom," 434.

18. Sickels, *Race, Marriage and the Law,* 115.

19. Shurtliff, interview, April 8, 1998; see also *New York Times,* February 13, 1972.

20. Requests to the Department of Justice and the Georgia attorney general's office for information pertaining to the case have been unsuccessful. I have not even been able to find the name of the assistant U.S. attorney assigned to the case.

21. Shurtliff, interview, April 8, 1998.

22. Shurtliff, interview, April 8, 1998.

23. Unofficial Opinion U83–31 of the Attorney General of the State of Georgia, June 22, 1983, Lexis Nexis online data base.

24. Beth Day, *Sexual Life Between Blacks and Whites: The Roots of Racism,* 15.

25. *(SC) State,* February 6, 1998, provided by Brad Jordan.

26. *(SC) State,* February 6, 1998, provided by Brad Jordan; Robert McNamara, Maria Tempenis, and Beth Walton, *Crossing the Line: Interracial Couples in the South,* 159–60; see http://www.leginfo.state.sc.us/housemembers/.

27. *Tampa Tribune,* October 16, 1997.

28. Cordell Maddox, interview by author, July 9, 1999.

29. Brad Jordan, interview by author, July 13, 1999; *Tampa Tribune,* October 16, 1997.

30. Maddox, interview, July 9, 1999.

31. *Charleston Post and Courier,* November 5, 1998.

32. McNamara, Tempenis, and Walton, *Crossing the Line,* 161.

33. George Clay, interview by author, August 30, 1999; Alvin Holmes, interview by author, September 14, 1999.

34. *London Independent,* June 27, 1999.

35. *New York Times,* November 5, 2000.

36. *New York Times,* November 5, 2000.

37. *Secession Room News,* http://www.srnews.com/sp/sp.html (accessed 1998).

38. *Burlington Free Press,* October 5, 2000.

39. *New York Times,* November 12, 2000.

20. Happily Ever After

1. *Jet,* November 9, 1992.

2. "Postscript," *Mr. and Mrs. Loving,* video recording, directed by Richard Friedenberg (Showtime, 1996).

3. Phil Hirschkop, interview by author, January 20, 1998.

4. "Postscript," *Mr. and Mrs. Loving.*

5. Leslie Houser, interview by author, December 2, 1998.

6. *Richmond Times Dispatch,* August 25, 1966.

7. Kenneth Edwards, interview by author, July 24, 1999.

8. "Postscript," *Mr. and Mrs. Loving.*

9. *Richmond Times Dispatch,* August 25, 1966.

10. Robert Pratt, speech, Columbus School of Law symposium, November 1997.

11. *Des Moines Register,* March 31, 1996; Houser, interview, December 2, 1998.

12. Houser, interview, December 2, 1998.

13. Leslie Houser, letter to author, September 13, 2000.

14. Pratt, speech.

15. "Postscript," *Mr. and Mrs. Loving.*

16. *Jet,* November 9, 1992.

17. *Charlotte Observer,* December 19, 1998, 1, 21; Houser, interview, December 2, 1998.

18. Pratt, speech; "Postscript," *Mr. and Mrs. Loving.*

19. Houser, interview, December 22, 2000.

20. Houser, interview, December 2, 1998.

21. Pratt, speech.

22. Mildred Loving, interview by author, April 27, 1999.

23. *Jet,* November 9, 1992.

24. Bernie Cohen, interview by author, April 27, 1999.

25. Houser, interview, December 2, 1998.

26. Cohen, interview, April 27, 1999; Hirschkop, interview, April 27, 1999; Loving, interview, April 27, 1999.

27. Cohen, interview, June 16, 1998.

28. Cohen, interviews, June 16, 1998, and April 27, 1999.

29. Hirschkop, interview, April 27, 1999.

30. Kenneth James Lay, "Sexual Racism: A Legacy of Slavery," 13 National Black Law Journal 161, 179.

31. *Chicago Tribune,* June 28, 1992.

32. Garnett Brooks, telephone conversation with author, February 2, 1998.

33. Edwards, interview, July 24, 1999.

34. Houser, interview, December 22, 2000.

35. *New York Times,* June 12, 1992.

36. Robert J. Sickels, *Race, Marriage and the Law,* 150.

37. Stan Beason, interview by author, April 28, 1999.

38. Pratt, speech.

39. *Washington Post,* June 12, 1992; *Chicago Tribune,* June 28, 1992.

40. *Washington Post,* June 12, 1992.

Bibliography

Books

American Civil Liberties Union. *New Dimensions . . . New Challenges: Annual Report for 1965/67.* New York, 1967.

American Jewish Congress and National Association for the Advancement of Colored People. *Civil Rights in the United States in 1951: A Balance Sheet of Group Relations.* New York, 1952.

Baker, Lee D. *From Savage to Negro: Anthropology and the Construction of Race, 1896–1954.* Berkeley: University of California Press, 1998.

Baker, Ray Stannard. *Following the Color Line: An Account of Negro Citizenship in the American Democracy.* New York: Doubleday, Page, 1908.

Bardaglio, Peter W. *Reconstructing the Household: Families, Sex, and the Law in the Nineteenth-Century South.* Chapel Hill: University of North Carolina Press, 1995.

Bartley, Numan V., ed. *The Evolution of Southern Culture.* Athens: University of Georgia Press, 1988.

Bell, Derrick. *Race, Racism and American Law.* 3rd ed. Boston: Little, Brown, 1992.

Berry, Mary Frances. *The Pig Farmer's Daughter and Other Tales of American Justice: Episodes of Racism and Sexism in the Courts from 1865 to the Present.* New York: Knopf, 1999.

Bickel, Alexander M. *The Least Dangerous Branch: The Supreme Court at the Bar of Politics.* New Haven: Yale University Press, 1962.

Bloch, J. M. *Miscegenation, Melaleukation, and Mr. Lincoln's Dog.* New York: Schaum, 1958.

Branch, Taylor. *Pillar of Fire: America in the King Years, 1963–65.* New York: Simon and Schuster, 1998.

Brink, William, and Louis Harris. *Black and White: A Study of U.S. Racial Attitudes Today.* New York: Simon and Schuster, 1966.

Brown, Kathleen M. *Good Wives, Nasty Wenches, and Anxious Patriarchs: Gender, Race, and Power in Colonial Virginia.* Chapel Hill: University of North Carolina Press, 1996.

Bryson, W. Hamilton. *Legal Education in Virginia, 1779–1979: A Biographical Approach.* Charlottesville: University Press of Virginia, 1982.

Bynum, Victoria E. "Misshapen Identity: Memory, Folklore, and the Legend of Rachel Knight." In *Discovering the Women in Slavery: Emancipating Perspec-*

tives on the American Past, edited by Patricia Morton. Athens: University of Georgia Press, 1996.

———. "Reshaping the Bonds of Womanhood: Divorce in Reconstruction North Carolina." In *Divided Houses: Gender and the Civil War,* edited by Catherine Clinton and Nina Silver. Oxford: Oxford University Press, 1992.

———. *Unruly Women: The Politics of Social and Sexual Control in the Old South.* Chapel Hill: University of North Carolina Press, 1992.

Carson, Clayborne. *In Struggle: SNCC and the Black Awakening of the 1960's.* Cambridge: Harvard University Press, 1981.

Cecelski, David S., and Timothy B. Tyson. *Democracy Betrayed: The Wilmington Race Riot of 1898 and Its Legacy.* Chapel Hill: University of North Carolina Press, 1998.

Chuman, Frank F. *The Bamboo People: Japanese-Americans, Their History and the Law.* Chicago: Japanese American Research Project, 1981.

Clinton, Catherine, and Michele Gillespie, eds. *The Devil's Lane: Sex and Race in the Early South.* New York: Oxford University Press, 1997.

Cohen, William. *At Freedom's Edge: Black Mobility and the Southern White Quest for Racial Control, 1861–1915.* Baton Rouge: Louisiana State University Press, 1991.

Cohodas, Nadine. *The Band Played Dixie: Race and the Liberal Conscience at Ole Miss.* New York: Free Press, 1997.

———. *Strom Thurmond and the Politics of Southern Change.* New York: Simon and Schuster, 1993.

Coleman, William T., Jr. "Mr. Justice Felix Frankfurter: Civil Libertarian as Lawyer and Justice; Extent to Which Judicial Responsibilities Affected his Pre-Court Convictions." In *Six Justices on Civil Rights,* edited by Ronald D. Rotunda. London: Oceana Publications, 1983.

Cott, Nancy F. "Giving Character to Our Whole Civil Polity: Marriage and the Public Order in the Late Nineteenth Century." In *U.S. History as Women's History: New Feminist Essays,* edited by Linda K. Kerber, Alice Kessler-Harris, and Kathryn Kish Sklar. Chapel Hill: University of North Carolina Press, 1995.

Cousins, Ralph E., et al. *South Carolinians Speak: A Moderate Approach to Race Relations.* South Carolina: Dillon Press, 1957.

Cray, Ed. *Chief Justice: A Biography of Earl Warren.* New York: Simon and Schuster, 1997.

Croly, Goodman David, and George Wakeman. *Miscegenation: The Theory of the Blending of the Races, Applied to the American White Man and Negro.* New York: H. Dexter Hamilton, 1864.

Currie, David P. *The Constitution in the Supreme Court: The First Hundred Years, 1789–1888.* Chicago: University of Chicago Press, 1985.

Daggett, Harriet Spiller. *Legal Essays on Family Law.* Baton Rouge: Louisiana State University Press, 1935.

Davis, Allison, Burleigh Gardner, and Mary R. Gardner. *Deep South: A Social Anthropological Study of Caste and Class.* Chicago: University of Chicago Press, 1941.

Day, Beth. *Sexual Life Between Blacks and Whites: The Roots of Racism.* New York: World, 1972.

Dollard, John. *Caste and Class in a Southern Town.* Garden City, NY: Doubleday Anchor Books, 1937.

Edgar, Walter. *South Carolina: A History.* Columbia: University of South Carolina Press, 1998.

Evers, Charles, and Andrew Szanton. *Have No Fear: The Charles Evers Story.* New York: Wiley, 1997.

Finkelman, Paul, ed. *Race, Law, and American History, 1700–1900.* Vol. 2, *Before Emancipation.* New York: Garland, 1992.

Forman, James. *The Making of Black Revolutionaries.* Seattle: Open Hand, 1985.

Fowler, David H. *Northern Attitudes Toward Interracial Marriage: Legislation and Public Opinion in the Middle Atlantic and the States of the Old Northwest, 1780–1930.* New York: Garland, 1987.

Garner, James Wilford. *Reconstruction in Mississippi.* Baton Rouge: Louisiana State University, 1968.

Gerber, David A. *Black Ohio and the Color Line: 1860–1915.* Urbana: University of Illinois Press, 1976.

Gilmore, Al-Tony. *Bad Nigger! The National Impact of Jack Johnson.* Port Washington, NY: Kennikat, 1975.

Gordon, Albert. *Intermarriage: Interfaith, Interracial, Interethnic.* Boston: Beacon Press, 1964.

Gossett, Thomas F. *Race: The History of an Idea in America.* Dallas: Southern Methodist University Press, 1963.

Grant, Joanne. *Ella Baker: Freedom Bound.* New York: Wiley, 1998.

Greenberg, Jack. *Crusaders in the Courts: How a Dedicated Band of Lawyers Fought for the Civil Rights Revolution.* New York: Basic Books, 1994.

———. *Race Relations and American Law.* New York: Columbia University Press, 1959.

Guild, June Purcell. *Black Codes of Virginia: A Summary of the Legislative Acts of Virginia Concerning Negroes from Earliest Times to the Present.* New York: Negro Universities Press, 1936.

Gunter, Gerald. *Learned Hand: The Man and the Judge.* New York: Knopf, 1994.

Hall, Fred S. *American Marriage Laws in Their Social Aspects.* New York: Russell Sage Foundation, 1919.

Henry, H. M. *The Police Control of the Slave in South Carolina.* New York: Negro Universities Press, 1968.

Hernton, Calvin. *Sex and Racism in America.* New York: Anchor Books, 1966.

Higginbotham, Leon A., Jr. *In the Matter of Color: Race and the American Legal Process; The Colonial Period.* New York: Oxford University Press, 1978.

Hodes, Martha, ed. *Sex, Love, Race: Crossing Boundaries in North American History.* New York: New York University Press, 1999.

———. *White Women, Black Men: Illicit Sex in the Nineteenth Century South.* New Haven: Yale University Press, 1997.

Holtzman, Elizabeth, with Cynthia L. Cooper. *Who Said It Would Be Easy? One Woman's Life in the Political Arena.* New York: Arcade, 1996.

Irons, Peter, and Stephanie Guitton, eds. *May It Please the Court: The Most Significant Oral Arguments Made Before the Supreme Court since 1955.* New York: New Press, 1993.

James, Marliese. *The People's Lawyers.* New York: Holt, Rinehart, and Winston, 1973.

Jenkins, Wilbert J. *Seizing the New Day: African-Americans in Post–Civil War Charleston.* Bloomington: Indiana University Press, 1998.

Johnson, Franklin. *The Development of State Legislation Concerning the Free Negro.* Westport, CT: Greenwood, 1919.

Johnston, James Hugo. *Race Relations in Virginia and Miscegenation in the South.* Amherst: University of Massachusetts Press, 1970.

Jordan, Winthrop D. *The White Man's Burden: Historical Origins of Racism in the United States.* London: Oxford University Press, 1974.

———. *White over Black: American Attitudes Toward the Negro, 1550–1812.* Chapel Hill: University of North Carolina Press, 1968.

Kennedy, Stetson. *Jim Crow Guide: The Way It Was.* Boca Raton: Florida Atlantic University Press, 1959.

Kinoy, Arthur. *Rights on Trial: The Odyssey of a People's Lawyer.* Cambridge: Harvard University Press, 1983.

Kitano, Harry. *Race Relations.* Englewood, NJ: Prentice-Hall, 1974.

Kluger, Richard. *Simple Justice.* New York: Vintage Books, 1975.

Knight, Ethel. *The Echo of the Black Horn.* Mississippi: Ethel Knight, 1951.

Kurland, Philip B., and Gerhard Casper, eds. *Landmark Briefs and Arguments of the Supreme Court: Constitutional Law.* Vol. 64. Arlington, VA: University Publications of America, 1975.

Larrowe, Charles P. *Harry Bridges: The Rise and Fall of Radical Labor in the United States.* New York: Lawrence Hill, 1972.

Larson, Edward J. *Sex, Race and Science: Eugenics in the Deep South.* Baltimore: Johns Hopkins University Press, 1995.

Larsson, M. Clotye, ed. *Marriage Across the Color Line.* Chicago: Johnson, 1965.

Lazarus, Edward. *Black Hills, White Justice: The Sioux Versus the United States, 1775 to the Present.* New York: Harper Collins, 1991.

Leverett, Rudy H. *Legend of the Free State of Jones.* Jackson: University of Mississippi Press, 1984.

Lewis, Earl, and Heidi Ardizzone. *Love on Trial: An American Scandal in Black and White.* New York: Norton, 2001.

Lewis, Sinclair. *Kingsblood Royal.* New York: Random House, 1947.

Loewen, James W. *Lies Across America: What Our Historic Sites Get Wrong.* New York: New Press, 1998.

Logan, Rayford W. *The Betrayal of the Negro.* New York: Collier Books, 1954.

Lyda, John W. *The Negro in the History of Indiana.* Terre Haute: Indiana Negro Historical Society, 1953.

Maltz, Earl. *Civil Rights, the Constitution and Congress, 1863–1869.* Lawrence: University of Kansas Press, 1990.

Mangum, Charles S., Jr. *The Legal Status of the Negro.* Chapel Hill: University of North Carolina Press, 1940.

Marsh, Charles. *God's Long Summer: Stories of Faith and Civil Rights.* Princeton: Princeton University Press, 1997.

Martin, John Bartlow. *The Deep South Says "Never."* Westport, CT: Negro Universities Press, 1957.

McNamara, Robert, Maria Tempenis, and Beth Walton. *Crossing the Line: Interracial Couples in the South.* Westport CT: Greenwood, 1999.

Montagu, Ashley. *Man's Most Dangerous Myth: The Fallacy of Race.* 6th ed. Walnut Creek, CA: AltaMira Press, 1997.

Morgan, Edward S. *American Slavery, American Freedom: The Ordeal of Colonial Virginia.* New York: Norton, 1975.

Murphy, Walter F. *Elements of Judicial Strategy.* Chicago: University of Chicago Press, 1964.

Murray, Pauli, ed. *States' Laws on Race and Color.* Athens, GA: Women's Division of Christian Service, 1950.

Muse, Benjamin. *Ten Years of Prelude: The Story of Integration since the Supreme Court's 1954 Decision.* Beaconsfield, PQ: Darwen Finlayson, 1964.

Myrdal, Gunnar. *An American Dilemma.* New York: Harper, 1944.

Peters, William. *The Southern Temper.* Garden City, NY: Doubleday, 1959.

Porterfield, Ernest. *Black and White Mixed Marriages.* Chicago: Nelson-Hall, 1978.

Quillin, Frank U. *The Color Line in Ohio: A History of Race Prejudice in a Typical Southern State.* Ann Arbor, MI: George Wahr, 1913.

Quint, Howard H. *Profile in Black and White: A Frank Portrait of South Carolina.* Westport, CT: Greenwood, 1958.

Roberts, Randy. *Papa Jack: Jack Johnson and the Era of White Hopes.* New York: Free Press, 1983.

Roberts, Robert E. T. "Black-White Inter-marriage in the United States." In *Inside the Mixed Marriage*, edited by Walton Johnson and D. Michael Warren. Lanham, MD: University Press of America, 1994.

Rogers, J. A. *Sex and Race: A History of White, Negro and Indian Miscegenation in the Two Americas.* Vol. 2, *The New World.* St. Petersburg, FL: Helga M. Rogers, 1942.

———. *Sex and Race: A History of White, Negro and Indian Miscegenation in the Two Americas.* Vol. 3, *Why White and Black Mix in Spite of Opposition.* St. Petersburg, FL: Helga M. Rogers, 1944.

Rowan, Carl T. *South of Freedom.* New York: Knopf, 1954.

Schwartz, Bernard. *Super Chief: Earl Warren and His Supreme Court—A Judicial Biography.* New York: New York University Press, 1983.

Sickels, Robert J. *Race, Marriage and the Law.* Albuquerque: University of New Mexico Press, 1972.

Smith, Bob. *They Closed Their Schools: Prince Edward County, Virginia, 1951–1964.* Chapel Hill: University of North Carolina Press, 1965.

Smith, John, ed. *Anti-Black Thought, 1863–1925.* Vols. 7 and 8. New York: Garland, 1993.

Spickard, Paul R. *Intermarriage and Ethnic Identity in Twentieth-Century America.* Madison: University of Wisconsin Press, 1989.

Stanton, Mary. *From Selma to Sorrow: The Life and Death of Viola Liuzzo.* Athens: University of Georgia Press, 1998.

Stember, Charles Herbert. *Sexual Racism: The Emotional Barrier to an Integrated Society.* New York: Elsevier, 1976.

Stephenson, Gilbert Thomas. *Race Distinctions in American Law.* New York: Appleton, 1910.

Stuart, Irving R., and Lawrence Edwin Abt, eds. *Interracial Marriage: Expectations and Realities.* New York: Grossman, 1973.

Taylor, Alrutheus Ambush. *The Negro in South Carolina During the Reconstruction.* New York: AMS Press, 1924.

————. *The Negro in the Reconstruction of Virginia.* New York: Russel and Russel, 1969.

Tindall, George Brown. *South Carolina Negroes, 1877–1900.* Baton Rouge: Louisiana State University Press, 1952.

Turner, Edward Raymond. *The Negro in Pennsylvania: Slavery—Servitude—Freedom, 1639–1861.* New York: Negro Universities Press, 1911.

Tushnet, Mark V. *Making Civil Rights Law: Thurgood Marshall and the Supreme Court, 1936–61.* New York: Oxford University Press, 1994.

Vernier, Chester G. *American Family Laws.* Vol. 1, Sect. 44. Stanford, CA: Stanford University Press, 1931 (supplement, 1983).

Vexler, Robert I. *Chronology and Documentary Handbook of the State of Louisiana.* Dobbs Ferry, NY: Oceana, 1978.

Wallace, David Duncan. *South Carolina: A Short History, 1520–1948.* Columbia: University of South Carolina Press, 1951.

Wasby, Stephen L, Anthony A. D'Amato, and Rosemary Metrailer. *Desegregation from Brown to Alexander.* Carbondale: Southern Illinois University Press, 1977.

Washington, Joseph R., Jr. *Marriage in Black and White.* Boston: Beacon Press, 1970.

Weiner, Marli F. *Mistress and Slaves: Plantation Women in South Carolina, 1830–1880.* Urbana: University of Illinois Press, 1998.

Williams, Juan. *Thurgood Marshall: American Revolutionary.* New York: Times Books, 1998.

Williamson, Joel. *After Slavery: The Negro in South Carolina During Reconstruction, 1861–1877.* Chapel Hill: University of North Carolina Press, 1965.

————. *New People.* New York: Free Press, 1980.

————, ed. *The Origins of Segregation.* Boston: Heath, 1968.

Wynes, Charles E. *Race Relations in Virginia, 1870–1902.* Charlottesville: University of Virginia Press, 1961.

Zack, Naomi. *Race and Mixed Race.* Philadelphia: Temple University Press, 1993.

Archival Materials

ACLU Archives. Seeley G. Mudd Manuscript Library, Princeton University.

Papers of the NAACP. Part 11: Special Subject Files, 1912–1939. Series B: *Harding, Warren B.,* through *YWCA,* Cleveland, Ohio.

Papers of the NAACP. Part 15: Segregation and Discrimination, Complaints and Responses, 1940–1955. Series B: General Office Files, Cleveland, Ohio.

Papers of the NAACP. Part 18: Special Subjects, 1940–1955. Series A: Legal Department Files, Cleveland, Ohio.

Periodicals

Alpert, Jonathan L. "The Origins of Slavery in the United States—The Maryland Precedent." *American Journal of Negro History,* 14, no. 1 (1970): 189–221.

Arendt, Hannah. "Reflections on Little Rock." *Dissent,* Winter 1959, 45–56.

Bickel, Alexander. "Integrated Cohabitation." *New Republic,* May 30, 1964, 4–5.

Booker, Simeon. "A Challenge for the Guy Smiths." *Ebony,* December 1967, 146–50.

———. "The Couple That Rocked the Courts." *Ebony,* September 1967, 78–84.

———. "The Crime of Being Married." *Time,* March 18, 1966, 85–91.

Brown, Phil. "Black-White Interracial Marriages: A Historical Analysis." *Journal of Intergroup Relations,* Fall-Winter 1989–90, 26–36.

Brown, Thomas. "The Miscegenation of Richard Mentor Johnson as an Issue in the National Election Campaign of 1835–36." *Civil War History* 32, no. 1 (March 1993).

Bynum, Victoria E. "'White Negroes' in Segregated Mississippi: Miscegenation, Racial Identity and the Law." *Journal of Southern History* 64, no. 2 (May 1998): 247–76.

Crane, Victoria Glenn. "Two Women, White and Brown in the South Carolina Court of Equity, 1842–1845." *South Carolina Historical Magazine* 96, no. 3 (July 1995): 198–220.

Cummins, Jerold C., and John L. Kane. "Miscegenation, the Constitution and Science." *Dicta* 38 (January–February 1961): 24–64.

Davenport, Charles B. "State Laws Limiting Marriage Selection." *Eugenics Record Office Bulletin* (Cold Spring Harbor, NY), no. 9 (June 1913).

Dorr, Gregory Michael. "Principled Expediency: Eugenics, *Naim v. Naim,* and the Supreme Court." *American Journal of Legal History* 42 (June 1997): 119.

Earl, Phillip I. "Nevada's Miscegenation Laws and the Marriage of Mr. and Mrs. Bridges." *Nevada Historical Quarterly* 34, no. 1 (Spring 1994): 1–17.

Francis Flaherty, "Wins Grow under State ERAs," *National Law Journal,* September 9, 1983.

Frederickson, Kari. "'The Slowest State' and 'Most Backward Community': Racial Violence in South Carolina and Federal Civil-Rights Legislation." *South Carolina Historical Magazine* 98, no. 2 (April 1997): 177–202.

Hardaway, Roger D. "Prohibiting Interracial Marriage: Miscegenation Laws in Wyoming." *Annals of Wyoming* 52 (Spring 1960): 55–60.

———. "Unlawful Love: A History of Arizona's Miscegenation Law." *Journal of Arizona History* 27, no. 4 (Winter 1986): 377–90.

Hodes, Martha. "The Sexualization of Reconstruction Politics." *Journal of the History of Sexuality* 3 (1993): 402–17.

"How the NAACP Stands on Intermarriage." *U.S. News and World Report,* September 2, 1963.

"Intermarriage and the Race Problem—As Leading Authorities See It." *U.S. News and World Report,* November 18, 1963, 84–93.

Jenks, Albert Ernest. "The Legal Status of Negro-White Amalgamation in the United States." *American Journal of Sociology* 21 (1916): 666–78.

Kaplan, Sidney. "The Miscegenation Issue in the Election of 1864." *Journal of Negro History* 34 (1949): 274–343.

Kennedy-Haflett, Cynthia. "'Moral Marriage': A Mixed-Race Relationship in Nineteenth-Century Charleston, South Carolina." *South Carolina Historical Magazine* 97, no. 3 (July 1996): 206–26.

Mayer, Milton. "The Issue Is Miscegenation." *Progressive,* June 1959, 8–18.

Mills, Gary B. "Miscegenation and the Free Negro in Antebellum 'Anglo' Alabama: A Reexamination of Southern Race Relations." *Journal of American History* 68, no. 1 (June 1981): 16–34.

Pascoe, Peggy. "Miscegenation Law: Court Cases, and Ideologies of 'Race' in Twentieth-Century America." *Journal of American History* 83, no. 1 (June 1996): 44–69.

———. "Race, Gender and Intercultural Relations: The Case of Interracial Marriage." *Frontiers* 12, no. 1: 5–15.

"A Race Purity Law." *Opportunity* 2, no. 18 (June 1924): 163–64.

Saks, Eva. "Representing Miscegenation Law." *Raritan* 8, no. 2 (Fall 1988): 39–69.

Sherman, Richard B. "'The Last Stand': The Fight for Racial Integrity in Virginia in the 1920s." *Journal of Southern History* 54, no. 1 (February 1988): 69–92.

Simkins, Francis. "Race Relations in South Carolina since 1865." *South Atlantic Quarterly* 20 (April 1921): 165–77.

Sollors, Werner. "Of Mules and Mares in a Land of Difference; or, Quadrupeds All?" *American Quarterly* 42 (June 1990): 167–90.

Spitz, David. "Politics and the Realm of Being." *Dissent,* Winter 1959, 56–65.

Tumin, Melvin. "Pie in the Sky." *Dissent,* Winter 1959, 65–71.

Valentine, Victoria. "When Love Was a Crime." *Emerge,* June 1997, 60–62.

Wallenstein, Peter. "Race, Marriage and the Supreme Court from *Pace v. Alabama* (1883) to *Loving v. Virginia* (1967)." *Journal of Supreme Court History* 2 (1998): 65–85.

———. "The Right to Marry: *Loving v. Virginia.*" *OAH Magazine of History,* Winter 1995, 37–41.

"Weddings: Mr. and Mrs. Smith." *Newsweek,* October 2, 1967, 23–24.

"What Negros Want Now." *U.S. News and World Report,* May 28, 1954, 54–59.

"What the South Really Fears about Mixed Schools." *U.S. News and World Report,* September 19, 1958, 76–90.

Woodson, C. G. "The Beginnings of Miscegenation of Whites and Blacks." *Journal of Negro History* 3, no. 4 (October 1918): 335–53.

Zabel, William D. "Interracial Marriage and the Law." *Atlantic Monthly,* October 1965, 75–79.

Theses and Dissertations

Arness, Frank F. "The Evolution of the Virginia Anti-miscegenation Laws." Master's thesis, Old Dominion College, 1966.

Banks, James. "Strom Thurmond and the Revolt Against Modernity." PhD thesis, Kent State University, 1970.

Beall, Charles Franklin, Jr. "With Malicious Intent: John McCray, Willie Tolbert and the Struggle for Equal Justice in South Carolina." Master's thesis, University of Virginia, 1987.

Colson, Julie Penrod. "Interracial Marriage in the United States: 1960 and 1970." Master's thesis, University of Kentucky, 1975.

Everett, Robert Burke. "Race Relations in South Carolina, 1900–1932." PhD diss., University of Georgia, 1969.

Gilmore, Al-Tony. "America's Reaction to Jack Johnson, 1908–1915." PhD diss., University of Toledo, 1972.

Halevi, Sharon. "The Path Not Taken: Class, Gender and Race in the South Carolina Backcountry, 1750–1800." PhD diss., University of Iowa, 1995.

Head, Joseph Lewis. "Attitudes Toward the Negro in South Carolina, 1670 to 1822." Master's thesis, University of Georgia, 1970.

Johnson, James Hugo. "Miscegenation in the Ante-Bellum South." PhD diss. (excerpt), University of Chicago, 1939.

Kantrowitz, Stephen David. "The Reconstruction of White Supremacy: Reaction and Reform in Ben Tillman's World, 1847–1918." PhD diss., Princeton University, 1995.

Kitchen, Deborah Lynn. "Interracial Marriage in the United States: 1900–1980." PhD diss., University of Minnesota, 1993.

Martyn, Byron Curti. "Racism in the United States: A History of Anti-miscegenation Legislation and Litigation." PhD diss., University of Southern California, 1979.

Newby, Idus A. "South Carolina and the Desegregation Issue, 1954–1956." Master's thesis, Georgia Teachers College, 1957.

O'Neill, Stephen. "From the Shadow of Slavery: The Civil Rights Years in Charleston." PhD diss., University of Virginia, 1994.

Robinson, Charles F., II. "The Antimiscegenation Conversation: Love's Legislated Limits (1868 1967)." PhD diss., University of Houston, 1988.

Romano, Renee Christian. "Crossing the Line: Black-White Interracial Marriage in the United States, 1945–1990." PhD diss., Stanford University, 1996.

Secrest, Andrew McDowd. "In Black and White: Press Opinion and Race Relations in South Carolina, 1954–1964." PhD diss., Duke University, 1971.

Sharfstein, Daniel Jacob. "In Search of the Color Line: *Ferrall v. Ferrall* and the Struggle to Define Race in the Turn-of-the-Century American South." BA honors thesis, Harvard College, 1994.

Sohn, Chang Moon. "Principle and Expediency in Judicial Review: Miscegenation Cases in the Supreme Court." PhD diss., Columbia University, 1970.

Tenofsky, Elliot. "Interest Groups and Litigation: The Commission on Law and Social Action of the American Jewish Congress." PhD diss., Brandeis University, 1979.

Thomson, Brian William. "Racism and Racial Classification: A Case Study of the Virginia Racial Integrity Legislation." PhD diss., University of California, Riverside, 1978.

Wallace, Meghan. "South Carolina Reacts to Desegregation: The Closing of Edisto Beach State Park." Paper for History 788, University of South Carolina, December 1997.

Wikramanayke, Ivy Marina. "The Free Negro in Ante-Bellum South Carolina." PhD diss., University of Wisconsin, 1966.

Law Review Articles

Applebaum, Harvey M. "Miscegenation Statutes: A Constitutional and Social Problem." 53 Georgetown Law Journal 49–91 (1964).

Avins, Alfred. "Anti-Miscegenation Laws and the Fourteenth Amendment: The Original Intent." 52 Virginia Law Review 1224–55 (1966).

Bank, Steven, A. "Anti-Miscegenation Laws and the Dilemma of Symmetry: The Understanding of Equality in the Civil Rights Act of 1875." 2 University of Chicago Law School Roundtable 303 (1995).

Bickel, Alexander. "The Original Understanding and the Segregation Decision." 69 Harvard Law Review 1–65 (November 1955).

Calhoun, John C. "Who Is a Negro?" Notes, 11 University of Florida Law Review 235–40 (1948).

Cohen, Harold. "An Appraisal of the Legal Tests Used to Determine Who Is a Negro." 34 Cornell Law Quarterly 246–55 (1948).

"Comments." 36 Yale Law Review 858–59 (1927).

"Constitutional Law—Domestic Relations—Miscegenation Laws Based Solely upon Race Are a Denial of the Due Process and Equal Protection Clauses of the Fourteenth Amendment." 13 New York Law Forum 170–78 (1967).

Conter, C. Michael. "Constitutional Law: Miscegenation Laws." 48 Marquette Law Review 616–20 (1965).

D.P.L. "Editorial Note: The Constitutionality of Miscegenation Statutes." 1 Howard Law Journal 88–100 (January 1955).

Drinan, Robert F. "The Loving Decision and the Freedom to Marry." 29 Ohio State Law Journal 358–98 (1968).

Ehrenzweig, Albert. "Miscegenation in the Conflict of Laws." 45 Cornell Law Quarterly 659–78 (1960).

Elman, Philip. "Essay Commemorating the One Hundredth Anniversary of the Harvard Law Review: The Solicitor General's Office, Justice Frankfurter, and Civil Rights Litigation, 1946–1960; An Oral History." 100 Harvard Law Review 817–52 (February 1987).

Ely, John Hart. "If at First You Don't Succeed, Ignore the Question Next Time? Group Harm in *Brown v. Board of Education* and *Loving v. Virginia*." 15 Constitutional Commentary 215–23 (1988).

Evans, Linwood S. "Constitutional Law—Miscegenation Statutes—Validity Sustained Against Due Process and Equal Protection Challenges." 19 South Carolina Law Review 253–60 (1967).

Finkelman Paul. "The Color of Law." 87 Northwestern University Law Review 935–91 (1993).

———. "The Crime of Color." 67 Tulane Law Review 2063–112 (1993).

Foster, William E. "A Study of the Wyoming Miscegenation Statutes." Notes, 10 Wyoming Law Journal 131–38 (Winter 1956).

Getman, Karen A. "Sexual Control in the Slaveholding South: The Implementation and Maintenance of a Racial Caste System." 7 Harvard Women's Law Review 115–52 (1984).

Gunther, Gerald. "The Subtle Vices of the 'Passive Virtues'—A Comment on Principle and Expediency in Judicial Review." 64 Columbia Law Review 1–25 (January 1964).

Higginbotham, A. Leon, Jr., and Barbara Kopytoff. "Racial Purity and Interracial Sex in the Law of Colonial and Antebellum Virginia." 77 Georgetown Law Journal 1967–2067 (August 1989).

Higgins, Scott T. "Casenotes: Constitutional Law—Due Process—Virginia's Miscegenation Statute Does Not Deny Due Process of Law and Equal Protection of Law." 8 Arizona Law Review 361 (1967).

"Hook v. Blanton." 12 Race Relations Law Reporter 2079–80.

"Intermarriage with Negroes—A Survey of State Statutes." 36 Yale Law Review 856–66 (1927).

Kennedy, Randall. "How Are We Doing with *Loving?*: Race, Law and Intermarriage." 77 Boston University Law Review 815 (1997).

Lay, Kenneth James. "Sexual Racism: A Legacy of Slavery." 13 National Black Law Review 165–83 (Spring 1993).

Lombardo, Paul A. "Miscegenation, Eugenics, and Racism: Historical Footnotes to *Loving v. Virginia.*" 21 University of California Davis Law Review 421–53 (1988).

Minor, James F., and Branaugh Minor. "Moon et al. v. Children's Home Society of Virginia." 17 Virginia Law Register 688–99 (January 1911).

"Notes: Constitutionality of Anti-Miscegenation Statutes." 58 Yale Law Review 472–82 (1949).

Phillips, Cyrus E., IV. "Miscegenation: The Courts and the Constitution." 8 William and Mary Law Review 133–42 (1966).

Pittman, R. Carter. "The Fourteenth Amendment: Its Intended Effect on Anti-Miscegenation Laws." 43 North Carolina Law Review 92–109 (1964).

Pratt, Robert A. "Crossing the Color Line: A Historical Assessment and Personal Narrative of *Loving v. Virginia.*" 41 Howard Law Journal 229–45 (Winter 1998).

Riley, Lloyd H. "Miscegenation Statutes—A Re-evaluation of Their Constitutionality in Light of Changing Social and Political Conditions." 32 Southern California Law Review 28–48 (1958).

Seidelson, David E. "Miscegenation Statutes and the Supreme Court: A Brief Prediction of What the Court Will Do and Why." 15 Catholic University Law Review 156–70 (1966).

Shokes, C. D. "The Serbonian Bog of Miscegenation." 21 Rocky Mountain Law Review 425 (1949).

"The Supreme Court, 1955 Term." 70 Harvard Law Review 98–104 (1956).

"The Supreme Court, 1964 Term." 79 Harvard Law Review 1965.

Tragen, Irving G. "Statutory Prohibitions Against Interracial Marriage." 32 California Law Review, September 1944, 269–79.

Wadlington, Walter. "The *Loving* Case: Virginia's Anti-miscegenation Statute in Historical Perspective." 52 Virginia Law Review 1189–223 (1966).

Wallenstein, Peter. "Race, Marriage, and the Law of Freedom: Alabama and Virginia, 1860's–1960's." 70 Chicago-Kent Law Review 371–437 (1994).

Walton, Edmund L., Jr. "The Present Status of Miscegenation Statutes." 4 William and Mary Law Review 28–35 (1963).

Weinberger, Andrew D. "A Reappraisal of the Constitutionality of Miscegenation Statutes." 42 Cornell Law Quarterly 208–22 (1957).

Wilharm, John H., Jr. "Racial Intermarriage—A Constitutional Problem." 11 Western Reserve Law Review 93–101 (December 1959).

Wright, Edward T. "Interracial Marriage: A Survey of Statutes and Their Interpretations." 1 Mercer Law Review 83–90 (1949).

Interviewees

Harry Ackerman
Harvey Applebaum
Charles Ares
Lawrence Aschenbrenner
William Bentley Ball
Fred Banks
Rims Barber
Stan Beason
William Beemer
Arthur Berney
Harold Braynon
David Carliner
Bernard Cohen
Marvin Cohen
William Coleman
Richard Daly
James D. Davis
Armand Derfner
Kenneth Edwards
Philip Elman
Robert Farmer
Norikko (Nikki) Flynn
Walter Gorman
Raymond Green
Jack Greenberg
Robert Hall
Terry Haskins
Casey Hayden
Philip Hirschkop
Alvin Holmes

Elizabeth Holtzman
Valen Honeywell
Brad Jordan
James Koons
Donald Kramer
Julian Lapides
Arthur Lazarus
Herbert Monte Levy
A. Jack Lilly
Mildred Loving
Kenneth MacDonald
Jesse Cordell Maddox
James Mahorner
William Marutani
John Maxey
Michael Meltsner
Roger Mills
Alan Mirman
Ottis Moore
James Nabrit III
Bert Neuborn
Lawrence Ollason
Henry Oyama
Louis Pollak
H. M. Ray
Paul Rees
Bruce Roberts
James Robertson
Alma Ross
Lawrence Ross
Jon Schneider
Richard Selph
Jonathan Shapiro
M. Karl Shurtliff
Constance Slaughter-Harvey
Frederick Stant
Mrs. Edward Stehl
Joseph Straub

Nicholas Valeriani
Robert Vaughn
Walter Wadlington
Joseph Wroten
William Zabel
Dorothy Zellner

Index

2283 motion, 139, 260n. 20

Ackerman, Harry, 81–83
adultery, 60, 61
aftermath of *Loving,* 193–94; Alabama, 206–9; Georgia, 209–13; interracial marriages, 194–96, 197–205; Mississippi, 197–205
Alabama, 6, 29, 42, 43, 47, 61–62 *(see also Jackson v. Alabama; Pace v. Alabama);* aftermath of *Loving,* 206–9; constitution, 4–5, 46, 210–11; fornication laws, 60–61; repeal of antimiscegenation law, 4, 212–13
Almond, J. Lindsay, Jr., 106
American Civil Liberties Union (ACLU), 3, 88; Arizona law and, 80–81, 84; custody cases, 70–71, 73; looks for test cases, 90, 94–97; *Loving v. Virginia* and, 147–54; *Naim v. Naim* and, 104–10; NatCap branch, 135–36, 150
American Dilemma, An (Myrdal), 28
American Jewish Congress (AJC), 3, 73, 77, 84, 90, 108, 155
amicus briefs, *Loving v. Virginia:* ACLU, 150–51, 153–54; Catholic organizations, 166–67; Japanese American Citizens League, 165–66; Legal Defense Fund, 161–63; NAACP, xii, 161, 163–64; North Carolina, 2, 171–72
Antieu, Chester (Chet), 139, 150
antimiscegenation statutes, 2–3 *(see also* extraterritorial marriages; historical context; penalties; racial definitions; repeal of antimiscegenation statutes; *individual statutes);* annulment of marriages, 34–35, 40–41, 44, 50, 55, 69, 104–5, 143–44, 224; constitutionality, 46–47; enforcement, 38–39; human toll of, 163, 184; non-black races, 32–

33; prohibitions against marrying interracial couples, 35, 38–42, 44, 50, 79, 117; reasons for, 25–28; by state, 227–31; support of interracial marriage as crime, 3, 35–36
Applebaum, Harvey, 150, 182–83
Ares, Charles, 80–81, 82, 83
Arizona, 3–4, 31, 42–43, 101; challenges to statute, 78–84; inheritance issues, 67–68
Arkansas, 41, 43, 44, 194
Army, 97, 206–7
Asians, 3, 32, 44, 59. *See also* Mongolians
Association of Immigration and Nationality Lawyers (AINL), 108–9, 155

Ball, William Bentley, 166, 168
Baltimore Afro-American, 18
Bangel, A. A., 104–5, 111
banishment, 15–16, 33–34, 39, 57
Banks, Fred, 199, 200
Bazile, Leon Maurice, 2, 14–15, 137–39, 142, 175, 187, 211
Beazely, Frank, 13–14, 138
Bell v. State, 45
Berney, Arthur, 151–54, 157, 173
Berry, Frank, 80, 82, 84
Bett, Phyllis, 206–10
Bill to Preserve the Integrity of the White Race, A, 174
Black, Hugo, 98–99, 112, 186–87, 201
blood, percentage of, 3, 33, 41, 48–50, 68–69, 93, 123; Florida, 117–18; Virginia, 29, 48–49
blood tests, 10, 27
Bolz, Sanford (Sandy), 90, 108
Boyd, Leona Eve, 194–95
Brennan, William, 186
Bridges, Harry, 4, 84–88
Bridges case, 84–88, 100, 101, 102, 171
Brooks, Garnett, 2, 11–12, 15, 218–19

Brown v. Board of Education, xii, 58, 89, 105, 107, 152; *Loving v. Virginia* and, 145, 148, 157, 184; *McLaughlin v. Florida* and, 120, 127, 130
Buck v. Bell, 143
Burger, Warren, 73
Button, Robert Y., 141, 144, 170
Butznor, John, 141, 142

Caldwell, Millard, 120–21, 194
California, 4, 45, 49, 74, 144; antimiscegenation laws, 75–78; challenges to statute, 75–78
Cameron, Lucille, 49
Carliner, David, 104–7, 108–11, 114–15, 136, 148, 150, 155, 206–7, 254n. 9
Caroline County, Virginia, 19
Carrico, Harry, 2, 144–46
Carter, Robert, 155, 163–64, 168
Catawba tribe, 58, 101, 174
Catholic Interracial Council, 75–77, 166
Catholics, 80, 81, 96, 166–67
Central Point, Virginia, 9–10, 13, 17–22
certiorari, 4, 99, 109–10, 113
Chappell, Michael, 212–13
Cherokees, 31, 33, 58–59, 172, 174
children, 101 (*see also* custody; inheritance); anthropological arguments, 153–54; as argument against interracial marriage, 28–29, 70–71, 130, 153, 156, 163–64, 180, 183; custody cases, 70–73; illegitimacy, 3, 26, 41, 69, 149, 194; pseudoscientific theories, 28–29, 41, 163–64; religious views, 166–67; servitude, 38, 45
Chinese, 27, 32, 42, 43, 49, 50
Chuman, Frank, 109
Civil Rights Act of 1866, 127–29, 169–70, 175, 179
Civil Rights Act of 1964, 135, 140, 155
civil rights movement, xii, 139, 140–41, 159
Clark, Tom, 112, 186
Clark case, 66
Clay, George, 212
cohabitation, interracial, 50, 58, 63; Flor-

ida statute, 117–18, 122, 127–29, 131, 162; Mississippi statute, 201–2
Cohen, Bernard S. (Bernie), 2, 18, 97, 135–36, 137–39, 144, 149, 151, 154, 189, 215, 259n. 1; career, 141, 158–59, 217–18; meeting with Lovings, 136–37; motion to vacate judgment, 137–38; oral argument, 175–77; rebuttal, 183–85; relationship with Hirschkop, 2, 139–40
Cohen, Marvin S., 81, 82
Coleman, William, 121, 128–29, 189
colonies, 37–38
Colorado, 35, 43, 49, 97, 101
comity, 142
common-law marriages, 61; as defense, 119, 122, 124, 128–29; inheritance and, 64–66, 69
communism, 59
concealment penalties, 35
concubinage, 30–31, 61, 63
Confederate Heritage, 212
Constitution, U.S., 99, 104. *See also* Fourteenth Amendment; state constitutions
Council of Conservative Citizens, 90
Council of Federated Organizations, 141
Cox, Harold, 200, 201–2
Creek Nation, 31–32, 91–92
cross burnings, 215
cruel and unusual punishment, 142–43
Culbertson, John Bolt, 95
Cummings, John D., 198, 200
custody, 64, 70–73, 158

Dalton, John, 171
Danville, Virginia, 139, 140
Davis, James, 144
Davis, Vernon, 198, 199, 201
Delaware, 38, 42, 194
Democratic Party, 48
Derfner, Armand, 199, 201
District of Columbia, 42, 46, 51, 53
Douglas, William O., 98–99, 112, 162, 186
Dred Scott v. Sanford, 1, 162
Dreyfus, Benson, 85
Drinan, Father, 151
due process clause, 58, 80, 106, 111, 143,

187–88; *Loving v. Virginia,* 137, 147, 149–50, 152–53, 156–57, 175–76, 187; *McLaughlin v. Florida* and, 119–22, 125; oral argument, 175–76

Edelman, Peter, 195
Emery, A. L., 90–92, 94
enforcement, 38–39
Ennis, Edward, 109
equal protection clause: clear and compelling reasons, 80–81; *Loving v. Virginia* and, 73, 147, 150–52, 154, 156–57, 176; *McLaughlin v. Florida* and, 119–22, 125; *Naim v. Naim* and, 106, 111; oral arguments, 174–75; *Perez* and, 77–78; Supreme Court ruling, 187–88
Estate of Monks case, 68
Etheridge, William, 200, 201
Ethiopians, 30
eugenics theories, 52, 54, 55, 106, 156
Europe, 25, 37
Evers, Charles, 197–98
expert witnesses, 67–68
extraterritorial marriages, 3, 10–11, 35, 40, 42, 104, 224; Virginia Code section 20–58, 11, 148, 161, 170, 178, 182–84

Fannin, Paul, 83
Farmer, Robert W., 11
Ferman, Irving, 105
Field, Stephen, 47
Fifth Amendment, 78
Finch, Cliff, 204
First Amendment, 76, 149
Florida, 4, 6, 40, 194 *(see also* Florida antimiscegenation statutes; *McLaughlin v. Florida);* constitution, 45, 118, 125; definition of Negro, 30, 117–18, 123–25, 127–28, 163, 225; penalties, 117–18, 123, 128–29, 225; percentage of blood, 117–18
Florida antimiscegenation statutes: cohabitation, 117–18, 122, 127–29, 131, 162, 225; fornication, 119, 122, 123; section 1.01, 124, 125, 128; section 741.11, 125; section 798.02, 123, 125,

225; section 798.05, 118, 122, 123–24, 125, 127
fornication, 4, 39, 44, 60–62, 98; Alabama statute, 98–99; Florida statute, 119, 122, 123
Fortas, Abe, 186
Fourteenth Amendment, 43–44, 58, 73, 76, 78, 104, 111, 138, 211; framers, 127, 130, 170, 179, 184–85, 188; LDF amicus brief, 161–63; legislative history, 129–30, 156, 169–70, 175, 185; *McLaughlin v. Florida* and, 119–22; not meant to cover miscegenation, 43–44, 156, 172, 175, 179; Oklahoma statute and, 91–92; as unconstitutional, 124, 127, 128, 130
Francovich, Sam, 85, 86, 87
Frankfurter, Felix, 112, 113
Freedmen's Bureau Bill, 127, 129, 169–70, 175, 179
Freedom Summer, 124, 140
Fuller v. Virginia, 137
full faith and credit clause, 104, 179

Garry, Charles, 85
Georgia, 31, 40, 42, 52–53, 96, 175, 194; aftermath of *Loving,* 209–13
Gezelin, Emile, 86–87
Givens, Viola, 85–86
Goldberg, Joe, 151–52, 156
Goodman, David, 26–27
Gordon, Albert, 154, 170, 171, 180–81, 184
Gorman, Walter, 207, 209
Graves, G. E., 118–20, 257n. 6
Graybill, Leo, 100
Greaves, Elmore, 198, 202, 203, 204
Green, Raymond, 11, 18
Greenberg, Jack, 28, 121–24, 155, 162–63, 167
Grossman, Harvey, 98
Grove, Weaver, 202
Gunther, Gerald, 99

Haltom, E. B., 98–99, 257n. 6
Harlan, John, 47, 129–30, 186
Hastie, William, 92
Hawaiians (Kanakans), xx, 3, 32, 43

Hendrick, Leon, 200
Higgs, Williams, 140
Hill, Garnet, 215, 217
Hill, Raymond, 217
Hindus, 3, 31, 32, 79
Hirschkop, Philip J. (Phil), 17, 97, 135, 144,
    151, 154, 185, 189–90, 193, 214, 259n.
    1; aftermath of *Loving* and, 193–94;
    background, 139–41; career, 159–60,
    217–18; oral argument, 174–75; rela-
    tionship with Cohen, 2, 139–40
"Hirschkop the Horrible: A '60's Lawyer in
    the '80s" (article), 159
historical context: 1600s, 37–39; 1700s,
    39–40; 1800s, 40–46; 1900s, 47–51;
    1913, 49–51; 1920s, 52–53; 1930s, 53–
    54; 1970s, 3, 5, 38, 102; Civil War pe-
    riod, 37–38
Hoffman, Connie, 116, 118
Holmes, Oliver Wendell, 156–57
Holtzman, Elizabeth, 124, 140–41
Houser, Brittany, 216
Houser, Leslie, 216
housing restrictions, 81, 106

Illinois, 40, 46, 49, 51
immigration law, 104, 108–9, 111
Inabinett, Curtis, 211–12
incest argument, 35, 44–45, 175–76
individual, marriage and, 77, 106, 119–21,
    163
inheritance, 79, 196; Arizona, 67–68; com-
    mon-law marriages and, 64–66, 69; le-
    gitimacy of children, 66–67, 69; Native
    Americans, 67, 91
*Intermarriage: Interfaith, Interracial, Inter-
    ethnic* (Gordon), 154, 170, 171
"Interracial Marriage and the Law" (Zabel),
    151
interracial marriages, post-*Loving,* 194–96,
    197–205
interreligious marriages, 180
interstate commerce, 140, 143

Jackson Clarion-Ledger/Daily News, 203,
    204

Jackson v. Alabama, 4, 98–99, 112, 113, 118,
    143
Jackson v. State, 107–8
Japanese, 27, 32, 49, 50, 69, 165; in Vir-
    ginia, 181–82
Japanese American Citizens League (JACL),
    3–4, 77, 90, 100, 101, 155; amicus brief,
    165–66
Japanese Americans, 81, 96–97, 168
Jenkins, Monroe, 197–98
Johnson, Jack, 49, 51, 100
Johnson, Roman Howard, 194–95
Jones v. Lorenzen, 97
Jordan, Brad, 211–12
Justice Department, 206–9

Kadish, Sanford, 95–96
Karpatkin, Marvin, 156
Kennedy, Robert F., 135
Kentucky, 6, 35, 40, 42, 43, 51, 194
Kinney's Case, 143
Kinoy, Arthur, 139, 140
Kirby v. Kirby, 67–68
Kirstein v. Board of Visitors, 159
Knight case, 92–94
Konvitz, Milton, 92
Koon, Larry, 211
Korean war brides, 90, 100
Kramer, Donald W., 165–66, 168, 173, 177
Krucker, Herbert, 82–83
Kunstler, William, 139, 140, 218

Lapides, Julian, 59, 102
Law Student Civil Rights Research Coun-
    cil (LSCRRC), 140, 151–52
Lawyers' Committee for Civil Rights un-
    der Law (LCCRUL), 157, 199
Lawyers Committee for Human Rights, 158
Lawyers' Constitutional Defense Commit-
    tee (LCDC), 199
Leary, Noreen, 198, 199, 201
Legal Defense Fund (LDF), xii, 99, 118,
    121, 199–200 (*see also* National Asso-
    ciation for the Advancement of Col-
    ored People); amicus brief in *Loving,*
    161–63

legislatures, 4–5

Lesser v. Lesser, 70–71

Levy, Herbert Monte, 95, 105–6, 108, 110–11, 114, 115

Lewers, William, 166, 168

Lewis, Oren, 141, 142

Lilly, Jack, 11, 13, 15, 18, 138

Linson, Berta, 198–205

lobbying, 99–100

Lomas v. State, 126

Louisiana, 32–33, 44, 46, 51, 55, 58, 65, 194

Loving, Mildred Dolores Jeter, xi, 1–2, 13, 189, 214–20 (*see also* Lovings); background, 9–10, 15; letter to Kennedy, 135–36

Loving, Richard Perry, xi, 1, 13, 137, 186–87 (*see also* Lovings); background, 9–10, 17–19; at news conference, 188–89, 214–15; quoted in Supreme Court, 176, 177

Lovings: arrest, 11–12; banishment to Washington, D.C., 15–16, 135–36, 141–42, 146; children, 15, 16, 215, 216; news conference, 188–89, 214–15; sentence, 14–15; wedding in Washington, D.C., 9–10

Loving v. Virginia, xii, 72, 90, 97, 141, 169 (*see also* amicus briefs, *Loving v. Virginia*); 2283 motion, 139, 260n. 20; appeal to Supreme Court, 137, 144, 147–48; Bazile's ruling, 142–43; Carrico's affirmation of Bazile, 145–46; Cohen's rebuttal, 183–85; due process clause and, 147, 149, 150, 152–53; equal protection clause and, 73, 150–52, 154, 156–57, 176; jurisdictional statement, 148–49, 169; motion to vacate judgment, 137–38; *Naim v. Naim* and, 145–46, 171, 175, 187; notice of appeal, 144, 147–48; oral arguments, 155, 173–81, 266n. 6; scientific arguments, 155–56, 177, 178, 182–83; sociological arguments, 153–54; state remedies and, 142–44; Supreme Court opinion, 186–90; suspended sentence, 15, 137, 144, 146; three-judge panel, 139, 142; Virginia's defense, 169–72, 175

Mahorner, James, 123, 124, 130–31

Malays, 27, 30, 53, 59, 75, 79

Man's Most Dangerous Myth: The Fallacy of Race (Montagu), 162

marriage, right to, 77–78, 147, 187, 188

marriage licenses, 40, 41, 48, 75–76, 97, 117, 207

Marshall, Daniel, 75–76

Marshall, John, 156–57

Marshall, Thurgood, 90–92, 105, 109

Marutani, William M., 155, 165–66, 168, 182, 266n. 6; oral argument, 173, 177–78

Maryland, 37–38, 101; attempts to repeal law, 59–60; repeal of antimiscegenation law, 5, 102, 160, 174; servitude penalty, 38, 45

Maslow, Will, 108, 114, 115, 255n. 30

Maxey, John, 199, 200, 201

Maynard v. Hill, 107

McDaniel, Herman, 195–96

McIlwaine, Robert D., III, 2, 141, 170–71, 181–84, 219; oral argument, 178–81

McLaughlin, Dewey, 116, 118

McLaughlin v. Florida, 4, 97, 117–31, 141, 143, 152, 189; *Brown v. Board of Education* and, 120, 127, 130; common-law marriage as defense, 119, 122, 124; equal protection clause, 119–22; Fourteenth Amendment and, 119–22, 125; jurisdictional statement, 121–22, 125; *Loving v. Virginia* and, 145, 147–48, 162, 169, 177–79, 187; NAACP brief, 124–26; *Pace* and, 118–22, 127, 130–31, 143; reply brief, 128–29; state's argument, 123–24, 126–27

media, 87–88

Meltsner, Michael, 161, 162–63, 167

Mexicans, 67–68

Michigan, 41, 46, 49–50, 51, 102

military, integration of, 22

military interference, 207–8

Mills, Roger, 198–205

Mirman, Alan S., 105, 109, 255n. 20

miscegenation, as term, 26–27

"Miscegenation: The Theory of the Blending of the Races, Applied to the American White Man and Negro" (pamphlet), 26–27

Mississippi, 3, 6, 27, 35–36, 40, 101–2; challenges to statute, 92–95; civil rights movement, 140–41; constitution, 44, 198, 200, 203, 205; post-*Loving* interracial marriages, 196, 197–205

Mississippi Code, 198, 200

Mississippi Sovereignty Commission, 94

Missouri, 29, 31, 40–41, 43, 49, 174–75, 194

Mitchell, Clarence M., III, 59, 102

Mitchell, John, 207, 208

Mongolians, 27, 30, 32, 43, 44, 45, 59, 75, 79

Montagu, Ashley, 156, 162, 185

Montana, 49, 69, 100–101

Moody, Ralph, 172

Moon v. Children's Home Society of Virginia, 70

Motley, Constance Baker, 94

Mr. and Mrs. Loving (film), xi, 21, 216, 217, 259n. 1

mulattoes, 30, 39, 75

Myrdal, Gunnar, 28, 157

Nabrit, James M., III, 124, 161

Naim, Ham Say, 103–4

Naim v. Naim, 4, 94, 103–16, 130, 137, 162; ACLU and, 104–10; annulment granted, 104–5; appeals, 106–10, 113; conferences, 113–14; *Jackson v. State* and, 107–8; *Loving v. Virginia* and, 145–46, 171, 175, 187; oral arguments, 106–7; per curiam decision, 112, 115–16; state's defense, 111–12; Supreme Court of Appeals of Virginia decision, 114–15

NatCap (ACLU), 135–36, 150

National Association for the Advancement of Colored People (NAACP), 3, 51, 84 (*see also* Legal Defense Fund); amicus briefs, xii, 161, 163–64; custody cases and, 71–73; *McLaughlin v. Florida* and, 118–19, 121–26; reluctance to get involved, 84, 90–92, 94; *Stevens v. United States,* 90–92

National Association for the Advancement of White People, 89

National Catholic Conference for Interracial Justice (NCCIJ), 3, 166–67

National Catholic Social Action Conference (NCSAC), 166–67

Native Americans, 3, 43, 48–49, 58–59, 79, 95, 101; inheritance and, 67, 91; in Virginia, 31–32, 39, 53, 178

Nebraska, 27, 49, 50, 100, 194

Negro, definitions of, 29–31, 53, 163; in Florida, 30, 117–18, 123–25, 127–28, 163, 225; in Virginia, 29, 31, 39, 48–49, 53, 70, 156, 174, 223

Nevada, 4, 42, 49, 101, 102; challenges to statute, 84–88; definition of white, 29–30

New Jersey, 50

New Mexico, 42, 46

New York, 50

New York Herald, 27

New York Times, 27, 174, 195, 203

Ng, Daniel R., 96

Ninth Amendment, 149

Norfolk Virginia Pilot, 146

North Carolina, 6, 38, 41, 44, 101, 102, 174, 210; constitution, 171–72, 194; *Loving* brief, 2, 171–72

North Dakota, 27, 49, 101

O'Connor, John J., 101

octaroons, 30

Ohio, 41, 42, 46, 50

Oklahoma, 6, 32–33, 48, 90–92, 174, 194; inheritance, 61, 69

Ollason, Lawrence, 81

O'Neill, Grayce Gibson, 80, 81

Oregon, 3, 32, 43, 46, 67, 100–101, 102

Oyama, Henry, 79–80, 82, 83–84

Oyama case, 79–84, 100, 101, 171

Pace, Tony, 46

Pace v. Alabama, 4, 46, 77, 98, 106, 152; *Loving v. Virginia* and, 143, 148; *McLaughlin*

v. Florida and, 118–22, 127, 130–31, 143; as outmoded, 107, 125, 165
Palmore case, 73, 158
Pamunkey tribe, 32, 53
parentage of couples, 56–57
Parker, Frank, 95
Patty, Kenneth C., 170
penalties, 10, 26, 31, 33–35, 84, 102; for cohabitation, 50, 58, 63, 117–18, 128–29; different for whites and non-whites, 39, 42, 44–45, 57, 73, 117–18; felonies, 3, 34, 44–45; fines, 3, 15, 34, 39–41; in Florida, 117–18, 123, 128–29, 225; historical context, 38–40; for issuing marriage license, 40–42, 50, 117; for performing marriages, 3, 35, 39–41, 44, 50, 79, 117, 224; prison terms, 3, 39–43, 55, 60–61, 92–93, 95; servitude, 38, 45; in Virginia, 10, 14–15, 38–39, 44, 137, 144, 146, 185
Pennsylvania, 5, 38, 40, 50, 51
Perez case, 75–78, 81, 85, 87, 90, 100–101, 145; *Loving v. Virginia* and, 171, 182
Perry, Marshall, 199, 200, 204–5
Phelps, M. T., 83
Philippine-white marriages, 48, 59
Phillips, Olin, 211
physical appearance, as racial definition, 30, 33, 42, 68, 92–93, 123–24
Plecker, William, 52, 56
Plessy v. Ferguson, 107, 145
Pocahontas clause, 31, 52–53, 172
Podret, Jack, 81
Pointer, Sam, 207, 208
Pollak, Louis (Lou), 121, 129–30, 189
polygamous marriages, 167, 175, 184
Pratt, Robert, 21, 215
pregnancy, as crime, 39, 101
Prescott, Joyce, 195–96
Price, L. V., 207, 208
privacy, right to, 120, 147, 165
pseudoscience, 33, 41, 52, 67–68, 76, 149, 170, 204 (*see also* scientific arguments); theories on children, 28–29, 41, 163–64
public facilities, 207, 208
public health arguments, 27

Rabkin, Sol, 110
racial definitions (*see also* Negro, definitions of): percentage of blood, 3, 33, 41, 48–50, 68–69, 93, 117–18; physical appearance, 30, 33, 42, 68, 92–93, 123–24; race as only reason for crime, 46–47, 125, 128, 148, 161–62, 177–78, 187–88; white person, 29–31, 183, 223–24
Racial Integrity Act of 1924 (Virginia), 52–54, 56, 104, 106, 183–84, 223–24. *See also* Virginia Code
racial purity arguments, 52, 78, 177
Reconstruction, 43–44
Rees, Paul, 80, 82, 83–84
Reiner, Andrea, 109
religion, free exercise of, 76, 78, 80–81, 166–67
repeal of antimiscegenation statutes, 40, 42–43, 45–46, 83, 100–102, 194; Alabama, 4, 212–13; Maryland, 5, 59–60, 102, 160, 174; Mississippi, 101–2; process, 99–100
Republic of New Africa, 203
Reynolds v. United States, 175, 184
Rhode Island, 40, 46
Richmond Times-Dispatch, 52
Rights of the Indigent, 198
Roberts, Bruce, 86–87
Roberts, H. W., 209
Rockwell, George Lincoln, 218
Rogers, J. A., 25
Rolfe, John, 31
Ross, Lawrence, 199, 201
Ross, Quitman, 92–94
Russell, John J., 166

Sawada, Noriko (Nikki), 84–88
Schifter, Richard, 109
Schmidt, Benno, 187
Schneider, Jon, 149, 151–52
schools, segregation and, 30, 46, 53, 89, 109–10, 183, 203
scientific arguments, 108, 111, 126, 153–54, 162–64 (*see also* pseudoscience); as irrelevant, 171–72; *Loving v. Virginia* and, 155–56, 177–78, 182–83

Scott v. Georgia, 28, 126, 163
seduction under promise of marriage, 56, 137
segregation, 5–6, 10, 28, 126, 130; schools and, 30, 46, 53, 89, 109–10, 183, 203
separate-but-equal principle, 127, 145, 148, 152, 163
sexuality, interracial, 26–28, 60–63. *See also* cohabitation; fornication
Sharp, W. G., 75
Sherrer, Wayne, 207–9
Shurtliff, M. Karl, 207–10
Sisson, John P., 166
Slaughter-Harvey, Constance, 199
slavery, 22, 38; as basis for antimiscegenation laws, 26, 149, 153, 156–57, 162, 174–75, 187
social welfare arguments, 76–78, 86
Sodaro, Anselm, 101
South Carolina, 31, 43, 101, 174, 194; constitution, 4, 44, 194, 211–12
Southern National Party (SNP), 198–200, 204, 213
southern states, 3, 28–32, 38, 43–44, 89–90, 174
Sparta, Virginia, 20
special interest groups, 3–4, 89–91, 108–9, 155, 157
Speiser, Lawrence (Larry), 97, 136, 150
Stangle, Joseph, 96
Stant, Frederick T. "Bingo," 105, 109
Starr, Kenneth, 203
state constitutions, 3, 5, 29, 34, 44–45, 66, 99; Florida, 45, 118, 125; Mississippi, 44, 198, 200, 203, 205; North Carolina, 171–72, 194; South Carolina, 4, 44, 194, 211–12; Tennessee, 43; Virginia, 137–38, 144
Statement on the Nature of Race (UNESCO), 162, 177, 181
states: control of marriage, 111–12, 120, 143, 145, 175, 179; legislative objectives, 77, 126, 130, 163–64; police power of, 106–7, 145; racial integrity motive, 111–12, 148–49
Stehl, Edward, III, 13–14

sterilization, 50
Stevens v. United States, 90–92
Stewart, Potter, 129–30, 162, 186
Story v. State, 89
support of interracial marriage, as crime, 3, 35–36
Supreme Court, 3–4, 73, 90, 187–88, 201 *(see also Loving v. Virginia; McLaughlin v. Florida; Naim v. Naim; Pace v. Alabama);* approaches to, 109–11
Supreme Court of Appeals of Virginia, 114–15, 141
Swartzfager, Paul, 93

Taney, Roger, 1, 162
Tennessee, 40, 43, 195–96
territories, 42–43, 44
Texas, 6, 41, 43, 62, 65–66, 194
Tompkins, John, 47
Traynor, Roger, 77–78
Trezise, Jack, 97

Udall, Morris, 82
Udall, Stewart, 82
UNESCO, *Statement on the Nature of Race,* 162, 177, 181
United Nations, 167
United States, stance against antimiscegenation laws, 206–8
United States v. Brittain, 46, 209
Universal Declaration of Human Rights, 167
unmarriable classes, 3, 29, 49, 75. *See also* Chinese; Hawaiians; Japanese; Malays; Mongolians; Native Americans
U.S. Catholic Conference, 166
U.S. Code, 109, 148
Utah, 96, 102

Vaughn, David, 195
Virginia, 52 *(see also* Racial Integrity Act of 1924); annulment of marriages, 143–44; antimiscegenation laws, 10, 39–40, 44; Bowling Green, 12–13, 19; Central Point, 9–10, 13, 17–22; penalties, 10, 14–15, 38–39, 44, 137, 144, 146, 185;

post-*Loving* interracial marriages, 194–95; prosecutions, 55–57; racial definitions, 29, 31, 39, 48–49, 53, 70, 156, 174, 223; registration of race, 29, 33, 176, 192, 223

Virginia Code, 223–24; 1900s, 48–49; 1924 revisions, 156, 174, 183–84; extraterritorial marriage, 35, 40, 148, 170, 224; Pocahontas clause, 31, 52–53, 172; Racial Integrity Act of 1924, 52–54, 56, 104, 106, 183–84, 223–24; section 20–54, 178, 182–85; section 20–57, 11; section 20–58, 11, 148, 161, 170, 178, 182–84; section 20–59, 170, 178, 182–85; slavery as origin of, 149, 156–57, 174–75

Virginia Constitution, section 1, 137–38, 144

Virginia Law of 1691, 38, 39, 149, 156

Virginia Marriage Requirements, 193–94

Voyer, Louis, 206–10

war brides, 90, 100

Warren, Earl, 75, 98–99, 112, 115–16, 128–29, 156, 178, 180, 186–87

Wasserman, Jack, 108–9

Watts, Rowland, 84, 95

Weidemeyer, C. Maurice, 60

Weinberger, Andrew, 163–64, 167–68

Weitzel, Frank, 97

Welcome, Verda, 59–60, 102

West Virginia, 31, 34–35, 45, 194

White, Byron, 131, 186

White, Walter, 94

White Citizens' Councils, 89–90, 195

white person, definition of, 29–31, 183, 223–24

white supremacy, 52, 120, 148–49, 157, 187, 188

Whitman, George, 26–27

Wilkins, Roy, 109

Wine, David, 83

Wines, Taylor, 86–87

Wisconsin, 50, 51

Wood, Martha, 197–98

Wright, Edward, 27

Wright, Marian, 195

Wulf, Melvin (Mel), 147, 151, 154, 155, 262n. 45

Wyoming, 27, 44–45, 51

Zabel, William, 73, 151, 152–54, 157–58, 173

Zarr, Melvyn, 161

Born in Astoria, New York, **Phyl Newbeck** lives in the foothills of the Green Mountains in northern Vermont. She directs the Vermont Teacher Diversity Scholarship program, a nonprofit program that recruits and trains students from diverse racial and ethnic backgrounds to be teachers in Vermont's public schools. She serves on the Board of Directors of the Jericho Underhill Land Trust and chairs the Jericho Development Review Board.

The complete paintings of

Picasso

Blue and Rose Periods

Introduction by **Denys Sutton**

Notes and catalogue by **Paolo Lecaldano**

Harry N. Abrams, Inc. *Publishers* New York

Standard Book Number 8109-5514-8
Library of Congress Catalogue
Card Number 70-92261
© Copyright in Italy by
Rizzoli Editore, 1968
Printed and bound in Italy

Table of contents

Denys Sutton	Introduction	5
Paolo Lecaldano	An outline of the artist's critical history	9
	The paintings in colour	15
	List of plates	16
	The works	81
	Exhibitions	82
	Bibliography	82
	Outline biography	83
	Catalogue of works	87
Appendix	Table of concordance	114
Indexes	Subjects	116
	Titles	116
	Topographical	117
	Previous owners	117
	French titles	118
	Prices	119

Photographic sources

Colour plates: Baltimore Museum of Art, Baltimore (Md.); Blauel, Munich; Brenwasser, New York; Conzett & Huber, Zürich; Göteborgs Museum, Göteborg; Goetz, Los Angeles (Cal.); Held, Ecublens; Hinz, Basle; Ides et Calendes, Neuchâtel; Mas, Barcelona; Mellon, Washington, DC; Merkel, Saõ Paulo; Metropolitan Museum of Art, New York; National Gallery of Art, Washington, DC; Nimatallah, Milan; Scott, Edinburgh; Service T.I.P., Liège; Solomon R. Guggenheim Museum, New York; Staatsgalerie, Stuttgart; Toledo Museum of Art, Toledo (Ohio); Virginia Museum of Fine Arts, Richmond (Va.); Warburg, New York; Whitney, New York. Black and white illustrations: most of these were supplied by the respective galleries or collections, or were already in the Rizzoli archives. Photographs nos. 49, 93 B, 149, 176, 177, 181, 238, 245 C, 246, 258 A, 275 A, 289 B, 298, were reproduced by kind permission of the authors and publishers, from *Picasso 1900–1906*, by Pierre Daix and Georges Boudaille, Neuchâtel 1966, Editions Ides et Calendes.

Introduction

If Pablo Picasso had died in 1906 he would have been only twenty-five but he would have left behind him a formidable body of work – the many paintings, water-colours, drawings and etchings from the Blue and Rose Periods which have rightly won him so many admirers. They are among the most enchanting pictures produced in the early years of this century and their vivacity and freshness have not diminished with the years.

One of Picasso's achievements at this time was to have taken the more or less conventional subject-matter of the *fin de siècle* and given it his own personal twist, elegant in style and often elegiac in mood. Yet his art, while reflecting the temper of the day, succeeded in being more than modish. He was already a master of paradox for, although often considered an extreme radical, he has invariably been a lover of earlier art and his connoisseur's eye has permitted him to look in many different directions, adapting to his own ends anything that has captured his fancy.

His intellectual and artistic appetite is displayed to the full in his salad days, when he was in touch with the intelligentsia and the artistic world of Barcelona, Madrid and Paris. He was one of the circle that gathered in the famous "Els 4 Gats", where he made spirited drawings of his companions, and in Madrid in 1901 he edited the avant-garde review *Arte Joven*. He numbered among his Spanish friends the painter Nonell, who was his senior and exerted a decided influence on him, Junyer, Manolo the sculptor, Ricardo Canals and the writer Utrillo. In Paris, which he visited for the first time in 1900 and where he settled in 1904, he formed valuable contacts with a lively circle which included Guillaume Apollinaire, Max Jacob and André Salmon and he owed much to his relationship with Fernande Olivier. It was thanks to these connexions, as well as to his own love of novelty, that he kept abreast of modern trends in literature, ideas and art.

Picasso grew up at the tail-end of historicism so it is small wonder that, during his artistic and intellectual *wanderjähre* (1900–6), he tapped so many different sources – Toulouse-Lautrec, Steinlen, Beardsley, Rosetti, El Greco and Iberian sculpture. He was an exponent of the theory of the "museum without walls" before it had been coined by André Malraux. The range of his borrowings has been examined in detail by Sir Anthony Blunt and Dr Phoebe Pool. Although some of their theories have been challenged by MM. Daix and Boudaille, the authors of the standard work on the early work of Picasso who reject the debt to Edvard Munch, their chief conclusions are valid.

So much emphasis is now placed on the merit of an artist who immediately casts off an inheritance, that it is sometimes overlooked that many painters in earlier times found nothing wrong in leaning on either their forbears or their contemporaries when formulating their own style. Such debts were not felt to hamper their own originality and there is no reason why they should do so. Rubens looked at Elsheimer, Correggio, Titian and Tintoretto, not to speak of the Antique, without in any way impairing the robustness of his own work. Another artist fond of "quoting" from the Old Masters was Sir Joshua Reynolds. Picasso therefore may be placed in a noble tradition; he is an aesthete who has got the best out of a period of aestheticism.

The old view that Spain in the 1890s and 1900s was an artistic backwater is now seen to be misleading. In fact, this period witnessed a considerable resurgence of intellectual life in Spain, and besides Picasso himself, reference may be made to Gaudí, Unamuno and Ortega y Gasset. The Catalan Renaissance, for instance, afforded a specific contribution to European culture which was international in character. Its exponents looked at the Spanish tradition obviously, but, also, at the achievements of France and, no less significantly, of the North. Wagner, Schopenhauer and Nietzsche were names to conjure with in Barcelona and Picasso is even said to have read in his teens most of the writings of the last-mentioned German philosopher. Picasso is well-read so that a literary flavour was only to be expected in his painting at this stage. He is one of the many artists and men of letters who succumbed to the then fashionable pessimism and who were fascinated by the problem of giving artistic expression to physical and psychological illness.

On arriving in Paris in 1900, Picasso adopted the traditional path of the tourist and was intrigued, understandably so, by the night life of the city; by places such as the Moulin de la Galette and the garishly dressed prostitutes with their feather boas. His approach resembles that of other masters of *la belle Epoque*; however, his early pictures of such subjects were endowed with a sense of psychological insight which was not to be found in those of many of his contemporaries. His themes and the mood of his pictures were then derived from the tradition of the French poets of urban life – Baudelaire, Verlaine and Laforgue and express nostalgia, a sense of pathos and melancholy. Yet Picasso was opposed to Naturalism and, unlike painters such as de Nittis or Raffaëlli, he did not paint mean streets in an anecdotal manner. The first Paris pictures reflect a youthful zest for strong colours and for black outlines that anticipate the procedures of Fauvism by some years.

Inevitably this impressionable painter responded to the willowy lines and decorative appeal of Art Nouveau, then such a dominant European style. The subject-matter he chose to paint – the nature of relations between the sexes as in *Life* (no. 89) – was also akin to the iconography of this movement. His closeness to Symbolism is no less evident. Cirici Pellicer, in his valuable account of the early Picasso, has drawn attention to the parallels existing between Picasso's painting and that of Maurice Denis; the differences between them are telling, however, for Denis aimed at rendering the bliss of domestic life and the consolations of religion, while Picasso produced works in which faith is conspicuously absent. As an heir to the Decadent tradition, he sought an artistic equivalent for nihilism and pessimism.

The sort of ideas that Picasso expressed in his early painting can be found in Unamuno's books, above all in *Del sentimiento trágico de la vida*, 1912, in which this influential thinker emphasised that man's life was a tragedy from birth to death. It is no less relevant that Ortega y Gasset's contact with German philosophy heightened the pessimism ventilated in *España invertebrada* (1921) and *La rebelión de las masas* (1930). It is significant that certain of Picasso's representa-

tions of women and children reveal affinities with those of Carrière. The connexion is based on their mutual love of pathos and their sympathy for the poor – evident in Picasso's pictures of beggars and Carrière's espousal of Socialism. However, their technique and concept of colour were different; Carrière restricted his palette practically to monochrome. Picasso clothed his works in blue. His almost exclusive use of this colour in 1902–3, as Sir Anthony Blunt and Dr Pool point out, "has never been satisfactorily explained". It has been attributed to the fact that he was too poor to buy other colours and that he worked by lamplight. However, a convincing explanation is that blue is the colour that was so much admired by Romantics and the Decadents. It is certainly one that well accorded with his themes and heightened their pervasive sense of mystery.

Picasso, who has never denied his debt to other artists, acknowledges the influence on him of Van Gogh which can be most effectively seen in the *Self-Portrait* (no. 21). His appreciation of El Greco is particularly interesting for this artist had only begun to be admired again in the 1890s – Sargent for one championed his work. There is no doubt that the manneristic twist, the elongations and the spiritual mood of the great Spanish painter were congenial to him. Picasso's unusual picture, *Burial of Casagemas* – a poet who had committed suicide in Paris – was indebted to El Greco's *Dream of Philip II* or *Burial of Count Orgaz*. There is a fascinating echo from Odilon Redon in Picasso's picture also; for the plunging horse must surely derive from one of this artist's illustrations to Flaubert's *Tentation de Saint-Antoine*. Picasso's interest in Spanish painting may also be observed in his pictures of bull-fights with their inevitable relationships with Goya and Lucas.

The stage has played a considerable role in Picasso's art but only since the publication of Douglas Cooper's important book on this topic has the importance of his contribution to the Russian ballet of Diaghilev been fully realised. This theatrical streak is evident in Picasso's early pictures, not only in their subject matter – harlequins and circus people (he loved the Cirque Médrano) – but in the disposition of space which often suggests that the protagonists in a picture are on the stage. Yet there is nothing at all naturalistic about his conception. The figures in *The Acrobats* (no. 192) seem to have strayed on to a stage from some dream world and it is easy to understand the deep appeal of this picture to Rilke; it inspired the celebrated opening of the fifth of his Duino elegies: "But tell me, who are they, these acrobats, even a little more fleeting than we ourselves – so urgently, ever since childhood wrung by an (oh for the sake of whom?) never-contented will?" Picasso's paintings of the circus and harlequins, as well as the Salome series, stress the exquisite side of his art: this dandy of art possesses a true Parisian chic. Another sign of his cult of elegance is his rose tones in many pictures of 1905.

Picasso was in touch with several of the men of letters, headed by Moréas, who in 1905–6 supported a return to the Antique world. Yet in turning in this direction, Picasso did no more than adhere to the tradition of idealistic painting associated with Puvis de Chavannes, Hans von Marées and (mixed with Celtic mystery) Augustus John. Picasso, in fact, is one of the last of the great nineteenth-century classicists – a breed which produced Rodin, Richard Strauss and Hugo von Hofmannsthal. Picasso appreciated the elegant linearism of Greek vase painting and the perfect pose of Archaic sculpture.

By 1905 significant changes may be detected in Picasso's art. The intricacies of his style at the period and the confused chronology of his evolution have been well analysed by MM. Daix and Boudaille. Picasso paid visits to Holland and to Gósol in Catalonia, where he spent the summer of 1906. Even if he did not see Iberian sculpture at Gósol (none in fact exists there), his painting was now moving in a different direction. The famous portrait of Gertrude Stein, for instance, shows a stronger, more brutal and more monumental treatment of form. It may well be that his concern with primitivism was a sign of a reaction against aestheticism.

How may the works of the Blue and Rose Periods be compared with those of the Cubist Period or with Picasso's later development? Do they seem to be old-fashioned and dated or is it that his expression of a vision, in which man's alienation from an increasingly mechanistic and impersonal world is conveyed with a melancholy and sweetness, has more to offer us than is often believed, more even than his Cubist and later pictures?

DENYS SUTTON

An outline of the artist's critical history

... Picasso's art is extremely young. Gifted with an observing eye that does not forgive people's weaknesses, he manages to plumb beauty even in the horrible, which he then puts down with the sobriety of a man who paints because he sees and not because he knows how to achieve this or that effect. . . .

In Paris they have given him a nickname: his appearance, his wide-brimmed hat which has endured the inclemencies of Montparnasse, his eyes – the bright eyes of a southerner who is also master of himself, his neck enveloped in fantastic, ultra-impressionistic scarves, have all inspired his French friends to call him "Little Goya".

We believe that he will not be false to his name physically: his intensity tells us that we are right. MIGUEL UTRILLO ("PINCELL"), review of the exhibition in the Sala Parés, in *Pèl i Ploma*, Barcelona, June 1901

... The recent Spanish flowering, which is wholly pictorial this time, is imbued above all with harsh, dark, corrosive imagery which can also be magnificent at times, but with a deliberately gloomy, violently autochthonous magnificence.

All these artists are, indeed, related by a marked family likeness: underneath their apparent influences one detects their great predecessors, and especially Goya, that sad, powerful genius: as, for example, in Picasso, the latest striking arrival on the scene.

Picasso is absolutely, decisively a painter, as his feeling for material is sufficient to show: like all true painters, he loves colour for itself, and every material has its own colour.

So that every subject arouses him, therefore, everything may become a subject for him. The dazzling explosion of flowers over the rim of a vase, towards light and the luminous atmosphere that enfolds them: the multicoloured surge of the crowd, the green of a race track, the dry sand of a bull-ring; the exposure of female bodies, of every kind of female body, or the concealment of them and the way they are defined, revealed as solid behind the soft layers of mothy stuffs . . . And the unexpected: the light green of one of the three dancing girls contrasting with the white of their petticoats, or the very stiff, masculine whiteness of the starched underclothes of the little girls; the white and yellow of a woman's hat: and so on.

Just as every part of a subject is a subject for him, so everything assists him to render it: slang, dialect, even his neighbour's vocabulary. And it is not difficult to discover the many probable influences on him. Delacroix, Manet (the most legitimate since he, too, derives something from the Spanish school), Monet, Van Gogh, Pissarro, Toulouse-Lautrec, Degas, Forain, maybe even Rops . . . But all of them in passing, dissipated almost before they are apprehended.

His impetuosity has clearly prevented him as yet from developing a style of his own: his personality is expressed precisely in this effusion, this youthfully furious spontaneity. (He is said to be not yet twenty years old, yet to complete three canvasses a day.) Herein, however, lies danger, in this very impetus which could direct him to facile virtuosity and even more facile success. "Prolific" and "fertile" are adjectives, just like "energetic" and "violent". It would be a shame, when he shows such exuberant virility. FÉLICIEN FAGUS, "L'Invasion espagnole: Picasso", in *La Revue Blanche*, Paris, 15 July 1901

... As for M. Picasso, who they tell me, is still very young, he marks his début with such élan that I am afraid for his future. One could make a list of the origins of all his paintings: their variety is too astonishing. This is not to deny his gift: but I should advise him, for his own good, not to paint more than one canvas a day. FRANÇOIS CHARLES, review of the exhibition at the Galerie Vollard, in *L'Ermitage*, Paris, September 1901

... Earlier a blazing riot of colour, Picasso is now concentrating his powers on the line of energy.

The absorbed, almost benumbed little girl with the stubborn, thin, serious brow and sick, mistrustful, pitiless eyes, painted entirely in light shades of blue, is poised like a character from history. The young girl who is standing upright in the tub to sponge herself, with slender legs and lean torso, has a rounded shoulder whence branches the arm that carries the sponge: she emerges as a fragile figurine, self-contained, extraordinarily peaceful. The courtesan whose outline is stamped on the thick azure background is unaware of her dignity. The feline twist of her shoulders and hands, and the fixity of her expression under the statuesque headgear of her wide hat with its nodding plume together make something hieratic of her, which is fully expressed in the golden-haired virgin (herself, or her sister?): she is just a young girl stretching down, her head erect and an absent-minded expression on her face; her short, feline nose is slightly wrinkled, between sniffing and breathing – a wonderful creature, almost a goddess, a sphinx. The whole is contained within an opacity which flashes with light and with open areas imprisoned inside perfectly conceived and considered perimeters, painted with great emphasis and command: a simplification which solidly confirms the impression aroused by these canvasses of stained glass. . . .

All these Spanish artists . . . have temperament, breeding and personality. Each one is an absolute master in his own field, exclusively his own, yet very closely related to his neighbour's. As yet, however, there is no great man among them; no one who dominates them, absorbing and recreating everything, whom they all depend upon and who is great enough to build a world of his own without any limits.

We may mention the names of Goya, Zurbarán, Herrera, who fight on the same side as our own Impressionists, Manet, Monet, Degas and Carrière. Which of them – and the time is ripe – will become their El Greco? FÉLICIEN FAGUS, "Peintres espagnols", in *La Revue Blanche*, Paris, September 1902

One of the extraordinary elements is the empty sadness whose weight is felt through the entire, already vast output of this young man. Picasso, who began to paint even before he learned to read, seems to have been commissioned to record the whole of our existence with his brush: he could be called a young god, come to build the world anew. But a dark god. The hundreds of faces he has painted are all sombre, not a smile amongst them and the world is no more habitable than are its leprosy-infected factories. His painting itself is diseased.

Incurably so? I do not know. We certainly stand here before a man of power, vocation, and real talent. Some of the drawings give the impression – like a simple crouching nude – of an already mature prodigy. Some compositions – such as the two spectators in a box, a man and woman, who look away from the stage where, in the distance, a ballerina is performing pirouettes – draw us and disturb us like some poem from the *Fleurs du Mal*. These are almost sexless beings, the demons of everyday, with desolate eyes, lolling heads and brows shadowed by despairing or criminal thoughts. . . .

Should we even wish that such painting should be cured? Or should this disconcertingly precocious young man be destined to consecrate with the title of masterpiece the negative feeling in life, whose suffering he, like all of us, shares? CHARLES MORICE, "Exposition", in *Mercure de France*, Paris, December 1902

. . . Picasso, too, can draw good likenesses: he is, one might say, a good enamellist. Some of his pastels are in metallic, acidulous shades, like chemicals, which he pursues obstinately; the lines are refined, enclosing pools of rose but especially blue, which are themselves flowers, wallpapers, or vests and shawls of anxious, pensive women. There is one painting of a woman dressed in pastel yellow, an angular music-hall *diseuse*, who is consumed by her own consumption. Herein we discern a painter watchful of the effect which the poverty of present times makes in the suburbs of Paris – members of secret sects, thieving couples, agitators, women, all on hard times, rejected, on strike, forgotten, going to pieces, eaten up, tossed about by life like flotsam and jetsam. MAURICE LE SIEUTRE, introduction to the catalogue of the exhibition at the Galerie Berthe Weill, Paris, 24 October–20 November 1904

. . . Blessed are the uneasy since solely for them is eternal peace reserved: Mir, Nonell, Xiró and Ruiz Picasso, who is now turning his attention to works that will surprise and even terrify us. EUGENIO D'ORS in *El poble catalá*, Barcelona, 10 December 1904

. . . He was not yet twenty years old, yet already possessed an astonishing sureness in his handling of colour relations, and of composition, such as artists of much longer experience are still striving to attain. CHARLES MORICE, preface to the catalogue of the exhibition at the Galerie Serrurier, Paris, 25 February–6 March 1905

. . . I have already had several reasons to speak of Picasso, to remark upon the outstanding gifts of this very young artist, at the same time deploring the negative approach of his concentration on empty misery and on his exacerbated vision of men and things.

But the new works he is showing indicate a fundamental change in his attitude. Not that no element of his turbid early portrayal remains: Picasso is Andalusian; his predilection for the images and accents of anguish are an indelible sign of his race to Spaniards. Nonetheless, his attitudes are lightening now; the elements are less wretchedly disposed; the canvasses are brightening. No longer is there a delight, for its own sake, in all that is sad and ugly. His premature twilight of hypochondria, which ought, logically, to have led to the black night of despair and death, has given way, by some happy illogicality, to a beam of light: the dawn of compassion, of salvation is born.

What we most disliked in Picasso's early works – which were, all the same, well differentiated by the sharp imprint of a powerful personality – was that not only did he not seem to feel compassion for poverty, he seemed to love it. But his sensibilities have now deepened, just as his technique has strengthened and become more refined. His structures are now more solid. CHARLES MORICE, review of the exhibition at the Galerie Serrurier, in *Mercure de France*, Paris, March 1905

It has been said that Picasso's works reveal his early disillusionment with life. I think the opposite.

He is, in fact, delighted with everything. The incontestable talent he has has been put, as it seems to me, to serve an imagination that mixes in just the right amounts the magnificent and the horrible, the crude and the refined. The scrupulous exactitude of his naturalism borders on that mysticism that is tucked away somewhere in the depths of all Spanish minds, even those least religious. Castelar, as we know, carried a rosary in his pocket: and if Picasso is not exactly religious, as to credo, I will wager that he nurses a stealthy respect for St Theresa or St Isidore.

During carnival in Rome, there are masques (with Harlequin, Columbine, the French cook . . .) in which, after an orgy that frequently ends in murder, everyone goes off in the morning to kiss St Peter's worn big toe. These people would certainly fascinate him greatly.

Beneath the gaudy tinsel of the dancers he paints we see, undoubtedly, the young; cunning, malicious, crafty, poor and liars. The mothers he depicts clench slender hands just like those that the young mothers of working people have. The pubic hair that classical painters disdain to show, and which is the touchstone of western shame, his women, however, reveal. GUILLAUME APOLLINAIRE, "Picasso, peintre et dessinateur", in *La Revue Immoraliste*, Paris, April 1905

If we possessed wisdom, all the Gods would wake up and get moving. Born out of the deep awareness that humanity looks after itself, the pantheisms that it worships and which are in its likeness have fallen asleep. But despite their eternal sleep, there are eyes in which are reflected whole humanities amounting to divine, joyous visions. Eyes, wide-awake, like flowers continually turned towards the sun. What joyous richness for those born to see with eyes like this.

Picasso has looked at the human images that vacillate in the blue haze of memory and that generate metaphysics, through their unity with the divine: pious heavens disturbed by scenes of rape: dim pervasive lights like those in caverns.

Wandering youths, without beliefs, halt while the rain evaporates: "Look: there are people who live outside this man-made world, people who wear tattered clothes." Young men who have never known an embrace, yet understand everything – oh mother, love me! – They can cut capers, and their cartwheels are like the whirling of minds.

There are women no longer loved, who remember. Too long have they contemplated their frail ideas; devoted to their memories, they do not pray: they crouch down in their twilight as if in some ancient church. Women who have given up weaving crowns of straw, whose fingers would fumble to do so now. Women who fall mute as dawn breaks, washed over by silence. Women who have opened countless doors. Mothers protect their babies from misfortune and see, when they lean over them, that the smile of their little ones tells them they are good. Women accustomed to giving thanks, whose forearms tremble like children.

Enveloped in icy mists, old men wait without thinking at all, since only the young think. . . . There are other beggars, whom life has worn out: feeble, stupid, the lees of life, they are stunned to have reached an end which is still blue, yet no longer the horizon. As they have grown old, a folly has seized them like that which overtakes kings who own too many heads of elephants and rule tiny states. Some are travellers who have confused the flowers and the stars.

Aged as oxen who have endured for twenty-five years, the young men lead girls who will be mothers under the moon.

In the purity of daylight, the women keep silent, their bodies like angels and their glances fluttering: deep inside they are smiling at danger; they await fear to confess their harmless sins.

For a whole year Picasso has lived this dewy life, blue like the damp bottom of the abyss, compassionate, with a compassion that has made him harsher.

The squares display hanged corpses stiff against the houses and leaning over the passers-by in expectation of some redeemer, on strings that hang miraculously straight under roofs ablaze with brilliant flowers. Enclosed in their rooms, impoverished artists draw velvet nudes by the light of a lamp: the abandoned shoes by the bed are a mark of tender attention.

After the frenzy, calm.

Under their rags, harlequins come to life, when the painter summons his colours together, and makes them burgeon or fade to show the strength and duration of passions, when the lines describing vests curve, break and rush together.

Paternity transfigures the harlequin framed in his room, while his wife washes herself in freezing water and is happy with herself, as slim and lithe as her husband is puppet-like, and a flicker of fire warms his caravan: sons are heard from far off, and soldiers pass by, cursing the day. Love is fine, once you get past it and the habit of living at home intensifies the fatherly feeling: children bring the father and mother, whom Picasso renders as glorious and immaculate, together again.

The mothers, bearing a child for the first time, were not expecting to do so: because of a chattering old crow, perhaps, or an unfavourable omen. Christmas! And so, they will give birth to future acrobats, a cross between tame monkeys and bear-like dogs.

Adolescent sisters, balancing immense balloons, imprint on the spheres the moving rays of the worlds: innocent adolescent sisters, in the anxiety of innocence, to whom animals reveal the religious mystery. And harlequins exalt the glory of their women, whom they also look like: neither male nor female.

Colours with the opacity of frescoes, decisive lines: but relegated to the fringes of life, the animals look like humans and their sexes become indistinct.

Hybrid hearts with the wisdom of Egyptian demi-gods: taciturn harlequins whose cheeks and foreheads are worn through morbid sensibility: it is not possible to accept these acrobats, used to the devout attention of those who watch their silent rites performed with rough agility, as mere players.

In this, this artist shows himself different from the Greek vases, of which his style is sometimes reminiscent. On painted earthen-ware, the bearded voluble priests sacrifice animals which are resigned and have no destiny. In Picasso, virility is beardless, but is revealed in the tendons of thin arms and the planes of faces, while the animals assume an air of mystery.

Picasso's predilection for the fugitive and transient penetrates to the core of things and changes them, producing utterly unique originals in flowing chalcographic lines, in which the general appearance of the world is not one whit altered by the light, which moulds the form as its colour changes.

More than all the poets, sculptors and other artists, this Spaniard leaves us breathless, as after a sudden ice-cold shower: his meditations reveal themselves in silence: and he comes from far off, from the harsh annals of the compositions and decorations of seventeenth-century Spain.

Anyone who has known him will remember his sudden trucu-lences, which went beyond experience. His obstinate pursuit of beauty has guided his steps and made him Latin in morality, but an Arab in rhythm.

GUILLAUME APOLLINAIRE, "Les jeunes: Picasso peintre", in *La Plume*, Paris, 15 May 1905

Sandricourt pointed his finger at a considerable painting full of flat, almost faded, colours [on the walls of the "Lapin Agile": see no. 197 of the *Catalogue*] and remarked:

"This Harlequin and Columbine are hungry. Look at their eyes . . . yet they haven't a penny, so they may not eat. That's why they drink. They aren't even looking at each other, yet we know they are in love. The dauber who splashed them on canvas in a couple of hours will become a genius, if Paris does not murder him first."

He must have been protesting because he had at once recognised the hand which had painted the yellowy-red and green lozenges of the vests of those wasted bodies.

"Dear Sir, the painter of this Harlequin is already well-known and soon . . . To remember him in some way, you may call him the Callot of acrobats. But you had much better learn his name. It is Picasso."

EUGÈNE MARSAN, *Sandricourt au pays des firmans. Histoire d'un Gouvernement*, Paris 1906

[1901–2]
. . . In Barcelona, and subsequently in Paris, Picasso created emotive pictures, invocations to sensibility, pursuing to the ex-treme every refinement of feeling. The world's images produced

in him states of mind of which the figures manifested by his brush are, in a way, visual representations, an essential reclothing by which everyone may relive them. It is by instinct, not on purpose, that he draws beings weighed down by precarious mental and physical health. That is why he is able to dwell on their complicated reactions so efficaciously. In his depiction of the unhappy and the disinherited, the artist gives an attention which is entirely sympathetic, which is thus responsible for the verity of those figures, not to mention the particular quality of those pictures to stimulate an attraction not aroused elsewhere. The singular charm bewitches the beholder and constantly turns him back into his memory.

It is the so-called "Blue Period". . . . Girls, cripples, couples either famished or clutching the glass of absinthe, blind men, sorrowing mothers, angular youths, lean faces, and deformed bodies are all witnesses to a humanity which knows no joy. Sometimes a face appears, reflecting subtle meditation, but generally the figures are ambiguous, marked with profound morbidity, immersed in dark deprivation.

One might have expected the intense search for expression to have led Picasso into over-emphasis. On the contrary, his works are always stylistically impeccable and dramatically intense. Anyone except him would have slithered into the pathetic and the affected. But Picasso even though so young, knew how to reinforce his skill in anecdote with purely plastic means.

The change in his conception of the external world, as the artist knew it, brings about a parallel change in his palette and manner of painting: he passes from warm colour to an almost cold range of grey-blues and this tendency towards impoverishment of colours determined in its turn, a simplification of their use. At first he adopted very fine touches, or else wide and short, or even very long ones. In some paintings the brush strokes seem very light, in others, by contrast, very heavy when the colours have not been applied with a spatula. In other words, the techniques employed in Picasso's paintings in 1900 and the first part of 1901 were various. With those of the "blue period" he achieves the height of simplicity: light and smooth touches which are not found in any earlier works.

[1903–4]
. . . During this period, Picasso is only interested in human values: apart from figures, nothing or almost nothing stimulates his brush. There is not a single still life with the exception of two views of Barcelona, landscape is only occasionally introduced into a background. When an artist is seized by an obsession about the mystery of human life, he hardly uses landscape at all unless as an essential backcloth. What is essential to Picasso is the emotion aroused by man himself: this element is one of the main characteristics of his spirit. Some time ago he had a discussion with the sculptor Laurens about the highest form an artist can aspire to, and he put landscape at the lowest level of his ambitions, with, in a rising sequence of importance, still life, man, and above him – the gods, and above all, goddesses. But, to be plain, Picasso did not mean that to achieve elevation an artist has to choose divinity as a subject. Rather that, when he has mastered the subtlest relationships between things, when he has himself risen above the attractiveness, the beauty and energy with which, at rare moments, men can clothe themselves, when he has fused intensity of passion with spiritual strength, only then can he raise

his mind to pure beauty and – if he has the technique at his command – to invisible beauty. From this Picasso derives his interest in human beings. The elevation of art implies every other elevation of the human spirit. To give expression to the gods and goddesses the artist must exert all his faculties to the utmost, an effort which necessarily demands a total impoverishment yet brings with it an immense enrichment. One can no longer tell what is material, what spiritual and a unity of contrasts is achieved which only the miracle of true art can work.

[1904–6]
. . . The "Blue Period" came to an end. Colour timidly reclaimed its rights. More varied and richer shades can be seen in "*Les noces de Pierrette*", *Contemplation* and *Woman with her Hair Up* [nos. 142, 140–1 and 131]. The figures of 1904 are drawn with greater accuracy, the treatment is both incisive and fully expressive. We should note the attention Picasso gives to the portrayal of the hand, whose fingers are disproportionately long, as in the Catalan primitives and, in fact, in Spanish art generally which loves to let hands speak, to make them express a feeling. . . .

At the same time Picasso achieves total mastery in his drawing and displays virtuosity which is both rare and dangerous. This sureness of touch is astonishing in one who is only twenty-three: there is not the slightest uncertainty in it. Anyone else but him might have made capital out of it, would have over-exercised it. But Picasso has been endowed with many other gifts beside that of drawing to perfection; he has received abilities commensurate with his ambitions and, although very young, has an exact knowledge of himself. However one looks at his work, one always finds in it a continuous movement towards inner vision, together with an awareness of never having fully expressed what he was feeling: a superhuman ambition which leaves him eternally unsatisfied and makes him turn constantly in new directions.

In 1905 he totally abandoned his earlier work, in spirit, subject and colour. And the dramas of the "Blue Period" are followed by quieter canvases in which humanity is seen less from its suffering aspect than in plastic values. Without modifying his intensity, he extends his vision of the outside world to circus people and strolling players. He paints a fantastic series of acrobats, jugglers, tightrope walkers, actors from peripheral folk-theatres and above all, those harlequins whom he has always chosen and through whom he has woven a subtle web of emotions. A parallel change can be seen in the composition of the paintings. At first Picasso only showed single figures or couples, and produced nothing comparable to the *Acrobats* [no. 192]. . . . During the "Blue Period" he put his vision directly on canvas, which explains why there are no preliminary drawings of the work that dates from that time . . . ([the few that are known] consist of different technical means of expressing exactly the same subject). . . . So the *Acrobats* is the exception to Picasso's rule to work in one stroke: moreover, the studies differ very little from the finished work. In fact, Picasso has always found it impossible – and still does – to advance a plastic resolution whose realisation demands extensive application, and long, deliberate work.

[1905–6]
. . . All Picasso's changes have resulted not from the demands of theory but rather from the strength of his need to transmit feeling. Without even enunciating precepts, by wrapping himself, on the

contrary, in silence, Picasso widens his vision and extends his own range. Ever since his youth he has aspired, through consecutive approaches, to the infinite. There have been unexpected links and inevitable breaks in the chain whose effects can be seen in his recent work. This should never be lost to sight if we want to explain the renewal Picasso brought about at the end of 1905. Success was already very close then, and anyone might have grabbed it with all their might. But not Picasso, who will break out on a new adventure.

Up until then he had always endowed his characters with subjective emotions, whose intensity was in perfect accord with his own temperament and strength of feeling. Now, he rejects that. He finds himself at fault, in having created a work that he considered excessively romantic. "It's mere sentiment", he said. In these last years I have sometimes heard him express sympathy for the paintings he did between the ages of twenty-two and twenty-five, and admit that their general attitude quite closely matched his own personality. But then he meant to eliminate from his own work every trace of sentimentality, in order to achieve objectivity. With time, a mistrust grew of his own innermost feelings, against which he has reacted with every ounce of energy, as the great number of still lifes painted between 1907 and the present time bear witness. But even the ruthless struggle he has undertaken since then against narrative constitutes a clear proof of Picasso's mistrust of personal feeling.

The same motive drove him, at the beginning of 1906, to give up his habit of transcribing humanity as exactly as his mastery enabled him to. And while he devotes himself to the elimination of episode and to the restraint of his own violent feeling, in order to gain power in plasticism, he tries to acquire something equivalent to nature, to assure himself some recital of life, and to affirm the essence of humanity with greater generalisation. That is why sentiment vanishes in the figures of the "Rose Period", together with the suppression of all that might insinuate itself, that might be of exclusive relevance. Picasso frees his figures from their personal histories, from the events of their daily lives, and endows them with a richer plasticity. Their surfaces are ampler, their bodily proportions are changed, we see many of them with a large head and body somehow shortened. The details become extremely simplified and often serve as architectural setting for the figure as a whole. Even colour is altered in the general move towards simplification. The characters of 1906 are bathed in light tenuous shades of rose. . . .

CHRISTIAN ZERVOS, *Pablo Picasso*, vol. I, Paris, 1932

. . . So it was that towards the end of 1901 Picasso reduced his palette to one single colour. The Blue Period began: the period of "soaked" painting, as Apollinaire put it, in which there is certainly no forced strangeness or originality, but the first stage towards cutting off short with the recent past, by starting to reject all the effects of atmosphere and light that colour can give, and, as a result, the very situation of the impressionistic subject, which is reduced to expeditious relations of mass and chiaroscuro. This kind of wounding of the self is an exact indication of the gradual atonement Picasso had to make to get back to a point which attracted him yet still remained veiled. His decision did not, in fact, derive from an abandonment to the calm fruits of formal procedure, but was a deliberate, planned act, in which the artist made a clean break and cleared the ground to see it more clearly.

He began by simplifying his technique, and through this simplified technique, the object itself. Or rather, he tried to shatter the formulation of the image on the object. This inverted process made form abstract, making it disposable, and, basically, unimportant. Hence the customary unconcern, almost kleptomaniac, in references to Degas, such as in *The Blue Room* [no. 9], to Daumier in *Two Women at a Bar* [no. 44] and to Gauguin in his *Life* [no. 89] where the nudes . . . have the nasty, slightly perspiring look of the Councils of the Levy. But it is not difficult to perceive that in these livid images Picasso was seeking not only to contrast a plastic vision with one of colour, taking ingredients wherever he could find them: not even a plastic vision might derive from a natural object which became pertinent and almost cohesive with the very blood circulation of man. And since this too had to be avoided, the conversion of chromatic to plastic became instrumental, and although circumscribed by formula, ended by losing interest in the question of form to the point of lapsing into the general style of the *Seated Woman with Arms Crossed* [no. 29] and the *Mother and Child* [no. 16], in which the chiaroscuro invests the figures in washes of a kind of thick brine.

But we can see another element in their pictorial introduction: what we might call a warning of social edification. In the impressionistic vision there was no time to feel separation from what the image represented. There was immediate participation whether it depicted ballerinas, or barmen, horse-races, cathedrals, pale in the dawn, or flaming in the sunset. To mark detachment, Picasso attempted to inject between image and consciousness the social division which the time already pointed to. By turning, however, to generalised, programmatic types, rather than the touching encounter of the individual with his own daily life, he idolised ambiguous originals of lost women, of humble street mothers, and of wasted beggars.

This was a humanity made up by the symbolist aesthetic in which profound interest in humanity and a mastering desire for form became, for so direct and aggressive a nature, gradually falsified. The initial relation with what exists, which first drove Picasso to an authoritive grip on it, was then imposed with sentimental reflection, kept the image back on the fringes of actual life. Almost as though an artist's interest in humanity should express itself only in compassion for the wretchedness of man.

But it was not long before Picasso realised his own equivocation and took stock again. . . .

Thus from the transient world of vagabonds, driven by need and hunger, Picasso moved on suddenly . . . to a much less Parisian, much more gypsy world of acrobats and jugglers. And this is not only a change of subject because once the social distress was swept away, the thick azure paste became clearer and the line tightened and thickened, evoking a vague, atmospheric feeling. Whoever considers the fascinating tempera of the *Young Man in Blue* [no. 227] might well think that at this moment Picasso had recourse to Impressionism. But the other numerous paintings of this period clarify the position a good deal. In reality Picasso is recovering certain means of expression that he had earlier discarded. The blue which he had to break, not so much with colour as with the situation of the impressionistic object, became rarer and thus admitted other colours which were clear and unmixed, milky spreads of gouache separated from each other without an infusion of air or a chink of light. These are the colours of Harlequin's patches, seen as a thing, as one object relating to another. They are still slightly extraneous to their surroundings, like the colouring of a print, delicately washed, sometimes almost too delicately, on to those contour lines full of crevices and trembling slightly under some invisible breath. As before, but now as a result of a less physical, more deliberate fusion, diverse veins flow together. Seurat, in his almost regrettable definition of forms and even in his choice of female nudes who are, without any ideal limitations, pleasant women of the day with slightly ill-formed busts and with the curve of their backs emphasised; Puvis de Chavannes, in a certain neatness of his profiles and even more in his clear and opaque colours; Degas again, but caught unexpectedly in that initial moment of compromise between an Ingres seen through the eyes of Puvis and with the sensualities of a Courbet. Finally, Cézanne, withered, but showing up wherever the contour is more vital and has more atmosphere. We see how mistrustful Picasso is of letting the object be moved by a breath of existence, almost as if by a gust of cold air coming from outside into a warm room. The same beauty of the faces, somewhat generic and statuesque, depicted with light touches, without aspiring to noble ideals is near enough to a type to negate the fresh impact of an individual: by caressing the senses he separates contact. Then the tender, visionary families of Harlequin are born, the acrobats resting in a silk vest, and youths leading horses to bathe. Here the young Spartans of Degas, dressed only in their androgynous softness, renew that inexplicable relation with horses which became a surprising element in some parts of the Panathenean games. This early glance at classical art is so discreet as almost to pass unnoticed (not, however, by Apollinaire). Yet it is to be found in the contrived unity of stress, in the difficult marriage of form with beauty. From it can arise that magnificent woman with the fan [no. 220] whose gesture is so charged with cleanness and majesty. And sometimes in certain shadows indicated by a sudden thickening, we also perceive some recall to the magnificent, spon-

taneous daubings of Corot. But yet, so much barer in its almost conventional colour: and so smooth as if by pumice stone. As we said, somewhat antique.

Now it is time he opened his eyes: an artist who is endowed with such an intuition for form, and is not apparently satisfied with it. Here is one year's work and already the so-called Rose Period shows a new variant. Yet they contain, these works, a manner and lucidity which would make sufficient foundation for an artist like Tiepolo so that he could furnish the land with similar, happy images for tens of years. . . .

By breaking with his harlequins and jugglers, Picasso was giving up his life.
CESARE BRANDI, *Carmine, o della pittura*, Florence 1947

If history were serious it would show that the Pablo Picasso of 1901–6 is always the most lively and interesting. . . .
LEONARDO BORGESE in *Corriere della sera*, Milan, 23 September 1953

The works he did between 1901 and 1906 are different according to the "Blue" or "Rose" Periods, just because the shade, more than the actual colour, drew his attention. Picasso's mind was occupied with drawing as a power of outline, a gradation of chiaroscuro and formal proportion. He painted neither landscapes nor still lifes. He was busy with the image of humanity either to characterise it with extreme realism and constant energy, or to idealise it with an obvious classical aspiration. His sympathy for poor people and their wretchedness and for circus clowns and their unhappiness was revealed with a finesse and concern which was pure tenderness. The rich fruit of those years is the regret of all those who do not like to break with tradition, and Picasso himself returns to it quite often in moments of relaxation. LIONELLO VENTURI, in the catalogue to the Picasso Exhibition, Rome, 1953

The paintings in colour

List of plates

HARLEQUIN LEANING ON HIS ELBOW [no. 3]
PLATE I   1901

CHILD HOLDING A DOVE [no. 5]
PLATE II   1901

MOTHER AND CHILD [no. 18]
PLATE III   1901

SLEEPING DRINKER [no. 27]
PLATE IV   1902

PORTRAIT OF CORINA ROMEU [no. 30]
PLATE V   1902

MOTHER AND CHILD [no. 35]
PLATE VI   1902

TWO WOMEN AT A BAR [no. 44]
PLATE VII   1902

THE SOLER FAMILY [no. 80]
PLATES VIII–IX   1903

ROOFS OF BARCELONA [no. 58]
PLATE X   1903

BARCELONA AT NIGHT [no. 57]
PLATE XI   1903

POOR PEOPLE ON THE SEASHORE [no. 86]
PLATE XII   1903

LIFE [no. 89]
PLATE XIII   1903

BLIND OLD MAN AND BOY [no. 91]
PLATE XIV   1903

THE OLD BLIND GUITAR PLAYER [no. 92]
PLATE XV   1903

THE BLIND MAN'S MEAL [no. 94]
PLATE XVI   1903

CELESTINA [no. 99]
PLATE XVII

WOMAN WITH LOCK OF HAIR [no. 71]
PLATE XVIII

MOTHER WITH SICK CHILD [no. 100]
PLATE XIX

BEGGAR MAN WITH DOG [no. 103]
PLATE XX

THE MADMAN [no. 108]
PLATE XXI

THE COUPLE [no. 119]
PLATE XXII

THE LAUNDRESS [no. 125]
PLATE XXIII

WOMAN WITH BRAIDED HAIR [no. 131]
PLATE XXIV

GIRL CHILD WITH CROW [no. 132]
PLATE XXV

PORTRAIT OF SUZANNE BLOCH [no. 136]
PLATE XXVI

THE ACTOR [no. 154]
PLATE XXVII

MOTHER AND CHILD [no. 167]
PLATE XXVIII

ACROBAT AND YOUNG HARLEQUIN [no. 170]
PLATE XXIX

YOUNG ACROBAT AND CHILD [no. 158]
PLATE XXX

THE HURDY-GURDY PLAYER AND YOUNG HARLEQUIN [no. 193]
PLATE XXXI

CLOWN AND YOUNG ACROBAT [no. 187]
PLATE XXXII

ACROBAT AND YOUNG EQUILIBRIST [no. 174]
PLATE XXXIII

FAMILY OF ACROBATS WITH APE [no. 165]
PLATE XXXIV

FAMILY OF ACROBATS [no. 180]
PLATE XXXV

THE ACROBATS [no. 192]
PLATES XXXVI–XXXVII

HARLEQUIN ON HORSEBACK [no. 196]
PLATE XXXVIII

YOUNG EQUESTRIENNE [no. 194]
PLATE XXXIX

AT THE "LAPIN AGILE" [no. 197]
PLATE XL

THE DEATH OF HARLEQUIN [no. 198]
PLATE XLI

THE KING [no. 179]
PLATE XLII

THREE DUTCH WOMEN [no. 199]
PLATE XLIII

PORTRAIT OF BENEDETTA CANALS [no. 211]
PLATE XLIV

PROFILE OF A YOUNG MAN WITH A LACE COLLAR [no. 213]
PLATE XLV

YOUNG MAN WITH A GARLAND OF ROSES [no. 217]
PLATE XLVI

WOMAN WITH A FAN [no. 220]
PLATE XLVII

ACROBAT AND STILL LIFE [no. 224]
PLATE XLVIII

YOUNG MAN IN BLUE [no. 227]
PLATE XLIX

BOY LEADING A HORSE [no. 235]
PLATE L

"LA COIFFURE" [no. 244]
PLATE LI

HORSES BATHING [no. 239]
PLATES LII–LIII

NUDE OF FERNANDE OLIVIER WITH CLASPED HANDS [no. 251]
PLATE LIV

TWO NAKED YOUTHS [no. 261]
PLATE LV

THE TWO BROTHERS [no. 257]
PLATE LVI

THE TWO BROTHERS [no. 258]
PLATE LVII

PORTRAIT OF FERNANDE OLIVIER WITH HEADSCARF [no. 265]
PLATE LVIII

HEAD AND SHOULDERS OF A YOUNG SPANIARD [no. 267]
PLATE LIX

"LA TOILETTE" [no. 270]
PLATE LX

THE HAREM [no. 274]
PLATE LXI

CATTLE DROVER WITH SMALL BASKET [no. 280]
PLATE LXII

THE BREAD CARRIER [no. 283]
PLATE LXIII

PORTRAIT OF GERTRUDE STEIN [no. 306]
PLATE LXIV

Cover:
Detail from *The Acrobats* [no. 192]

The arabic numeral in square brackets after the title of each work refers to the numbering of the paintings adopted in the Catalogue *(pages 87–113).*

In the captions at the foot of the plates the corresponding actual size (width) of the picture, or part of the picture reproduced in them, is given in centimetres.

PLATE I   HARLEQUIN LEANING ON HIS ELBOW   New York, Metropolitan Museum of Art
Whole (60.5 cm.)   1901

PLATE II   CHILD HOLDING A DOVE London, The Dowager Lady Aberconway Collection
Whole (54 cm.)

PLATE III   MOTHER AND CHILD Los Angeles, Goetz Collection
Whole (60 cm.)

PLATE IV   SLEEPING DRINKER Glarus (Switzerland), Huber Collection
Whole (62 cm.)

PLATE V   PORTRAIT OF CORINA ROMEU   Property of the Artist
Whole (49 cm.)

PLATE VI   MOTHER AND CHILD   Edinburgh, Scottish National Gallery of Modern Art
Whole (33 cm.)

PLATE VII   TWO WOMEN AT A BAR   New York, Chrysler Collection
Whole (91.5 cm.)

PLATES VIII-IX THE SOLER FAMILY Liège, Musée des Beaux-Arts
Whole (200 cm.)

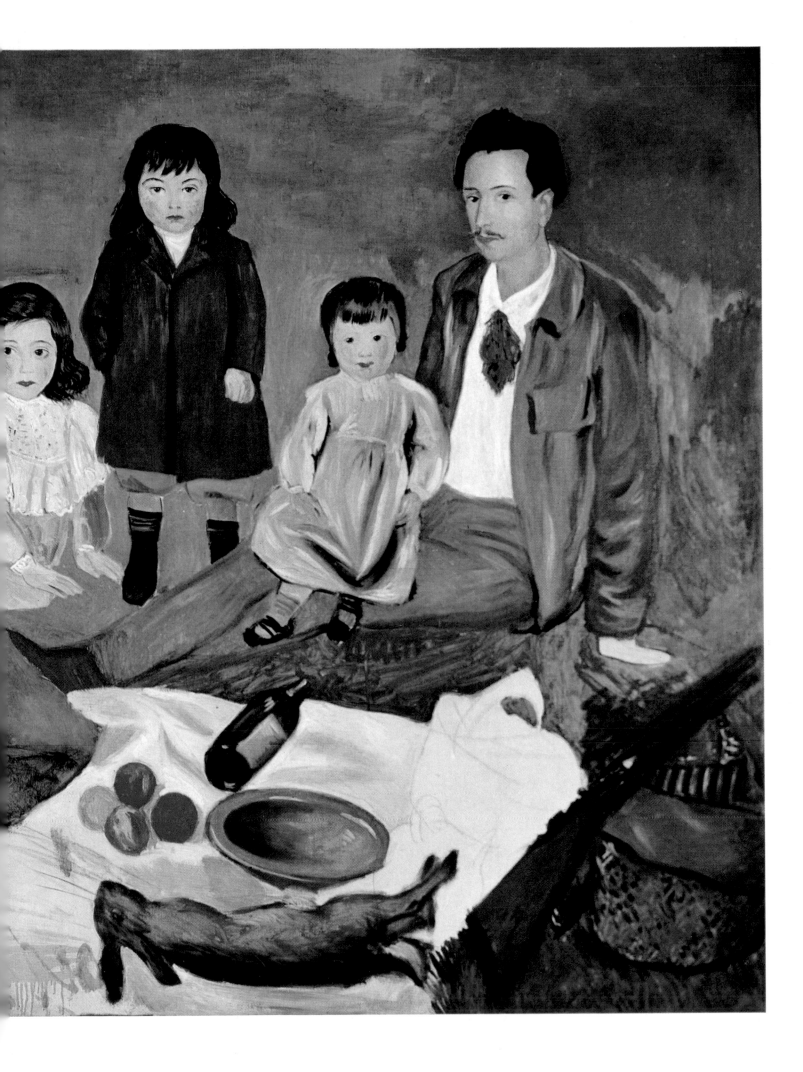

PLATE X   ROOFS OF BARCELONA Property of the Artist
Whole (110 cm.)

PLATE XI   BARCELONA AT NIGHT   Zurich, Bührle Foundation
Whole (50 cm.)

PLATE XII   POOR PEOPLE ON THE SEASHORE   Washington, DC, National Gallery of Art
Whole (69 cm.)

PLATE XIV   BLIND OLD MAN AND BOY Moscow, Pushkin Museum
Whole (92 cm.)

PLATE XV   THE OLD BLIND GUITAR PLAYER Chicago (Ill.), Art Institute
Whole (82 cm.)

PLATE XVI THE BLIND MAN'S MEAL New York, Metropolitan Museum of Art
Whole (94.5 cm.)

Picasso

PLATE XVII   CELESTINA Paris, Private collection
Whole (56 cm.)

PLATE XVIII   WOMAN WITH LOCK OF HAIR Barcelona, Picasso Museum
Whole (37 cm.)

PLATE XIX   MOTHER WITH SICK CHILD   Barcelona, Picasso Museum
Whole (41 cm.)

PLATE XX   BEGGAR MAN WITH DOG New York, Thannhauser Collection
Whole (21 cm.)

PLATE XXI

THE MADMAN Barcelona, Picasso Museum
Whole (36 cm.)

PLATE XXII THE COUPLE Ascona, Private collection
Whole (81 cm.)

PLATE XXIII   THE LAUNDRESS New York, Thannhauser Collection
Whole (72.5 cm.)

PLATE XXIV   WOMAN WITH BRAIDED HAIR   Chicago (Ill.), Art Institute
Whole (31 cm.)

PLATE XXV   GIRL CHILD WITH CROW   Toledo (Ohio), Museum of Art
Whole (49.5 cm.)

PLATE XXVI   PORTRAIT OF SUZANNE BLOCH São Paulo, Museu de Arte
Whole (54 cm.)

PLATE XXVII   THE ACTOR New York, Metropolitan Museum of Art
Whole (112 cm.)

PLATE XXVIII   MOTHER AND CHILD Stuttgart, Staatsgalerie
Whole (69.5 cm.)

PLATE XXIX   ACROBAT AND YOUNG HARLEQUIN Belgium, Private collection
Whole (76 cm.)

PLATE XXX   YOUNG ACROBAT AND CHILD   New York, Thannhauser Collection
Whole (18 cm.)

PLATE XXXI   THE HURDY-GURDY PLAYER AND YOUNG HARLEQUIN   Zürich, Kunsthaus
Whole (70 cm.)

PLATE XXXII   CLOWN AND YOUNG ACROBAT Baltimore (Ma.), Museum of Art
Whole (47 cm.)

PLATE XXXIII   ACROBAT AND YOUNG EQUILIBRIST Moscow, Pushkin Museum
Whole (95 cm.)

Picasso

PLATE XXXIV   FAMILY OF ACROBATS WITH APE Göteborg, Konstmuseum
Whole (75 cm.)

PLATE XXXV   FAMILY OF ACROBATS Baltimore (Ma.), Museum of Art
Whole (30.5 cm.)

PLATES XXXVI-XXXVII   THE ACROBATS   Washington, DC, National Gallery of Art
Whole (229.5 cm.)

PLATE XXXVIII   HARLEQUIN ON HORSEBACK Washington, DC, Mellon Collection
Whole (96 cm.)

PLATE XXXIX   YOUNG EQUESTRIENNE   Property of the Artist
Whole (78 cm.)

PLATE XL   SELF-PORTRAIT IN THE DRESS OF A HARLEQUIN IN A CAFÉ New York, Payson Collection
Whole (100.5 cm.)

PLATE XLI   THE DEATH OF HARLEQUIN   Washington, DC, Mellon Collection
Whole (95 cm.)

PLATE XLII   THE KING Stuttgart, Staatsgalerie
Whole (45 cm.)

PLATE XLIII THREE DUTCH WOMEN Paris, Musée National d'Art Moderne
Whole (66 cm.)

PLATE XLIV   PORTRAIT OF BENEDETTA CANALS Barcelona, Picasso Museum
Whole (70.5 cm.)

PLATE XLV   PROFILE OF A YOUNG MAN WITH A LACE COLLAR Worcester (Mass.), Art Museum
Whole (59.5 cm.)

PLATE XLVI   YOUNG MAN WITH GARLAND OF ROSES New York, Whitney Collection
Whole (79 cm.)

PLATE XLVII   YOUNG WOMAN WITH RAISED ARM New York, Harriman Collection
Whole (81.5 cm.)

PLATE XLVIII   ACROBAT AND STILL LIFE Washington, DC, National Gallery of Art
Whole (70 cm.)

PLATE XLIX
YOUNG MAN IN BLUE   New York, Warburg Collection
Whole (55.5 cm.)

PLATE L   NUDE YOUNG MAN WITH HORSE New York, Paley Collection
Whole (130 cm.)

"LA COIFFURE" New York, Metropolitan Museum of Art
Whole (99.5 cm.)

PLATES LII-LIII   HORSES BATHING Worcester (Mass.), Art Museum
Whole (58 cm.)

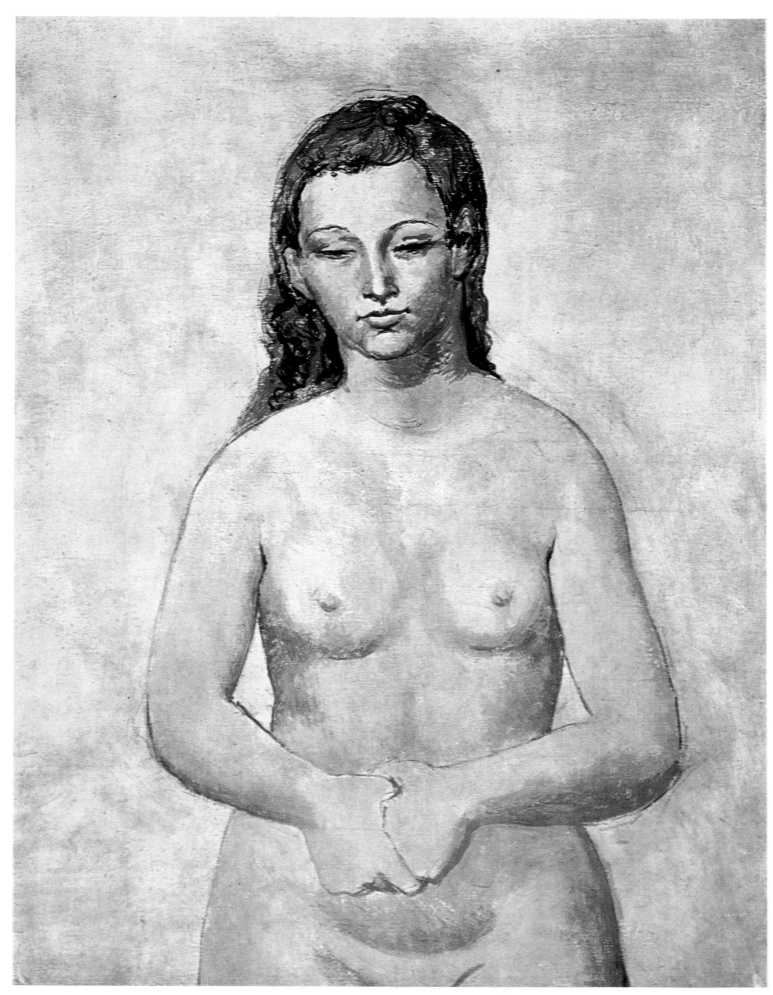

PLATE LIV   NUDE OF FERNANDE OLIVIER WITH CLASPED HANDS   Toronto, Zacks Collection
Whole (75.5 cm.)

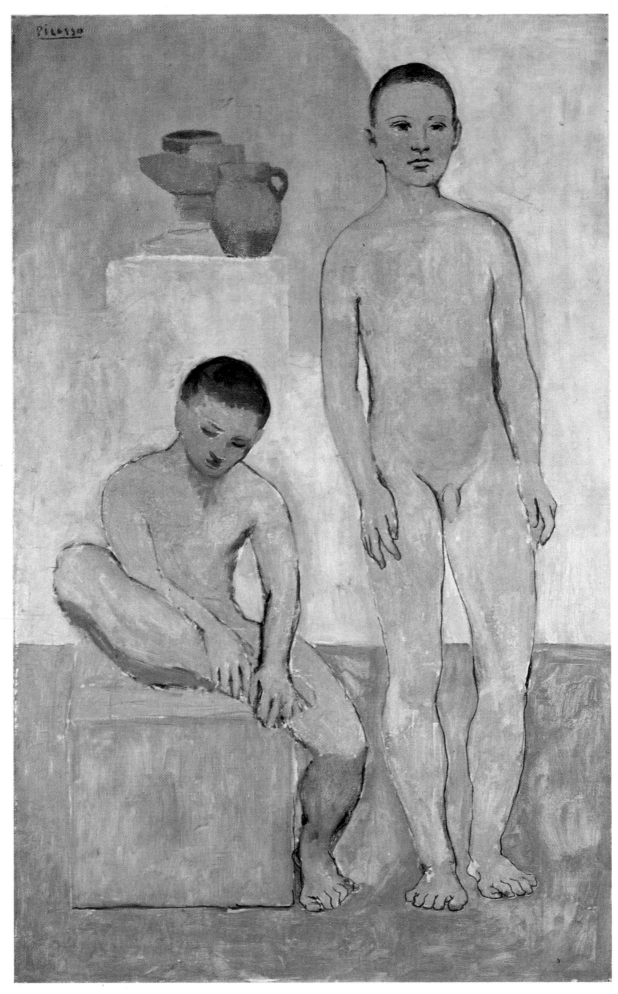

PLATE LV TWO NAKED YOUTHS Washington, DC, National Gallery of Art
Whole (93.5 cm.)

PLATE LVI   THE TWO BROTHERS Property of the Artist
Whole (60 cm.)

PLATE LVII   THE TWO BROTHERS Basle, Kunstmuseum
Whole (97 cm.)

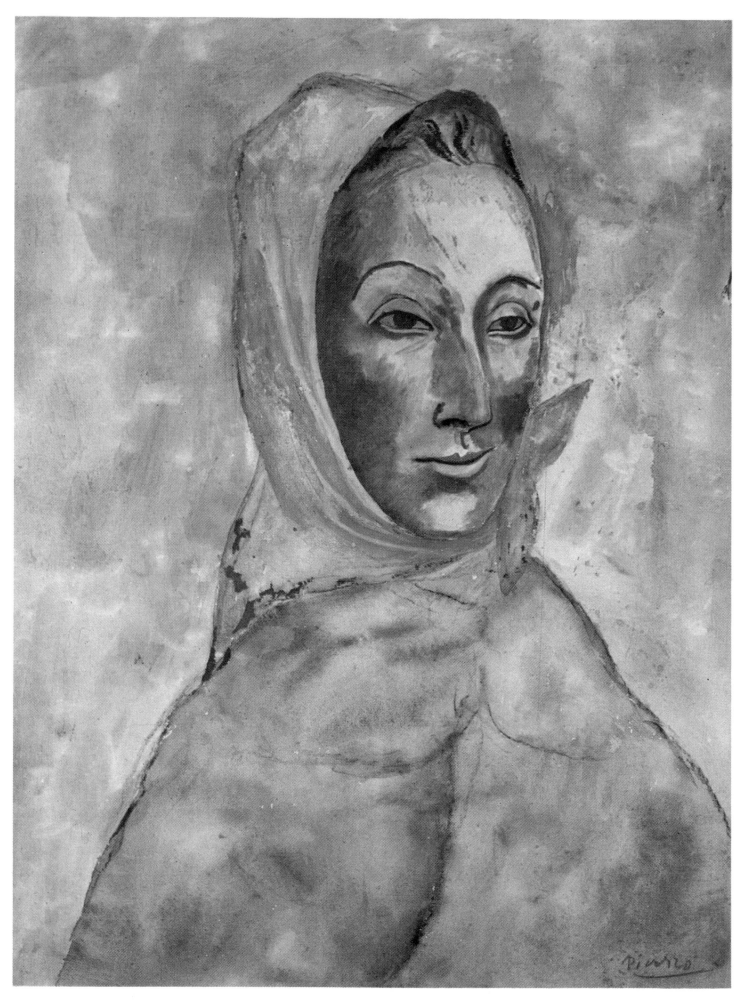

PLATE LVIII   PORTRAIT OF FERNANDE OLIVIER WITH HEADSCARF   Richmond (Va.), Virginia Museum of Fine Arts
Whole (49.5 cm.)

PLATE LIX   HEAD AND SHOULDERS OF A YOUNG SPANIARD Göteborg, Konstmuseum
Whole (48 cm.)

PLATE LX "LA TOILETTE" Buffalo (NY), Albright-Knox Gallery
Whole (99 cm.)

PLATE LXI   THE HAREM   Cleveland (Ohio), Museum of Art
Whole (109.5 cm.)

PLATE LXIII   THE BREAD CARRIER   Philadelphia (Pa.), Museum of Art
Whole (70 cm.)

PLATE LXIV   PORTRAIT OF GERTRUDE STEIN New York, Metropolitan Museum of Art
Whole (81 cm.)

The works

So that the essential elements in each work may be immediately apparent, each note is headed first by a number (following the most reliable chronological sequence) which is given every time the work is quoted throughout the book, and then by a series of symbols. These refer to: 1) The technique and support used; 2) The presence or absence of signature and date; 3) The whereabouts of the work. The numbers inserted between the first and second symbols indicate, in centimetres or metres, the dimensions of the painting: above, its height; below, its width. Between the second and third symbols are indicated: above, the place where the work was executed; below the date of execution.

Technique and support

⊕ Oil on canvas

⊕ Oil on wood

⊕ Oil on paper or card

⊕ Gouache on canvas

⊕ Gouache on paper or card

⊕ Watercolour on paper or card

⊕ Pastel on paper or card

⊕ Mixed techniques on paper or card indicated in text

Additional data

▤ Unsigned and undated

▤ Signed

▤ Dated

▤ Signed and dated

Whereabouts

⋮ Public collection

⋮ Private collection

82 ⋮ Unknown

Exhibitions

There have been a vast number of exhibitions of Picasso's works, both one-man and combined with the works of other artists, over the last seventy years. They began with the first collections on view in Paris at the Galeries Ambroise Vollard in June and July 1901, and at the Galerie Berthe Weill in April, June, November and December 1902; and culminated in the great *Hommage à Pablo Picasso* held in Paris from November 1966 to February 1967. This exhibition was divided between three buildings; paintings at the Grand Palais, drawings, sculpture and ceramics at the Petit Palais, and typography at the Bibliothèque Nationale. In this monograph, however only twenty of these exhibitions are referred to – the most important, and, above all, those where works belonging to the two periods under consideration here, were extensively represented. The following table indicates the symbols given in the text for those exhibitions referred to in this catalogue.

13 M 1913 Munich, Moderne Galerie H. Thannhauser, *Pablo Picasso*.
32 P 1932 Paris, Galerie G. Petit, *Picasso*.
32 Z 1932 Zurich, Kunsthaus, *Picasso*.
36 NY 1936 New York, J. Seligman & Co. Gallery, *Picasso, Blue and Rose Periods*.
37 C 1937 Chicago (Ill.), Art Institute, *Watercolors and Gouaches by Picasso*.
38 B 1938 Boston (Mass.), Museum of Modern Art, *Picasso and Matisse*.

39 NY 1939–40 New York, Museum of Modern Art, *Picasso: Forty Years of his Art*; then, in part: Chicago (Ill.), Art Institute; Boston (Mass.), Museum of Fine Arts; Saint Louis (Miss.) City Art Museum; Cincinnati (Ohio), Museum of Art; Cleveland (Ohio), Museum of Art; San Francisco (Cal.), Museum of Art.
47 NY 1947 New York, Knoedler Gallery, *Picasso before 1907*.
53 L 1953 Lyons, Musée des Beaux-Arts, *Picasso*.
53 M 1953 Milan, Palazzo Reale, *Picasso*.
54 P 1954 Paris, Maison de la Pensée Française, *Picasso, oeuvres des musées de Leningrad et de Moscou, 1900–1914*.
55 P 1955 Paris, Musée des Arts Décoratifs, *Picasso, peintures 1900–1955*.
55 M 1955 Munich, Haus der Kunst, *Picasso 1900–1955*.
57 NY 1957 New York, Museum of Modern Art, *Picasso, 75th Anniversary Exhibition* (then to Chicago, Art Institute).
58 P 1958 Philadelphia (Pa.), Museum of Art, *Picasso, a Loan Exhibition*.
59 M 1959 Marseilles, Musée Cantini, *Picasso*.
60 L 1960 London, Tate Gallery, *Picasso*.
60 P 1960 Paris, Musée National d'Art Moderne, *Les sources du XXᵉ siècle: les arts en Europe de 1814 à 1914*.
64 T 1964 Toronto, Art Gallery, *Picasso and Man*.
66 P 1966–7 Paris, Grand Palais, Petit Palais and Bibliothèque Nationale, *Hommage à Pablo Picasso*.

Bibliograpny

The literature on Picasso is vast. Even discounting the general works, the list of monographs is certainly impressive. In this catalogue therefore, references are given only to the most important of these works; and those which are concerned specifically with the same period of his art as we are here. The references listed under each work described or cited speak for themselves, but a special mention must be made of the great catalogues of Zervos (1932 and 1954), and also of the work of Daix and Boudaille to whom this book is particularly indebted. Their book *Picasso 1900–1906* is the first systematic study of Picasso's work before Cubism since Cirici Pellicer's great essay on the subject. In view of the importance of these works and in recognition of their authority on the subject, a concordance of them both and the catalogue provided here is given in the tables on pages 114–5. The following is a list of quoted works and their respective symbols.

R 21 Maurice Raynal, *Picasso*, Munich 1921.
L 28 André Level, *Picasso*, Paris 1928.
D 30 Eugenio d'Ors, *Pablo Picasso*, Paris 1930.
Z 32 Christian Zervos, *Pablo Picasso*, vol. 1: *Oeuvres de 1895 à 1906*, Paris 1932.

S 38 Gertrude Stein, *Picasso*, Paris 1938.
B 39 Alfred H. Barr, Jr., *Picasso, Forty Years of his Art* (in catalogue NY 39).
C 40 Jean Cassou, *Picasso*, Paris 1940.
M 42–48 Joan Merli, *Picasso, el artista y la obra de nuestro tiempo*, Buenos Aires 1942 (second edition 1948).
B 46 Alfred H. Barr, Jr., *Picasso, Fifty Years of his Art*, New York 1946.
S 46–53 Jaime Sabartés, *Picasso, portraits et souvenirs*, Paris 1946 (Spanish edition: *Picasso, retratos y recuerdos*, Madrid 1953).
S 48–55 Denys Sutton, *Picasso, Paintings of the Blue and Rose Periods*, London 1948 (second edition 1955).
CP 50 Alejandro Cirici Pellicer, *Picasso avant Picasso* (French edition revised from *Picasso antes de Picasso*, Barcelona 1946).
G 51 Maurice Gieure, *Initiation à l'oeuvre de Picasso*, Paris 1951.
L 52–54 William S. Lieberman, *Picasso, Blue and Rose Periods*, New York 1952 (second edition 1954).
R 53 Maurice Raynal, *Picasso*, Geneva 1953.
S 54 Jaime Sabartés, *Picasso, documents iconographiques*, Geneva 1954.
Z 54 Christian Zervos, *Pablo Picasso*, vol. VI: *Supplément aux volumes I à V*, Paris 1954.
B 55 Wilhelm Boeck, *Picasso*, Paris 1955 (with a preface by Jaime

Sabartés).
EM 55 Frank Elgar and Robert Maillard, *Picasso*, Paris 1955.
KP 55 Daniel-Henry Kahnweiler and Hélène Parmelin, *Picasso, œuvres des musées de Léningrad et Moscou*, Paris 1955.
E 56 Frank Elgar, *Picasso, époques bleue et rose*, Paris 1956.
B 57 Alfred H. Barr, Jr., *Picasso, 75th Anniversary* (in catalogue NY 57).
C 58 Jean Cassou, *Picasso*, Paris 1958.
P 58 Roland Penrose, *Picasso, his Life and Work*, London 1958.
C 59 Raymond Cogniat, *Picasso, figures*, Lausanne 1959.
D 60 Gaston Diehl, *Picasso*, Paris 1960.
D 61 David Douglas Duncan, *Picasso's Picassos*, Lausanne 1961.
BP 62 Anthony Blunt and Phoebe Pool, *Picasso, The Formative Years, A Study of his Sources*, London 1962.
S 63 Jaime Sabartés, *Picasso, les bleus de Barcelone*, Paris 1963.
B 64 Georges Boudaille, *Picasso, sa première époque, 1881–1906*, Paris 1964.
D 64 Pierre Daix, *Picasso*, Paris 1964.
J 64 Hans L. C. Jaffé, *Picasso*, New York 1964.
K 65 Helen Kay, *Picasso's World of Children*, New York 1965.
DB 66 Pierre Daix and Georges Boudaille, *Picasso, 1900–1906*, Neuchâtel 1966.
P 66 Josep Palau i Fabre, *Picasso en Cataluña*, Barcelona 1966.

Outline biography

1881 25 October
Picasso was born in the Merced district of Malaga, at 11.15 p.m., the firstborn son of Don José Ruiz Blasco and Doña Maria Picasso y López. The child was christened Pablo, Diego, José, Francisco de Paula, Juan Nepomuceno, Maria de los Remedios, Crispín, Crispiniano de la Santísima Trinidad Ruiz y Picasso. His father was professor of drawing at the San Telmo school of arts and crafts, and keeper of the local museum.

1884 25 December The birth of his sister Lola.

1887 The birth of his sister Conchita.

1891 September Don José was appointed professor of drawing at the La Guarda school of arts and crafts, at Corunna in Galicia. The family moved to Corunna in September, travelling by sea from Malaga to Vigo. They moved into the second floor of no. 14 Calle Payo Gómez and Pablo was enrolled as a pupil in the junior section of the La Guarda school.

1891 Conchita died soon after the arrival of the family at Corunna.

1891–4 The Ruiz family continued to live in Corunna. Pablo attended the La Guarda school where he designed and edited hand-written newsletters *(La Coruña, Azul y Blanco)*. He displayed such a marked pictorial talent that his father decided to give up his own painting, which he personally regarded as mediocre, and concentrate solely on furthering his son's work. He even made him a present of his own palette and brushes.

1895 Don José gave up his appointment at the La Guarda school to his colleague Ramón Navarra García. On 16 April he received instead an appointment to the La Lonja school of fine arts in Barcelona. He moved at once to Barcelona to take up the appointment.

1895 Don José was granted leave of absence, and rejoined his family, who were still living in Corunna.

1895 July The Ruiz family visited Madrid, where Pablo saw the Prado for the first time.

1895 The whole family spent a holiday in Malaga, staying at the house of Don José's mother

1895 Mid-September The family moved to Barcelona, travelling by sea from Malaga. They lived for a short while in the Calle de la Reina Cristina; but later moved to no. 4 Calle Llauder, which was in the port area not far from the La Lonja school.

1895 September Pablo took the examination for the Senior classes of painting and life-drawing at La Lonja, for which the minimum age of admission was twenty. He passed, and was enrolled as a student despite the fact that he was only fourteen. It is said that he completed the tests, which usually took a whole month, in a single day: this story however is disproved by two drawings, known to have been done for this purpose, dated 25 September and 30 September.

1895–6 Pablo attended the courses at La Lonja and made friends with his classmates Manuel Pallarés y Grau and Manuel Hugué (Manolo), the brothers Angel, Mateu and Wenceslao Fernández de Soto, the brothers Carlo and Sebastián Junyer Vidal, Sebastián Junyent and Carlos Casagemas.

1896 Recognising his son's amazing precocity and independent nature, his father rented a room for him in Calle de la Plata, where Pablo could work by himself. There, among other works he executed a self-portrait dressed in the clothes of an eighteenth-century gentleman.

1896 April His picture *First Communion* is accepted for the municipal exhibition of Barcelona.

1896 25 May The newspaper *Diario de Barcelona* reported favourably on this picture by an artist who was not yet fifteen years old.

1896 At the end of the year the Ruiz family moved into a new house in the same neighbourhood of the port no. 3 Calle de la Merced.

1897 8 June The young man's picture *Science and Charity* was sent to the national exhibition of fine arts in Madrid, where it was well received. (It was later also exhibited at the local exhibition in Malaga, where it was awarded a gold medal.)

1897 12 June Opening of the café "Hostal d'Els Quatre Gats" (abbreviated to "Els 4 Gats"), which became a centre of the young intellectual life of Barcelona. It was built in the neo-Gothic style by the architect Puig y Cadafalch, and was situated in the Carreras' house on the corner of the Calle Montesion and the Calle Patriarca, half-way between the Cathedral and the Plaza de Cataluña This "meeting place of intellectuals with a wine-bar, restaurant and a room for puppet-shows", consisted of a huge room with two arches on one side and five on the other; it extended at the rear to form a salon for exhibitions. It was founded by the ex-painter Pere Romeu in imitation of the "Taverne du Chat-Noir" in Paris, as a rendezvous for the *avant-garde* young artists and writers of the city: which indeed it quickly became. Pere Romeu also started a literary review of the arts, originally also called *Els 4 Gats*, but soon changed to *Pèl i Ploma*. This review was illustrated by Ramón Casas and edited by the Spanish writer and painter Miguel Utrillo (who was later to give his name to Suzanne Valadon's son Maurice Utrillo).

1897 Summer The whole family spent the holiday once again in Pablo's grandmother's house in Malaga.

1897 October Pablo went to Madrid where he successfully passed the entrance examination for the senior classes of the Real Academia de San Fernando, "La Casona". (It is said that in these examinations too, he repeated the exploit which was attributed to him in September 1895.)

1897 October–April **1898** Madrid: the young man changed his lodgings repeatedly. He moved from the Calle de San Pedro Mártir, to the Calle de Jesus y Maria, and finally to the Calle Lavapies. He visited the Prado frequently, studying the masterpieces there at the expense of his courses at the "Casona".

1898 June Madrid; he became ill with scarlet fever.

1898 Mid-June He returned to Barcelona frustrated and exhausted.

1898 Late June He went to Horta de Ebro, travelling there by train as far as Tortosa and the rest of the way on horseback. He went with a friend Manuel Pallarés who was a native of the village and who owned a house there (in the higher part at no. 11 Calle de Grau). The village of Horta de Ebro is situated in the middle of the province of Tarragona, 500 metres above sea-level. In 1919 it was renamed San Juan.

1898 Summer–Winter **1899** Pablo stayed in Horta de Ebro, frequently going off for long spells into the mountains with Pallarés. He sometimes spent the night in caves, drawing and painting from nature. As a result he acquired a freedom he could never have achieved by copying Old Masters in the Prado. (Later he was to acknowledge this himself: "All that I know I learnt in Horta de Ebro".) He became so fluent in the Catalan dialect that he adopted it as if his own. It was during this period that he painted, among other things, the picture *Aragonese Customs*; this was awarded the medal for third place at the national exhibition of fine arts in Madrid, and the gold medal at the local exhibition in Malaga.

1899 April Return to Barcelona

1899 April–December Disagreements with his family caused him to leave their house and share lodgings and a studio

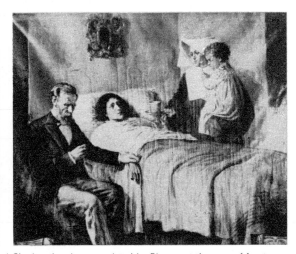

The First Communion *and* Science and Charity, *the pictures painted by Picasso at the ages of fourteen and fifteen, which were accepted for the exhibitions at Barcelona and Madrid (property of the artist).*

Portraits of Picasso until 1906. (From top to bottom, and left to right; first row.) At the age of fifteen (photograph, Barcelona 1896; self-portrait in the dress of an eighteenth-century gentleman, oil, id.; self-portrait, id.). At the age of seventeen (self-portrait at his easel, charcoal, Barcelona, 1898). (Second row.) At the age of twenty (self-portrait with Sebastián Junyer Vidal in the Parody of Manet's "Olympia", ink and coloured pencil, Barcelona, 1901; self-portrait, charcoal, id.; portrait painted by Ramón Casas, published in Pèl i Ploma, 14–17 June 1901). (Third row.) At the age of twenty (self-portrait in front of the Moulin-Rouge, ink and coloured pencil, Paris 1901; self-portrait: "Yo Picasso", oils id.; self-portrait, chalk and watercolour, id.; self-portrait in top hat, oils, id.). (Fourth row.) At the age of twenty (self-portrait with beard, id.); at twenty-one (self-portrait on the beach, ink and coloured pencil, Barcelona 1902) and at twenty-two (self-portrait with moustache, ink and water-colour, id., 1903). (Bottom row.) At the same age (self-portrait with moustache, ink, 1903), at the age of twenty-three (portrait in front of his picture Life [no. 89] painted by Sebastián Junyer Vidal, Barcelona 1904; photograph, Paris 1904) and at twenty-five (self-portrait, in Paris 1906).

with other artists. Finally he lived in a small room in a studio belonging to the brother of the sculptor José Cardona y Turró, at no. 1 Calle de Escudillers Blancs. Mateu Fernández de Soto brought the young poet Jaime Sabartés (1881–1968) to visit him there. Sabartés was to remain in close contact with Picasso for the rest of his life; for many years he was his private secretary. At this time he was living in considerable poverty among the young Bohemian intellectuals of Barcelona. He frequented "Els 4 Gats" where he made many new acquaintances and friends including Rafael Moragas, Ramón Pitxot and the brothers Ramón and Cinto Reventós. He joined a literary circle which met on Sunday afternoons at the house of Carlos Casagemas and in the evenings at that of Juan Vidal Ventosa. He stayed at a brothel for a few weeks where he decorated the walls of his room.

1900 Barcelona: at the beginning of the year he moved with Carlos Casagemas to a new studio at no. 17 Calle della Riera de Sant Joan, where he stayed until the end of September. The studio was bare; on its walls Picasso painted the furniture it lacked. It was a period of intense activity; he made a living by giving drawing lessons.

1900 1 February A one-man show of his drawings and paintings was opened in the exhibition room of "Els 4 Gats" They consisted largely of portraits of well-known Barcelona characters, executed in pencil, charcoal or water-colour, the subjects included the painters Santiago Rusiñol and Joaquín Mir; and his friends Jaime Sabartés, Cinto Reventós, Juan Vidal Ventosa, Angel and Mateu Fernández de Soto, Alejandro Riera, etc. Some of these were bought, largely by the subjects themselves, for one or two pesetas each.

1900 3 February The Barcelona newspaper *Vanguardia* published a long review of his exhibition at "Els 4 Gats". The review was unsigned but was probably written by Rodríguez Codolá, a professor at La Lonja.

1900 12 July The review *Joventut* (Barcelona, no. 22 page 345) published an illustration of Picasso's for the first time. This illustration was for Juan Oliva Bridgman's short poem *El clam de les verges.* This was followed by a second illustration on 16 August for another poem of Bridgman's, this time entitled *Ser o no ser.*

1900 6 September The review *Catalunya Artística* (Barcelona, no. 13 page 208) published one of his portraits of the poet Antón Busquets y Punset, and on 4 October (no. 17 page 268) an illustration of his for the story *La loca* by Suninyac Senties was published. However other drawings submitted to various periodicals were rejected including one Picasso sent to the review *L'Esquella de la Torratxa.*

1900 Late October Picasso made his first trip to Paris with Carlos Casagemas and Manuel Pallarés. He stayed with the

Barcelona painter Isidro Nonell in his studio at 49 Rue Gabrielle. It was during this first period in Paris that Picasso altered his signature from "Pablo Ruiz Picasso" or "P. Ruiz Picasso", to "Pablo R. Picasso" or "P. R. Picasso".

1900 December He returned to Barcelona with Carlos Casagemas.

1900 30 December–January **1901** Picasso visited Malaga with Casagemas in an attempt to get over an unhappy love affair.

1901 January Picasso arrived in Madrid and took lodgings in an attic in no. 4 Calle Caballera de Gracia, but later moved to Calle Zurbaran. He began to adopt the straightforward and definitive signature "Picasso".

1901 February Carlos Casagemas returned alone to Paris, and in despair over an unhappy love affair took his own life in the café "L'Hippodrome" in the Boulevard de Clichy.

1901 31 March Issue of the first of five published numbers of the Madrid review *Arte Joven*, begun and edited by the Catalan writer Francisco de Assis Soler, and illustrated by "Pablo Ruiz Picasso".

1901 Mid-May The experiment of *Arte Joven* failed and Picasso returned to Barcelona.

1901 25 June–14 July An exhibition of Picasso's pastels, executed mostly in Paris, was held in the Sala Parés, the most important gallery in Barcelona. The exhibition was promoted by the review *Pèl i Ploma*.

1901 Review by Miguel Utrillo (under the pseudonym of "Pincell") of the exhibition at the Sala Parés; this appeared in the June number of *Pèl i Ploma*, whose issue was delayed (see page 9).

1901 Mid-June Picasso made his second visit to Paris at the invitation of Pedro Manyac, a young Catalan who lived in Paris and was involved in the world of commercial art. He offered Picasso a contract giving him 150 francs a month in return for exclusive rights to the whole of Picasso's output. He also guaranteed him an exhibition with the important dealer Ambroise Vollard. Manyac installed Picasso, with his friend Jaime Andreu Bonsons who had come with him to Paris, in a studio at no. 130C Boulevard de Clichy, close to the café in which Carlos Casagemas had committed suicide four months earlier.

1901 25 June–14 July Paris: Exhibition at the Galeries Vollard of "Tableaux de F. Iturrino and P. R. Picasso": the latter was represented by 64 paintings, largely in oil, and an unspecified number of drawings. In the exhibition catalogue, which included a preface by the playwright Gustave Coquiot, various pictures appeared as already sold, and the names of the buyers are given (Fabre, Ackermann, Personnas, Virenca, Sainsère, Blot, Coll, Mme Besnard and Mme Kollwitz).

The literary café "Els 4 Gats" at Barcelona. (First row, left to right.) Portrait of Pere Romeu by Picasso (ink); self-portrait (in the foreground) with (from left to right) Pere Romeu, Roquerol, Fontbona, Angel Fernández de Soto, and Sabartés (ink, Barcelona 1902); poster designed by Picasso, showing the entrance to "Els 4 Gats" (Barcelona 1899). (Second row.) The interior of the restaurant (photograph); another interior, with the brothers de Soto (far left and right, and Pere Romeu in the centre (photograph).

Many others were sold during the exhibition. Max Jacob visited the exhibition and was interested in getting to know the painter; their friendship dates from this time.

1901 15 July An article by Félicien Fagus, "L'invasion espagnole: Picasso", appeared in the *Revue Blanche* (see page 9).

1901 September A brief review of the exhibition at the Galeries Vollard, signed by François Charles, appeared in the review *L'Ermitage* (see page 9). Picasso met André Salmon at this time.

1901 October Jaime Sabartés arrived in Paris, and was met at the Gare d'Orsay by Picasso (who had now grown a beard).

1901 Autumn The so-called Blue Period of Picasso's work

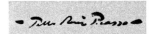

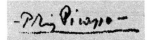

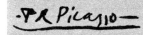

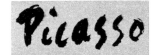

Development of Picasso's signature. (From top to bottom.) "Pablo Ruiz 'Picasso", used until October 1900; "P. Ruiz Picasso" or "P.R.Picasso", at the end of 1900, and the final "Picasso", from January 1901.

began in Paris with the painting *Seated Child* (no. 19), and the portraits of Jaime Sabartés (no. 22) and Mateu Fernández de Soto (no. 23). This period was to continue until the spring of 1904.

1902 January Picasso returned to Barcelona. In view of his straightened circumstances he went to live with his family, with whom he had become completely reconciled, in the Calle de la Merced. He rented a studio at no. 6 Calle del Conde de Asalto with his friend Angel Fernández de Soto.

1902 Winter–Spring Period of financial difficulties. Picasso frequented the "Guayaba" (Walhalla), a group which met at the studio of the engraver Juan Vidal Ventosa at no. 4 Plaza de l'Oli. Members of the circle included Cinto Reventós (who later became one of the most famous doctors in Barcelona), the narrator Ramón Reventós, the essayist Eugenio d'Ors, the painter Isidro Nonell and the brothers Fernández de Soto. Picasso executed a poster of Harlequin and Columbine for a certain Lecitina Agell and designed a card announcing the birth of their son for Pere and Corina Romeu. His precarious financial position was relieved somewhat by a friend of his, a tailor, J. M. Soler called "Retallet": this man had a shop in the Plaza Santa Maria and sometimes commissioned works from promising young artists and provided clothes in exchange for drawings and paintings.

1902 1–15 April Pedro Manyac organised an exhibition of "Tableaux et pastels de Louis Bernard-Lemaire et de Picasso" at the Galerie Berthe Weill at no. 25 Rue Victor-Massé. Picasso exhibited fifteen paintings which he had left in the care of Manyac on his departure for Barcelona the previous January.

1902 April Jaime Sabartés also

returned to Barcelona.

1902 2–15 June A "Group Exhibition" was held in Paris again at the Galerie Berthe Weill, including works by Matisse and Picasso's picture *Grand Prix d'Auteuil*, which had been left in the case of Manyac. The catalogue contained a preface by Emile Seyden.

1902 Summer In Barcelona Picasso produced a poster for "Els 4 Gats".

1902 1 September A review by Félicien Fagus of the exhibition held at the Galerie Berthe Weill the preceeding April, appeared in the *Revue Blanche* in Paris.

1902 September Picasso's third visit to Paris accompanied by Sebastián Junyer Vidal. They stayed first in the Hôtel du Maroc (now the Hôtel Louis XV), then at the Hôtel des Ecoles in the Rue Champollion. Picasso finally shared a room with Max Jacob on the fourth floor of a house in the Boulevard Voltaire, which faced the "Paris-France" dress shops where Jacob was working It was a time of great hardship; they had only one bed and Picasso was forced to work during the night while Jacob slept, and sleep during the day when Jacob went to work in the shop.

1902 15 November–15 December "Exposition: Peintures, pastels et dessins de MM. Girieud, Launay, Picasso et Pichot" again at the Galerie Berthe Weill. Picasso was represented by nine pictures and various drawings. The catalogue opened with a preface signed by "Harlor".

1902 December A review by the symbolist poet Charles Morice, the friend of Gauguin, of the exhibition at the Galerie Berthe Weill (see page 10), appeared in the *Mercure de France*.

1902 December–January **1903** Exhausted by hardship and cold Picasso decided to return to Barcelona (in Paris he had had to burn numerous works – drawings, watercolours and gouaches in order to heat his room). He succeeded in selling a poster to Mme Besnard, one of his clients (possibly the *Mother and Child on the Sea Shore* [no. 36]) and with the sixty francs he received for it, he bought his railway ticket. He left for Barcelona leaving all his works which had escaped burning in the care of his friend Pichot.

1903 Late January Picasso returned to Barcelona and again stayed with his family in Calle de la Merced and used the studio at no. 17 Riera de Sant Joan, which he had shared with Carlos Casagemas. This time he shared it with Angel Fernández de Soto, called "Patas". He stayed there until the end of the year.

1903 Barcelona: the Blue Period continued. Picasso began to enjoy a certain success.

1904 New Year Picasso succeeded in obtaining his own studio in the Calle del Comercio; and also his own room in the same street where he moved leaving his family's house.

1904 January–April Among other works Picasso decorated the walls of Jaime Sabartés' studio in Barcelona which was situated on the top floor of no. 37 Calle del Consulado. The decoration (now lost) included a virile negro hanging upside down from a tree under which a naked couple were embracing, recalling a current performance of *Othello* in Barcelona given by Ermete Zacconi.

1904 April Picasso returned to Paris again with Sebastián Junyer Vidal: this time he settled there permanently. He

85

lived in a dilapidated tenement at no. 13 Rue de Ravignan in Montmartre, where his friend, the sculptor Paco Durio was already living. Also lodging there were Kees van Dongen, Pierre Mac Orlan, André Salmon, Max Jacob and Jacques Vaillant. Max Jacob later christened the house "Le Bateau Lavoir" ("The Floating Laundry") and it became a very lively gathering place for young artists. Picasso stayed there until October 1909. The Blue Period came to an end.

1904 Picasso became a friend of a young woman, Fernande Olivier, who also lived in the "Bateau Lavoir". His relationship with her lasted until 1912. She appears in nos. 154, 247–251, 265, 295 and 303 of the *Catalogue*. He executed the engraving *A Frugal Repast*.

1904 24 October–20 November "Exposition de peintures, aquarelles, pastels et dessins par MM. Charbonnier, Clary-Baroux, Duty (Raoul), Girieud, Picabia, Picasso, Thiesson", at the Galerie Berthe Weill. Picasso was represented by eleven pictures and various drawings, all prior to 1904, except for a drawing entitled *The Fool*. The catalogue included a preface by Maurice Le Sieutre.

1904 10 December In the fifth issue of the review *El poble catalá* there appeared a forecast about Picasso by Eugenio d'Ors (see page 10).

1905 The so-called Rose Period of Picasso's art began with the picture *The Actor* (no. 154). . Picasso and his friends began smoking opium in the studio at the "Bateau Lavoir", but gave it up when one of them, the German painter Wiegels, became an addict. Picasso became a friend of Guillaume Apollinaire and also of the rich Americans Leo and Gertrude Stein, who bought pictures from him for eight hundred francs (see nos. 229 and 306). Picasso produced his series of dry points and etchings of acrobats but a limited printing of them, edited by Delâtre, had little success. The originals were later bought

Friends of the young Picasso. (From top to bottom and left to right; first row.) Self-portrait with Francisco de Asís Soler (publicity drawing in Arte Joven, *Madrid, June 1901); self-portrait with Jaime Andreu Bonsons on their arrival in Paris in June 1901 (ink and coloured pencil). (Second row.) Portrait of Manuel Pallarés (ink, Barcelona 1895); portrait of Carlos Casagemas (charcoal, Barcelona 1900). (Third row.) Portrait of Angel Fernández de Soto (ink and watercolour, Barcelona 1900); portrait of Jaime Sabartés (charcoal and watercolour, Barcelona 1899–1900); portrait of Miguel Utrillo (part of a pen and coloured pencil drawing, Barcelona 1902). (Fourth row.) Portrait of Pedro Manyac (oils, Paris 1901); portrait of Max Jacob (ink, Paris 1904–5); portrait of Guillaume Apollinaire (ink and charcoal, Paris 1905). (Bottom row.) The "Bateau-Lavoir" (photograph, 1905); Fernande Olivier, Picasso and Ramón Reventós at Barcelona (photograph 1906).*

by Ambroise Vollard who had them steel-faced and re-printed them in 1913, together with the *Frugal Repast* of 1904, in a limited edition of 279 copies.

1905 25 February–6 March In Paris, "Exposition des peintres Trachsel, Gérardin, Picasso" took place at the Galerie Serrurier, 37 Boulevard Haussman. Picasso exhibited twenty-eight pictures, six engravings (of acrobats) and a portfolio of drawings, all recent works, executed in 1904 or the first two months of 1905. The catalogue opened with a preface by Charles Morice (see page 10).

1905 Charles Morice also reviewed the Exhibition at the Galerie Serrurier in the *Mercure de France* (see page 10).

1905 *La Revue Immoraliste* published an article by Guillaume

The Frugal Repast *(etching, Paris 1904).*

Apollinaire, "Picasso, peintre et dessinateur" (see p. 11). Another article by Guillaume Apollinaire in the review *La Plume*, "Les jeunes: Picasso peintre" (see p. 11).

1905 Summer Picasso visited Holland as the guest of the writer Tom Schilperoort.

1905 Autumn Picasso met Henri Matisse through Gertrude Stein.

1906 Late April Picasso went to Barcelona with Fernande Olivier.

1906 May–August He stayed with Fernande Olivier in the medieval village of Gósol, at an altitude of 1500 metres in the province of Lérida. They stayed in the Can Tempanada Inn. Picasso did a great deal of work there mostly drawings and gouaches but also a few paintings: among them "La Toilette" and *The Harem* (nos. 270 and 274). It was at this time that he produced the album of sketches known as the *Carnet catalán* published in facsimile in 1958 by Berggruen & Co., with notes by Douglas Cooper (see nos. 239, 254, 255 and 265). The original is in the possession of the author.

1906 Mid-August An epidemic of typhoid broke out and Picasso and Fernande Olivier left Gósol for Paris.

1906 Autumn End of the Rose Period. The novel *Sandricourt* by Eugène Marsan appeared, in which a reference to Picasso testifies to the popularity he had achieved before his Cubist phase (see page 11).

Catalogue of works

The present *Catalogue* lists the pictorial works of Picasso between 1901 and 1906.

In the period we are concerned with at the beginning of his working life, his work can be broadly grouped into two "periods", both stylistically and chronologically: first the Blue Period which lasted roughly from the autumn of 1901 to the spring of 1904 — and then the Rose Period whose development can be traced between the early months of 1905 and the autumn of 1906.

Of the three hundred and seven works described in this book, the one hundred and twenty-four pictures here catalogued from no. 19 to no. 142 are assignable to the first period; while the hundred and thirty-two, here catalogued from no. 158 to no. 289, can be classified as belonging to the second. These include all the known works. However the catalogue also lists works which do not strictly belong to either period — the first eighteen pictures described here precede those which are truly of the Blue Period; the fifteen from no. 143 to no. 157 illustrate the transition between the two phases belonging absolutely to neither, and the final eighteen works here, catalogued from no. 290 to no. 307, were painted after the conclusion of the true Rose Period and herald the beginnings of a new stylistic approach. There are also another fifty-one pictures included here, which cannot strictly be classified as belonging to either of the two periods, but which nevertheless are relevant in some way.

In the years with which we are concerned, there is a definite Pre-Blue Period which is already Blue in some way, and a Post-Rose Period which is still Rose in certain respects; and there are also pictures which demonstrate characteristics of both periods yet belong to neither. It is also impossible to impose absolute limits chronologically; since quite often a painting is quite different in mood from those executed before and after — which may be similar in both style and feeling and can quite naturally be grouped together.

In the *Catalogue*, as we have said, the entire known output of Picasso relevant to the Blue and Rose Periods is listed. This does not, however, exclude the possibility that he executed other relevant works in the early years of the century; which for one reason or another have remained unknown, possibly in the artist's own possession.

We have also said "pictorial works". In fact although drawings (executed without any subsidiary media in pencil, charcoal or pen) and etchings have been excluded, the term "pictorial" has nevertheless been interpreted in a very wide sense. It includes not only oils and tempera (i.e. gouaches) but also pastels, watercolours and works executed in mixed media, as well as drawings heightened with colour. Several drawings have also been included in the *Catalogue* and reproduced, whenever they seem in some way relevant to the paintings, or capable of being related to them.

1 ⊘ 82/66 ▤ Paris 1901 ⁝

Portrait of Jaime Sabartés
Moscow, Pushkin Museum.
Previous owners: Kahnweiler, Paris; Shchukine, Moscow; Museum of Modern Western Art, Moscow.
Exhibitions: 54 P, 66 P.
Bibliography: R 21, Z 32 no. 97, S 46–53, CP 50, B 55, KP 55, P 58, D 64, DB 66 VI no. 19.

Jaime Sabartés, in his *Picasso, Retratos y recuerdos,* relates:
"Without knowing it, I was serving as a model for a picture. ... Picasso finished painting me as he saw me at the café. The canvas was turned towards the wall when I entered. In the mirror over the easel, I was surprised to see myself just as he had caught me unaware, in a fleeting moment of my journey through life. I saw myself, I gazed at myself fixed upon the canvas, and I understood what I had suggested to the restless observation of my friend: the vision of my solitude, seen from without. The look is lost in a gloom which it does not succeed in penetrating, the thought wanders uncertainly; and·both the look and the thought unite in losing themselves in vacuity, because the eyes, myopic and blank, do not see, and the thought does not reveal itself in the look. The effect upon me of looking at myself in this marvellous blue mirror was profound: it was as if the waters of a great lake retained something of myself because I found my reflection in it."

2 ⊘ 63/46 ▤ Paris 1901 ⁝

Portrait of Mateu Fernández de Soto
Winterthur, Oskar Reinhart Foundation.
Previous owner: Private collection, Hamburg.
Bibliography: Z 32 no. 94, S 48–55, CP 50, DB 66 VI no. 21.

3 ⊘ 80/60,5 ▤ Paris 1901 ⁝

Harlequin Leaning on his Elbow
New York, Metropolitan Museum of Art.
Previous owners: Suermondt, Aachen; Neuer Kunstsalon, Munich; Quinn, New York; Anderson, New York; McIlhenny, Philadelphia (Pa.); Clifford, Radnor (Pa.); Loeb, New York.
Exhibitions: 13 M, 36 NY, 38 B, 39 NY, 59 M.
Bibliography: Z 32 no. 79, S 38, B 39, M 42–48, B 46, L 52-54, EM 55, P 58, C 59, DB 66 VI no 22.

It would appear that the signature and date were added by the artist in 1927. See Plate I. The painting was given to the Metropolitan by Mrs Loeb.

4 ⊘ 73/60 ▤ Paris 1901 ⁝

Harlequin and his Companion
Moscow, Pushkin Museum.
Previous owners: Vollard, Paris; Morosov, Moscow; Museum of Modern Western Art, Moscow.
Exhibitions: 54 P.
Bibliography: Z 32 no. 92, S 48-55, KP 55, D 60, D 64, DB 66 VI no. 20.
Bought in 1908 for 300 francs.

5 ⊘ 73/54 ▤ Paris 1901 ⁝

Child Holding a Dove
London, The Dowager Lady Aberconway Collection.
Previous owners: Rosenberg, Paris; Reid, London; Workman, London; Courtauld, London.
Exhibitions: 60 L, 64 T, 66 P.
Bibliography: L 28, Z 32 no. 83, S 48-55, CP 50, B 55, EM 55, C 58, J 64, K 65, DB 66 VI no. 14.
See plate II.

6 ⊘ 41,5/33 ▤ Paris 1901 ⁝

Woman in a Bonnet
Property of the artist.
Bibliography: Z 32 no. 101, C 40, DB 66 VI no. 12.

7 ⊘ 81,5/54 ▤ Paris 1901 ⁝

Exhausted Nude
Paris, Private collection.
Previous owners: Vollard, Paris; Joseph von Sternberg, Hollywood; Sarlie, New York; Maguy, Paris.
Bibliography: Z 32 no. 104, DB 66 VI no. 18.
Sold at Parke-Bernet's, New York in 1949 for $3,500 and at Sotheby's, London, on 12 October 1960 for £30,000.

8 ⊘ 46,5/33 ▤ Paris 1901 ⁝

Nude with Bathrobe
Property of the Artist.
Bibliography: Z 32 no. 102, M 42-48, DB 66 VI no. 13.

9 ⊘ 51/62,5 ▤ Paris 1901 ⁝

The Blue Room
Washington, DC, Phillips Collection.
Previous owners: Uhde, Paris; Bignou, Paris; Reid, London.
Exhibitions: 36 NY, 39 NY, 47 NY.
Bibliography: Z 32 no. 103, B 39, B 46, L 52-54, R 53, B 55, EM 55, P 58, DB 66 VI no. 15.

The painting depicts Picasso's studio in the Boulevard de Clichy. On the back wall, at the right-hand side, is a poster done by Toulouse-Lautrec for May Milton.

10 ⊘ 75/51 ▤ Paris 1901 ⁝

Woman with a Chignon
Cambridge (Mass.), Harvard University, Fogg Art Museum.
Previous owners: Quinn, New York; Bakwin, New York; Wertheim, New York.
Exhibitions: 36 NY.
Bibliography: Z 32 no. 96, DB 66 VI no. 23.

On the back of the canvas is the oil-painting *Child in a Bonnet,* painted shortly before.

11 ⊘ 73/54 ▤ Paris 1901 ⁝

The Aperitif
Leningrad, Hermitage.
Previous owners: Shchukine, Moscow; Museum of Modern Western Art. Moscow.
Bibliography: Z 32 no. 98, S 48-55, CP 50, KP 55, DB 66 VI no. 24.

1

2

3 [Plate I]

4

5 [Plate II]

6

7

8

9

10

11

12

12 ⊗ 77/61 ▤ Paris 1901 ⋮

The Absinthe Drinker
Geneva, Obersteg Collection.
Previous owners: Bollag, Zurich.

Bibliography: Z 32 no. 100, C 40, CP 50, DB 66 VI no. 25.

On the back of the canvas is the oil-painting *Woman in a Theatre Box,* painted shortly before.

13 ⊗ 49,5/25,5 ▤ Paris 1901 ⋮

The Laundress
New York, Metropolitan Museum of Art, Stieglitz Collection.

Previous owners: Sabartés, Paris; Stieglitz, New York.

Bibliography: S 46-53, EM 55, DB 66 VI no. 27.

The dedication in the top right-hand corner reads: "a Jacobus Sabartés".

14 ⊗ 100/73 ▤ Paris 1901 ⋮

Mother and Child
Paris, Niarchos Collection.
Previous owners: Vollard, Paris; Schmits, Wuppertal; Thannhauser, New York; Kirkeby, New York.

Bibliography: K 65, DB 66 X no. 9.

15 ⊗ 92/65 ▤ Paris 1901 ⋮

Mother and Child
Whereabouts unknown.
Previous owner: Oppenheim, Paris.

Bibliography: Z 32 no. 117, DB 66 VI no. 31.

16 ⊗ 110,5/96,5 ▤ Paris 1901 ⋮

Mother and Child
Cambridge (Mass.), Harvard University, Fogg Art Museum.
Previous owners: Quinn, New York; Fukushima, Paris; Wertheim, New York.

Exhibitions: 39 NY.

Bibliography: D 30, Z 32 no. 115, B 39, B 46, CP 50, B 55, P 58, BP 62, K 65, DB 66 VI no. 30.

17 ⊗ 46,5/31 ▤ Paris 1901 ⋮

Mother and Child
Küsnacht, Private collection.
Previous owners: Thannhauser, Munich; Laya, Geneva; Georg Reinhart, Winterthur.

Exhibitions: 32 Z.

Bibliography: Z 32 no. 110, CP 50, DB 66 VI no. 29.

Sold by the Peau de l'Ours, Paris, on 2 March 1914, for 1,350 francs.

18 ⊗ 91,5/60 ▤ Paris 1901 ⋮

Mother and Child
Los Angeles (Cal.), Goetz Collection.
Previous owners: Vollard, Paris; Bernheim de Villiers, Paris; Salz, New York.

Exhibitions: 32 P, 32 Z, 60 L.

Bibliography: Z 32 no. 109, CP 50, G 51, B 55, EM 55, K 65, DB 66 VI no. 28.

See Plate III.

19 ⊗ 65/54,5 ▤ Paris 1901 ⋮

Seated Child
Merion (Pa.), Barnes Foundation.

Bibliography: Z 32 no. 116, K 65, DB 66 VI no. 32.

This is the first painting which can be ascribed without qualification to the Blue Period.

20 ⊗ 52/60 ▤ Paris 1901 ⋮

Woman with a White Mantilla
New York, Lasker Collection.
Previous owners: Guillaume, Paris; Mme Walter, Paris.

Bibliography: Z 54 no. 733, DB 66 XV no. 42.

Acquired by the present owner in 1950, for $22,000.

21 ⊗ 81/60 ▤ Paris 1901 ⋮

Self-Portrait with Cloak
Property of the Artist.

Exhibitions: 32 P, 32 Z, 60 L, 66 P.

Bibliography: Z 32 no. 91, CP 50, G 51, S 54, EM 55, P 58, D 61, BP 62, B 64, DB 66 VI no. 35.

22 ⊗ 44,5/37 ▤ Paris 1901 ⋮

Portrait of Jaime Sabartés
Property of the Artist.

Bibliography: Z 32 no. 87, M 42-48, S 46-53, DB 66 VI no. 34.

23 ⊗ 45/37 ▤ Paris 1901 ⋮

13

19

20

Portrait of Mateu Fernández de Soto
Property of the Artist.

Bibliography: Z 32 no. 86, CP 50, DB 66 VI no. 33.

24 ⊗ 63,5/50 ▤ Barcelona 1902 ⋮

Crouching Woman
Stockholm, Nathhorst Collection.
Previous owners: Vollard, Paris; Lewisohn, New York; Sarlie, New York.

Exhibitions: 36 NY.

Bibliography: Z 32 no. 160, R 53, DB 66 VII no. 4.

Sold at Sotheby's, London, on 12 October 1960 for £48,000.

14

15

16

17

18 [Plate III]

25 ⊘ 101/66 ▤ Barcelona 1902 ⋮

Crouching Beggar
Toronto, Art Gallery.
Previous owners: Thannhauser, Munich; Mendel, Saskatoon (Canada).
Exhibitions: 64 T.
Bibliography: Z 32 no. 121, BP 62, D 64, DB 66 VII no. 5.

26 ⊘ 90/71 ▤ Barcelona 1902 ⋮

Crouching Woman
Stuttgart, Staatsgalerie.
Previous owners: Gertrude Stein, Paris; Gaspari, Munich; Muthmann, Nassau; Nathan, Zurich.
Exhibitions: 55 M.
Bibliography: R 21, Z 32 no. 119, S 48-55, CP 50, BP 62, DB 66 VII no. 2.
On the back of the canvas is painted the gouache *Mother and Child* of 1905 (no. 167).

27 ⊘ 80/62 ▤ Barcelona 1902 ⋮

Sleeping Drinker
Glarus (Switzerland), Huber Collection.
Previous owners: Gertrude Stein, Paris; Troplowitz, Hamburg; Kunsthalle, Hamburg.
Exhibitions: 53 M.
Bibliography: Z 32 no. 120, CP 50, EM 55, DB 66 VII no. 3. P 66.
This picture which was confiscated by the Nazis in 1937, was auctioned on 30 June 1939 at the Fischer Gallery of Lucerne in the sale of pictures and sculptures by modern masters from German museums, and was bought for 80,000 Swiss francs. See Plate IV.

28 ⊘ 100/69 ▤ Barcelona 1902 ⋮

Seated Woman with a Scarf on her Shoulders
Detroit (Mich.), Private collection.
Previous owner: Guillaume, Paris.
Exhibitions: 32 P, 32 Z, 36 NY.
Bibliography: Z 32 no. 133, S 48-55, CP 50, DB 66 VII no. 6.

29 ⊘ 81/60 ▤ Barcelona 1902 ⋮

Seated Woman with Arms Crossed
Chicago (Ill.), McCormick Collection.
Previous owner: Private collection, Berlin.
Exhibitions: 32 Z, 36 NY, 39 NY.
Bibliography: R 21, Z 32 no. 105, B 39, B 46, S 48-55, CP 50, Z 54 no. 543, DB 66 VII no. 7.

30 ⊘ 60/49 ▤ Barcelona 1902 ⋮

Portrait of Corina Romeu
Property of the Artist.
Exhibitions: 32 P, 32 Z, 66 P.
Bibliography: Z 32 no. 130, CP 50, G 51, EM 55, DB 66 VII no. 15.
Corina was the wife of the painter Pere Romeu, landlord of the literary café of Barcelona "Els 4 Gats". See Plate V.

31 ⊘ 46/41 ▤ Barcelona 1902 ⋮

30 [Plate V]

31

32

33

Portrait of Germaine Pichot
New York, Jonas Collection.
Previous owner: Guillaume, Paris.
Bibliography: DB 66 VII no. 8.
The subject was the wife of the Catalan painter Ramón Pichot.

32 ⊘ 60/49 ▤ Barcelona 1902 ⋮

Woman with a Fringe
Baltimore (Md.), Museum of Art, Cone Collection.
Previous owners: Gertrude Stein, Paris; Cone, Baltimore.
Bibliography: R 21, Z 32 no. 118, S 48-55, DB 66 VII no. 10.

33 ⊘ 65/54 ▤ Barcelona 1902 ⊙

Woman with a Scarf on her Shoulders
Property of the Artist.
Exhibitions: 32 P, 32 Z, 66 P.
Bibliography: Z 32 no. 155, DB 66 VII no. 9.

34 ⊘ 37/45 ▤ Barcelona 1902 ⊙

The Offering
Toronto, Crang Collection.
Previous owners: Gertrude Stein, Paris; Sternheim, Paris; Von Ripper, Paris; Knoedler, New York.
Exhibitions: 47 NY, 64 T.
Bibliography: Z 32 no. 131,

S 38, S 48-55, CP 50, K 65, DB 66 VII no. 11.

Some preliminary drawings of this picture are known, which present three variations on the theme. In the first, 34 A (Z 32 no. 192, pencil, 24 × 29·5 cm), a small sheet with more sketches, the offering is given by a man, and the scene in the background conceived with three people. In the second, 34 B (DB 66 VII no. D1, Indian ink, 25 × 26 cm, signed and dated 1902), to which Daix and Boudaille gave the title *L'Offrande,* a man and a young girl are depicted. In the third, 34 C, and the fourth, 34 D (Z 54 nos. 418 and 420, both pen drawings and 24 × 24 cm

21

22

23

24

25

26

27 [Plate IV]

28

29

and 24 × 19 cm respectively), the offering is made by a woman to a little boy and a little girl. The second belongs to Berggruen, Paris; the whereabouts of the other three is not given by Zervos.

35 ⊘ 40,5/33 ▤ Barcelona 1902 ⋮

Mother and Child
Edinburgh, Scottish National Gallery of Modern Art.
Previous owners: Gaffé, Brussels; Berggruen, Paris; Tooth, London; Maitland, Edinburgh; National Gallery of Scotland, Edinburgh.
Bibliography: DB 66 VII no. 18.
See Plate VI.

36 ⊘ 46/31 ▤ Barcelona 1902 ⊙

Mother and Child on the Seashore
Whereabouts unknown.
Previous owners: Besnard, Paris; Rosenberg, Paris.
Exhibitions: 32 Z.
Bibliography: Z 32 no. 381, CP 50, DB 66 VII no. 21.
This is probably the pastel painting which Picasso succeeded in selling in January 1903 in Paris, to a certain Mme Besnard, the wife of a paint merchant (and already a client of his since his first exhibition at Vollard's in June–July 1901), for sixty francs, with which he was able to buy his railway ticket and return to Barcelona.

37 ⊘ 83/60 ▤ Barcelona 1902 ⋮

Mother and Child on the Seashore
New York, Private collection.
Previous owners: Fontbona, Barcelona.
Bibliography: CP 50, Z 54 no. 478, K 65, DB 66 VII no. 20.
The dedication, not in Picasso's hand, is to "Dr Fontbona". Sold at Sotheby's, London, on 26 April 1967, for £190,000, the largest sum ever realised for a work by a living artist. A drawing, 37 A, in ink and coloured pencil on a sheet of notepaper, 14 × 9 cm, dating from the same period, and signed over the cancellation of a previous signature of doubtful authenticity (Z 32 no. 151 and DB 66 VII D 9; *Miséreuse au bord de la mer;* CP 50: *Mendiante à la plage*), is reminiscent of this picture. The former property of Junyer Vidal, Barcelona, it now belongs to Gustave Kahnweiler, London.

38 ⊘ 46,5/38 ▤ Barcelona 1902 ⋮

Farewell to the Fisherman

34

34 A

34 B

34 C

34 D

35 [Plate VI]

36

37

37 A

38

90

Küsnacht, Private collection.
Previous owner: Doetsch-Benzinger, Basle.
Bibliography: DB 66 VII no. 19.

39 ⊛ 152 / 100 ▤ Barcelona 1902 ⋮

The Two Sisters
Leningrad, Hermitage.
Previous owners: Shchukine, Moscow; Museum of Modern Western Art, Moscow.
Exhibitions: 64 T.
Bibliography: Z 32 no. 163, CP 50, KP 55, DB 66 VII no. 22.

Two drawings for this picture are known. The first, 39 A (Z 54 no. 436; DB 66 VII no. D 4), in sepia, 29 × 13·5 cm, with the inscription *Les deux sœurs* was formerly at the Rosengart Gallery, Lucerne; the actual whereabouts of the second, 39 B (Z 54 no. 435; DB 66 VII no. D 6), in pencil, 16 × 11 cm, is not known.

40 ⊛ 27,5 / 20 ▤ Barcelona 1902 ⋮

Crouching Nude with Green Stocking
Paris, Private collection.
Previous owners: Gertrude Stein, Paris; Schoeller, Paris.
Bibliography: B 55, EM 55, DB 66 VII no. 16.
See also, for comparison, no. 68.

41 ⊛ 46 / 40 ▤ Barcelona 1902 ⋮

Nude Woman from Behind
Paris, Private collection.
Previous owner: Rothschild, Paris.
Exhibitions: 53 L, 55 P.
Bibliography: CP 50, Z 54 no. 449, EM 55, D 60, B 64, DB 66 VII no. 17, P 66.

42 ⊛ 30,5 / 38,5 ▤ Barcelona 1902 ⋮

Couple in a Café
New York, Ault Collection.
Bibliography: DB 66 VII no. 12.
Authenticated by Picasso on 3 September 1965.

43 ⊛ 43 / 33 ▤ Barcelona 1902 ⋮

Seated Couple from Behind
Buenos Aires, De Ganay Collection.
Exhibitions: 55 P, 55 M.
Bibliography: DB 66 VII no. 14.
Authenticated by Picasso on 3 September 1965.

44 ⊛ 80 / 91,5 ▤ Barcelona 1902 ⋮

Two Women at a Bar
New York, Chrysler Collection.

39

40

39 A

39 B

Previous owner: Gertrude Stein, Paris.
Exhibitions: 38 B, 39 NY, 60 L.
Bibliography: Z 32 no. 132, S 38, B 39, B 46, S 48-55, CP 50, EM 55, BP 62, DB 66 VII no. 13.
See Plate VII.

45 ⊛ 50,5 / 40,5 ▤ Barcelona 1902 ⋮

The Blue House
New York, owned by the heirs of Gertrude Stein.

Previous owner: Gertrude Stein, Paris.
Exhibitions: 32 P, 32 Z.
Bibliography: S 48-55, DB 66 VII no. 1.
Sold at the Peau de l'Ours, Paris, on 2 March 1914, for 550 francs.

46 ⊛ 88,5 / 76,5 ▤ Barcelona 1902 ⋮

Man in Blue
Property of the Artist.
Exhibitions: 32 P, 32 Z.
Bibliography: L 28, Z 32 no. 142, C 40, CP 50, G 51, DB 66 VIII no. 1.

47 ⊛ 31 / 23,5 ▤ Paris 1902 ⋮

Portrait of the Poet Cornuti with Female Figure
Whereabouts unknown.
Previous owner: Lefèvre, Paris.
Bibliography: Z 32 no. 182, CP 50, DB 66 VIII no. 2.

On the back of this water-colour the following note is handwritten by Max Jacob: "This portrait depicts a poet called Cornuty [sic] whom Picasso had known in Barcelona, and whom I too had known, emaciated and starving beneath his locks of hair; he enunciated his words in a hollow voice, and extended a slender hand with the fingers pointing forward to the infinite. He had an admiration for Flaubert, which he pronounced 'Flobert': 'If only Flobert had translated Gorki....' he said to me at the time when Gorki was all the rage, about 1900. His father was the director of a store at Montpellier, and Cornuty despised him because he used to scratch himself in an indecent manner. He had abandoned his family, and armed with a cudgel, a Lavallière cravat, a cloak and a soft hat, went on foot to attend a socialist meeting in the city. There had been a gendarme to inform them to ask for alms at the farmhouses: 'There can't be all that many like him' he exclaimed, clearing his throat and placing the stress of the

sentence on 'all that many', while the 'like him' was lost in a sort of heavy breathing. He spent a night out in the countryside, with frozen feet, and his companions of the haystacks carried him to a blacksmith's fire, 'at the risk of killing me', he said. One day he met his uncle, who went round selling lengths of cloth to the singers at the café-concerts of the period, and who invited him to dine at the Alcazar. Because his uncle had introduced him as a poet, a woman singer wished to drink a toast to 'The Arts'. I do not record Cornuty's verses, but he had written a comedy in which the leading character was an impoverished nobleman who took the part of his own valet and of himself alternately. Cornuty died at a very early age: he died of starvation, in Catalonia I think." Sold at the Peau de l'Ours, Paris, on 2 March 1914, for 400 francs.

48 ⊛ 37 / 46 ▤ Paris 1902 ⋮

The Two Mothers
Paris, Private collection.
Previous owner: Level, Paris.
Exhibitions: 55 P.
Bibliography: Z 32 no. 180, CP 50, C 58, DB 66 VIII no. 3.
Sold at the Peau de l'Ours, Paris, on 2 March 1914, for 700 francs.

49 ⊛ 37,5 / 27 ▤ Paris 1902 ⋮

The Mistletoe Seller
Paris, Berggruen Collection.
Bibliography: DB 66 VIII no. 5.
Indian ink and watercolour on paper. A study for the gouache is given under the following number.

50 ⊛ 55 / 38 ▤ Paris 1902 ⋮

The Mistletoe Seller
Paris, Private collection.
Previous owner: Pellequer, Paris.
Exhibitions: 55 P.
Bibliography: Z 32 no. 123, CP 50, B 55, DB 66 VIII no. 4.

See also the previous number, as well as no. 212.

51 ⊗ — ▭ Barcelona 1903? ⦂

Prone Nude
Whereabouts unknown.
Previous owner: Dutilleul, Paris.
Bibliography: Z 54 no. 413, DB 66 X no. 7.
Dimensions unknown.
Zervos gives the date as 1902 or 1903; Daix and Boudaille were inclined to date it even later than 1903. Sold by auction in Paris on 9 December 1960, for 95,000 francs.

52 ⊗ 45,5 / 55 ▭ Barcelona 1903 ⦂

Nude Lying on her Side
Worcester (Mass.), Higgins Collection.
Previous owner: Bucher, Paris.
Bibliography: Z 54 no. 479, DB 66 X no. 8.
Executed on a canvas already painted on by others. High up in the background of the picture there was another female figure belonging to a previous picture; Picasso disowned it in May 1935, but he had already written on the back of the canvas a signed declaration: "Bien entendu ce tableau est de moi, Picasso, Paris le 17 Novembre XXXIV".

53 ⊗ 55 / 38 ▭ Barcelona 1903 ⦂

Seated Woman
Zurich, Bollag Collection.
Exhibitions: 32 Z.
Bibliography: Z 54 no. 476, DB 66 IX no. 10.
Gouache and watercolour on glued paper.

54 ⊗ 46 / 38 ▭ Barcelona 1903 ⦂

Profile of a Woman
Solothurn, Private collection.
Previous owner: Müller, Solothurn.
Bibliography: Z 54 no. 467, C 59, DB 66 X no. 10.
Signed on the back of the frame.

55 ⊗ 29 / 28,5 ▭ Barcelona 1903 ⦂

Head of a Woman
New York, J. K. Thannhauser Collection.
Bibliography: Z 32 no. 206, S 48-55, DB 66 IX no. 8.

56 ⊗ 61 / 38 ▭ Barcelona 1903 ⦂

Street in Barcelona
London, Private collection.

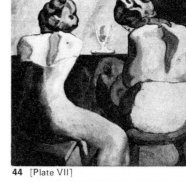

42

43

44 [Plate VII]

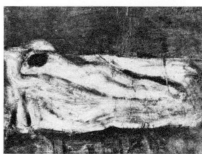

45

47

Autograph of Max Jacob on reverse of no. 47.

48

51

52

Previous owners: Stransky, New York; Astor, London.
Exhibitions: 60 L.
Bibliography: Z 32 no. 122, DB 66 IX no. 1.
In the background, the old Palace of Fine Arts, which was demolished in 1940 and stood in the Paseo de la Industria, opposite the Parque de la Ciudadela.

57 ⊗ 67 / 50 ▭ Barcelona 1903 ⦂

Barcelona at Night
Zurich, Bührle Foundation.

Previous owners: Wildenstein, Paris–New York; Schweppe, New York.
Exhibitions: 55 P, 55 M.
Bibliography: DB 66 IX no. 3, P 66.
Like the *Roofs of Barcelona* (no. 58), this also is a view from the studio in the Riera de Sant Joan; in the middle ground on the left is the roof of the Church of Santa Marta. According to a report noted in the book *Festschrift zu Ehren von Emil G. Bührle zur Eröffnung des Kunsthaus-Neubaus und Katalog der Sammlung Emil G. Bührle*, Kunsthaus–Zurich,

June–September 1958, this painting belonged originally to Picasso's mother. See Plate XI.

58 ⊗ 70 / 110 ▭ Barcelona 1903 ⦂

Roofs of Barcelona
Property of the Artist.
Exhibitions: 32 P, 32 Z, 66 P.
Bibliography: L 28, Z 32 no. 207, CP 50, DB 66 IX no. 2.
This view, like that of the preceeding picture, was taken from Picasso's studio in the Riera de Sant Joan, which has now disappeared.
See plate X.

59 ⊗ 26 / 35 ▭ Barcelona 1903 ⦂

Guitar Player at the Inn
Zurich, Bührle Foundation.
Previous owners: Junyer Vidal, Barcelona; Dereppe, Lugano.
Bibliography: Z 32 no. 178, CP 50, DB 66 IX no. D 18.
Indian ink and coloured pencil on card. An authentic signature; cancellation of an earlier signature of doubtful authenticity.

60 ⊗ 37 / 27 ▭ Barcelona 1903 ⦂

46

49

50

53

54

91

55

Peasants
Wuppertal. Von der Heydt-Museum.
Previous owners: Lefèvre, Paris; Bernados, Geneva; Von der Heydt, Ascona.
Bibliography: DB 66 IX no. D 19.
Indian ink and watercolour on yellow card. On the back, drawing of a nude woman, and sketches of figures.

61 ⊕ 26/35 ▤ Barcelona 1903

Peasants Dancing the Jota
Whereabouts unknown.
Previous owner: Viñes, Paris.
Bibliography: Z 32 no. 186, DB 66 IX no. D 20.
The pair of dancers on the left appear in the *Peasants* described above. A pen and ink sketch of the man in a hood in the centre, 61 A, 29 × 12 cm (DB 66 IX no. D 21), is in the hands of a private collector in Lausanne.

62 ⊕ 31,5/22,5 ▤ Barcelona 1903

Catalan Peasants
San Antonio (Tex.), Koogler McNay Collection.
Previous owners: Bignou, Paris; Quest, Chicago.
Bibliography: Z 32 no. 376, DB 66 IX no. D 16.

63 ⊕ 31,5/22 ▤ Barcelona 1903

The Idiot
Zurich, Private collection.
Previous owner: Bollag, Zurich.
Bibliography: Z 54 no. 482, DB 66 IX no. D 17.
Indian ink and watercolour on paper.

64 ⊕ 31/22 ▤ Barcelona 1903

Strolling Guitar Player
Turgovia (Switzerland), Private collection.
Previous owners: Bollag, Zurich; Lion, Steckborn (Switzerland).
Bibliography: Z 54 no. 481, DB 66 IX no. D 15.

65 ⊕ 81,5/65,5 ▤ Barcelona April 1903

Couple in a Cafe
Oslo, Nasjonalgalleriet
Previous owners: Vilaró, Barcelona; Flechtheim, Düsseldorf; Gold, Copenhagen.
Bibliography: Z 32 no. 167, S 48-55, DB 66 IX no. 9.
In the top right-hand corner is signed and dated: "Picasso, 1903, avril".

66 ⊕ 23,5/17 ▤ Barcelona May 1903

Blind Woman
Heino (Holland), Hannema–De Stuers Foundation.
Bibliography: DB 66 IX no. D 6.
Indian ink and watercolour on paper; dated on the back: "23 Mayo 1903". A pen and ink drawing, 66 A, 23 × 17 cm, whereabouts unknown (Z 54 no. 451), has a comparable theme.

67 ⊕ ▤ Barcelona 1903

Nude with Flowing Hair
Whereabouts unknown.
Previous owner: Junyent, Barcelona.

56

57 [Plate XI]

Bibliography: CP 50, Z 54 no 462, DB 66 IX no 18.
Dimensions unknown; it does not appear to be signed.

68 ⊕ ▤ Barcelona 1903

Nude with Crossed Legs
Whereabouts unknown.
Bibliography: Z 32 no. 181, CP 50, DB 66 IX no. 19.
The dimensions are variously given as 58 × 44 and 60 × 46 cm. See no. 40.

69 ⊕ 40,5/35,5 ▤ Barcelona 1903

Head of a Woman
New York, on loan from the Milton de Groot Collection to the Metropolitan Museum of Art.
Previous owners: Fukushima, Paris; Milton de Groot, New York.
Bibliography: Z 54 no. 548, DB 66 IX no. 16.

70 ⊕ 50/36 ▤ Barcelona 1903

Woman with a Kerchief round her Neck
Leningrad, Hermitage.
Previous owners: Shchukine, Moscow; Museum of Modern Western Art, Moscow.
Bibliography: Z 32 no. 166, BP 62, B 64, DB 66 IX no. 14.

---

58 [Plate X]

71 ⊕ 50/37 ▤ Barcelona 1903

Woman with Lock of Hair
Barcelona, Picasso Museum.
Previous owners: Plandiura, Barcelona; Museo de Arte Moderno, Barcelona.
Exhibitions: 60 P.
Bibliography: Z 32 no. 165, CP 50, S 63, DB 66 IX no. 15, P 66.
See Plate XVIII.

72 ⊕ 125,5/91,5 ▤ Barcelona June 1903

Portrait of Sebastián Junyer Vidal with Female Figure
Los Angeles (Cal.), Museum of Art.
Previous owners: Junyer Vidal, Barcelona; Bright, Los Angeles.
Exhibitions: 32 P, 57 NY, 66 P.
Bibliography: Z 32 no. 174, CP 50, B 57, DB 66 IX no. 21, P 66.
The dedication at the bottom right-hand corner reads: "A Sebastián Juñer/Picasso/Junio 1903".

73 ⊕ 27/20 ▤ Barcelona 1903

Portrait of Angel Fernández de Soto with Female Figure
Düsseldorf, Forberg Collection.
Previous owners: Junyent, Barcelona; Rosengart, Lucerne.
Bibliography: DB 66 IX no.

D 9.
Indian ink, watercolour and coloured pencil on paper. Signature of doubtful authenticity on the right. Authenticated by Picasso on 10 November 1955, and signed on the left.

74 ⊕ 69,5/55 ▤ Barcelona 1903

Portrait of Angel Fernández de Soto
New York, Stralem Collection.
Previous owners: Mendelssohn, Berlin; Thannhauser, Lucerne; Taylor, Lucerne.
Exhibitions: 47 NY, 64 T.
Bibliography: Z 32 no. 201, S 48-55, EM 55, DB 66 IX no. 20.

75 ⊕ 36/27 ▤ Barcelona 1903

Head of a Woman
Paris, owned by the heirs of Guillaume Apollinaire.
Previous owner: Guillaume Apollinaire, Paris.
Bibliography: Z 32 no. 205, S 48-55, CP 50, DB 66 IX no. 17.

76 ⊕ 21,5/14 ▤ Barcelona 1903

Man with a Dog
Whereabouts unknown.
Previous owner: Junyer Vidal, Barcelona.
Bibliography: Z 32 no. 194,

59

60

61

61 A

62

63

64

66

66 A

67

68

69

70

71 [Plate XVIII]

73

74

75

76

81

CP 50, DB 66 IX no. D 8.

Indian ink and watercolour on paper.

77 21 / 15 Barcelona 1903

Portrait of the Tailor Soler Dressed in Riding Clothes
Pittsburgh (Pa.), Heinz Collection.
Previous owners: Soler, Barcelona; Berggruen, Paris.
Bibliography: DB 66 IX no. D 7.
Indian ink and watercolour on paper; the signature is of doubtful authenticity. See no. 80.

78 100 / 70 Barcelona 1903

Portrait of the Tailor Soler
Leningrad, Hermitage.
Previous owners: Soler,

Barcelona; Shchukine, Moscow; Museum of Modern Western Art, Moscow.
Bibliography: Z 32 no. 199, S 48-55, CP 50, B 64, DB 66 IX no. 22, P 66.
See also the two following numbers.

79 100 / 73 Barcelona 1903

Portrait of Madame Soler
Munich, Neue Pinakothek,
Previous owners: Soler, Barcelona; Kahnweiler, Paris; Thannhauser, New York.
Bibliography: Z 32 no. 200, S 48-55, DB 66 IX no. 21, P 66.
See also the two preceding numbers and the following one. Bought in 1964 by the Bavarian state for 1,200,000 francs.

80 150 / 200 Barcelona Summer 1903

The Soler Family
Liège, Musée des Beaux-Arts.
Previous owners: Soler, Barcelona; Kahnweiler, Paris; Wallraf-Richartz-Museum, Cologne.
Exhibitions: 53 L, 60 L, 66 P.
Bibliography: Z 32 no. 203, CP 50, EM 55, P 58, K 65, DB 66 IX no. 23, P 66.
This picture originally had a plain background. At the request of Soler (a tailor of Barcelona with whom Picasso exchanged paintings for clothing), the artist agreed that Sebastián Junyer Vidal should set the group in a landscape. We reproduce here a photograph (published in Z 32 no. 204) of the picture altered in this way. Picasso altered it again in 1913 when the painting was hung in the Museum at Cologne, restoring the original background. The picture was confiscated by the Nazis in 1937 and was auctioned on 30 June 1939 at the Fischer Gallery in Lucerne, at a sale of pictures and sculptures of modern masters coming from German museums. See the article "Les aventures d'un tableau de Picasso" in *Arts* of 15 November 1946; see also the two previous numbers. Finally, see Plates VIII–IX.

81 31,5 / 43 Barcelona 1903

Family at Table
Buffalo (NY), Albright-Knox Art Gallery.
Previous owners: Gertrude Stein, Paris; Perls, Paris; Watson, London; French Art Galleries, New York.
Bibliography: CP 50, Z 54 no. 563, K 65, DB 66 IX no. D 13.
Indian ink and watercolour on paper.

82 47 / 36 Barcelona 1903

The Poor Wretches
Wuppertal, Von der Heydt-Museum.
Previous owners: Von der Heydt, Ascona.
Bibliography: DB 66 IX no. D 1.
A study for the oil painting given under no. 85.

83 37,5 / 26,5 Barcelona 1903

The Poor Wretches
University of Manchester, Whitworth Art Gallery.
Previous owners: Anderson, New York.
Bibliography: DB 66 IX no. 4.
Indian ink and watercolour on paper: sketch for the oil painting given under no. 85.

84 Barcelona 1903

The Poor Wretches
Whereabouts unknown.
Bibliography: Z 32 no. 198.
Dimensions unknown. See the two previous numbers and the two following numbers.

85 59,5 / 49,5 Barcelona 1903

Poor Wretches on the Seashore
Northampton (Mass.), Smith College, Museum of Art.
Previous owners: Stransky, New York; Dexter, Abbott (Maine).
Bibliography: Z 32 no. 197, DB 66 IX no. 5.
See also the three previous numbers and the following number. Sold in 1933 for $3,000.

86 105,5 / 69 Barcelona 1903

Poor People on the Seashore
Washington, DC, National Gallery of Art, Dale Collection.
Previous owners: Schubert, Bochum (Germany); Dale, New York.
Bibliography: Z 32 no. 208,

65

72

77

78

79

80 [Plates VIII–IX]

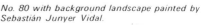

No. 80 with background landscape painted by Sebastián Junyer Vidal.

82 83 84 85 86 [Plate XII]

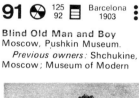

87 88 89 [Plate XIII] 89 A 89 B

S 38, C 40, S 48-55, CP 50, G 51, EM 55, K 65, DB 66 IX no. 6.

See the four previous numbers and Plate XII, for which the photographic originals were kindly supplied by the National Gallery of Art in Washington.

87 ⊘ — ▤ Barcelona 1903

The Embrace
Whereabouts unknown.
Previous owner: Thann-hauser, Paris.
Bibliography: Z 32 no. 162, DB 66 IX no. 11.
Dimensions unknown. A study in pastels for the following picture.

88 ⊘ 98/57 ▤ Barcelona 1903

The Embrace
Paris, Musée de l'Orangerie, Walter-Guillaume Collection.
Previous owners: Vollard, Paris; Guillaume, Paris; Walter, Paris.
Exhibitions: 60 P, 66 P.
Bibliography: Z 32 no. 161, S 48-55, CP 50, EM 55, DB 66 IX no. 12, P 66.
See the previous number.

89 ⊘ 197/127,5 ▤ Barcelona 1903

Life
Cleveland (Ohio), Museum of Art, Hanna Collection.
Previous owners: Vollard, Paris; Bignou, Paris; Thann-hauser, Lucerne; Rhode Island School of Design, Providence (R.I.).
Exhibitions: 32 P, 32 Z, 39 NY, 47 NY, 60 L, 66 P.
Bibliography: D 30, Z 32 no. 179, B 39, C 40, B 46, S 48-55, CP 50, G 51, L 52-54, B 55, EM 55, P 58, BP 62, J 64, DB 66 IX no. 13, P 66.

At least two preparatory sketches are known for this picture, which ranks among Picasso's most important works: the first, 89 A (Z 54 no. 534; DB 66 IX D 4; P 66), in ink, 15·7 × 11 cm, its whereabouts is unknown; the second, 89 B (DB 66 IX D 5; P 66), in pencil, 26·7 × 19·7 cm, is in London, owned by Penrose. The latter, drawn on the back of a letter, bears the date 2 May 1903 in Picasso's handwriting; in the

sketch, the male figure has the features of Picasso himself, while in the finished picture on the other hand it has those of Casagemas (this was noted by Pierre Daix in an article "La période bleue de Picasso et le suicide de Carlos Casagemas" in *Gazette des Beaux-Arts* of April 1967). See Plate XIII.

90 ⊘ — ▤ Barcelona 1903

The Blind Beggar
Whereabouts unknown.
Previous owners: Pellequer, Paris.
Bibliography: Z 32 no. 188.
Dimensions unknown.

91 ⊘ 125/92 ▤ Barcelona 1903

Blind Old Man and Boy
Moscow, Pushkin Museum.
Previous owners: Shchukine, Moscow; Museum of Modern

Western Art, Moscow.
Exhibitions: 54 P, 60 L.
Bibliography: L 28, Z 32 no. 175, EM 55, KP 55, P 58, DB 66 IX no. 30.

On the back of the picture is written: "Picasso / calle de la Merced 3 / piso 2° / Barcelona". A preparatory design for this painting, 91 A, in coloured pencil (in blue and rose tones), 35 × 26 cm, signed over the cancellation of an earlier signature (Z 32 no. 170; DB 66

90 91 [Plate XIV] 91 A 92 [Plate XV]

93 93 A 93 B 94 [Plate XVI]

94

IX no. 29), is in existence and belongs to a private collector living in Switzerland. See Plate XIV.

92 [symbol] 121/82 [symbol] Barcelona 1903 [symbol]

The Old Blind Guitar Player
Chicago (Ill.), Art Institute, Bartlett collection.
Previous owners: Vollard, Paris; Quinn, New York; Bartlett, Chicago.
Exhibitions: 36 NY, 39 NY.
Bibliography: Z 32 no. 202, B 39, B 46, CP 50, L 52-54, P 58, BP 62, B 64, DB 66 IX no. 34, P 66.
See Plate XV.

93 [symbol] 51,5/34,5 [symbol] Barcelona 1903 [symbol]

The Blind Man
Cambridge (Mass.), Harvard University, Fogg Art Museum.

100 [Plate XIX]

Previous owners: Kahnweiler, Paris; Museum of Art, Toledo (Ohio); Wertheim, New York.
Bibliography: R 21, Z 32 no. 172, M 42-48, DB 66 IX no. 31.
Several sketches relating to this picture are known. One of them, 93 A (Z 54 no. 533), in ink, 11·5 × 6·5 cm, present location unknown, is dated by Zervos October 1903. It shows only the head and shoulders of the blind man. Another, 93 B (DB 66 IX no D 23), in pencil and pastel, 36 × 26 cm, owned by Maguy, Paris, is rather closer to the finished painting. It was recently signed and authenticated by the artist.

94 [symbol] 95/94,5 [symbol] Barcelona 1903 [symbol]

The Blind Man's Meal
New York, Metropolitan Museum of Art.
Previous owners: Vollard, Paris; Thannhauser, Munich and then New York; Private collection, Westphalia; Haupt, New York.
Exhibitions: 13 M, 57 NY, 58 F, 60 L.
Bibliography: Z 32 no. 168, CP 50, L 52-54, P 58, DB 66 IX no. 32, P 66.
We learn from a letter of Picasso's, now in the possession of the Barnes Foundation, Merion (Pa.), that in the early stages of the execution of this picture, the figure of a dog gazing at the blind man was introduced. Compare with no. 106. See also Plate XVI. The painting was donated to the Metropolitan Museum in 1950 by Mrs Ira Haupt.

95 [symbol] 130/97 [symbol] Barcelona 1903 [symbol]

The Ascetic

Merion (Pa.), Barnes Foundation.
Previous owner: Guillaume, Paris.
Bibliography: Z 32 no. 187, CP 50, DB 66 IX no. 33.

96 [symbol] 32/18 [symbol] Barcelona 1903 [symbol]

Old Woman with a Shawl
Whereabouts unknown.
Bibliography: Z 32 no. 230, S 48-55, DB 66 IX no. 27.
The picture does not appear to be signed.

97 [symbol] 32,5/24 [symbol] Barcelona 1903 [symbol]

Old Woman with a Hat
Buffalo, Kenefick Collection.
Previous owners: Junyent, Barcelona; Goodyear, New York.
Exhibitions: 36 NY.
Bibliography: CP 50, Z 54 no. 600, DB 66 IX no. 28, P 66.
Indian ink and watercolour on paper. The subject is a native of Horta de Ebro.

98 [symbol] 55/37 [symbol] Barcelona 1903 [symbol]

Old Woman with Nude Figures
Küsnacht, Kirchheimer Collection.
Previous owners: Bollag, Zurich.
Bibliography: Z 54 no. 578, DB 66 IX no. D 11.
Indian ink and watercolour on paper.

99 [symbol] 70/56 [symbol] Barcelona 1903 [symbol]

Celestina
Paris, Private collection.
Previous owner: Pellequer, Paris.
Exhibitions: 32 P, 32 Z, 66 P.
Bibliography: Z 32 no. 183, CP 50, G 51, B 55, EM 55, D 64, J 64, DB 66 IX no. 26, P 66.
On the back of the picture, on the frame, is written: "Carlota Valdivia/Calle Conde Asalto 12/4°/1ª Escalera interior", and the date, March 1904, which is not however that of the picture. There is a sketch for this famous painting in charcoal and coloured pencil, 99 A 27 × 23·5 cm, signed over the cancellation of an earlier apocryphal signature, formerly the property of Junyer Vidal, Barcelona, and now of Motte, Geneva (Z 32 no 191; DB 66 IX no. 25; P 66). In this sketch (where the subject appears to be far more sordid and to have more in common with the character of the comedy of Fernando de Rojas, compared with the idealisation of the subject in the picture) there are two other figures: another woman on the

95

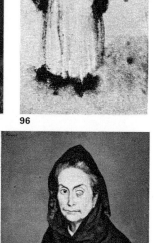

96

97

98

99 [Plate XVII]

left, and on the right a caricature of Sebastián Junyer Vidal. See Plate XVII.

100 [symbol] 47,5/41 [symbol] Barcelona 1903 [symbol]

Mother with Sick Child
Barcelona, Picasso Museum.
Previous owners: Plandiura, Barcelona; Museum of Modern Art, Barcelona.
Bibliography: Z 32 no. 169, CP 50, D 60, BP 62, S 63, DB 66 IX no. 7, P 66.
See Plate XIX.

101 [symbol] 31,5/22 [symbol] Barcelona 1903 [symbol]

Beggar Man and Child
Whereabouts unknown.
Bibliography: Z 54 no. 483.

102 [symbol] 26/36 [symbol] Barcelona 1903 [symbol]

"Caridad"
Brussels, Mabille Collection.
Previous owner: Junyer Vidal, Barcelona.
Bibliography: CP 50, Z 54 no. 438, DB 66 IX no. D 22.
Indian ink and coloured pencil on paper. Authentic signature; cancellation of an earlier apocryphal signature. The sheet contains various brief sketches:

the subject in the left background, with the classical wreath, has the profile of Picasso himself; on the right-hand side is a sketch of the *Beggar Man with Dog*, which relates to the following picture.

103 [symbol] 29/21 [symbol] Barcelona 1903-4 [symbol]

Beggar Man with Dog
New York, J. K. Thannhauser Collection.
Previous owners: Vines, Paris.
Bibliography: Z 32 no. 184, DB 66 X no. 5.
The inscription in the top right-hand corner reads: "El loco" (the madman). A sketch for this watercolour is on the sheet mentioned under the previous number. See Plate XX, for which the photographic originals were kindly furnished by the Guggenheim Museum, with the permission of the Thannhauser Foundation.

104 [symbol] — [symbol] Barcelona 1903-4 [symbol]

Head of a Poor Man
Whereabouts unknown.
Bibliography: Z 54 no. 544, DB 66 X no. 4.
Dimensions unknown.

99 A
Possibly a sketch for the paintings given under the three following numbers. It is comparable, however, also to nos. 101 to 103 and no. 108.

105 [symbol] 24,5/34,5 [symbol] Barcelona 1903-4 [symbol]

The Poor Man's Meal
Paris, Private collection.
Previous owners: Gertrude Stein, Paris; Seligmann, New York; Sachs, Paris.
Bibliography: S 38, Z 54 no. 684, DB 66 X no. 3.
The signature was added later. See also the previous number and the following two numbers.

106 [symbol] 24/33 [symbol] Barcelona 1903-4 [symbol]

The Poor Man's Meal
Whereabouts unknown.
Previous owners: Level, Paris; Lefèvre, Paris.
Bibliography: Z 32 no. 209, K 65, DB 66 X no. 1.
See the two previous numbers. It is possible that this was the first version of the watercolour described under the following number. See also no. 94.

107 [symbol] 27/35 [symbol] Barcelona 1903-4 [symbol]

101

102

103 [Plate XX]

104

105   106   107   108 [Plate XXI]

The Poor Man's Meal
Detroit (Mich.), Private collection.
Previous owner: Pellequer, Paris.
Bibliography: L 28, Z 32 no. 210, DB 66 X no. 2.
Indian ink and watercolour on paper. See the three previous numbers.

108 ⊕ 86 36 ▤ Barcelona 1904 ⦂

The Madman
Barcelona, Picasso Museum.
Previous owners: Junyent, Barcelona; Plandiura, Barcelona; Museo de Arte Moderno, Barcelona.
Exhibitions: 60 P.
Bibliography: Z 32 no. 232, CP 50, B 55, S 63, D 64, DB 66 X no. 6, P 66.
The dedication on the left reads: "A mi buen/amigo Sebastián/Junyent/Picasso" Executed on two sheets of yellowish paper gummed together. See Plate XXI.

109 ⊕ 49,5 38 ▤ Barcelona 1904 ⦂

Portrait of Jaime Sabartés
Oslo, Private collection.
Previous owner: Sabartés, Paris.
Bibliography: Z 54 no. 653, DB 66 X no. 11.

The dedication in the top left-hand corner reads: "Al amigo Sabartés/Picasso 1904".

110 ⊕ 45 24,5 ▤ Barcelona March 1904 ⦂

Portrait of Luis Vilaro
Switzerland, Private collection.
Previous owners: Vilaro, Barcelona; has been on loan to the Kunsthaus, Zurich, since 1965, from the present owner.
Bibliography: Z 32 no. 164, S 48-55, DB 66 X no. 12.
The inscription on the back reads: "Al amigo/recuerdo de/Picasso/15 Mz 1904".

111 ⊕ 36 26 ▤ 1904 ⦂

Solitude
New York, Chrysler Collection.
Previous owner: Perls, New York.
Bibliography: DB 66 XI no. D 2.
Executed in Barcelona or Paris.

112 ⊕ 36 26 ▤ Paris 1904 ○○

Old Man with Child
Whereabouts unknown.
Previous owner: Lefèvre, Paris.
Bibliography: Z 32 no. 237, DB 66 XI no. D 3.

109   110

111   112

113 ⊕ 36 26,5 ▤ 1903 o 1904 ⦂

Poor Children
New York, J. K. Thannhauser Collection.
Previous owner: Thannhauser, Lucerne.
Bibliography: Z 32 no. 185, DB 66 XI no. D 1.
Executed in Barcelona or Paris.

114 ⊕ — ▤ Paris 1904 ○○

Boy with Bucket
New York, owned by the heirs of Gertrude Stein.
Previous owner: Gertrude Stein, Paris.
Bibliography: Z 32 no. 227, S 48-55, DB 66 XI no. 1.
Dimensions not given.

115 ⊕ ▤ Paris 1904 ○○

Poor Children
Whereabouts unknown.
Previous owner: Vömel, Düsseldorf.
Bibliography: Z 32 no. 219, DB 66 XI no. D 2.
Indian ink and watercolour on paper. Dimensions unknown. It is similar in composition to the watercolour described under the following number.

116 ⊕ 37 27 ▤ Paris 1904 ⦂

Poor Children
New York, Museum of Modern Art.
Previous owners: Level, Paris; Leperrier, Paris; Pellequer, Paris; Eumorphopoulos, London; Thannhauser, New York; Knoedler, New York; Josten, New York.
Exhibitions: 57 NY.
Bibliography: L 28, Z 32 no. 218, B 57, K 65, DB 66 XI no. 3.
The same composition as the painting described above. On the back of the sheet which is used the other way up, is the watercolour *Woman Leaning on Folded Arms*, which is described here under the following number. Sold at Sotheby's, London, in 1940 for £210.

117 ⊕ 27 37 ▤ Paris 1904 ⦂

Woman Leaning on Folded Arms
New York, Museum of Modern Art.
Exhibitions: 57 NY.
Bibliography: L 28, Z 32 no. 231, B 57, DB 66 XI no. 4.
On the back of the watercolour *Poor Children* described above, where the list of previous owners is given. The sheet, here, is used the other way up.

118 ⊕ 36 26 ▤ Paris 1904 ○○

The Suicide
Zurich, Bollag Collection.
Bibliography: Z 54 no. 617, DB 66 XI no. D 9.
Indian ink and watercolour on paper.

119 ⊕ 100 81 ▤ Paris 1904 ○○

The Couple
Ascona, Private collection.
Previous owners: Thannhauser, Munich; Mayer, Zurich.
Exhibitions: 32 Z, 53 M.
Bibliography: L 28, Z 32 no. 224, C 40, S 48-55, R 53, EM 55, DB 66 XI no. 5.
See Plate XXII.

120 ⊕ 34,5 23,5 ▤ Paris 1904 ○○

Couple with Child
Whereabouts unknown.
Previous owner: Lefèvre, Paris.
Bibliography: Z 32 no. 238, DB 66 XI no. D 4.
Indian ink and watercolour on paper.

121 ⊕ 37 26 ▤ Paris 1904 ○○

Couple with Children
Whereabouts unknown.
Previous owner: Dutilleul,

124   125 [Plate XXIII]

Paris.
Bibliography: Z 54 no. 615, DB 66 XI no. D 5.
Indian ink and watercolour on paper.

122 ⊕ 35,5 26 ▤ Paris 1904 ⦂

Couple with Child
Marseille, Private collection.
Exhibitions: 59 M.
Pencil and watercolour on paper.

123 ⊕ ▤ Paris 1904 ⦂

The Eviction
Paris, Private collection.
Previous owner: Lewisohn, New York.
Bibliography: DB 66 XI no. D 7.
Indian ink and gouache on card: dimensions not known.

124 ⊕ 37 51,5 ▤ Paris 1904 ○○

The Laundress
New York, Chrysler Collection.
Previous owner: Hessel, Paris.
Bibliography: Z 32 no. 248, DB 66 XI no. D 11.

125 ⊕ 116 72,5 ▤ Paris 1904 ○○

The Laundress
New York, J. K. Thannhauser Collection.
Previous owner: Thannhauser, Munich.
Exhibitions: 39 NY, 57 NY.
Bibliography: L 28, Z 32 no. 247, B 39, B 46, CP 50, L 52-54, B 57, B 64, D 64, DB 66 XI no. 6.
See Plate XXIII for which the photographic originals were kindly provided by the Guggenheim Museum with the permission of the Thannhauser Foundation.

126 ⊕ 46 31 ▤ Paris 1904 ⦂

The Blind Old Man and Little Girl, Both Nude
Küsnacht, Burgauer Collection.
Previous owner: Bollag, Zurich.
Bibliography: G 51, Z 54 no. 631, DB 66 XI no. D 20.
Indian ink and watercolour on paper.

127 ⊕ 35 26,5 ▤ Paris 1904 ⦂

Nude Woman and Child
Cambridge (Mass.), Harvard University, Fogg Art Museum.
Previous owners: Matisse, New York; Wertheim, New York.
Bibliography: Z 32 no. 239, K 65, B 66 XI no. D 19.
Coloured pencil and watercolour on paper.

128 ⊕ 35,5 25,5 ▤ Paris 1904 ⦂

Mother and Child
Budapest, Szépművészeti Múzeum.
Previous owner: Hatvany, Budapest.
Bibliography: DB 66 XI

no. 21.
Indian ink and watercolour on paper.

129   Paris 1904

Mother and Child Adorned with Garlands
Paris, Private collection.
Previous owner: Pellequer, Paris.
Bibliography: Z 32 no. 229, DB 66 XI no. 20.

130   Paris 1904

Portrait of Sebastián Junyer Vidal
Barcelona, Picasso Museum.
Previous owners: Plandiura, Barcelona; Museo de Arte Moderno, Barcelona.
Exhibitions: 53 L.
Bibliography: Z 32 no. 214, M 42-48, CP 50, S 63, DB 66 XI no. 15, P 66.
This picture bears an apocryphal signature.

131  Paris 1904

Woman with her Hair Up
Chicago (Ill.), Art Institute.
Previous owners: Gold, Berlin; Johnson, Chicago; Brewster, Chicago.
Exhibitions: 36 NY, 37 C, 39 NY, 57 NY.
Bibliography: R 21, Z 32 no. 233, B 39, B 46, S 48-55, CP 50, B 55, EM 55, B 57, DB 66 XI no. 7.
See Plate XXIV.

132 Paris 1904

Girl Child with Crow
Toledo (Ohio), Museum of Art.
Previous owners: Guillaume, Paris; Drummond Libbey, Toledo (Ohio).
Exhibitions: 32 P, 32 Z, 36 NY, 37 C, 39 NY, 53 L, 53 M, 57 NY.
Bibliography: Z 32 no. 240, B 39, B 46, CP 50, EM 55, DB 66 XI no. 10.
Gouache and pastel on paper stuck to cardboard. The model for it was the young girl Margot, daughter of the landlord of the "Lapin Agile", Frédé (see no. 197), who later married Pierre Mac Orlan, and died in 1963. See also the following number. See Plate XXV, for which the photographic originals were kindly provided by the Museum of Art at Toledo, to which the painting was donated by Mr Edward Drummond Libbey.

133   Paris 1904

Girl with Crow
Whereabouts unknown.
Previous owner: Sainsère, Paris.
Exhibition: 66 P.
Gouache and pastel on paper. A copy of the work described above, executed "after a few days' interval", according to the catalogue of a show in Paris in 1966–7, where this painting was mentioned for the first time.

134 Paris 1904

Portrait of Gaby Baur
Paris, Private collection.
Previous owners: Junyer Vidal, Barcelona; Matthiesen London.
Exhibitions: 60 L.

113

114

115

116

117

118

119 [Plate XXII]

120

121

122

123

126

127

128

129

130

131 [Plate XXIV]

132 [Plate XXV]

133

97

134

137

138

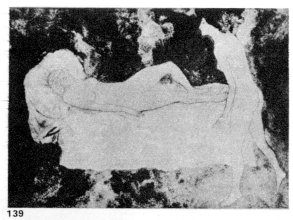

139

140

141

142

147

Bibliography: Z 32 no. 215, CP 50, DB 66 XI no. 17.

This picture bears an apocryphal signature. The subject depicted was the wife of the actor Harry Baur.

135 ⊕ 14,5 13,5 ☰ Paris 1904 ⦂

Portrait of Suzanne Bloch
Ascona, Neuburg-Coray Collection.

Bibliography: DB 66 XI no. 16.

Indian ink and watercolour on paper. This picture is also called, wrongly, *Portrait of Colette.* See the following number.

---

136 ⊕ 65 54 ☰ Paris 1904 ⦂

Portrait of Suzanne Bloch
São Paulo, Museu de Arte.

Previous owners: Sichowski, London; Bieber, Lugano.

Exhibitions: 13 M.

Bibliography: D 30, Z 32 no. 217, S 48-55, C 58, C 59, DB 66 XI no. 18.

Suzanne Bloch was the sister of the violinist Henri Bloch and a well known Wagnerian singer. See Plate XXVI.

137 ⊕ 34 24 ☰ Paris 1904 ⦂

Kneeling Nude

Liège, Graindorge Collection.

Previous owners: Poissonnier, Paris; Thompson, Pittsburgh (Pa.).

Bibliography: Z 54 no. 632, DB 66 XI no. D 21.

Coloured pencil and watercolour on paper.

138 ⊕ 55 38 ☰ Paris 1904 ⦂

The Friends
Paris, Private collection.

Previous owner: Richet, Paris.

Exhibition: 55 P.

Bibliography: S 48-55, Z 54 no. 652, EM 55, DB 66 XI no. 8.

A variation of the theme is shown in the watercolour under the following number.

139 ⊕ — ☰ Paris 1904 ⦂

The Friends
Whereabouts unknown.

Bibliography: DB 66 XI no. 9.

Dimensions unknown. See also the preceding number.

140 ⊕ 36 26 ☰ Paris 1904 ⦂

Contemplation
Paris, Helft Collection.

Bibliography: Z 32 no. 234, DB 66 XI no. 11.

Indian ink and watercolour on paper signed in 1924. The same theme with variations is depicted in the painting given under the following number.

141 ⊕ 37 27 ☰ Paris 1904 ⦂

Contemplation
New York, Bertram Smith Collection.

Previous owners: Pellequer, Paris; Furthman, New York.

Exhibitions: 36 NY, 57 NY, 58 F, 64 T.

Bibliography: L 28, Z 32 no. 235, CP 50, B 57, P 58, DB 66

XI no. 12.

Indian ink and watercolour on paper: the male figure is a self-portrait. See also the preceeding number.

142 ⊕ 95 145 ☰ Paris 1904 ⦂

"Les Noces de Pierrette"
Whereabouts unknown.

Previous owners: Stransky, New York; Renand, Paris.

Bibliography: Z 32 no. 212, BP 62, DB 66 XI no. 22.

With this picture which, according to information given in DB 66, has in fact been destroyed, the Blue Period ends.

---

143 ⊕ 61,5 47 ☰ Paris 1904 ⦂

Vase with Flowers
Los Angeles (Cal.), Goetz Collection.

Previous owner: Salz, New York.

Bibliography: DB 66 XI no. 14.

Written on the back in Picasso's own hand is the inscription "Collection privée de l'artiste".

144 ⊕ 61,5 47 ☰ Paris 1904 ⦂

Vase with Flowers
Rochester (NY), Rochester University, Memorial Art

135

136 [Plate XXVI]

146

151

143

144

148

149

Gallery.

Previous owners: Guillaume, Paris; Stransky, New York; Sibley Watson, Rochester.

Bibliography: Z 32 no. 241, DB 66 XI no. 13.

Gouache and watercolour on paper.

145 ⊕ 36/26 ▤ Paris 1904 ⁞

Profile of a Woman
New York, J. K. Thannhauser Collection.

Previous owner: Gaffé, Brussels.

Bibliography: Z 32 no. 221, DB 66 XI no. D 12.

146 ⊕ 37,5/26,5 ▤ Paris 1904 ⁞

The Kiss
Göteborg, Konstmuseum.

Previous owner: Turitz, Göteborg.

Bibliography: DB 66 XI no. 19.

On the painting, in Picasso's own hand, is the date "7 Septiembre 1904".

147 ⊕ 54,5/44 ▤ Paris 1904 ⁞

"Hôtel de l'Quest"
Los Angeles (Cal.), Goetz Collection.

Previous owners: Libaude, Paris; Perls, Paris; Chrysler, New York.

Bibliography: Z 32 no. 213, DB 66 XI no. D 16.

Pencil and watercolour on paper. An inscription in the artist's hand in the bottom left-hand corner: "Esquisse pour/ Hôtel de l'Quest, Chambre 22". This project for a poster, which was not carried out, was for the comedy of the same name by G. Coquiot and J. Lorrain, given at the Grand Guignol, Paris, on 28 May 1904.

148 ⊕ 73/60 ▤ Paris 1904 ⁞

"Sainte Roulette"
USA, Private collection.

Previous owner: Perls, New York.

Bibliography: Z 54 no. 616, DB 66 XI no. D 14.

This project was for a poster, which was not carried out, for the comedy *Sainte Roulette* by G. Coquiot and J. Lorrain, given in Paris at the Théâtre Molière, on 10 October 1904. See also the following number.

149 ⊕ — ▤ Paris 1904 ⁞

"Sainte Roulette"
Whereabouts unknown.

Bibliography: DB 66 XI no. D 15.

Dimensions unknown. See the poster given under the preceeding number. This is a second sketch for the same project.

150 ⊕ 37/27 ▤ Paris 1904 ⁞

Portrait of Manuel Hugué
Property of the artist.

Bibliography: L 28, Z 32 no. 211, CP 50, D 61, DB 66 XI no. D 10.

Indian ink with a watercolour background on paper. Manuel (Manolo) Hugué, a long standing friend of Picasso, was a Spanish sculptor who had made his home among the artists of Montmartre.

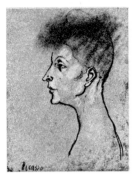

145

151 ⊕ 43,5/34,5 ▤ Paris 1904 ⁞

Portrait of Angel Fernández de Soto with Female Figure
Columbus (Ohio), Gallery of Fine Arts.

Previous owners: Dudensing, New York; Howald, Columbus (Ohio).

Bibliography: DB 66 XI no. D 18.

The signature is possibly apocryphal.

152 ⊕ — ▤ Paris 1904 ⁞

154 [Plate XXVII]

155

156

150

154 A

155 A

157

Self-Portrait with Pipe
Whereabouts unknown.

Previous owner: Junyent, Barcelona.

Bibliography: S 54, DB 66 XI no. D 28.

Indian ink and watercolour on paper. Dimensions unknown. The inscription at the top reads: "A Sebastiá Junyent/Picasso"; and the one at the bottom left reads: "Paris Diciembre/1904"; and below that is written: "Mi retrato".

153 ⊕ 17/10,5 ▤ Paris — ⁞

152

Self-Portrait with Pipe
Paris, whereabouts unknown.

Previous owner: Maar, Paris.

Bibliography: DB 66 XI no. D 29.

Indian ink and watercolour on paper. Executed in the winter of 1904–5.

154 ⊕ 194/112 ▤ Paris ⁞

The Actor
New York, Metropolitan Museum of Art.

Previous owners: Leffmann, Cologne; Private collection, Germany; Perls, New York; Rosenberg, Paris; Knoedler, New York; Chrysler Foy, New York.

Exhibition: 39 NY.

Bibliography: R 21, Z 32 no. 291, B 39, L 52-54, EM 55, P 58, B 64, DB 66 XII no. 1.

Executed in the winter of 1904–5.

A sketch for this painting, 154 A, in pencil, 47 × 31·5 cm, signed, previously belonging to Gertrude Stein (Paris), Alice Toklas (Paris), Valentin (New York) and Rockefeller (New York), and now in the hands of a private collector in New York, was shown in the exhibitions 57 NY and 58 F, and was published in Z 54 no. 681, B 57, BP 62 and DB 66 XII no. 2. On the same sheet, together with other brief sketches, are two female profiles: these are the first known sketches of Fernande Olivier (see no. 247). See Plate XXVII. The painting was donated to the Metropolitan Museum by Mrs Thelma Chrysler Foy in 1952.

155 ⊕ 65/50,5 ▤ Paris 1905 ⁞

Mother and Child
Paris, Private collection.

Previous owners: Sainsère, Paris; Richet, Paris.

Exhibition: 66 P.

Bibliography: S 48-55, B 55, B 64, K 65, DB 66 XII no. 4.

Related to this picture is the sketch, 155 A, in pencil, *Mother and Child with a study of hands*, 34·4 × 26·6 cm which is well known and more often illustrated (Z 32 no. 220; K 65; DB 66 XI no. D 26), and is today in the Fogg Art Museum, Harvard University, Cambridge (Mass.). It is signed and dated 1904.

156 ⊕ 106/76 ▤ Paris 1905 ⁞

Seated Nude
Paris, Musée National d'Art Moderne.

Previous owners: Gertrude Stein, Paris; Matisse, New York; Chrysler, New York.

Bibliography: Z 32 no. 257,

153

C 40, S 48-55, C 59, D 60, DB 66 XII no. 3.

157 ⊕ 72,5/60 ▤ Paris 1905 ⁞

Woman Wearing a Chemise
London, Tate Gallery.

Previous owners: Kahnweiler, Paris; Flechtheim, Berlin; Stoop, London.

Exhibitions: 32 P, 32 Z, 60 L, 66 P.

Bibliography: Z 32 no. 307, S 48-55, G 51, EM 55, C 58, K 65 DB 66 XII no. 5.

158 [Plate XXX]

158 ⊕ 23,5/18 ▤ Paris 1905 ⁞

Young Acrobat and Child
New York, J. K. Thannhauser Collection.

Bibliography: Z 54 no. 718, K 65, DB 66 XII no. 15.

Gouache and watercolour on paper. The inscription at the bottom right reads: "A Mlle./A. Nachmann/Picasso/Paris 26 March 05". This is the first painting which belongs completely to the Rose Period. See Plate XXX, for which the photographic originals were kindly provided by the Guggenheim Museum, with the

159

160

161

162

163

164

165 [Plate XXXIV]

165 A

Paris, Private Collection.
Previous owners: Bignou,
Paris; Rothschild, Paris.
Bibliography: DB 66 XII
no. 10.
Indian ink and watercolour on
paper. Dimensions unknown.
Reproduced in the periodical *La
Plume* of 15 May 1905.

169 ⊗ 31,5 / 23,5 ▤ Paris 1905 ⁞

The Acrobat's Meal
New York, Private collection.
Previous owners: Reber,
Lausanne; Clark, New York.
Exhibition: 36 NY.
Bibliography: Z 32 no. 292,
DB 66 XII no. 14.
Gouache and watercolour on
paper.

170 ⊗ 105 / 76 ▤ Paris 1905 ⁞

**Acrobat and Young
Harlequin**
Belgium, Private collection.
Previous owner: Städtisches
Museum, Wuppertal.
Exhibition: 66 P.
Bibliography: Z 32 no. 297,
C 59, DB 66 XII no. 9.
This picture was reproduced
in *La Plume* of 15 May 1905.
It was confiscated by the
Nazis in 1937 and was put on
sale on 30 June 1939 at the
Fischer Gallery, Lucerne, in an
auction sale of paintings and
sculptures of modern masters
from German museums. See
Plate XXIX.

171 ⊗ 57 / 41 ▤ Paris 1905 ⁞

Small Child with Dog
Leningrad, Hermitage.
Previous owners: Shchukine,
Moscow; Museum of Modern
Art, Moscow.
Bibliography: Z 32 no. 306,
K 65, DB 66 XII no. 16.

permission of the Thannhauser
Foundation.

159 ⊗ 69 / 54 ▤ Paris 1905 ⁞

**Harlequin and his
Companion**
USA, Private collection.
Previous owner: Fleischmann,
Zurich.
Bibliography: Z 54 no. 702,
DB 66 XII no. 12.

160 ⊗ 29,5 / 21 ▤ Paris 1905 ⁞

Harlequin's Family
New York, Payson Collection.
Previous owners: Private
collection, Cologne; Knoedler,
New York.
Bibliography: Z 32 no. 244,
BP 62, DB 66 XII no. 11.
Indian ink and watercolour on
paper. Sold at Sotheby's,
London, on 25 November 1959,
for £12,000.

161 ⊗ 58 / 43,5 ▤ Paris 1905 ⁞

Harlequin's Family
Washington, DC, Eisenstein
Collection.
Previous owner: Lewisohn,
New York.
Exhibitions: 36 NY, 39 NY.
Bibliography: D 30, Z 32 no.
298, B 39, L 52-54, B 55, EM 55,
K 65, DB 66 XII no. 6.
Indian ink and gouache on
paper. Picasso made the etching
La Toilette de la mère in 1905
on the same theme.

162 ⊗ 22 / 29 ▤ Paris 1905 ⁞

A Family of Acrobats
Germany, Private collection.
Previous owner: Schnitzler,
Frankfurt.
Bibliography: Z 32 no. 289,
DB 66 XII no. 13.

163 ⊗ 50 / 32 ▤ Paris 1905 ⁞

The Ape
Baltimore (Md.), Museum of
Art, Cone Collection.
Previous owner: Cone,
Baltimore.
Exhibitions: 57 NY, 58 F.
Bibliography: B 57, DB 66
XII no. D 1.
Indian ink and watercolour on
paper. This could be a study for
no. 165.

164 ⊗ 16 / 14 ▤ Paris 1905 ⁞

166

166

**Violinist with Family and
Ape**
Baltimore (Md.), Museum of
Art, Cone Collection.
Previous owner: Cone,
Baltimore.
Bibliography: DB 66 XIII
no. 7.
Indian ink and watercolour on
paper.

165 ⊗ 104 / 75 ▤ Paris 1905 ⁞

Family of Acrobats with Ape
Göteborg, Konstmuseum.
Previous owner: Pineus,
Göteborg.
Exhibition: 66 P.
Bibliography: Z 32 no. 299,
S 38, S 48-55, EM 55, P 58,
BP 62, K 65, DB 66 XII no. 7.
Indian ink, gouache, water-
colour and pastel on cardboard.
There could well be a relation-
ship between this painting and
the ink drawing, 165 A, signed,
18·5 × 12·5 cm, owned by a
private collector in the United
States (DB 66 XII no. D 3), from
which in the same year 1905
Picasso incised on the reverse a
dry point with the title *La
Famille de Saltimbanques au
macaque.* See also the previous
two numbers. See Plate
XXXIV.

166 ⊗ 16,5 / 10 ▤ Paris 1905 ⁞

**Actress with Child at her
Breast**
Preston, Kessler Collection.
Previous owner: Stoop,
London.
Bibliography: DB 66 XII
no. D 8.
Indian ink and watercolour on
paper.

167 ⊗ 90 / 71 ▤ Paris 1905 ⁞

Mother and Child
Stuttgart, Staatsgalerie.
Previous owners: Gertrude

Stein, Paris; Gaspari, Munich;
Muthmann, Nassau; Nathan,
Zurich.
Exhibition: 55 M.
Bibliography: R 21, Z 32 no.
296, S 48-55, B 55, K 65,
DB 66 XII no. 8.
On the back of the canvas is
painted the oil painting
Crouching Woman of 1902 (no.
26). See Plate XXVIII.

168 ⊗ — ▤ Paris 1905 ⁞

Seated Harlequin

167 [Plate XXVIII]

170 [Plate XXIX]

169

174 [Plate XXXIII]

172 ⊘ 105,5 / 75 ▤ Paris 1905 ⁞

Young Harlequin and Child with Dog
New York, Burden Collection.
Previous owners:
Thannhauser, Paris; Ludington, Santa Barbara (Cal.).
Exhibitions: 39 NY, 57 NY.
Bibliography: Z 32 no. 300, B 39, B 46, L 52-54, EM 55, B 57, K 65, DB 66 XII no. 17.
Reproduced in the periodical *La Plume* of 15 May 1905.

173 ⊘ 54 / 44 ▤ Paris 1905 ⁞

The Athlete
Paris, Private collection.
Previous owners: Sainsère, Paris; Richet, Paris.
Exhibitions: 55 P, 66 P.
Bibliography: EM 55, DB 66 XII no. 20.
The dedication in the top left-hand corner reads: "A Paul Fort/Picasso". There is a signed study for this picture in the Museum of Art in Baltimore, 173 A (DB 66 XII no. D 21), in pen and watercolour, 31 × 24 cm.

174 ⊘ 147 / 95 ▤ Paris 1905 ⁞

Acrobat and Young Equilibrist
Moscow, Pushkin Museum.
Previous owners: Gertrude Stein, Paris; Kahnweiler, Paris; Morosov, Moscow; Museum of Modern Western Art, Moscow.
Exhibitions: 54 P, 60 L.
Bibliography: R 21, L 28, Z 32 no. 290, S 38, S 48-55, EM 55, KP 55, P 58, D 60, BP 62, B 64, D 64, K 65, DB 66 XII no. 19.
In 1913 this picture was sold for 16,000 francs. See Plate XXXIII.

175 ⊘ 70 / 54 ▤ Paris 1905 ⁞

Young Clown
Paris, Private collection.
Previous owner: Rothschild, Paris.
Bibliography: Z 32 no. 293, DB 66 XII no. 26.
He also depicted this sitter in one of his first bronzes, modelled in the same year, 1905 – 175 A, the *Tête de Fou*, 41 cm. high (Z 32 no. 322).

176 ⊕ ▤ Paris 1905 ⁞

Young Clown with Child
Paris, owned by the heirs of Guillaume Apollinaire,
Previous owner: Guillaume Apollinaire, Paris.
Bibliography: DB 66 XII no. D 4.
Indian ink and coloured pencil on paper. Dimensions not given. A dedication in the artist's hand reads: "Picasso/à Guillaume/Apollinaire/1905".

177 ⊕ 16,5 / 12,5 ▤ Paris 1905 ⁞

The Clown's Family with Accordion
Washington DC, Bliss Collection.
Previous owners: Fernande Olivier, Paris; Sarah Stein, Paris.
Bibliography: DB 66 XII no. D 5.
Indian ink, coloured pencil and watercolour on paper. The

171

172

173

173 A

dedication in the top right-hand corner reads: "Pour Fernande/Pablo".

178 ⊘ 190,5 / 108 ▤ Paris 1905 ⁞

Young Clown and Small Harlequin
Merion (Pa.), Barnes Foundation.
Bibliography: Z 32 no. 301, DB 66 XII no. 25.

179 ⊘ 51 / 39,5 ▤ Paris 1905 ⁞

The King
Stuttgart, Staatsgalerie.
Previous owner: Borst, Stuttgart.
Bibliography: Z 32 no. 245, BP 62, DB 66 XII no. 21.
In Z 32 no. 246 is published a sketch in pencil, 17 × 10 cm, formerly in the Museum of Modern Western Art and now in the Pushkin Museum in Moscow. This deals with the same subject, but in this case the crown, which is closed in on top almost in the form of a tiara, is decorated with nude figures.

See Plate XLII.

180 ⊕ 24 / 30,5 ▤ Paris 1905 ⁞

Family of Acrobats
Baltimore (Md.), Museum of Art, Cone Collection.
Previous owner: Cone, Baltimore.
Exhibitions: 57 NY, 58 F.
Bibliography: L 52-54, R 53, EM 55, B 57, K 65, DB 66 XII no. 18.
Indian ink and watercolour on paper. Engraved by Picasso as a

dry point in same year of 1905. See Plate XXXV. See also no. 182.

181 ⊕ 18 / 11,5 ▤ Paris 1905 ⁞

Young Clown and Actress with Amphora
New York, Lehman Collection.
Previous owner: Knoedler, New York.
Bibliography: DB 66 XII no. D 6.
Indian ink and watercolour on paper.

175

175 A

179 [Plate XLII]

179 A

176

177

178

181

180 [Plate XXXV]

182

183

185

185 A

189

190

191

192 [Plates XXXVI–XXXVII]

192 A

192 B

193 [Plate XXXI]

182 ⊕ 9.5 / 10.5 ▤ Paris 1905 ⦂

Family of Acrobats
Wuppertal, Von der Heydt-Museum.
Previous owner: Flechtheim, Dusseldorf.
Bibliography: Z 32 no. 281, CP 50, DB 66 XII no. D 2.
Indian ink and watercolour on paper. Zervos lists it as a study for painting no. 180.

183 ⊕ 19 / 13 ▤ Paris 1905 ○ ○

Ex-Libris of Guillaume Apollinaire
Whereabouts unknown.
Previous owners: Guillaume Apollinaire, Paris; Flechtheim, Berlin; Cooper, London; Buchholz, New York; Chrysler, New York.
Exhibitions: 32 Z, 39 NY.
Bibliography: Z 32 no. 225, B 39, BP 62, DB 66 XII no. D 9.
Indian ink and watercolour on paper. It is signed with the words "Picasso/fecit" and is inscribed along the bottom "Ex-libris". In the top right-hand corner there also appears the name "Apollinaire". It is possible that the photograph does not reproduce the entire page, and it is probable that "Guillaume" was written in the top left-hand corner, before the surname.

184 ⊕ 23 / 15 ▤ Paris 1905 ○ ○

Seated Clown
Whereabouts unknown.
Previous owner: Perls, New York.
Bibliography: Z 54 no. 734, B 55, DB 66 XII no. D 18.
Indian ink and watercolour on paper. The same composition was incised by Picasso, in the same year of 1905, as a dry point entitled *Le Saltimbanque au repos*. As in nos. 186, 188, 190 and 192, the figure of the clown is drawn from real life in the circus. In DB 66 XII no. 30 is reproduced an ink sketch, 184 A, 25·5 × 21·5 cm, owned by Hault, New York. In this sketch the same subject appears brandishing a rapier (whence the title *Bouffon à la rapière*).

and there is an inscription in Picasso's hand reading "Eltio Pepe Don José/a 40 años". In addition, and apart from the one indicated in no. 188 A, three other designs in which the same model appears are known: 184 B, in pencil, signed, and authenticated by the artist on 17 October 1960, 14·5 × 12 cm, once the property of Bollag, Zurich, then of the Rosengart Gallery, Lucerne, and now owned by Sprengel, Hanover. The clown is depicted full-length, giving a sweeping gesture with his right arm (DB 66 XII no. D 20); 184 C, in pencil and indian ink, 31 × 20 cm, in an unknown collection, where Uncle Pepe, without his clown's cap, is drawn seated (Z 54 no. 691); 184 D, in ink, 19 × 17·5 cm, this is also in an unknown collection, and shows a family scene, with Uncle Pepe without his cap, and three or four other figures.

185 ⊕ 32.5 / 24 ▤ Paris 1905 ⦂

Family with Crow
New York, Museum of Modern Art, Newberry Collection.
Previous owners: Berggruen, Paris; Private collection, Basle; Newberry, New York.
Exhibition: 64 T.
Bibliography: Z 54 no. 703, B 55, DB 66 XII no. D 7.
Indian ink and coloured pencil on paper. The same group can be seen, together with another figure relative to the acrobats no. 192, in a pencil sketch, 185 A, 30·5 × 23·5 cm, in an unknown collection (Z 32 no. 279).

186 ⊕ 66 / 56 ▤ Paris 1905 ○ ○

Clown and Young Acrobat
USA, Private collection.
Previous owners: Lichnowsky, Kuchelna (Czechoslovakia); Perls, New

York.
Bibliography: Z 32 no. 284, DB 66 XII no. 28.
Gouache and pastels on paper. See no. 184.

187 ⊕ 60 / 47 ▤ Paris 1905 ⦂

Clown and Young Acrobat
Baltimore (Md.), Museum of Art, Cone Collection.
Previous owners: Thannhauser, Lucerne; Rosengart, Lucerne; Cone, Baltimore.
Bibliography: Z 32 no. 283, EM 55, BP 62, K 65, DB 66 XII no. 29.
Charcoal, pastel and watercolour on paper. See no. 184 and also Plate XXXII.

188 ⊕ 29 / 18.5 ▤ Paris 1905 ⦂

Clown and Young Girl
New York, J. K.

Thannhauser Collection.
Bibliography: Z 54 no. 697, DB 66 XII no. D 19.
See no. 184. In Z 54 no. 689 is published an ink sketch, 188 A, 31 × 24 cm, in an unknown collection, which relates to this watercolour.

189 ⊕ 70.5 / 47.5 ▤ Paris 1905 ⦂

Girl Child with Dog
Los Angeles (Cal.), Goetz Collection.
Previous owners: Thannhauser, Lucerne; Sykes, Cambridge; Kaye, London; Beatty, London; Salz, New York.
Exhibition: 32 Z.
Bibliography: Z 32 no. 286, K 65, DB 66 XII no. 31.
Gouache and pastel on paper. A study for no. 192.

190 ◕ 51 / 61 ▤ Paris 1905 ⦂

184

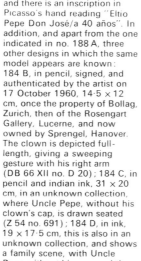
186

187 [Plate XXXII]

188

184 A

184 B

184 C

184 D

188 A

Sketch for "The Acrobats"
Moscow, Pushkin Museum.
Previous owners: Shchukine, Moscow; Museum of Modern Western Art, Moscow.
Bibliography: Z 32 no. 287, DB 66 XII no. 33.
See no. 192.

191 ⊘ 67/51 ▤ Paris 1905 ⁝

Young Woman from Majorca
Moscow, Pushkin Museum.
Previous owners: Shchukine, Moscow; Museum of Modern Western Art, Moscow.
Exhibition: 54 P.
Bibliography: Z 32 no. 288, KP 55, DB 66 XII no. 34.
A study for *The Acrobats* described under the following number.

192 ⊘ 213/229,5 ▤ Parigi 1905 ⁝

The Acrobats
Washington, DC, National Gallery of Art, Dale Collection.
Previous owners: Level, Paris; La Peau de l'Ours, Paris; Koenig, Munich; Dale, New York.
Bibliography: L 28, Z 32 no. 285, B 46, S 48-55, CP 50, G 51, L 52-54, B 55, EM 55, C 58, BP 62, K 65, DB 66 XII no. 35.
For the forerunners of this painting, which ranks as one of the most important of Picasso's early period, see previous numbers, from no. 189 onwards. Another sketch, 192 A, appears in red chalk, *Young boy with Wine Cask*, signed, 49·5 × 31·5 cm, formerly the property of Suermondt, Aachen, and Fine Arts Associates, New York, and now in the possession of Pulitzer, St Louis (Mo.) (DB 66 XII no. 32). Yet another sketch, 192 B, is related to this picture. This is published in Z 32 no. 280, accompanied by the information that it was once in the possession of Level, Paris. See Plates XXXVI–XXXVII.

193 ⊘ 100/70 ▤ Paris 1905 ⁝

The Hurdy-Gurdy Player and Young Harlequin
Zurich, Kunsthaus.
Exhibitions: 53 M, 60 P, 66 P.
Bibliography: Z 54 no. 798, EM 55, BP 62, K 65, DB 66 XII no. 22.
The traditional date is 1906, but stylistically it relates to 1905. The title assigned to it at the big exhibition in Milan in 1953 was: *Seated Acrobat with Young Boy*. Bought in 1942 for 10,000 Swiss francs. See Plate XXXI.

194 ⊘ 59/78 ▤ Paris 1905 ⁝

Young Equestrienne
Property of the Artist.
Exhibitions: 32 P, 32 Z, 66 P.
Bibliography: G 51, DB 66 XII no. D 15.
An ink sketch of the same subject, 23·9 × 30·9 cm (DB 66 XII no. D 14), is to be found in the Cone Collection at the Museum of Art in Baltimore. (Md.). See Plate XXXIX.

195 ⊘ 22/13 ▤ Paris 1905 ⊙

194 [Plate XXXIX]

Picasso

194 A

Harlequin on Horseback
Whereabouts unknown.
Previous owner: Lefèvre, Paris.
Bibliography: DB 66 XII no. D 11.
A study for the painting described under the following number.

199 · [Plate XLIII]

200

201

195

196 [Plate XXXVIII]

196 ⊘ 100/69 ▤ Paris 1905 ⁝

Harlequin on Horseback
Washington, DC, Mellon Collection.
Previous owners: Level, Paris; Mermod, Lausanne.
Exhibitions: 32 Z.
Bibliography: L 28, Z 32 no. 243, S 48-55, B 55, C 58, C 59, DB 66 XII no. 24.
See also the previous number as well as Plate XXXVIII.

197 ⊘ 99/100,5 ▤ Paris 1905 ⁝

At the "Lapin Agile"
New York, Payson Collection.
Previous owners: Gérard, Paris; Flechtheim, Berlin; De Maré, Stockholm.
Exhibition: 59 M.
Bibliography: Z 32 no. 275, S 48-55, P 58, C 59, BP 62, DB 66 XII no. 23.
This picture was given by the artist to Frédé, the proprietor of the "Lapin Agile" (who is depicted in the background playing the guitar). It remained for a long time hung on the wall of the well-known café in Montmartre. This picture is referred to in *Sandricourt* by Eugène Marsan, where, however, due to a slip of the writer's memory, the woman is called "Columbine". The extract is reproduced on page 11. See Plate XL.

198 ⊘ 65/95 ▤ Paris 1905 ⊙

The Death of Harlequin
Washington, DC, Mellon Collection.
Previous owners: Bought from the artist himself in 1905–6 by W. Uhde, who lent it to Rainer Maria Rilke; then to a private collector in Westphalia; Thannhauser, New York; Somerset Maugham, Cap-Ferrat.
Exhibition: 13 M.
Bibliography: Z 32 no. 302, S 48-55, EM 55, BP 62, K 65, DB 66 XII no. 27.
The signature appears to date from 1911. On the back is an oil painting of 1901 of a *Seated Woman in a Garden*. It was sold

200 ⊘ 78/67,5 ▤ Schoorldam 1905 ⊙

Nude of Young Dutch Girl with Cap

197 [Plate XL]

198 [Plate XLI]

at Sotheby's, London, on 10 April 1962 for £80,000. See Plate XLI.

199 ⊘ 76/66 ▤ Schoorldam 1905 ⁝

Three Dutch Women
Paris, Musée National d'Art Moderne.

202

204

Previous owners: La Peau de l'Ours, Paris; Level, Paris; Lefèvre, Paris.
Exhibition: 66 P.
Bibliography: L 28, Z 32 no 261, DB 66 XIII no. 2.
Written on the back is: "Picasso/Schoorl/1905". See Plate XLIII.

Brisbane, Queensland Art Gallery.
Previous owners: Durio, Barcelona; Thannhauser, Paris; Stang, Oslo; Freshfield, London; Gollancz, London; De Vahl Rubin, London.
Exhibition: 60 L.

203

205

Bibliography: Z 32 no. 260, B 46, S 48-55, B 55, DB 66 XIII no. 1.
Oil, gouache and blue gesso on paper. The dedication in the top left-hand corner reads: "A mi querido amigo/Paco Durio/Picasso/Schoorl".

201 ⊘ 75,5/60 ▤ Schoorldam 1905 ⊙

Full Length Nude with Cap
Whereabouts unknown.
Previous owner:

103

209

210

211 [Plate XLIV]

208 ⊕ 12/19 ▤ Paris 1905 ⋮

The Lovers
New York, Serger Collection.
Previous owners: Christian
Diòr, Paris; Dubourg, Paris.
Bibliography: DB 66 XIII
no. D 5.
   Authenticated by the artist on
14 March 1960. It was a sketch
for the etching *L'étreinte*
executed by Picasso in the same
year of 1905. The watercolour,
which is not reproduced here,
is given in DB 66 page 281.

209 ⊕ — ▤ Paris 1905 ⋮

Profile of a Woman
Baltimore (Md.), Museum of
Art, Cone Collection.
Previous owner: Cone,
Baltimore.
Bibliography: DB 66 XIII
no. D 9.
   Indian ink and watercolour on
paper.

210 ⊕ 36/26,5 ▤ Paris 1905 ⋮

Portrait of Alice Derain
Lucerne, Rosengart Collection.
Previous owner: Von der
Heydt, Ascona.
Exhibition: 32 Z.
Bibliography: Z 32 no. 251,
D 60, B 64, DB 66 XIII no. D 6.
   Indian ink and watercolour on
paper. There is an autographed
dedication in the bottom left-
hand corner: "A Alice!/
Picasso/1905".

211 ⊕ 90,5/70,5 ▤ Paris 1905 ⋮

Portrait of Benedetta Canals
Barcelona, Picasso Museum.
Previous owners: Canals,
Barcelona; Plandiura,
Barcelona; Museo de Arte
Moderno, Barcelona.
Exhibition: 66 P.
Bibliography: Z 32 no. 263,
DB 66 XIII no. 9, P 66.

222

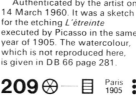

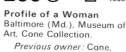

223

218

219

220 [Plate XLVII]

Thannhauser, Paris.
Bibliography: Z 32 no. 255,
DB 66 XIII no. 4.
   The signature in the bottom
left-hand corner is possibly
apocryphal.

202 ⊕ 81/65 ▤ Paris 1905 ⋮

"La Coiffure"
Baltimore (Md.), Museum of
Art, Cone Collection.
Previous owners: Sainy,
Paris; Rosenberg, Paris; Cone,
Baltimore.
Exhibitions: 32 P, 32 Z.
Bibliography: L 28, Z 32,
no 309, G 51, DB 66 XIII no. 3.

203 ⊕ 55/50 ▤ Paris 1905 ⋮

**Nude with her Hand in her
Hair**
Whereabouts unknown.
Previous owner: Gertrude
Stein, Paris.
Bibliography: Z 32 no. 259,
S 48-55, EM 55, DB 66 XIII
no. 5.

204 ⊕ 41/27 ▤ Paris 1905 ⋮

**Nude Woman Dressing her
Hair**
Basle, Staechelin Collection.
Bibliography: DB 66 XIII
no. D 3.

205 ⊕ 39,5/27 ▤ Paris 1905 ⋮

**Seated Nude Dressing her
Hair**
Baltimore (Md.), Museum of
Art, Cone Collection.
Previous owner: Cone,
Baltimore.
Exhibition: 64 T.
Bibliography: DB 66 XIII
no. D 1.

206 ⊕ 26,5/21 ▤ Paris 1905 ⋮

Nude Figures Embracing

Copenhagen, Statens Museum
for Kunst.
Previous owners: Guillaume,
Paris; Tetzen, Lund
(Switzerland).
Bibliography: Z 32 no. 228,
DB 66 XIII no. 6.
   Gouache and watercolour on
paper. This painting, which is
not reproduced here, is shown in
DB 66 page 276.

207 ⊕ — ▤ Paris 1905 ⋮

The Lovers
Paris, owned by heirs of

Guillaume Apollinaire.
Previous owner: Guillaume
Apollinaire, Paris.
Bibliography: DB 66 XIII
no. 7.
   Dimensions not given. The
dedication in the artist's own
hand in the bottom right-hand
corner reads: "A mon cher ami/
Guillaume Apollinaire/Picasso/
1905". This painting which is
not reproduced here is given in
DB 66 page 276. Two studies in
watercolour, signed, 11·5 × 18
cm, are in the possession of
Poissonnier, Paris.

The beautiful Benedetta, who
came from Rome, was the wife
of the Catalan painter Ricardo
Canals who lived in
Montmartre. She had already
been a model for Degas and Paul-
Albert Bartholomé, and in 1895
had posed for the celebrated
Monument to the dead, now at
Père-Lachaise. See Plate XLIV.

212 ⊕ 45/37 ▤ Paris 1905 ⋮

Profile of a Young Boy
Property of the Artist.
Bibliography: Z 32 no. 216,

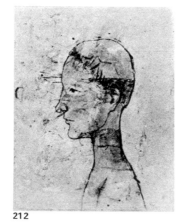

212

213 [Plate XLV]

214

215

216

217 [Plate XLVI]

217 A

221

104

S 48-55, D 61, DB 66 XIII
no. D 11.

Under this painting, but with
the sheet used the other way
up, there are traces of earlier
figures, among which is a
sketch of the *Mistletoe Seller* of
1903, described under no. 50,

213 ⊗ 79,5 / 59,5 ▤ Paris 1905 ⦂

**Profile of a Young Man with
a Lace Collar**
Worcester (Mass.), Art Museum,
on loan from the Dial Collection.
Previous owners: Guillaume,
Paris; Dial, Boston.
Exhibitions: 36 NY, 37 C.

224 [Plate XLVIII]

Bibliography: Z 32 no. 276,
S 48-55, EM 55, DB 66 XIII
no. 19.
See Plate XLV for which the
photographic originals were
kindly provided through the Art
Museum in Worcester

214 ⊗ 77,5 / 65,5 ▤ Paris 1905 ⦂

**Young Man with a Lace
Collar**
New York, Meyer Collection.
Previous owner: Haldsdurk,
Berlin.
Bibliography: Z 32 no. 273,
DB 66 XIII no. 18.

215 ⊗ 54 / 34 ▤ Paris 1905 ⦂

Young Man with Vase
Glens Falls (NY), Hyde
Collection.
Previous owners: Durio,
Barcelona; Flechtheim,
Düsseldorf.
Bibliography: Z 32 no. 272,
S 48-55, DB 66 XIII no. 17.

216 ⊗ 64,5 / 54 ▤ Paris 1905 ⦂

**Young Man with Bunch of
Flowers**
Villanova (Pa.), Wintersteen

225

227 [Plate IL]

228

Collection.
Previous owner: McIlhenny,
Philadelphia (Pa.).
Exhibitions: 47 NY, 58 F,
64 T.
Bibliography: Z 32 no. 262,
DB 66 XIII no. 12.

217 ⊗ 99 / 79 ▤ Paris 1905 ⦂

**Young Man with Garland of
Roses**
New York, Whitney Collection.
Previous owner:
Mendelssohn, Berlin.
Exhibitions: 57 NY, 58 F,
60 L, 66 P.
Bibliography: Z 32 no. 274,
S 48-55, L 52-54, B 57, C 58,
DB 66 XIII no. 13.
This was painted originally as
a portrait of a young Paris
worker. André Salmon in *La
jeune peinture française*, Paris
1912, recounts that: "One
evening Picasso left his friends
and returned to his studio where
he took up a canvas which had
been left neglected for a month,
and added to the figure a crown
of roses. By a sublime caprice,
he had transformed the work
into a masterpiece." An ink
sketch, 217 A, 30 × 23 cm,
signed (DB 66 XIII no. D 10), is

to be found in the Cone
Collection in the Museum of
Art in Baltimore. See Plate
XLVI.

218 ⊕ 14 / 12 ▤ Paris 1905 ⦂

Nude Mother with Child
Baltimore (Md.), Museum of
Art, Cone Collection.
Previous owner: Cone,
Baltimore.
Bibliography: K 65, DB 66
XIII no. D 8.
Indian ink and watercolour on
paper.

219 ⊗ 152 / 65 ▤ Paris 1905 ⦂

**Nude Girl with Basket of
Flowers**
New York, owned by the heirs of
Gertrude Stein.
Previous owners: Leo and
Gertrude Stein, Paris.
Exhibitions: 32 P, 32 Z, 54 P,
59 M, 60 L.
Bibliography: R 21, Z 32 no.
256, S 38, C 40, S 48-55, EM 55,
KP 55, D 60, D 64, DB 66 XIII
no. 8.
The picture is signed. On the
back of the canvas is the
inscription: "Picasso/13 rue

Ravignan/1905". Bought from
Clovis Sagot in 1905 for 150
francs.

220 ⊗ 99 / 81,5 ▤ Paris 1905 ⦂

Woman with a Fan
New York, Harriman Collection.
Previous owners: Gertrude
Stein, Paris; Rosenberg, Paris.
Exhibitions: 32 P, 36 NY,
39 NY, 60 L, 66 P.
Bibliography: R 21, Z 32 no.
308, B 39, G 51, B 55, EM 55,
P 58, DB 66 XIII no. 14.
See Plate XLVII.

221 ⊗ 51 / 41 ▤ Paris 1905 ⦂

**Head and Shoulders of a
Young Boy**
Baltimore, Museum of Art, Cone
Collection.
Previous owner: Cone,
Baltimore.
Bibliography: Z 54 no. 688,
K 65, DB 66 XIII no. 10.

222 ⊗ 70,5 / 52 ▤ Paris 1905 ⦂

Actor and Young Boy
New York, Clark Collection.
Bibliography: Z 32 no. 295,
L 52-54, B 64, DB 66 XIII no. 11.

223 ⊕ 17,5 / 15,5 ▤ Paris 1905 ⦂

Sheet of Sketches
Property of the artist.
Bibliography: DB 66 XIII
no. D 12.
Indian ink and watercolour on
paper. On the back is the
inscription in the artist's own
hand: "Paris 24 décembre 1905/
media noche/Paris Paris Paris".
The sheet contains the sketch
of an acrobat surrounded by
sketches of various other people,
among which is a caricature of
Guillaume Apollinaire.

224 ⊗ 100 / 70 ▤ Paris 1905 ⦂

Acrobat and Still Life
Washington, DC, National
Gallery of Art, Dale Collection.
Previous owner: Dale, New
York.
Bibliography: Z 32 no. 294,
DB 66 XIII no. 20.
See Plate XLVIII for which the
photographic originals were
kindly provided by the National
Gallery of Art in Washington.

225 ⊗ 35 / 24 ▤ Paris 1905 ⦂

Head of a Young Harlequin
Düsseldorf, Private collection.

Previous owner: Vömel,
Düsseldorf.
Exhibitions: 32 Z, 55 M.
Bibliography: L 28, Z 32 no.
252, DB 66 XIII no. 16.

226 ⊗ 41,5 / 32 ▤ Paris 1905 ⦂

Head of a Young Harlequin
Detroit (Mich.), Private
collection.
Previous owners: Doucet,
Paris; Seligmann, New York.
Exhibition: 32 P.
Bibliography: G 51, Z 54 no.
686, DB 66 XIII no. 15.

229

227 ⊗ 99,5 / 55,5 ▤ Paris 1905 ⦂

Young Man in Blue
New York, Warburg Collection.
Previous owners: Flechtheim,
Berlin; Lichnowsky, Kuchelna
(Czechoslovakia); the German
Embassy in London; on loan to
the Kronprinz Palace, Berlin;
Valentin, New York.
Exhibitions: 13 M, 32 P,
36 NY, 38 B, 39 NY.
Bibliography: Z 32 no. 271,
B 39, DB 66 XIII no. 21.
See Plate XLIX.

228 ⊗ 74 / 59,5 ▤ Paris 1906 ⦂

Portrait of Allan Stein
Baltimore (Md.), Museum of
Art, Cone Collection.
Previous owners: Michael
Stein, Vaucresson (Paris);
Cone, Baltimore.
Bibliography: Z 32 no. 353,
S 48-55, K 65, DB 66 XIV no. 2.
Allan was the son of Michael
Stein the brother of Leo and
Gertrude. See also the following
number.

229 ⊗ 27,5 / 17 ▤ Paris 1906 ⦂

230

231

232

233

234

Portrait of Leo Stein
Baltimore (Md.), Museum of Art, Cone Collection.
Previous owners: Leo and Gertrude Stein, Paris; Cone, Baltimore.
Exhibitions: 57 NY, 58 F, 64 T.
Bibliography: Z 32 no. 250, S 48-55, B 57, DB 66 XIV no.
See also *Outline biography,* **1905.**

230 ⊗ 51/34,5 ▤ Paris 1905-6 ⦂

Young Equestrienne and Young Man
Whereabouts unknown.
Previous owner: Tietz, Cologne.
Bibliography: Z 32 no. 269, M 42-48, S 54, DB 66 XIV no. 3.

231 ⊗ 50/32 ▤ Paris 1905-6 ⦂

Young Man with a Horse
London, Tate Gallery.
Previous owner: Stoop, London.
Exhibition: 60 L.

Bibliography: Z 32 no. 270, E 56, DB 66 XIV no. 4.

232 ⊗ 68/52 ▤ Paris 1905-6 ⦂

Nude Young Man
Leningrad, Hermitage.
Previous owner: Museum of Modern Western Art, Moscow.
Bibliography: Z 32 no. 268, DB 66 XIV no. 8.
See also the following numbers up to no. 239.

233 ⊗ 23,5/16,5 ▤ Paris 1905-6 ⦂

Nude Young Man with Horse
Baltimore (Md.), Museum of Art, Cone Collection.
Previous owner: Cone, Baltimore.
Bibliography: DB 66 XIV no. 5.
Pencil and watercolour on paper. A sketch for the composition *Horses Bathing,* no. 239.

234 ⊗ 49/32 ▤ Paris 1905-6 ⦂

Nude Young Man with Horse
Baltimore (Md.), Museum of Art, Cone Collection.
Previous owners: Michael Stein, Vaucresson (Paris); Cone, Baltimore.
Bibliography: G 51, L 52-54, DB 66 XIV no. 6.
A sketch for the composition *Horses Bathing,* no. 239.

235 ⊗ 221/130 ▤ Paris 1905-6 ⦂

Boy Leading a Horse
New York, Paley Collection.
Previous owners: Vollard, Paris; Thannhauser, Lucerne.
Exhibitions: 39 NY, 57 NY.
Bibliography: L 28, Z 32 no. 264, S 38, B 39, C 40, M 42-48, S 48-55, B 55, EM 55, B 57, P 58, BP 62, K 65, DB 66 XIV no. 7.
The first detailed working out of a study for the *Horses Bathing,* no. 239. In Z 32 no. 266 is published a sketch, signed, 24 × 16 cm, of unknown date and whereabouts. See Plate L.

Monte-Carlo.
Bibliography: S 48-55, DB 66 XIV no. 9.
A study for the composition *Horses Bathing,* no. 239.

238 ⊗ 31/49 ▤ Paris 1906 ⦂

Horses Bathing
Paris, Berggruen Collection.
Bibliography: DB 66 XIV no. 15.
A final study before the painting described under the following number.

236 ⊗ 44/30 ▤ Paris 1906 ⦂

Nude Young Man on Horseback
Kusnacht, Kirchheimer Collection.
Previous owner: Bollag, Zurich.
Exhibition: 32 Z.
Bibliography: Z 54 no. 683, DB 66 XIV no. 10.
A study for the composition *Horses Bathing,* no. 239.

237 ⊗ 55/38 ▤ Paris 1906 ⦂

Nude Young Man on Horseback
France, Private collection.
Previous owner: Van Dongen,

239 ⊗ 37,5/58 ▤ Paris 1906 ⦂

Horses Bathing
Worcester (Mass.), Art Museum lent by the Dial Collection.
Previous owners: Flechtheim, Berlin; Dial, Boston.
Exhibitions: 37 C, 39 NY.
Bibliography: Z 32 no. 265, B 39, B 46, EM 55, E 56, DB 66 XIV no. 16.
This picture is the last known stage of the preparatory studies for a projected picture *The Watering-Place* (which was never executed). Apart from the other studies described above (from no. 232 onwards), four other preparatory studies are known. Two of these, 239 A

235 [Plate L]

235 A

240

236

237

241

242

238

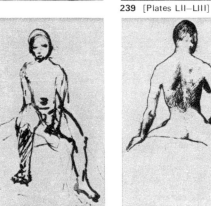

239 [Plates LII–LIII]

239 D

106

239 A

239 B

239 C

239 E

239 F

243

244 [Plate LI]

244 A

244 B

244 C

245

245 A

245 B

245 C

245 D

246

246 A

246 B

247

249

250

248

and B are found on pages 23 and 25 of the *Carnet Catalan* (DB 66 XIV nos. 12 and 13). See also the *Outline biography*. **1906.** The other two are: 239 C, *Horseman from Behind* in charcoal on grey paper, 46·5 × 30·5 cm, signed, once in the possession of Matisse, New York, and now owned by Warrington, Cincinnati (Ohio), exhibited in 39 NY, 57 NY, 58 F and 64 T, published in B 39 and 46, L 52-54, Z 54 no. 682 and DB 66 XIV no. 11: and 239 B *Nude Figures and Horses,* in pencil, 29 × 49·5 cm, once the property of Lewisohn, New York, and now of Chrysler, New York, published in L 52-54 and DB 66 XIV no. 14. Further in

Z 32 no. 267, is published another drawing, 239 E, of a young nude horseman, 30·5 × 23·5 cm, with no indication of the medium, formerly in the possession of Liebman, New York. Lastly a sheet of ink sketches, 239 F, signed and dated "P. 06", 40·5 × 32·5 cm, formerly owned by Gertrude Stein, Paris, then by Curt Valentin, New York, and now by a private collector in New York. It is published in Z 54 no. 864 and DB 66 XIV no. D 1, and includes two caricatures and a brief sketch of a naked horseman which suggests that it may have been executed in relation to this series. From this *Horses Bathing* Picasso made a dry point. See Plates LII–LIII.

240 ⊕ 62/45 ▤ Paris 1906 ○ ○

Vase with Roses
Whereabouts unknown.
Previous owner: Bollag, Zurich.
Bibliography: DB 66 XIV no. D 7.

241 ⊕ 26/21 ▤ Paris 1906 ○ ○

Nude Figures with Child
Whereabouts unknown.
Previous owner: Bollag, Zurich.
Bibliography: DB 66 XIV no. D 5.
Indian ink and coloured pencil on paper. A sketch for the *Blue Vase* described under the following number.

242 ⊕ 31,5/24,5 ▤ Paris 1906 ● ●

The Blue Vase
Zurich, Bollag Collection.
Bibliography: DB 66 XIV no. D 6.
Indian ink and blue pencil on yellow paper. See also the preceding number which is also possibly a preparatory study for a picture which was never executed.

243 ⊕ 25/17 ▤ Paris 1906 ● ○

"La Coiffure"
Los Angeles (Cal.), Private collection.
Previous owner: McLane, Los Angeles.
Bibliography: Z 54 no. 744, DB 66 XIV no. 19.
Gouache and pencil on paper. Possibly a preliminary idea for the painting next described.

244 ⊕ 175/99,5 ▤ Paris 1906 ● ●

"La Coiffure"
New York, Metropolitan Museum of Art.
Previous owners: Vollard, Paris; Perls, Paris; Matisse, New York; Clark, New York; Museum of Modern Art, New York.
Exhibitions: 39 NY, 66 P.
Bibliography: L 28, Z 32 no. 313, B 39, M 42-48, EM 55, BP 62, B 64, DB 66 XIV no. 20.
Although traditionally dated 1905, on stylistic grounds the more probable date is the summer of 1906. The Barnes Foundation in Merion (Pa.) possesses two preparatory sketches for this painting which are still unpublished. Two other sketches relate to this painting: 244 A, ink on paper, signed, 30·9 × 23·9 cm, Cone Collection, Museum of Art, Baltimore (DB 66 XIV no. 17), where only the seated woman with long hair is shown; and 244 B, in pencil and Indian ink on grey paper, signed, 18 × 30

cm, once the property of Jarvis, Portland (G B), and now in the possession of Michael Smith, London (Z 54 no. 741 and DB 66 XIV no. 18). In this study there is a third woman with a child at her breast in addition to the two female figures. Lastly, in Z 32 no. 282 is published a sketch, 244 C, 16·5 × 10·5 cm, once owned by Level, Paris, which is of the same theme, but here the woman is standing. See also the preceding number and Plate LI.

245 ⊕ — ▤ Gósol 1906 ○ ○

Head of a Peasant Woman
Whereabouts unknown.
Previous owner: Stevenson,
Chicago.
Bibliography: Z 54 no. 763, DB 66 XV no. 55.
Gouache and ink on paper: dimensions unknown. Sold at Parke-Bernet's, New York on 4 May 1967 for $6,000. There are four ink sketches relating to this gouache which have been published: 245 A, 21 × 13·5 cm, in the possession of the artist (Z 54 no. 762); 245 B, whose dimensions are not given, also in the possession of the artist (Z 54 no. 764); 245 C, 59 × 43 cm, signed, once the property of Bollag, Zurich, and now in an unknown collection (DB 66 XV no. D 38); 245 D,

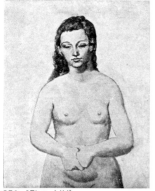

251 [Plate LIV]

252

253

259

21 × 13·5 cm, signed, in the ownership of Berggruen, Paris (DB 66 XV no. D 37).

246 40/30 Gósol 1906
Profile of a Woman
Paris, Berggruen Collection.
Bibliography: DB 66 XV no. D 33.

Indian ink and watercolour on paper. The same profile is found in two published sketches: 246 A, in black gesso, 59·5 × 45 cm, signed twice on the back, once the property of Huldschinsky (Berlin), Furstenberg (Amsterdam), Wildenstein (London), and since 1953 in the National Gallery of Canada in Ottawa, which was exhibited in 64 T and reproduced in DB 66 XV no. D 36, where there is a full-length portrait of the complete female figure; 246 B, ink, 23·5 × 32 cm, signed, and owned (in 1962) by Marlowe, New York, and reproduced in Z 54 no. 633, a sheet of sketches depicting the head and shoulders of a woman, and various other figures.

247 100/81 Gósol 1906
Portrait of Fernande Olivier Bareheaded
Cambridge (Mass.), Private collection.
Previous owner: Saint, Paris.
Exhibition: 39 NY.
Bibliography: L 28, Z 32 no. 254, B 39, B 46, S 48-55, EM 55, DB 66 XV no. 41.

Signed on the back. For other portraits of the same subject see nos. 154, 248–51, 265, 295 and 303, and the *Outline biography*, **1904**.

248 37,5/33 1906
Portrait of Fernande Olivier Bareheaded

260

USA, Private collection.
Bibliography: S 48-55, Z 54 no. 749, DB 66 XV no. 21.

Probably painted at Gósol.

249 81,5/60 Gósol 1906
Portrait of Fernande Olivier with White Headdress
Whereabouts unknown.
Bibliography: Z 54 no. 893, DB 66 XV no. 44.

261 [Plate LV]

250 100/81 Gósol 1906
Portrait of Fernande Olivier with Black Headdress
New York, J. K. Thannhauser Collection.
Bibliography: Z 32 no. 253, DB 66 XV no. 43.

This picture is mentioned in Z 32 (and from that reference in S 54 and in DB 66) with no indication whether it is signed.

251 96/75,5 Gósol 1906
Nude of Fernande Olivier with Clasped Hands
Toronto, Zacks Collection.
Previous owner: Rosengart, Lucerne.
Exhibition: 64 T.
Bibliography: R 21, Z 32 no. 310, M 42-48, S 48-55, DB 66 XV no. 28.

The dedication on the back reads: "A mon vrai ami/ Picasso/ 1er Janvier 1907" The person to whom this dedication was intended is not known. The painting can be assigned to the summer of 1906 although it is more usually dated in 1905. See Plate LIV.

252 48,5/29 Gósol 1906
Nude with Clasped Hands
London, Private collection.
Previous owner: Vollard, Paris.
Bibliography: Z 32 no. 258, P 58, DB 66 XV no. 19.

253 63/48,5 Gósol 1906
Three Nude Figures
New York, Hillman Collection.
Previous owner: Pellequer, Paris.
Bibliography: Z 32 no. 340, M 42-48, DB 66 XV no. 18.

It includes the following rough notes, in Picasso's hand, for a projected picture never in fact carried out. "The walls decorated with murals of landscapes, flowers and fruit"; "a room painted pink – white curtains – a cane sofa such as one finds in Maña – on it large purple cushions – a marble topped table – on it some glasses and a small mirror"; "maybe some muslin drapes"; "the woman holds a cigarette in her hand"; "he has a wine flask in his hand – there a plate of fruit".

254 — Gósol 1906
Nude Young Man
Paris, Berggruen Collection.
Bibliography: Z 54 no. 662, DB 66 XV no. 2.

Indian ink and watercolour on paper: dimensions not given. A study for *The Two Brothers*, no. 258 and for *The Young Men*, no. 259. A preparatory sketch for this is given on page 16 of the *Carnet Catalan* (DB 66 XV no. 1).

255 18/12 Gósol 1906

256

Nude Young Man and Children
London, Roland Collection.
Previous owners: Mayor, London; Coltman, London.
Bibliography: Z 54 no. 713, DB 66 XV no. 4.

Pencil and watercolour on paper. A study for *The Two Brothers*, no. 258. A preparatory sketch is given on page 27 of the *Carnet Catalan* (DB 66 XV no. 3).

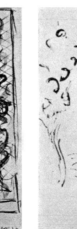

254

254 A

255

255 A

257 [Plate LVI]

258 [Plate LVII]

258 A

258 B

256 ⊘ 31/24 ▤ Gósol 1906 ⋮

Head of a Young Man
Cleveland (Ohio), Museum of Art, Hanna Collection.
Previous owners: Gertrude Stein, Paris; Bohrmann, Berlin; Doucet, Paris; Hanna, New York.
Bibliography: Z 32 no. 303, DB 66 XV no. 7.
On the picture is written the date 1905, but it was probably added by the artist at a later time, and may well be erroneous, since this gouache, because of the subject's identity, would seem to relate rather to the time of the sketches of the *Two Brothers* (no. 258).

257 ⊘ 80,5/60 ▤ Gósol 1906 ⋮

The Two Brothers
Property of the artist.
Exhibitions: 32 P, 32 Z, 66 P.
Bibliography: Z 54 no. 720, DB 66 XV no. 8.
A sketch for *The Two Brothers* described under the following number. See Plate LVI.

258 ⊘ 142/97 ▤ Gósol 1906 ⋮

The Two Brothers
Basle, Kunstmuseum, lent by the Staechelin Foundation.
Exhibition: 55 M.
Bibliography: Z 32 no. 304, M 42-48, D 64, K 65, DB 66 XV no. 9.
This picture is traditionally dated 1905, but it also relates to the time Picasso spent in Gósol. Apart from the other sketches previously given here beginning with no. 254, two other studies relative to this picture are known: 258 A, Indian ink on paper with a red background, 32·5 × 25·5 cm, signed, in the hands of a private Swiss collector (DB 66 XV no. 5), where the two young men are portrayed from behind; 258 B, Indian ink, 30 × 24 cm, signed, once the property of Cone, Baltimore, and now in the Cone Collection at the Museum of Art in that same city (DB 66 XV no. 6), where the two figures are sketched in the same pose in which they are depicted in this oil painting. See Plate LVII.

259 ⊘ 157/117 ▤ Gósol 1906 ⋮

The Young Men
Paris, Walter-Guillaume Collection.
Previous owners: Vollard, Paris; Guillaume, Paris; Walter, Paris.
Exhibitions: 32 P, 32 Z, 36 NY.

262

263

264

265 [Plate LVIII]

265 A

265 B

265 C

265 D

265 E

265 F

265 G

266

267 [Plate LIX]

Bibliography: Z 32 no. 324, M 42-48, S 48-55, DB 66 XV no. 11, P 66.
See the preceding numbers, beginning with no. 254.

260 ⊘ 100/81 ▤ 1906 ⋮

Nude Figure with Pottery
Whereabouts unknown.
Previous owner: Engelhorn, Ziegelhausen (Heidelberg).
Exhibition: 55 M.
Bibliography: DB 66 XV no. 24.
Probably painted at Gósol.

261 ⊘ 151,5/93,5 ▤ Gósol 1906 ⋮

Two Naked Youths
Washington, DC, National Gallery of Art, Dale Collection.
Previous owners: Vollard, Paris; Helft, Paris; Dale, New York.
Exhibition: 32 P.
Bibliography: L 28, Z 32 no. 305, C 40, M 42-48, Z 54 no. 715, BP 62, DB 66 XV no. 10.
Whether or not this picture was the last in chronological order, it concludes the series of nude male youths begun in no. 254. See Plate LV.

262 ⊘ 42/29 ▤ Gósol 1906 ⋮

Still Life with Pottery and Milk Jug
Basle, Staechelin Collection.
Bibliography: DB 66 XV no. 12.

263 ⊘ 82/100,5 ▤ Gósol 1906 ⋮

Still Life with Pictures
Washington, DC, Phillips Collection.
Previous owners: Kahnweiler, Paris; Robeyn, Brussels.
Bibliography: Z 32 no. 342, DB 66 XV no. 14.
On the wall to the right is a sketch for *The Two Brothers*, no. 258, which, as it includes (as does the previous and the following numbers) a *porrón*, the typical Catalan wine flask, is clearly related to the series of nude male youths (nos. 254–61) of the time of Gósol.

264 ⊘ 38,5/56 ▤ Gósol 1906 ⋮

Still Life with Wine Flask
Leningrad, Hermitage.
Previous owners: Shchukine, Moscow; Museum of Modern Western Art, Moscow.
Bibliography: Z 32 no. 343, S 48-55, KP 55, DB 66 XV no. 13.
The date was added to the picture by the artist in 1911.

265 ⊘ 66/49,5 ▤ Gósol 1906 ⋮

Portrait of Fernande Olivier with Headscarf
Richmond (Va.), Virginia Museum of Fine Arts, Catesby Jones Collection.
Previous owners: Dudensing, New York; Catesby Jones, New York.
Exhibitions: 39 NY, 47 NY, 64 T.
Bibliography: Z 32 no. 319, B 39, S 48-55, DB 66 XV no. 45.
Gouache and charcoal on paper. In Z 54 nos. 754, 755, 756 and 760 are published four preparatory sketches, 265 A, B, C and D, in the possession of the artist of which only the dimensions of the second one are given: 21 × 13 cm. Three other studies for this portrait, 265 E, F and G are given on pages 10, 47 and 70 of the

268

269

270 [Plate LX]

270 A

270 B

270 C

109

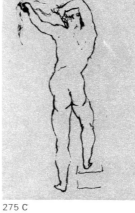

271　　**272**　　272 A　　**273**

275

275 A

?75 B　　　　　　275 C

Bibliography: DB 66 XV
no. D 13.

This picture relates in some
degree to the watercolour given
under the following number.

272 ✹ 146/114 ▤ Gósol : 1906

**Nude Young Woman with
Goat and Child**
Merion (Pa.), Barnes
Foundation.
Bibliography: L 28, Z 32 no.
249, M 42-48, DB 66 XV no. 35.
A sketch in pencil, 272 A, of a
*Nude Young Woman Doing Her
Hair,* 12 × 7·5 cm, in the
possession of the artist (DB 66
XV no. 36), is related to this
picture. The figure of the young
girl to be found in *The Harem,*
no. 274.

273 ✹ 64/49 ▤ Gósol : 1906

**Nude Woman Leaning
Forward**
Cleveland (Ohio), Museum of
Art, Hurlbut Collection.
Previous owner: Hurlbut,
Cleveland.
Exhibitions: 36 NY, 39 NY.
Bibliography: Z 32 no. 320,
B 39, M 42-48, B 46, DB 66
XV no. 38.
This figure is to be found in
the centre of the picture *The
Harem,* no. 274.

274 ✹ 154,5/109,5 ▤ Gósol : 1906

The Harem
Cleveland (Ohio), Museum of
Art, Hanna Collection.
Previous owners: Quinn,
New York; Hanna, New York.
Exhibition: 36 NY.
Bibliography: Z 32 no. 321,
M 42-48, DB 66 XV no. 40,
P 66.
There is a well-known design
in pencil, 247 A, 57·5 × 46 cm,
in an unknown collection
(Z 54 no. 657; EM 55; DB 66
XV no. 39), which contains a
complete sketch of this painting.

Carnet Catalan (DB 66 XV
nos. D 25, D 26, D 27). See
Plate LVIII.

266 ✹ 38/25,5 ▤ Gósol : 1906

Head of a Young Man
New York, Ault Collection.
Previous owners: Saint,
Paris; Dudensing, New York.
Bibliography: Z 32 no. 331,
Z 54 no. 781, B 55, BP 62,
DB 66 XV no. 17.

274 [Plate LXI]

274 A

267 ✹ 61,5/48 ▤ Gósol : 1906

**Head and Shoulders of a
Young Spaniard**
Goteborg, Konstmuseum.
Previous owner: Halvorsens,
Oslo.
Bibliography: Z 32 no. 318,
DB 66 XV no. 37, P 66.
Gouache and watercolour on
paper; signed on the back.
Wrongly believed to be a
portrait of Fernande Olivier, it
depicts in fact a young peasant
of Gósol. See Plate LIX.

268 ✹ 25,5/16,5 ▤ Gósol : 1906

Sketch for ''La Toilette''
New York, Chrysler Collection.
Previous owners: Leo Stein,
Paris; Sullivan, New York.
Bibliography: DB 66 XV
no. 31.
See no. 270.

269 ✹ 52/31 ▤ Gósol : 1906

''La Toilette''
São Paulo, Museu de Arte.
Previous owners: Stang,
Oslo; Warburg, New York.
Exhibition: 36 NY.
Bibliography: Z 54 no. 736,
DB 66 XV no. 33.
The first completed version of
the important work described
under the following number.

270 ✹ 151/99 ▤ Gósol : 1906

''La Toilette''
Buffalo (NY), Albright-Knox
Art Gallery.
Previous owner: Quinn, New
York.
Exhibitions: 36 NY, 38 B,
39 NY, 60 L, 64 T, 66 P.
Bibliography: L 28, Z 32 no.
325, B 39, M 42-48, L 52-54,
EM 55, C 58, B 64, D 64,

DB 66 XV no. 34, P 66.
Apart from the paintings given
under the two previous numbers,
three sketches relating to this
picture are also known: the
first, 270 A, in ink, signed,
25 × 17 cm (DB 66 XV no. 29);
the second, 270 B, in charcoal,
signed, 24 × 15 cm (DB 66 XV
no. 30); both previously in the
ownership of Bollag, Zurich,
and now in an unknown
collection. A third sketch, 270 C,
in charcoal on beige paper,

62 × 40·5 cm, signed and dated
1906 (L 52-54; DB 66 XV no.
32), once the property of
Flechtheim and then Stinnes
(both of Berlin), is now in the
collection of the Hillmann
Corporation in New York. See
Plate LX.

271 ✹ 41/27 ▤ Gósol : 1906

**Nude Figure seen from
Behind Doing her Hair**
Basle, Staechelin Collection.

276　　　276 A　　　276 B　　　276 C

278　　　　　**279**

See also the two preceding numbers. See Plate LXI.

275 ⊕ 37 24,5 ▦ Gósol 1906 ○

Nude Woman from the Side
Whereabouts unknown.
Previous owner: Guillaume, Paris.
Bibliography: Z 32 no. 226, M 42-48, DB 66 XV no. D 7.
In DB 66 are published, among others, three very convincing sketches relating to this watercolour: 275 A, pencil, 16·5 × 10·5 cm, signed, once the property of Cherbsky, Paris and now belonging to Georges Charensol, Paris (XV no. D 4; but see also in this catalogue under no. 271), on the back of

277

which is the painting given under no. 298; 275 B, in black gesso work, 31·5 × 25 cm, signed, once the property of Brewster, Chicago, and now in the Art Institute of the same city (XV no. D 5), in which there is also a sketch of two joined hands, like those of the woman and child in no. 276; 275 C, in ink, 40 × 29 cm, signed on the back, once the property of Roede and now in the hands of a private collector, both in Oslo (XV no. D 14).

276 ⊕ 24 16 ▦ Gósol 1906 ○

Nude Woman from Behind with Child
Whereabouts unknown.
Previous owner: Bollag, Zurich.
Bibliography: Z 54 no. 719, DB 66 XV no. D 3.
At least three sketches in charcoal are known which are definitely related to this watercolour: 276 A, 22 × 10 cm, signed, in the ownership of Josefowitz, Geneva (DB 66 XV no. D 1); 276 B, 31·1 × 23·9 cm, signed, in the Cone Collection of the Museum of Art in Baltimore (DB 66 XV no. D 2); 276 C, 24 × 15 cm, signed, once in the ownership of the Bollag Gallery, Zurich, and now owned by Kirchheimer, Küsnacht (DB 66 XV no. D 6), the last of which shows the child alone. See also the preceding number.

277 ⊕ — ▦ Gósol 1906 ○

Mother and Naked Child
Whereabouts unknown.
Previous owner: Bonnet, Paris.
Bibliography: Z 32 no. 315, DB 66 XV no. D 8.
This picture is noted only in the work of Zervos, the dimensions are unknown, and it is not certain whether it was signed. Zervos dates it Paris 1905, but it would seem more convincing to assign it to the time of Gósol.

278 ⊕ 54 38,5 ▦ Gósol 1906 :

Houses in Gósol
Copenhagen, Statens Museum for Kunst.
Previous owner: Tetzen, Lund (Sweden).
Bibliography: Z 32 no. 316, DB 66 XV no. 50.
The signature of the artist is on the back of the picture.

287

288

289

289 A

289 B

289 C

279 ⊕ 70 99 ▦ Gósol 1906 :

View of Gósol
New York, Private collection.
Previous owner: Spingold, New York.
Exhibition: 57 NY.
Bibliography: Z 54 no. 732, DB 66 XV no. 48.

280 ⊕ 62 47 ▦ Gósol 1906 :

Cattle Drover with Small Basket

Columbus (Ohio), Gallery of Fine Arts.
Previous owner: Dudensing, New York.
Bibliography: Z 32 no. 338, B 46, DB 66 XV no. 56.
See Plate LXII, for which the photographic originals were kindly provided by the Gallery of Fine Arts, Columbus.

281 ⊕ 24 31,5 ▦ Gósol 1906 :

Cockerels
San Francisco (Cal.), Museum of Art.
Previous owner: Levy, San Francisco.
Exhibition: 39 NY.
Bibliography: B 39, Z 54 no. 725, DB 66 XV no. 49.

282 ⊕ 24 31 ▦ Gósol 1906 :

Fowls
Baltimore (Md.), Museum of Art, Cone Collection.
Previous owner: Cone, Baltimore.
Bibliography: DB 66 XV no. 51.
Indian ink and watercolour on paper.

283 ⊕ 100 70 ▦ Gósol 1906 :

The Bread Carrier
Philadelphia (Pa.), Museum of Art.
Previous owners: Vollard, Paris; Caussignac, Paris; Guillaume, Paris; Harriman, New York; Ingersoll, Chestnut Hill (Pa.).
Exhibitions: 36 NY, 39 NY, 58 F, 66 P.
Bibliography: S 48-55, Z 54 no. 735, EM 55, DB 66 XV no 46, P 66.

Dated by Picasso at a later time and erroneously as 1905. See Plate LXIII.

284 ⊕ — ▦ Gósol 1906 :

Vase and Flowers
Winnipeg (Canada), McAuley Collection.
Bibliography: DB 66 XV no. 15.
Dimensions not given.

280 [Plate LXII]

281

282

284

285

286

283 [Plate LXIII]

Letter from Picasso and Fernande Olivier to Leo Stein, containing drawing no. 289 C.

285 ⊗ 70,5 / 54 ▦ Gósol 1906 ⦂

Pottery and Vase with Flowers
New York, J. K. Thannhauser Collection.
Previous owner: Thannhauser, Paris.
Bibliography: Z 54 no. 889, DB 66 XV no. 16.

286 ⊗ 40 / 30 ▦ Gósol 1906 ⦂

Vase with Flowers
Zurich, Bollag Collection.
Bibliography: Z 54 no. 723, DB 66 XV no. D 42.
Indian ink and watercolour on paper.

287 ⊗ 63 / 46,5 ▦ Gósol 1906 ⦂

The Peasants
Toronto, Zacks Collection.
Previous owners: Vollard, Paris; Harriman, New York; Knoedler, New York; Perls, New York.
Exhibitions: 57 NY, 58 F, 64 T.
Bibliography: Z 32 no. 311, B 46, B 57, DB 66 XV no. 60.
Indian ink and watercolour on paper. The first of three compositions with the same theme: see the next two numbers.

288 ⊗ 69 / 47 ▦ Gósol 1906 ⦂

The Peasants
Paris, Walter-Guillaume Collection.
Previous owners: Guillaume, Paris; Walter, Paris.
Bibliography: Z 32 no. 312, DB 66 XV no. 61.
The second of three compositions on the same theme.

289 ⊗ 218,5 / 129,5 ▦ Paris 1906 ⦂

The Peasants
Merion (Pa.), Barnes Foundation.
Previous owner: Vollard, Paris.
Bibliography: Z 32 no. 384, DB 66 XV no. 62.
This is the definitive painting of the series of *The Peasants* (see the two previous numbers) which was inspired by the style of El Greco. In DB 66 are published two preparatory sketches in ink: 289 A, 63 × 48 cm, signed, once in the ownership of Mrs S. B. Resor, New York, who in 1950 donated it to the Museum of Modern Art in that city (XV no. 58); 289 B, 18 × 12 cm, signed on the back, once in the Bollag Gallery, Zurich and the current property of Kirchheimer, Künacht (XV no. 57). A third sketch, 289 C, also in ink, contained in a letter (DB 66 XV no. 59 page 339) written by Picasso and Fernande Olivier to Leo Stein on 17 August 1906 from Paris: ("I am in the middle of painting a man with a young woman carrying flowers in a basket, with two bulls and a cornfield on one side"). The letter is preserved at Yale University and is documentary evidence that the series probably begun at Gósol was completed in Paris. On the following page all four sheets of this letter are reproduced. This picture terminates the Rose Period.

290 ⊗ 62 / 47 ▦ Gósol 1906 ⦂

Head of a Woman with Sleek Hair
Whereabouts unknown.

290

291

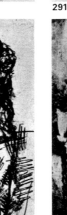
298

299

Previous owner: Vollard, Paris.
Bibliography: Z 32 no. 332, DB 66 XV no. 20.
A study for the *Nude Woman with Clasped Hands* described under no. 294.

291 ⊗ 61,5 / 43,5 ▦ 1906 ⦂

Head of a Woman with her Hair Down her Back
USA, Private collection.
Previous owners: Vollard, Paris; Museum of Art, Toledo

292

293

294

294 A

294 B

294 C

296

297

297 A

297 B

297 C

112

295

303

301

300

301 A

302

304

305

(Ohio); Knoedler, New York.
Exhibition: 36 NY.
Bibliography: Z 32 no. 333, M 42-48, DB 66 XV no. 22.
Probably painted at Gósol.

292 21 / 13 Gósol 1906

Nude Woman with Triangular Background
Whereabouts unknown.
Bibliography: Z 54 no. 887.

293 26 / 18 Gósol 1906

Nude Woman in an Archway
Merion (Pa.), Barnes Foundation.
Bibliography: Z 32 no. 326, S 48-55, DB 66 XV no. 26.
A sketch for the *Nude Woman with Clasped Hands* described under the following number.

294 153 / 94 Gósol 1906

Nude Woman with Clasped Hands
New York, owned by the heirs of Gertrude Stein.
Previous owner: Gertrude Stein, Paris.
Exhibitions: 54 P, 59 M.
Bibliography: D 30, Z 32 no.

327, M 42-48, S 48-55, KP 55, D 64, DB 66 XV no. 24.
Apart from the gouache and the small oil painting given under nos. 290 and 293, there exists a pencil sketch, 294 A, also a study for this nude figure: 62 × 47·5 cm; signed, once the property of Gertrude Stein, Paris; Perls, New York and Chrysler, New York, and now in the possession of Block, Chicago; published in Z 54 no. 779 and DB 66 XV no. 25. A further sketch of a nude woman with clasped hands, 294 B, also occurs in a pencil sketch, 17 × 11 cm, signed, owned by Rosengart, Lucerne, and published in DB 66 XV no. D 17; a variation on the head of the same model, 294 C, occurs in a pencil sketch, 21·5 × 13·5 cm, which is in the possession of the artist and is reproduced in Z 54 no. 852.

295 47,5 / 61,5 Gósol 1906

Reclining Nude (Fernande)
Cleveland (Ohio), Museum of Art.
Previous owners: Guillaume, Paris; Straight, Washington DC.
Exhibition: 64 T.

Bibliography: Z 32 no. 317, DB 66 XV no. 47.

296 40,5 / 35 Gósol 1906

Head of a Peasant
Philadelphia (Pa.), Meyer de Schauensee Collection.
Previous owner: Slater, Paris.
Bibliography: Z 32 no. 346, DB 66 XV no. 52.
Gouache and watercolour on rice paper.

297 45 / 40,5 Gósol 1906

Head of a Peasant
New York, Schoenborn-Marx Collection.
Previous owner: Marx, Chicago.
Bibliography: Z 54 no. 769, B 55, DB 66 XV no. 53.
Three sketches relating to this picture are known: 297 A, pencil, 35 × 22·5 cm, given in 1906 by the artist to his landlord at Gósol and which is at present in an unknown collection (Z 54 no. 770; DB 66 XV no. 54); 297 B, ink, 31·5 × 24·5 cm, in the possession of the artist (Z 54 no 765); 297 C, pencil, 25·5 × 20 cm, also in the

possession of the artist.

298 16,5 / 10,5 Gósol 1906

Head of a Woman
Paris, Georges Charensol Collection.
Previous owner: Cherbsky, Paris.
Bibliography: DB 66 XV no. D 21.
Indian ink and watercolour on paper. On the back is outlined the sketch (see no. 275A).

299 75 / 55 Paris 1906

Woman Sewing
France, Private collection.
Previous owner: Bienert, Hamburg.
Bibliography: Z 32 no. 314, S 48-55, DB 66 XVI no. 3.

300 47 / 31 1906

Head of a Woman
Zurich, Private collection.
Previous owner: Bollag, Zurich.
Bibliography: Z 54 no. 787, DB 66 XVI no. D 4.
Gouache and watercolour on paper. Probably executed in Paris, on his return from Gósol.

301 62 / 47 Paris 1906

Two Heads of Women
Houston (Tex.), on loan from the Hogg Collection to the Museum of Fine Arts.
Previous owner: Hogg, Houston.
Bibliography: Z 32 no. 335, DB 66 XVI no. 1.
A study for this gouache is given in a sketch, 301 A, in pencil and Indian ink, 17 × 11 cm, signed, the property of Rosengart, Lucerne, and published in Z 54 no. 753 and in DB 66 XVI no. D 1, on the back of which is outlined the sketch which has been referred to under no. 294.

302 51 / 39,5 Paris 1906

Bowed Head of a Woman
Stuttgart, Staatsgalerie
Previous owners: Mendelssohn, Berlin; Marlborough Gallery, London.
Exhibition: 55 M.
Bibliography: Z 32 no. 351, S 48-55, DB 66 XVI no. 4.
Signed on the back.

303 32 / 40 Paris 1906

Profile of Fernande Olivier
Stockholm, Prins Eugens Gemäldegalerie
Bibliography: DB 66 XVI no. 2.
Sold by the Svensk-Franska Konstgalleriet, in Stockholm in 1921.

304 21 / 13,5 Paris 1906

Two Nude Figures
Düsseldorf, Liesenfeld Collection.
Previous owners: Bernheim de Villiers, Paris; Rosenberg, Paris; Berggruen, Paris.
Bibliography: DB 66 XVI no. 11.
Indian ink and watercolour on paper. Signed "Picasso fecit". On the back of the sheet is a sketch of a hand.

306 [Plate LXIV]

305 100 / 81 1906

Nude Woman with Water Jug
London, James Collection.
Previous owners: Rober, Lausanne; Richet, Paris.
Exhibition: 60 L.
Bibliography: Z 32 no. 330, M 42-48, DB 66 XV no. 23.
Probably executed in Paris, after his return from Gósol.

306 100 / 81 Paris 1906

Portrait of Gertrude Stein
New York, Metropolitan Museum of Art.
Previous owner: Gertrude Stein, Paris, who bequeathed it to the Metropolitan Museum.

307

Exhibitions: 39 NY, 47 NY, 55 P, 57 NY, 58 F, 66 P.
Bibliography: Z 32 no. 352, S 38, B 39, C 40, M 42-48, B 46, L 52-54, B 55, EM 55, B 57, P 58, B 64, D 64, J 64, DB 66 XVI no. 10.
This picture was begun in the winter of 1905–6. In the spring Picasso painted out the head and in the autumn on his return from Gósol he re-painted it in the form of a mask, without seeing the model again. Nevertheless, Gertrude Stein herself (1938) wrote: "I was and still am completely satisfied with this portrait. For me, it is me; and it is the only representation of me which always will be me." See *Outline biography,* **1905.** See also Plate LXIV.

307 92 / 73 Paris 1906

Self-Portrait with Palette
Philadelphia (Pa.), Museum of Art, Gallatin Collection.
Previous owner: Gallatin, New York.
Exhibitions: 39 NY, 55 P, 55 M, 57 NY, 58 F, 60 L, 64 T, 66 P.
Bibliography: Z 32 no. 375, B 39, B 46, S 54, EM 55, B 57, D 64, DB 66 XVI no. 28.
Painted in autumn 1906.

113

Table of Concordance

This table shows the concordance between the catalogue given in this book, and those provided in two volumes (the first and the sixth) of the monumental work by Christian Zervos (Paris, 1932 and 1954) concerning the early years of Picasso's output, and also in the definitive work of Daix and Boudaille, Picasso 1900–1906 (Neuchâtel 1966).

CWA	Zervos	Daix & Boudaille	CWA	Zervos	Daix & Boudaille	CWA	Zervos	Daix & Boudaille
1	32 97	VI 19	59	32 178	IX D 18	115	32 219	XI 2
2	32 94	VI 21	60	— —	IX D 19	116	32 218	XI 3
3	32 79	VI 22	61	32 186	IX D 20	117	32 231	XI 4
4	32 92	VI 20	A	— —	IX D 21	118	54 617	XI D 9
5	32 83	VI 14	62	32 376	IX D 16	119	32 224	XI 5
6	32 101	VI 12	63	54 482	IX D 17	120	32 238	XI D 4
7	32 104	VI 18	64	54 481	IX D 15	121	54 615	XI D 5
8	32 102	VI 13	65	32 167	IX 9	122	54 704	XI D 6
9	32 103	VI 15	66	— —	IX D 6	123	— —	XI D 7
10	32 96	VI 23	A	54 451	— —	124	32 248	XI D 11
11	32 98	VI 24	67	54 462	IX 18	125	32 247	XI 6
12	32 100	VI 25	68	32 181	IX 19	126	54 631	XI D 20
13	— —	VI 27	69	54 548	IX 16	127	32 239	XI D 19
14	— —	X 9	70	32 166	IX 14	128	— —	XI 21
15	32 117	VI 31	71	32 165	IX 15	129	32 229	XI 20
16	32 115	VI 30	72	32 174	IX 21	130	32 214	XI 15
17	32 110	VI 29	73	— —	IX D 9	131	32 233	XI 7
18	32 109	VI 28	74	32 201	IX 20	132	32 240	XI 10
19	32 116	VI 32	75	32 205	IX 17	133	— —	— —
20	54 733	XV 42	76	32 194	IX D 8	134	32 215	XI 17
21	32 91	VI 35	77	— —	IX D 7	135	— —	XI 16
22	32 87	VI 34	78	32 199	IX 22	136	32 217	XI 18
23	32 86	VI 33	79	32 200	IX 24	137	54 632	XI D 21
24	32 160	VII 4	80	32 203	IX 23	138	54 652	XI 8
25	32 121	VII 5	A	32 204	— —	139	— —	XI 9
26	32 119	VII 2	81	54 563	IX D 13	140	32 234	XI 11
27	32 120	VII 3	82	— —	IX D 1	141	32 235	XI 12
28	32 133	VII 6	83	— —	IX 4	142	32 212	XI 22
29	32 105	VII 7	84	32 198	— —	143	— —	XI 14
30	32 130	VII 15	85	32 197	IX 5	144	32 241	XI 13
31	— —	VII 8	86	32 208	IX 6	145	32 221	XI D 12
32	32 118	VII 10	87	32 162	IX 11	146	— —	XI 19
33	32 155	VII 9	88	32 161	IX 12	147	32 213	XI D 16
34	32 131	VII 11	89	32 179	IX 13	148	54 616	XI D 14
A	32 192	— —	A	54 534	IX D 4	149	— —	XI D 15
B	— —	VII D 1	B	— —	IX D 5	150	32 211	XI D 10
C	54 418	— —	90	32 188	— —	151	— —	XI D 18
D	54 420	— —	91	32 175	IX 30	152	— —	XI D 28
35	— —	VII 18	A	32 170	IX 29	153	— —	XI D 29
36	32 381	VII 21	92	32 202	IX 34	154	32 291	XII 1
37	54 478	VII 20	93	32 172	IX 31	A	54 681	XII 2
A	32 151	VII D 9	A	54 533	— —	155	— —	XII 4
38	— —	VII 19	B	— —	IX D 23	A	32 220	XI D 26
39	32 163	VII 22	94	32 168	IX 32	156	32 257	XII 3
A	54 436	VII D 4	95	32 187	IX 33	157	32 307	XII 5
B	54 435	VII D 6	96	32 230	IX 27	158	54 718	XII 15
40	— —	VII 16	97	54 600	IX 28	159	54 702	XII 12
41	54 449	VII 17	98	54 578	IX D 11	160	32 244	XII 11
42	— —	VII 12	99	32 183	IX 26	161	32 298	XII 6
43	— —	VII 14	A	32 191	IX 25	162	32 289	XII 13
44	32 132	VII 13	100	32 169	IX 7	163	— —	XII D 1
45	— —	VII 1	101	54 483	— —	164	— —	XIII D 7
46	32 142	VIII 1	102	54 438	IX D 22	165	32 299	XII 7
47	32 182	VIII 2	103	32 184	X 5	A	— —	XII D 3
48	32 180	VIII 3	104	54 544	X 4	166	— —	XII D 8
49	— —	VIII 5	105	54 684	X 3	167	32 296	XII 8
50	32 123	VIII 4	106	32 209	X 1	168	— —	XII 10
51	54 413	X 7	107	32 210	X 2	169	32 292	XII 14
52	54 479	X 8	108	32 232	X 6	170	32 297	XII 9
53	54 476	IX 10	109	54 653	X 11	171	32 306	XII 16
54	54 467	X 10	110	32 164	X 12	172	32 300	XII 17
55	32 206	IX 8	111	— —	XI D 2	173	— —	XII 20
56	32 122	IX 1	112	32 237	XI D 3	A	— —	XII D 21
57	— —	IX 3	113	32 185	XI D 1	174	32 290	XII 19
58	32 207	IX 2	114	32 227	XI 1	175	32 293	XII 26

CWA	Zervos	Daix & Boudaille	CWA	Zervos	Daix & Boudaille	CWA	Zervos	Daix & Boudaille
A	32 322	— —	228	32 353	XIV 2	G	— —	XV D 27
176	— —	XII D 4	229	32 250	XIV 1	266	32 331	XV 17
177	— —	XII D 5	230	32 269	XIV 3	267	32 318	XV 37
178	32 301	XII 25	231	32 270	XIV 4	268	— —	XV 31
179	32 245	XII 21	232	32 268	XIV 8	269	54 736	XV 33
A	32 246	— —	233	— —	XIV 5	270	32 325	XV 34
180	— —	XII 18	234	— —	XIV 6	A	— —	XV 29
181	— —	XII D 6	235	32 264	XIV 7	B	— —	XV 30
182	32 281	XII D 2	A	32 266	— —	C	— —	XV 32
183	32 225	XII D 9	236	54 683	XIV 10	271	— —	XV D 13
184	54 734	XII D 18	237	— —	XIV 9	272	32 249	XV 35
A	— —	XII 30	238	— —	XIV 15	A	— —	XV 36
B	— —	XII D 20	239	32 265	XIV 16	273	32 320	XV 38
C	54 691	— —	A	— —	XIV 12	274	32 321	XV 40
D	54 690	— —	B	— —	XIV 13	A	54 657	XV 39
185	54 703	XII D 7	C	54 682	XIV 11	275	32 226	XV D 7
A	32 279	— —	D	— —	XIV 14	A	— —	XV D 4
186	32 284	XII 28	E	32 267	— —	B	— —	XV D 5
187	32 283	XII 29	F	54 864	XIV D 1	C	— —	XV D 14
188	54 697	XII D 19	240	— —	XIV D 7	276	54 719	XV D 3
A	54 689	— —	241	— —	XIV D 5	A	— —	XV D 1
189	32 286	XII 31	242	— —	XIV D 6	B	— —	XV D 2
190	32 287	XII 33	243	54 744	XIV 19	C	— —	XV D 6
191	32 288	XII 34	244	32 313	XIV 20	277	32 315	XV D 8
192	32 285	XII 35	A	— —	XIV 17	278	32 316	XV 50
A	— —	XII 32	B	54 741	XIV 18	279	54 732	XV 48
B	32 280	— —	C	32 282	— —	280	32 338	XV 56
193	54 798	XII 22	245	54 763	XV 55	281	54 725	XV 49
194	— —	XII D 15	A	54 762	— —	282	— —	XV 51
A	— —	XII D 14	B	54 764	— —	283	54 735	XV 46
195	— —	XII D 11	C	— —	XV D 38	284	— —	XV 15
196	32 243	XII 24	D	— —	XV D 37	285	54 889	XV 16
197	32 275	XII 23	246	— —	XV D 33	286	54 723	XV D 42
198	32 302	XII 27	A	— —	XV D 36	287	32 311	XV 60
199	32 261	XIII ?	B	54 633	— —	288	32 312	XV 61
200	32 260	XIII 1	247	32 254	XV 41	289	32 384	XV 62
201	32 255	XIII 4	248	54 749	XV 21	A	— —	XV 58
202	32 309	XIII 3	249	54 893	XV 44	B	— —	XV 57
203	32 259	XIII 5	250	32 253	XV 43	C	— —	XV 59
204	— —	XIII D 3	251	32 310	XV 28	290	32 332	XV 20
205	— —	XIII D 1	252	32 258	XV 19	291	32 333	XV 22
206	32 228	XIII 6	253	32 340	XV 18	292	54 887	— —
207	— —	XIII 7	254	54 662	XV 2	293	32 326	XV 26
208	— —	XIII D 5	A	— —	XV 1	294	32 327	XV 27
209	— —	XIII D 9	255	54 713	XV 4	A	54 779	XV 25
210	32 251	XIII D 6	A	— —	XV 3	B	— —	XV D 17
211	32 263	XIII 9	256	32 303	XV 7	C	54 852	— —
212	32 216	XIII D 11	257	54 720	XV 8	295	32 317	XV 47
213	32 276	XIII 19	258	32 304	XV 9	296	32 346	XV 52
214	32 273	XIII 18	A	— —	XV 5	297	54 769	XV 53
215	32 272	XIII 17	B	— —	XV 6	A	54 770	XV 54
216	32 262	XIII 12	259	32 324	XV 11	B	54 765	— —
217	32 274	XIII 13	260	— —	XV 24	C	54 772	— —
A	— —	XIII D 10	261	32 305	XV 10	298	— —	XV D 21
218	— —	XIII D 8	262	— —	XV 12	299	32 314	XVI 3
219	32 256	XIII 8	263	32 342	XV 14	300	54 787	XVI D 4
220	32 308	XIII 14	264	32 343	XV 13	301	32 335	XVI 1
221	54 688	XIII 10	265	32 319	XV 45	A	54 753	XVI D 1
222	32 295	XIII 11	A	54 754	— —	302	32 351	XVI 4
223	— —	XIII D 12	B	54 755	— —	303	— —	XVI 2
224	32 294	XIII 20	C	54 756	— —	304	— —	XVI 11
225	32 252	XIII 16	D	54 760	— —	305	32 330	XV 23
226	54 686	XIII 15	E	— —	XV D 25	306	32 352	XVI 10
227	32 271	XIII 21	F	— —	XV D 26	307	32 375	XVI 28

Indexes

Index of Subjects

Acrobats, 158, 162, 165, 169, 170, 174, 180, 182, 186, 187, 190, 223, 224.
Actors 154, 166, 181, 222
Animals 5, 59, 61, 76, 80, 82, 102, 103, 105, 106, 132, 133, 163, 164, 165, 171, 172, 180, 185, 189, 190, 194, 195, 196, 223, 230, 231, 233, 234, 235, 236, 237, 238, 239, 242, 272, 280, 281, 282, 289
Apollinaire 183, 223

Beggars 25, 90, 91, 92, 93, 101, 102, 103, 104, 105, 106, 107, 108
Blind People 66, 90, 91, 92, 93, 94, 126

Cafés 1, 2, 3, 4, 10, 11, 12, 27, 42, 44, 65, 72, 73, 74, 151, 197
Canals (Benedetta) 211
Children 5, 9, 113, 114, 115, 116, 132, 133, 158, 171, 172, 174, 189, 194, 212, 213, 214, 215, 216, 217, 221, 227, 230, 231, 256, 257, 266
Clowns 175, 176, 177, 178, 181, 184, 186, 187, 188, 190, 192
Cornuti (Poet) 47.
Couples 4, 42, 43, 65, 72, 73, 87, 88, 89, 98, 119, 140, 141, 146, 151, 159, 173, 181, 188, 197, 206, 207, 208, 241, 242, 287, 288, 289

Derain (Alice) 210
De Soto — see Fernández

Ex-Libris 183

Families 80, 81, 82, 83, 84, 85, 86, 120, 121, 122, 123, 160, 161, 162, 164, 165, 177, 180, 182, 185
Fernande Olivier 247, 248, 248, 250, 251, 265, 295, 303 (see also no. 154)
Fernández de Soto (Angel) 73, 74, 151
Fernández de Soto (Mateu) 2, 23
Flowers 143, 144, 216, 217, 219, 240, 242, 284, 285, 286, 287
Frédé (landlord of the "Lapin Agile") 197

Harlequins 3, 4, 142, 159, 160, 161, 168, 170, 172, 178, 180, 192, 193, 195, 196, 197, 198, 225, 226
Hugué (Manuel [Manolo]) 150

Interiors 9, 48, 59, 81, 123, 161, 162, 177, 299

Junyer Vidal (Sebastián) 72, 130

Lapin Agile 197
Laundresses 13, 124, 125

Manolo — see Hugué
Men 1, 2, 21, 22, 23, 46, 59, 75, 90, 92, 93, 94, 95, 102, 111, 118, 267, 280, 296, 297
Men and Children 49, 50, 62, 63, 64, 91, 101, 105, 106, 107, 112, 169, 170, 173, 174, 176, 186, 187, 193, 222
Nudes, Child 126, 127, 219, 232, 233, 234, 235, 236, 237, 238, 239, 241, 242, 244, 254, 255, 257, 258, 259, 261, 276
Nudes, Female 7, 8, 9, 40, 41, 52, 65, 67, 68, 69, 87, y8, 89, 98, 102, 127, 137, 138, 139, 140, 146, 156, 200, 201, 203, 204, 205, 206, 207, 208, 241, 242, 251, 252, 253, 260, 268,
269, 270, 271, 272, 273, 274, 275, 276, 292, 293, 294, 295, 304, 305
Nudes, Male 87, 88, 89, 98, 126, 156, 206, 207, 208, 241, 242, 253, 274

Olivier — see Fernande

Pichot (Germaine) 31
Portraits, Child 80, 228
Portraits, Female 30, 31, 79, 80, 99, 132, 133, 134, 135, 136, 210, 211, 247, 248, 249, 250, 251, 265, 295, 303, 306
Portraits, Male 1, 2, 21, 22, 23, 47, 72, 73, 74, 77, 78, 80, 102, 109, 110, 130, 141, 150, 151, 152, 153, 197, 229, 307
Posters 147, 148, 149

Romeu (Corina) 30

Sabartés (Jaime) 1, 22, 109
Self-Portraits 21, 102, 141, 152, . 153, 197, 307
Soler (various members of the family) 77, 78, 79, 80
Stein (Allan) 228
Stein (Gertrude) 306
Stein (Leo) 229
Still Lifes 262, 263, 264, 285

Uncle Pepe (see no. 184)

Various Groups 60, 61, 62, 64, 80, 89, 142, 147, 148, 149, 180, 190, 192, 198, 238, 239, 253
Views 45, 56, 57, 58, 278, 279
Vilaro (Luis) 110

Women 6, 10, 11, 12, 13, 20, 24, 25, 26, 27, 28, 29, 30, 31, 32, 33, 39, 44, 53, 54, 55, 70, 71, 75, 96, 97, 98, 99, 117, 124, 125, 131, 145, 157, 191, 199, 202, 209, 220, 243, 244, 245, 246, 268, 269, 270, 274, 283, 290, 291, 298, 299, 300, 301, 302
Women and Children 14, 15, 16, 17, 18, 34, 35, 36, 37, 38, 48, 89, 100, 128, 129, 155, 166, 167, 218, 277

Index of Titles

Absinthe Drinker, The, 12
Acrobat and Still Life 224
Acrobat and Young Equilibrist 174
Acrobat and Young Harlequin 170
Acrobats, The 192
Acrobat's Meal, The 169
Actor, The 154
Actor and Young Boy 222
Actress with Child at her Breast 166
Ape, The 163
Apéritif, The 11
Ascetic, The 95
At the "Lapin Agile" 197
Athlete, The 173

Barcelona at Night 57
Beggar Man and Child 101
Beggar Man with Dog 103
Blind Beggar, The 90
Blind Man 93
Blind Man's Meal, The 94
Blind Old Man and Little Girl, Both Nude 126
Blind Old Man and Boy 91
Blind Woman 66
Blue House, The 45
Blue Room, The 9
Blue Vase, The 242
Bowed Head of a Woman 302
Boy with Bucket 114
Boy Leading a Horse 235
Bread Carrier, The 283

"Caridad" 102
Catalan Peasants 62
Cattle Drover with Small Basket 280
Celestina 99
Child Holding a Dove 5

Clown and Young Acrobat 186, 187
Clown and Young Girl 188
Clown's Family with Accordion, The 177
Cockerels 281
Contemplation 141
Couple, The 119
Couple in a Café 42, 65
Couple with Child 120, 122
Couple with Children 121
Crouching Beggar 25
Crouching Nude with Green Stockings 40
Crouching Woman 24, 26
Death of Harlequin, The 198

Embrace, The 87, 88
Eviction, The 123
Exhausted Nude 7
Ex-Libris of Guillaume Apollinaire 183

Family of Acrobats 162, 180, 182
Family of Acrobats with Ape 165
Family with Crow 185
Family at Table 81
Farewell to the Fisherman 38
Fowls 282
Friends, The 138, 139
Full Length Nude with Cap 201

Girl with Crow 133
Girl Child with Crow 132
Girl Child with Dog 189
Guitar Player at the Inn 59

Harem, The 274
Harlequin and his Companion 4, 159
Harlequin on Horseback 195, 196
Harlequin Leaning on his Elbow 3
Harlequin's Family 160, 161
Head and Shoulders of a Young Boy 221
Head and Shoulders of a Young Spaniard 267
Head of a Peasant Woman 245
Head of a Poor Man 104
Head of a Woman 55, 69, 75, 298, 300
Head of a Woman with her Hair down her Back 291
Head of a Woman with Sleek Hair 290
Head of a Young Harlequin 225, 226
Head of a Young Man 256, 266
Hurdy-Gurdy Player and Young Harlequin, The 193
Horses Bathing 238, 239
"Hôtel de l'Ouest" 147
Houses in Gósol 278

Idiot, The 63

King, The 179
Kiss, The 146
Kneeling Nude 137

"La Coiffure" 202, 243, 244
"La Toilette" 269, 270
Laundress, The 13, 124, 125
"Les Noces de Pierrette" 142
Life 89
Lovers, The 207, 208

Madman, The 108
Man in Blue 46
Man with a Dog 76
Mistletoe Seller, The 49, 50
Mother and Child 14, 15, 16, 17, 18, 35, 128, 155, 167
Mother and Child Adorned with Garlands 129
Mother and Child on the Seashore 36, 37
Mother and Naked Child 277
Mother and Sick Child 100

Nude with Bathrobe 8
Nude with Clasped Hands 252
Nude with Crossed Legs 68
Nude of Fernande Olivier with Clasped Hands 251
Nude Figure Seen from Behind Doing her Hair 271

Nude Figure with Pottery 260
Nude Figures with Child 241
Nude Figures Embracing 206
Nude with Flowing Hair 67
Nude Girl with Basket of Flowers 219
Nude with her Hand in her Hair 203
Nude lying on her Side 52
Nude Mother with Child 218
Nude Woman in an Archway 293
Nude Woman from Behind 41
Nude Woman from Behind with Child 276
Nude Woman and Child 127
Nude Woman with Clasped Hands 294
Nude Woman Dressing her Hair 204
Nude Woman Leaning Forward 273
Nude Woman from the Side 275
Nude Woman with Triangular Background 292
Nude Woman with Water Jug 305
Nude of a Young Dutch Girl with Cap 200
Nude Young Man 232, 254
Nude Young Man and Children 255
Nude Young Man with Horse 233, 234
Nude Young Man on Horseback 236, 237

Offering, The 34
Old Blind Guitar Player, The 92
Old Man with Child 112
Old Woman with Hat 97
Old Woman with Nude Figures 98
Old Woman with Shawl 96

Peasants, The 60, 287, 288, 289
Peasants Dancing the Jota 61
Poor Children 113, 115, 116
Poor Man's Meal, The 105, 106, 107
Poor People on the Seashore 86
Poor Wretches, The 82, 83, 84
Poor Wretches on the Seashore 85
Portrait of Alice Derain 210
Portrait of Allan Stein 228
Portrait of Angel Fernández de Soto 74
Portrait of Angel Fernández de Soto with Female Figure 73, 151
Portrait of Benedetta Canals 211
Portrait of Corina Romeu 30
Portrait of Fernande Olivier Bare Headed 247, 248
Portrait of Fernande Olivier with Black Headdress 250
Portrait of Fernande Olivier with Headscarf 265
Portrait of Fernande Olivier with White Headdress 249
Portrait of Gaby Baur 134
Portrait of Germana Pichot 31
Portrait of Gertrude Stein 306
Portrait of Jaime Sabartés 1, 22, 109
Portrait of Leo Stein 229
Portrait of Luis Vilaro 110
Portrait of Madam Soler 79
Portrait of Manuel Hugué 150
Portrait of Mateu Fernández de Soto 2, 23
Portrait of the Poet Cornuti with Female Figure 47
Portrait of Sebastián Junyer Vidal 130
Portrait of Sebastián Junyer Vidal with Female Figure 72
Portrait of Suzanne Bloch 135, 136
Portrait of the Tailor Soler 78
Portrait of the Tailor Soler Dressed in Riding Clothes 77
Pottery and Vase with Flowers 285
Profile of Fernande Olivier 303

Profile of a Woman 54, 145, 209, 246
Profile of a Young Boy 212
Profile of a Young Man with a Lace Collar 213
Prone Nude 51

Roofs of Barcelona 58

"Sainte Roulette" 148, 149
Seated Child 19
Seated Clown 184
Seated Couple from Behind 43
Seated Harlequin 168
Seated Nude 156
Seated Nude Dressing her Hair 205
Seated Woman 53
Seated Woman with Arms Crossed 29
Seated Woman with a Scarf on her Shoulders 28
Self-Portrait with Cloak 21
Self-Portrait with Palette 307
Self-Portrait with Pipe 153
Sheet of Sketches 223
Sketch for "La Toilette" 268
Sketch for "The Acrobats" 190
Sleeping Drinker 27
Small Child with Dog 171
Soler Family, The 80
Solitude 111
Still Life with Pictures 263
Still Life with Pottery and Milk Jug 262
Still Life with Wine Flask 264
Street in Barcelona 56
Strolling Guitar Player 64

Three Dutch Women 199
Three Nude Figures 253
Two Brothers, The 257, 258
Two Heads of Women 301
Two Mothers, The 48
Two Naked Youths 261
Two Nude Figures 304
Two Sisters, The 39
Two Women at a Bar 44

Vase with Flowers 143, 144, 284, 286
Vase with Roses 240
View of Gósol 279
Violinist with Family and Ape 164

Woman in a Bonnet 6
Woman with her Hair Up 131
Woman with a Chignon 10
Woman with a Fan 220
Woman with a Fringe 32
Woman with a Kerchief round her Neck 70
Woman Leaning upon Folded Arms 117
Woman with Lock of Hair 71
Woman with a Scarf on her Shoulders 33
Woman Sewing 299
Woman Wearing a Chemise 157

Young Acrobat and Child 158
Young Clown 175
Young Clown and Actress with Amphora 181
Young Clown with Child 176
Young Clown and Small Harlequin 178
Young Equestrienne 194
Young Equestrienne and Young Man 230
Young Harlequin and Child with Dog 172
Young Man in Blue 227
Young Man with Bunch of Flowers 216
Young Man with Garland of Roses 217
Young Man with a Horse 231
Young Man with a Lace Collar 214
Young Man with Vase 215
Young Men, The 259

Topographical Index

Ascona
Neuberg-Coray Collection 135
Private collection 119

Baltimore (Md.)
Museum of Art 32, 163, 164, 180, 187, 202, 205, 209, 218, 221, 228, 229, 233, 234, 282

Barcelona
Picasso Museum 71, 100, 108, 130, 211

Basle
Kunstmuseum 258
Staechelin Collection 204, 262, 271

Belgium
Private collection 170

Brisbane
Queensland Art Gallery 200

Brussels
Mabille Collection 102

Budapest
Szépmüvészeti Múzeum 128

Buenos Aires
De Ganay Collection 43

Buffalo (NY)
Albright-Knox Art Gallery 81, 270
Kenefick Collection 97

Cambridge (Mass.)
Fogg Art Museum 10, 16, 93, 127
Private collection 247

Cannes
Property of the Artist 6, 8, 21, 22, 23, 30, 33, 46, 58, 150, 194, 212, 223, 257

Chicago (Ill.)
Art Institute 92, 131
McCormick Collection 29

Cleveland (Ohio)
Museum of Art 89, 256, 273, 274, 295

Columbus (Ohio)
Gallery of Fine Arts 151, 280

Copenhagen
Statens Museum for Kunst 206, 278

Detroit (Mich.)
Private collection 28, 107, 226

Düsseldorf
Forberg Collection 73
Liesenfeld Collection 304
Private collection 225

Edinburgh
Scottish National Gallery of Modern Art 35

France
Private collection 237, 299

Germany
Private collection 162

Glarus (Switzerland)
Huber Collection 27

Glens Falls (NY)
Hyde Collection 215

Göteborg
Konstmuseum 146, 165, 267

Heino (Holland)
Hannema-De Stuers Foundation 66

Houston (Tex.)
Museum of Fine Arts 301

Küsnacht
Burgauer Collection 126
Kirchheimer Collection 98, 236
Private collection 38

Leningrad
Hermitage 11, 39, 70, 78, 171, 232, 264

Liège
Graindorge Collection 137
Musée des Beaux-Arts 80

London
Dowager Lady Aberconway Collection 5
James Collection 305
Private collection 56, 252
Roland Collection 255
Tate Gallery 157, 231

Los Angeles (Cal.)
Goetz Collection 18, 143, 147, 189
Museum of Art 72
Private collection 243

Lucerne
Rosengart Collection 210

Manchester
Whitworth Art Gallery 83

Marseille
Private collection 122

Merion (Pa.)
Barnes Foundation 19, 95, 178, 272, 289, 293

Moscow
Pushkin Museum 1, 4, 91, 174, 190 191

Munich
Neue Pinakothek 79

New York
Ault Collection 42, 266
Bertram Smith Collection 141
Burden Collection 172
Chrysler Collection 44, 111, 124, 268
Clark Collection 222
Harriman Collection 220
Heirs of Gertrude Stein Collection 45, 114, 219, 294
Hillmann Collection 253
Jonas Collection 31
Lasker Collection 20
Lehman Collection 181
Metropolitan Museum of Art 3, 13, 69, 94, 154, 244, 306
Paley Collection 235
Payson Collection 160, 197
Private collection 37, 169, 279
Schoenborn-Marx Collection 297
Serger Collection 208
Stralem Collection 74
J. K. Thannhauser Collection 55, 103, 113, 125, 145, 158, 188, 250, 285
Warburg Collection 227
Whitney Collection 217

Northampton (Mass.)
Smith College Museum of Art 85

Oslo
Nasjonalgalleriet 65
Private collection 109

Paris
Berggruen Collection 49, 238, 246, 254
Georges Charensol Collection 298
Heirs of Guillaume Apollinaire Collection 75, 176, 207
Helft Collection 140
Musée de l'Orangerie 88
Musée National d'Art Moderne 156, 199
Niarchos Collection 14
Private collection 7, 40, 41, 48, 50, 99, 105, 123, 129, 134, 138, 153, 155, 168, 173, 175

Walter-Guillaume Collection 259, 288

Philadelphia (Pa.)
Meyer de Schauensee Collection 296
Museum of Art 283, 307

Pittsburgh (Pa.)
Heinz Collection 77

Preston (GB)
Kessler Collection 166

Richmond (Va.)
Virginia Museum of Fine Arts 265

Rochester (NY)
Memorial Art Gallery 144

San Antonio (Texas)
Koogler McNay Collection 62

San Francisco (Cal.)
Museum of Art 281

São Paulo
Museu de Arte 136, 269

Solothurn (Switzerland)
Private collection 54

Stockholm
Nathhorst Collection 24
Prins Eugens Gemäldegalerie 303

Stuttgart
Staatsgalerie 26, 167, 179, 302

Switzerland
Private collection 110

Toledo (Ohio)
Museum of Art 132

Toronto
Art Gallery 25
Crang Collection 34
Zacks Collection 251, 287

Turgovia (Switzerland)
Private collection 64

United States
Private collections 148, 159, 186, 248, 291

Villanova (Pa.)
Wintersteen Collection 216

Washington, DC
Bliss Collection 177
Eisenstein Collection 161
Mellon Collection 196, 198
National Gallery of Art 86, 192, 224, 261
Phillips Collection 9, 263

Whereabouts unknown
15, 36, 47, 51, 61, 67, 68, 76, 84, 87, 90, 96, 101, 104, 106, 112, 115, 120, 121, 133, 139, 142, 149, 152, 183, 184, 195, 201, 203, 230, 240, 241, 245, 249, 250, 260, 275, 276, 277, 290, 292, 299

Winnipeg
McAuley Collection 284

Winterthur
Oskar Reinhart Foundation 2

Worcester (Mass.)
Art Museum 213, 239
Higgins Collection 52

Wuppertal
Von der Heydt-Museum 60, 82, 182

Zurich
Bollag Collection 53, 118, 242, 286
Bührle Foundation 57, 59
Kunsthaus 193
Private collection 63, 300

Previous Owners

Abbot, Dexter (Maine) 85
Anderson, New York 3, 83
Apollinaire (Guillaume), Paris 75, 176, 183, 207
Astor, London 56
Bakwin, New York 10
Bartlett, Chicago (Ill.) 92
Beatty, London 189
Berggruen, Paris 35, 77, 185, 304
Bernados, Geneva 60
Bernheim de Villiers, Paris 18, 304
Besnard, Paris 36
Bieber, Lugano 136
Bienert, Hamburg 299
Bignou, Paris 9, 62, 89, 168
Bohrmann, Berlin 256
Bollag, Zurich 12, 63, 64, 98, 126, 236, 240, 241, 276, 300
Bonnet, Paris 277
Borst, Stuttgart 179
Brewster, Chicago (Ill.) 131
Bright, Los Angeles (Cal.) 72
Bucher, Paris 52
Buchholz, New York 183
Canals, Barcelona 211
Catesby Jones, New York 265
Caussignac, Paris 283
Cherbsky, Paris 298
Chrysler, New York 147, 156, 183
Chrysler Foy, New York 154
Clark, New York 169, 244
Clifford, Radnor (Pa.) 3
Coltman, London 255
Cone, Baltimore (Md.) 32, 163, 164, 180, 187, 202, 205, 209, 218, 221, 228, 229, 233, 234, 282
Cooper, London 183
Courtauld, London 5
Dale, New York 86, 192, 224, 261
De Maré, Stockholm 197
Dereppe, Lugano 59
De Vahl Rubin, London 200
Dial, Boston (Mass.) 213, 239
Dior (Christian), Paris 208
Doetsch-Benziger, Basle 38
Doucet, Paris 226, 256
Drummond Libbey, Toledo (Ohio) 132
Dubourg, Paris 208
Dudensing, New York 151, 265, 266, 280
Durio, Barcelona 200, 215
Dutilleul, Paris 51, 121
Engelhorn, Ziegelhausen (Heidelberg) 260
Eumorphopoulos, London 116-7
Flechtheim, Berlin and Düsseldorf 65, 157, 182, 183, 197, 215, 227, 239
Fleischmann, Zurich 159
Fontbona, Barcelona 37
French Art Galleries, New York 81
Freshfield, London 200
Fukushima, Paris 16, 69
Furthman, New York 141
Gaffé, Brussels 35, 145
Gallatin, New York 307
Gaspari, Monaco 26, 167
Gérard, Paris 197
German Embassy in London 227
Gold, Copenhagen and Berlin 65, 131
Gollancz, London 200
Goodyear, New York 97
Guillaume, Paris 20, 28, 31, 88, 95, 132, 144, 206, 213, 259, 275, 283, 288, 295
Haldsdurk, Berlin 214
Halvorsens, Oslo 267
Hanna, New York 256, 274
Harrimann, New York 283, 287
Hatvany, Budapest 128
Haupt, New York 94
Helft, Paris 261
Hessel, Paris 124
Hogg, Houston (Tex.) 301
Howald, Columbus (Ohio) 151
Hurlbut, Cleveland (Ohio) 273
Ingersoll, Chestnut Hill (Pa.) 283

Johnson, Chicago (Ill.) 131
Josten, New York 116-7
Junyent, Barcelona 67, 73, 97, 108, 152
Junyer Vidal, Barcelona 59, 72, 76, 102, 134
Kahnweiler, Paris 1, 79, 80, 93, 157, 174, 263
Kaye, London 189
Kirkeby, New York 14
Knoedler, New York 34, 116-7, 154, 160, 181, 287, 291
Koenig, Munich 192
Kronprinz Palace, Berlin 227
Kunsthalle, Hamburg 27
La Peau de l'Ours, Paris 192, 199
Laya, Geneva 17
Lefèvre, Paris 47, 60, 106, 112, 120, 195, 199
Leffmann, Cologne 154
Leperrier, Paris 116-7
Level, Paris 48, 106, 116-7, 192, 196, 199
Levy, San Francisco (Cal.) 281
Lewisohn, New York 24, 123, 161
Libaude, Paris 147
Lichnowsky, Kuchelna (Czechoslovakia) 186, 227
Lion, Steckborn (Switzerland) 64
Loeb, New York 3
Ludington, Santa Barbara (Cal.) 172
Maar, Paris 153
Maguy, Paris 7
Maitland, London 35
Marlborough, London 302
Marx, Chicago 297
Matisse, New York 127, 156, 244
Matthiesen, London 134
Maugham (Somerset), Cap-Ferrat 198
Mayer, Zurich 119
Mayor, London 255
McIlhenny, Philadelphia (Pa.) 3, 216
McLane, Los Angeles (Cal.) 243
Mendel, Saskatoon (Canada) 25
Mendelssohn, Berlin 74, 217, 302
Mermod, Lausanne 196
Milton de Groot, New York 69
Morosov, Moscow 4, 174
Muller, Solothurn (Switzerland) 54
Museo de Arte Moderno, Barcelona 71, 100, 108, 130, 211
Museum of Art, Toledo (Ohio) 93, 291
Museum of Modern Art, New York 244
Museum of Modern Western Art, Moscow 1, 4, 11, 39, 70, 78, 91, 171, 174, 190, 191, 232, 264
Muthmann, Nassau 26, 167
Nathan, Zurich 26, 167
National Gallery of Scotland, Edinburgh 35
Neuer Kunstsalon, Munich 3
Newberry, New York 185
Olivier (Fernande), Paris 177
Oppenheim, Paris 15
Pellequer, Paris 50, 90, 99, 107, 116-7, 129, 141, 253
Perls, New York and Paris 81, 111, 147, 148, 154, 184, 186, 244, 287
Pineus, Göteborg 165
Plandiura, Barcelona 71, 100, 108, 130, 211
Poissonnier, Paris 137
Quest, Chicago (Ill.) 62
Quinn, New York 3, 10, 16, 92, 270, 274
Reber, Lausanne 169, 305
Reid, London 5, 9
Reinhart (Georg), Winterthur 17
Renand, Paris 142
Rhode Island School of Design, Providence (RI) 89
Richet, Paris 138, 155, 173, 305
Robeyn, Brussels 263

Rosenberg, Paris 5, 36, 154, 202, 220, 304
Rosengart, Lucern 73, 187, 251
Rothschild, Paris 41, 168, 175
Sabartés (Jaime), Paris 13, 109
Sachs, Paris 105
Sainsère, Paris 133, 155, 173
Saint, Paris 202, 247, 266
Salz, New York 18, 143, 189
Sarlie, New York 7, 24
Schmits, Wuppertal 14
Schnitzler, Frankfurt 162
Schoeller, Paris 40
Schubert, Bochum (Germany) 86
Schweppe, New York 57
Seligmann, New York 105, 226
Shchukine, Moscow 1, 11, 39, 70, 78, 91, 171, 190, 191, 264
Sibley Watson, Rochester (NY) 144
Sichowski, London 136
Slater, Paris 296
Soler, Barcelona 77, 78, 79, 80
Spingold, New York 279
Städtisches Museum, Wuppertal 170
Stang, Oslo 200, 269
Stein, Paris 26, 27, 32, 34, 40, 44, 45, 81, 105, 114, 156, 167, 174, 203, 220, 256, 294, 306 (Gertrude); 268 (Leo); 219, 229 (Gertrude and Leo); 228, 234 (Michael); 177 (Sarah)
Sternheim, Paris 34
Stevenson, Chicago (Ill.) 245
Stieglitz, New York 13
Stoop, London 157, 166, 231
Straight, Washington, DC 295
Stransky, New York 56, 85, 142, 144
Suermondt, Aachen 3
Sullivan, New York 268
Sykes, Cambridge 189
Taylor, Lucerne 74
Tetzen, Lund (Sweden) 206, 278
Thannhauser, Lucerne, Munich, New York and Paris 14, 17, 25, 55, 74, 79, 87, 89, 94, 103, 113, 116–7, 119, 125, 158, 172, 187, 189, 198, 200, 201, 235, 285
Thompson, Pittsburg (Pa.) 137
Tietz, Cologne 230
Tooth, London 35
Troplowitz, Hamburg 27
Turitz, Göteborg 146
Uhde, Paris 9, 198
Valentin, New York 227
Valentine, see Dudensing
Van Dongen, Monte Carlo 237
Vilaro, Barcelona 65, 110
Vine, Paris 61, 103
Vollard, Paris 4, 7, 14, 18, 24, 88, 89, 92, 94, 235, 244, 252, 259, 261, 283, 287, 289, 290, 291
Vömel, Düsseldorf 115, 225
Von der Heydt, Ascona 6, 62, 210
Von Ripper, Paris 34
Von Sternberg (Joseph), Hollywood 7
Wallraf Richartz-Museum, Cologne 80
Walter, Paris 20, 88, 259, 288
Warburg, New York 269
Watson, London 81
Wertheim, New York 10, 16, 93, 127
Wildenstein, Paris and New York 57
Workman, London 5

French Titles

L'absinthe 47
Acrobate à la boule 174
Acrobate et jeune Arlequin 170
L'acteur 154
Les adieux du pêcheur 38
Les adolescents 259
Les amants 208
Angel de Soto au café 73
Angel Fernández de Soto 74
L'apéritif 11, 151
Arlequin accoudé 3
Arlequin à cheval 195, 196, 236
Arlequin assis, au fond rouge 168
Arlequin au verre 197
Arlequin et femme 159
Arlequin et femme à l'amphore 181
Arlequin et femme dans un café 197
Arlequin et sa compagne 4
Arlequin se maquillant 159
Artiste de cirque et enfant 166
L'ascète 95
L'athlète 173
Au bord de la mer 84
Au Lapin Agile 197
Autoportrait 21
Autoportrait à la palette 307
Autoportrait à la pipe 152, 153
L'aveugle 93, 94, 126
La baiser 146
Baladins 167, 178
Barcelone la nuit 57
Bateleur à la nature morte 224
Bateleur, esquisses et portrait-charge d'Apollinaire 223
Les bateleurs 190, 192
Le bock 1
La boîte au lait 114
Bouffon assis 184
Bouffon et jeune acrobate 186, 187
Bouffon et jeune fille 188
La buveuse assoupie 27
Buste de garçonnet 221
Buste de femme 33, 67
Buveuse d'absinthe 12, 27
Célestine 99
La chambre bleue 9
Charité 102
Chevaux au bain 238, 239
Le Christ de Montmartre 118
Clown à cheval 196
La coiffure 202, 244
Comédien et enfant 222
Comédiens 178
Composition: les paysans 288, 289
Confidences 39
Contemplation 141
Le coq 282
Les coqs 281
Corina Pere Romeu 30
Coupe, cruche et boîte à lait 262
Le couple 119
Couple assis vu de dos 43
Couple au café 66
Couple et enfant 120, 121
Couple nu et femme avec enfant 89
La couseuse 299
Cruche avec fleurs 284
Le déjeuner sur l'herbe 80
Le déjeuner sur l'herbe de la famille Soler 80
Deux adolescents 261
Les deux amies 138, 139
Deux Arlequins 158, 178
Deux femmes au bar 44
Deux femmes nues 304
Les deux frères 258
Deux frères, de face 257
Les deux saltimbanques 4
Deux saltimbanques avec un chien 172
Les deux sœurs 39
Deux têtes de femmes 301
Élégie 29
L'embrassement 88, 146
Enfant à la pipe 217
Enfant assis sur une chaise 19
L'enfant au pigeon 5
L'enfant et l'acrobate 193
L'enfant malade 100
Enfants 116

Enfants de la rue 113
L'entrevue 39
Esquisse pour "Hôtel de l'Ouest" 147
L'étrangleur 148
L'étreinte 87, 88, 207
Étude pour "La coiffure" 243
Étude pour "La toilette" 268, 269
Étude pour "Les bateleurs" 182, 185, 189, 190, 191
Étude pour "Vase bleu" 241
Ex-libris pour Guillaume Apollinaire 183
Famille au corbeau 185
Famille au singe 164
Famille au souper 81
La famille d'acrobates 162, 165
Famille d'acrobates au singe 165
Famille d'acrobates avec singe 165
Famille d'Arlequin 160, 161
Famille de bateleurs 180, 182
Famille de fou 175
Famille de saltimbanques 192
La famille Soler 80
Femme accoudée 117
Femme accroupie 24, 53
Femme accroupie et enfant 16
Femme accroupie près de la mer 26
Femme à la chemise 157
Femme à la corneille 132
Femme à la mantille blanche 20
Femme à la mèche 71
La femme à l'éventail 220
Femme assise au capuchon 26
Femme assise au fichu 28
Femme assise, les bras croisés 29
Femme assise se coiffant 205
La femme au café 11
Femme au casque de cheveux 131
Femme au châle 31
La femme au chignon 10
La femme au corbeau 133
Femme au fichu bleu 33
La femme au mouchoir de cou 70
Femme au peignoir de bain 8
Femme aux cheveux frangés 32
La femme aux pains 283
Femme aveugle 66
La femme borgne 99
La femme de l'acrobate 131
Femme de l'Île de Majorque 191
Femme de profil 157
Femme en chemise 157
La femme endormie 141
Femme en rose 291
Femme et enfant nu 277
Femme et fillette 127
Femme nue debout 294
Femme nue de dos 275
Femme nue, de dos, et enfant 276
Femme nue se coiffant, de dos 271
Femme nue se coiffant, de face 204
Femmes assises, vues de dos 43
Femmes au bar 44
Femmes et enfants 48
Fernande 295, 303
Fernande à la mantille 249
Fernande à la mantille noire 250
Fernande au mouchoir de tête 265
Figure d'homme 130
Figures en rose 274
La fille à la tignasse 71
Fille aux bras croisés 12
Fillette à cheval 230
Fillette au chien 189
Fillette au panier de fleurs 219
Fillette nue à la corbeille fleurie 219
Fleurs dans un vase bleu 144
Fleurs et cruche 286
Le fou 108, 175
Le fou au chien 103
Fou tenant un enfant 176
Gaby 134
Garçon à la collerette 214

Garçon à la pipe 217
Le garçon au chien 171
Le garçon bleu 227
Garçon de profil, à la collerette 213
Garçon nu 232
Garçon tenant un vase 215
Genoveva 67
La gommeuse 7
Grand nu rose 294
Le guitariste 59
Le harem 274
Hollandaise à la coiffe 200
L'homme au chien 76
Homme en bleu 6
L'idiot 63
Intimité 48
Jaime Sabartés 22
Jeune acrobate et enfant 158
Jeune Arlequin 225
Le jeune cavalier 236
Jeune écuyère 194
Jeune espagnol 267
Jeune femme accoudée 117
Jeune fille à la chèvre 272
Jeune garçon nu 254
Jeune garçon nu, à cheval 237
Jeune homme 228
Jeune homme à la boîte à lait 114
Jeune homme au bouquet 216
Jeune homme au cheval 231, 234
Jeune homme et enfants 255
La joie pure 88
La jota 61
Joueur de guitare 64
Le joueur d'orgue de Barbarie 193
Madame Canals 211
La Madone à la guirlande 129
Maison à Barcelone 45
La maison bleue 45
Maisons de Gosol 278
Le marchand de gui 49, 50
Les marins 62
Maternité 17, 18, 120, 155, 218
Maternité au bord de la mer 37
Mateu F. de Soto 23
Méditation 141
La mélancolie 28
Ménage de pauvres 65
Ménage et enfant 122
Mendiant 90
Mendiante à la plage 37
Le meneur de cheval 233
Meneur de cheval, nu 235
Mère et enfant 14, 15, 18, 35, 128, 167
Mère et l'enfant 34
Mère et enfant au bord de la mer 36
Mère et enfant au fichu 100
Mère et enfant de profil 37
Les misérables 83, 119
Les misérables au bord de la mer 84
La miséreuse accroupie 25
Miséreuse au bord de la mer 37
La mort d'Arlequin 198
Nature morte au tableau 263
Nature morte au vase 264
Nature morte: fleurs dans un vase 285
Les noces de Pierrette 142
Nocturne barcelonais 57
Nu accroupi au bas vert 40
Nu à genoux 137
Nu à la chevelure tirée 203
Nu assis 156
Nu au bonnet 201
Nu au pichet 305
Nu aux jambes croisées 68
Nu aux mains croisées 252
Nu aux mains serrées 251
Nu couché 52, 295
Nu couché sur le ventre 51
Nu debout, à la voûte rouge 293
Nu de dos 41
Le nu endormi 140, 141
Nu, étude pour "Le harem" 273
Nus enlacés 206
Nus roses 274
L'offrande 34
Les parias 86
Les pauvres 82, 105
Les pauvres au bord de la mer 86
Paysage de Barcelone 58

Paysage de Gosol 279
Les paysans 287
Paysans espagnols 60
Le peintre Sebastián Junyer 72
Petits gueux 115, 116
Pierreuses au bar 44
Le poète Cornuti 47
Le poète Sabartés 1
Le porrón 264
La porteuse de pains 283
Portrait 32
Portrait d'Alice Derain 210
Portrait d'Allan Stein 228
Portrait de Colette 135
Portrait de Corina Pere Romeu 30
Portrait de Fernande 247, 267
Portrait de Gaby 134
Portrait de Germaine Pichot 31
Portrait de Gertrude Stein 306
Portrait de l'artiste 21, 307
Portrait de Leo Stein 229
Portrait de Luis Vilaro 110
Portrait de Madame Soler 79
Portrait de Mateu F. de Soto 2, 23
Portrait de Sabartés 1, 22, 109
Portrait de Sebastián Junyer Vidal 72, 130
Portrait de Suzanne Bloch 135, 136
Portrait d'homme 46
Portrait d'une femme 136
Portrait d'une femme, sur carton 134
Portrait du sculpteur Manolo 150
Portrait du tailleur Soler 78
Profil au chignon 145
Profil de femme au chignon 145
Projet d'affiche 149
Le repas 107
Le repas de l'acrobate 169
Le repas de l'aveugle 94
Le repas des laboureurs 81
Le repas du gueux 107
Le repas du mendiant 105
Le repas du pauvre 106
La repasseuse 13, 124, 125
Le roi 179
Le roi Dagobert 179
Roses 240
Rue à Barcelone et Palais des Beaux-Arts 56
Sainte Roulette 148, 149
La saisie 123
Saltimbanques 230
Les saltimbanques au bord de la mer 84
Saltimbanques au repos 184
Scène de café 42
Scène d'intérieur 48
Le sculpteur Manolo 150
Le singe 163
Soler en tenue d'équitation 77
Solitude 111
La soupe 34
Le suicidé 118
Tête d'Arlequin 225, 226
Tête de femme 32, 55, 69, 75, 245, 298, 300
Tête de femme au chignon 290
Tête de femme de profil 54, 209, 246, 303
Tête de femme: Fernande 248
Tête de femme inclinée 302
Tête de femme, les cheveux dans le dos 291
Tête de garçon 212
Tête de jeune homme 256, 266
Tête de mendiant 104
Tête de paysan 297
Tête d'homme 296
La toilette 270
Toits de Barcelone 58
Torse de jeune fille 260
Les trois commères 199
Les trois hollandaises 199
Trois nus 253
Le tub 9
Vacher au petit panier 280
Les va-nu-pieds 113
Vase bleu 242
Vase de fleurs 143
Vendeurs de fleurs 287
La vie 89
Le veillard 91
Le veillard à l'enfant 111
Vieillard et fillette 126

118

Le vieille 96
Vieille femme au chapeau 97
Vieille femme endimanchée 97
Vieille femme et deux nus 98
Le vieux guitariste 92
Le vieux juif 91
Le violoniste 164

Prices

In nos. 4, 7, 17, 20, 24,
27, 36, 37, 45, 47, 48, 51, 79,
85, 116–7, 160, 174, 193,
198, 200, 219, 245, 296 and
303 are mentioned some of
the prices which Picasso's
works have fetched at
various times and in several
countries.